PERSONALITY AND LEARNING THEORY

Raymond B. Cattell, Ph.D., D.Sc., London University, is one of the world's leading personality theorists and researchers. As Distinguished Research Professor at the University of Illinois for thirty years he spearheaded a team of internationally acclaimed scholars in their innovative, pioneering research on personality and motivation. This work has been heralded for its creative contributions to personality concepts, psychometric advances, behavioral genetic methods, and clinical, social, and cultural research.

Among Dr. Cattell's many awards are the Darwin Fellowship, the Wenner Gren Prize of the New York Academy of Sciences, distinguished foreign honorary membership in the British Psychological Society, and presidentship of the Society of Multivariate Experimental Psychology. Among his 35 books are the *Handbook of Multivariate Experimental Psychology*, *Personality and Social Psychology*, *Prediction of Achievement and Creativity*, *Abilities: Their Structure, Growth and Action*, and *Meaning and Measurement of Neuroticism and Anxiety*. He has made over 400 contributions to scientific journals.

Personality and Learning Theory (Volumes 1 and 2) is the crowning work of one of this century's most distinguished psychologists. He has undertaken to heal the gulf between personality theory and learning theory which has troubled many, but so far has been comprehensively attacked by none. This two-volume work may well be remembered as the point at which learning theory, in a new synthesis, turned a corner into a more profitable and potent structured learning theory.

Forthcoming Volume 2, building on the personality theory and structures presented in this first volume, unravels the learning principles by which these structures are acquired.

PERSONALITY AND LEARNING THEORY

Volume 1

The Structure of Personality in Its Environment

Raymond B. Cattell

Distinguished Research Professor in Psychology, Emeritus;
University of Illinois

SPRINGER PUBLISHING COMPANY

New York

Springer Publishing Company, Inc.
200 Park Avenue South
New York, N.Y. 10003

79 80 81 82 83 / 10 9 8 7 6 5 4 3 2 1

Library of Congress Cataloging in Publication Data

Cattell, Raymond Bernard, 1905-
  The structure of personality in its environment.

  ([His] personality and learning theory ; vol. 1)
  Bibliography: p.
  Includes index.
  1. Personality. I. Title. II. Series.
[DNLM: 1. Personality. 2. Personality development.
3. Learning. 4. Psychological theory. BF698 C368p]
BF698.C323   Vol. 1   155.2s [155.2]   79-593
ISBN 0-8261-2120-9
ISBN 0-8261-2121-7 pbk.

Printed in the United States of America

To Dr. Robert K. Graham
and the Foundation for the Advancement of Man
for their help and encouragement
in research underlying this book.

CONTENTS

LIST OF TABLES

The present book covers the theory of personality structure and personality development (by learning and maturation) with due regard to environment and culture. For the convenience of the reader, in sheer handling and in instructional courses, it has been divided into two volumes.

The theory is a growth of twentieth century, experimental, quantitative psychology and integrates much that has been in more than a thousand scattered research articles and books by the present writer, a hundred co-workers and many other multivariate and bivariate researchers here and abroad. This construction differs from many other theories still taught, principally in the extensiveness of its welding to a quantitative experimental foundation and in the degree to which its syntax takes the form of integration by mathematical equations. The theory has the widely ramifying framework of a mathematical model, permitting at countless points tests of its internal consistency and its fit to facts.[1]

The first volume deals with personality and environment *in being*, but even here it is not a static "individual difference" treatment. It deals with the dynamics of the existing mechanisms, with the flow of states and processes, and the various ways in which the personality-environment interactions need to be analyzed.

The second volume, which will be explained in more detail in its own preface, is more revolutionary in character than the first. It propounds *structured learning theory* which is a substantial departure from learning theory in a reflexological framework as it is now commonly taught. Psychology has reason to be proud of two major edifices: psychometry and learning theory, which stand like the cathedrals of devoted builders that they are, amidst the shacks and intellectual slums of endless popular and undisciplined writing on psychological topics. Here the giants labored, in the persons of Galton, Spearman, Thurstone, Burt and their successors in the psychometric illumination of personality, and of Pavlov, Wundt, Thorndike, Hull and their successors in the field of process, in perception and learning.

These two pillars have long awaited a pediment to give entrance to the single hall of knowledge that psychology was intended to be. As one learns to expect from the history of science, proposals for integration are generally actually resisted. There are inbreedings and vested interests—as occurred for example in the resistances of medical men to an outsider like Pasteur—which resist bridge building long after its desirability has become rationally evident. I do not expect, therefore, that many psychometrists will drop their pre-occupations to keep me company in this novel incursion into learning theory. Nor do I expect that dyed-in-the-wool reflexological learning theorists will give unbiased attention to the contention of structured learning theory that present learning ideas are trying to put the jig-saw picture together with half the pieces missing.

The account of personality in being, in Volume 1, which gives an indispensable set of reference points for Volume 2, on growth, rests in the main on well checked and systematically carried forward programmatic work over the last half century. The building in Volume 2 is unfortunately much less complete and more speculative. Only in the last 15 years before retirement was the present writer ready to direct researches into the concepts of the dynamic calculus and multivariate analyses of learning. It is an absurdity, that only certain ivory tower philosophers would adopt, to think that theories can be extensively developed far ahead of experiment. An experiment can trip up a theory at the very first step, and though a good theorist can build up alternatives according to whether future experiments say yes or no at consecutive choice points, those alternative theoretical structures soon become impracticably numerous. Sincere theory advances hand in hand with experiment, and, being denied the resources and computer hours for the necessary complex and crucial needed experimental designs, I am compelled to substitute in Volume 2, for the complete experiments which characterize Volume 1, an appeal to others to "carry on."

Even in Volume 1 I have not set out all equations in full dress, though that can always be done. For the sake of good communication with averagely statistically trained psychologists I have presented simplified forms at times, or forms with simplifying assumptions, that the strict psychometrist may not like. For example, I have, with a warning note, left specific ("unique") factors off several equations where our concern is with broad common factors. I beg indulgence and understanding for dropping full dress: the interruptions of the text to meet the elaborations the more meticulous psychometrist might expect might well destroy the interest of the psychologist in the concepts as such.

The level of communication here is aimed at the graduate student and the scholar, though I see no reason, where majors in psychology are taught for ultimate professional work, why they should not get down to these basic principles straight away at an undergraduate stage—with competent teaching. Communication requires attention, however, to some systematic difficulties in introducing students with certain backgrounds to this area. These difficulties show up again and again in that part of the criticism of presentations like this that have no real substance. One difficulty, for years, has been mechanical repetitions of criticism of factor analysis as such, for example, that "factors are mere abstractions"; that "one only gets out of factor analysis what one puts in," and that factor analysts cannot agree among themselves. When these straw men are demolished by careful measuring they rise again with a persistence which suggests that they are defenses of the numerous psychologists who were allowed, a decade or more ago, to obtain a Ph.D. with no knowledge of those multivariate experimental methods and concepts, which are indispensable to a multivariate science. If the onlooker is bothered by what are unnecessary differences in reported factor analytic results the sooner he gains competence in the area to see just what the experimental flaws are that lead to these apparent discrepancies the better. Another obstacle reported by some critics, or, at least, reviewers, is the fact that new technical terms have to be learnt. The present writer has replied that he has never introduced a new term for a trait or a technical concept except where a genuinely new concept has been unearthed. Unfortunately, psychologists have been cheated for generations, as William James pointed out, by writers out to create an illusion of technical progress by calling old things by new names. A well thought out and precise technical vocabulary is both a necessity and a pleasurable elegance in good communication and calculation. Psychologists have been far too much bogged down in problems that have no existence except in semantics, or that arise from clinging to the battered coinage of popular terms. Unfortunately, the student has often been taught that the dignity of scholarship requires polysyllabic terms preferably from the classical languages. The time has come to end this posturing and one welcomes the computer scientist talking precisely about a "bit" of information, or the nuclear physicist defining a "quark." In the developments in my own area, where an important trait has been uniquely defined factorically (such as surgency, premsia, or autia) I have sought terms with interpretive meaning that are as economical as the formulae with which they go. And concepts, such as *P*-technique, trait view theory, fluid intelligence, the MAVA method, exvia, erg, cortertia, data box, dynamic lattice, IHD spiral, modulation index, scree test, SOR versus SR, syntality, tri-vector learning analysis, VIDA model, are kept as exact as their operational definition by crisp new terms. Of wanton innovation, with no cash of discovery to meet the check of subjective labelling, we have had enough; but the student who learns a genuine, precise scientific language finds himself in a new world of elegant and effective communication.

As to desirable background the reader should have (a) a course in general statistics extending at least to an acquaintance with multivariate thinking and the logic of factor analysis (but not necessarily to the detailed calculations). (2) A first degree of familiarity with existing, for example, Freudian, Jungian, etc. personality theory, and the new concepts of temperament and dynamic structure from the last 30 years of multivariate experiment. (3) For Volume 2 a corresponding familiarity with the existing main concepts of classical learning theory. Actually, the presentation here *does* run sufficiently over (2) and (3) before proceeding, but earlier, more extended contact would help. (4) That intangible qualification, a disciplined mind, permitting the reader to absorb compactly-stated propositions and to enjoy certain real conceptual complexities. Unless this last is more thoroughly inculcated than in many present-day undergraduate texts, psychologists must surely soon encounter a crisis where practitioners are quite underqualified for the complexities of their jobs. There could be a day of reckoning when society demands proof of the worth of the technological claims of psychology. Eysenck, for one, has pioneered by asking bluntly, "Do psychiatrists or psychotherapists do any good?" The U.S. Government has passed a law demanding that any tests used in industry shall demonstrate predictive *criterion validity.* How long before it demands proof that clinical therapy does something for the patient? Psychologists are being challenged to meet some of the standards of physics and engineering students, who are required to reason realistically and to read relatively complex mathematics in their *undergraduate* texts, because telephones have to work and bridges have to stand up. The price of true control and effectiveness in clinic, school, and society by psychologists is an earlier weaning of the undergraduate from merely verbal and sometimes almost anecdotal presentations in favor of *more precisely expressed* models and simple but real calculations.

As to advice on order of reading the chapters, the best is the order given. It would certainly be unprofitable, for example, to tackle Volume 2 on learning without first absorbing the concepts of Volume 1 on personality theory. *The reader is particularly urged to study carefully the summaries arranged at the end of each chapter,* which have been carefully prepared to test, by their condensed statement, the reader's grasp of the chapter itself. The bibliography has the double purpose of documenting the scientific foundations as such and providing a more expanded explanation of matters dealt with here in what must seem a condensed fashion to readers to whom all is new.

Concerning this documentation one must recognize that the bibliography over such a wide spectrum of personality and learning theory would have been enormous had I not resorted to representing the articles and books of many eminent contributors by the one or two most prominent of their contributions, from the bibliographies of which their other developments can be traced. Documentation has been used most heavily for *research* sources, but with adequacy, one hopes, concerning *general* reading expanding the various areas. Finally, effective use requires—since condensation has been centered on principles and models—that the skillful teacher should prepare to put flesh on the bones by expanding on illustrations for which the text had no space. For example, in Volume 1, it would be of interest and help to the student to dwell on the theoretical, *psychological nature* of the principal primary traits and states, their clinical relevancies, and the criterion relations found for them in applied psychology.

Finally in this preface I am moved to express warm gratitude to those many colleagues and graduate students who by reminders, helped me to achieve a synoptic view of a breadth that no individual alone could hope to complete in accurate detail. Most of those colleagues are in the author index. Further I wish to thank certain young instructors and professors who combined painstaking thoroughness in knowledge of their fields with an openness to new viewpoints, and as representative of whom I would gratefully mention Heather Birkett, Charles Burdsal, Dan Blaine, Jerry Brennan, Neil Dorans, Velma Kameoka, Sam Krug, and, outstandingly, John Horn, Jim Laughlin, John Nesselroade, John Sigurdson, Larry Sine and Robert Woliver.

No author can be trusted to evaluate soundly the significance of his own book relative to those of others, but he may more reliably evaluate it relative to other books of his own. And here I can only say that over the years I feel this has been my most important single presentation of findings and ideas.

NOTE

[1] Anyone disciplined in the old sciences and with some knowledge of the history of scientific theory cannot but deplore, with some disgust, what has long been, and still continues to be, served up to the student as "personality theory." Had Hamlet wanted a better example of "an unweeded garden that grows to seed" he would have found it in the pompous, pseudo-scholarly verbiage and name-dropping, and the untestable and dull speculation that fills symposia on this area of psychology. Skinner, the present writer, Thurstone, Eysenck and to some extent Guilford, have been accused by reviewers of being "atheoretical," but if the above circular semantic playgrounds are their idea of theory, what a compliment they have paid us!

It is a sorry trick of "progress" that just when psychologists began to mature into real concern for theory based on careful experiment and genuine internal syntax, the book market was hit by a new plague of writing psychological best sellers, often with the aid of journalist ghost writers. When the students' demand for the easiest picture book began to fix the standards of teaching it was inevitable that there would be a relapse from precise models and statistical testing into theory as kaffee-klatsch intellectualism. The curricula of universities recognize courses in science adapted to students of literature and journalism, and other liberal arts students who want only a general idea of what is going on in science. But they also recognize the need *from the first undergraduate years* of textbooks of a more disciplined and realistic standard for those who are going on to reach professional standards in physics, chemistry, engineering or medicine. The catastrophe that hit psychology is that, due to its popularity (every human being is a psychologist), the undergraduate oriented to a graduate career has been sacrificed to his more dilettante and numerous fellow travellers. If we honestly believe that psychology students are not the escapees from the harder subjects, and that they are prepared intelligently to face difficulties, then a book like the present volume should be taken at the undergraduate level by psychology majors. It is time that certain faculty members ceased insulting the intelligence, and misdirecting the intellectual growth, of serious students in psychology, by assuming that they cannot calculate, or use a technical vocabulary, or think steadily and analytically, but must instead have their minds filled with a verbiage of anecdotal speculation.

PERSONALITY AND LEARNING THEORY

CHAPTER 1

FOCUSING STRUCTURE: TYPES, PROCESSES, SURFACE AND SOURCE TRAITS

1-1. The Present Status of Scientific Personality Study

Literary studies of personality help us understand other personalities through our own experiences and introspections. The scientific study of personality seeks to understand personality as one would the mechanism of a watch, the chemistry of the life processes in a mammal, or the spectrum of a remote star. That is to say, it aims at objective insights; at the capacity to predict and control what will happen next; and at the establishment of scientific laws of a perfectly general nature. In the scientific approach the fact that the investigator is himself human may turn out, curiously enough, to be as much a hindrance as a help. In any case the undertaking presents a tremendous challenge to imagination and method, for the human mind is the most complex entity man has met in his universe.

Psychology has been slow to realize what older sciences have learned, namely, that progress in laws and principles begins only after measurement and description—*taxonomy* as it is broadly defined—have reached exact levels. As Francis Bacon pointed out long ago, the immature student begins by asking enormous questions and developing elaborate explanatory theories; but the mature investigator realizes that we must describe thoroughly before we can begin to explain. So in psychology *before we can get anywhere we have to be able to describe a given personality at a given moment of its psychological states, in an accurately described environment, in meaningful measurements.* As we watch a stirring drama at a movie theater, we seldom stop to reflect that the movement is produced by a succession of "stills"—some 16 to the second—going through the projector. Just so have psychologists tended to forget, in elaborating their dynamic and developmental theories, that the proof of such theory is possible only by measuring and describing the person accurately at two points (at least) in time. And this measurement, as we shall see, will need, at least in the beginning, to refer to a few hundred meaningful, unitary structures, for without such condensation on essentials we should get lost in the infinite possible bits of behavior that could be measured.

Broadly divided, the entities that can be described and studied in psychology, as in most sciences, fall into *structures*—traits, characteristics, attributes—and *processes*, in which a pattern of change over time is recognized. Language handles the first in nouns and adjectives and the latter basically by verbs and adverbs, although we can use nouns, such as *adolescence, disappointment, education, involution,* to describe the pattern of a process or state. Indeed, a process is a *structure in time,* so that the term structure covers both time patterns of response and the potential in an individual to respond to environmental stimuli; these might be called respectively *behaviorial structures* and *behavior potential structures.* The basis of a process or state behavior structure, incidentally, is also a behavior potential structure, as in a trait, and a trait often expresses itself in some process; but in the actual process there is always also a particular sequence of environmental stimuli concerned—one that is optimum in interlocking with the internal structure to produce the required process. The presence of structure is inferred from observed recurrent behavior, just as we infer the presence of a bulb in a flashlight from the reappearance of a beam of light, or a particular engine structure in a car from the car's movement and the kind of noise it makes.

Traits, processes, and the organism that integrates them are equally vital and indispensable concepts to a predictive psychology. Most important in an organism, of course, is the nervous system, but when we speak of structure it is initially only an abstraction from behavior. Any enquiry about relations of a behavioral structure to a neural structure is a second area of study. And although the accurate description, which is the basis of all advance in theory, *can* pick up either trait structures or processes first—their interdependence being like warp and weft in the texture of the behavioral tapestry—the movie analogy suggests it is strategically more profitable to begin with traits.

Historically, the location and description of traits did in fact begin with cross-sectional "stills" at a given moment in time, by what we shall later define as R-technique, which recognizes trait structures by comparing behavior across many individuals. On the other hand, one cannot measure a learning process, for example, without comparing what exists at two separate points in time.

Modern, experimental researchers on personality understand these principles well. But clinical and humanistic psychology—and preexperimental literary psychologists in general—have been too eager to get to grand theorizing to take time for this disciplined construction of a foundation of descriptive psychometric concepts and means of meaningful measurement. Such writers have used trait terms, but given no demonstration psychometrically that the ego and the superego, or the authoritarian personality, or whatever, *are* distinct and unitary traits. In some textbooks a section is some-times given to "trait theories of personality," as if there were other theories. In the sense of words used here, a trait theory simply means a theory of structure—a *recognition that organisms have attributes*—in which there can be diverse kinds of traits and states: source traits, surface traits, and, of course, transient states. The only logical meaning of a "non-trait theory" is that personality attributes do not exist and that no systematic differences can be observed among people or in the same person in different situations. It is a confession that the writer's methods offer him no escape from chaos and that science has to dissolve into complete lawlessness. An excellent account of the interface between the more philosophical aspects of this question and the actual methodologies and operational concepts developed here for traits has recently been given by Buss (1977).

My strategy of advance in research and conceptualization there-fore has two steps, which are reflected in the division of this book into two volumes. The first volume, containing eight chapters, has to do with description and measurement, initially of traits and later of states and processes. In the second volume I attempt to explain, by principles of genetics and learning (the latter including the study of the sociocultural environment), the trait and state structures found. I take the structures and their development, as demonstrated in the first volume, and seek their origins in terms of sophisticated models of genetic maturation and learning.

In this first descriptive phase I shall develop precise models and formulae and relate them to substantive discoveries in the field of trait and state structure. Pessimists have said that psychology students will not take studies on pure taxonomy any more enthusiastically than medical students take courses on bodily anatomy. But both are vitally necessary to any real understanding of *function*. In any case, in studying the psychometry of personality structure there are mathematically elegant developments that no scientifically oriented student who grasps them can fail to enjoy. In statistical analysis I shall lean on ANOVA and correlational methods (CORAN), but particularly on that final development of CORAN that is called factor analysis. However, the student with only rough ideas of what these methods involve will be led by easy steps, because I aim to introduce the statistical procedures in close connection with the psychological model concepts they serve.

Corresponding to these more sophisticated concepts in the model I shall use technical terms going beyond the popular language of, say, novelists and some "humanistic" psychologists. As medical science and physics have long known, nothing but confusion results from mixing popular words with strictly defined terms. So the reader should not express surprise if new ideas require him or her to learn a new vocabulary. For example, the dimension exvia-invia is defined as a unique second-order factor (page 78). This is the scientific concept behind the rough and uncertain ideas bandied about by journalists since the degeneration of Jung's terms "extraversion-introversion" (in his time never statistically defined—hence the degeneration). Correct scientific terms for clear and pointed discussion do not have to be long and pretentious. For example, the term *erg* (rhymes with berg) is briefer than "instinct structure" and *ergic* (rhymes with allergic) has an operational meaning that would be lost in the historical trail of misunderstandings about "instinctual." Erg is precise in its connotations in the various fields in which "drive" has been more loosely used.

In general the newer terms are both shorter and more exactly definable. But one should not let this reference to terminology, as related to models and formulae, suggest that we are to enter an orgy of academic pedantry in subjectively defining hundreds of technical terms. Psychology has suffered much from subjectivity of viewpoint. Biologists today blush a little at the scholarly volumes that appeared in the seventeenth century on the natural history of the unicorn or the anatomy of the dragon, but some current works on the ego, on needs, on frustration and aggression, and even on such technical-sounding themes as "approach-avoidance behavior" and the "genesis of the self-concept" are not much different.[1] Closely examined, they are no less fanciful in assuming structural entities where no proof of a unitary tendency, in process or structure, has first been experimentally given. New words, like new bank notes, should appear only after the gold of new entities or concepts has been confirmed to back them up.

Only in the last 50 years has a science of psychometry developed that has made "meaningful measurement at a given moment"—and therefore an ensuing science of development and learning concerning the structures found—a genuine possibility. However, the sometimes difficult specialty we call *psychometry*—behavioral measurement—must, by logical necessity, be encountered relatively early in this book if the taxonomic concepts are to be given a backbone. As promised above, we shall ease our way into it, accepting simplified statements first and qualifying with more recondite models as we proceed (which means that the reader must not charge the writer with inconsistency of an earlier with a later statement, explicitly stated to be more developed). It would help if the student would acquire the habit from the beginning of paralleling a verbal statement or definition with a more concise statement in a formula. All readers, hopefully, will then learn to appreciate the elegance of formulae, but if anyone later finds some formulae going beyond his familiarity with symbols, he can still hold on to the logical verbal statement of the relations until formulae become a part of his language.

All we have said about personality as such so far is that *there is structure in behavior.* This can be formulated as:

$$a_{hijk} = (f)a_{h'ij'k'} + u \tag{1-1}$$

which says that a measure of a of one kind of behavior j of a person i, in response to a stimulus h in situation k, is functionally related to a measure of some other bit of his behavior $a_{j'}$ in some other situation k', to a stimulus h', at some other time. (There is some unique part, u, in a_{hijk}.) Even the repetition of the very *same* behavior in the same situation hk would be evidence of structure, though narrower. The second piece of behavior, on the repetition, is recognized never to be completely predictable from the first because of some unknowable fraction u. Structure is thus operationally defined initially simply as something persisting in the individual that helps to predict his behavior at one time and place from his behavior in another. The function (f) could be a single regression coefficient for a linear relation, or some more complex nonlinear algebraic relation.

The next basic proposition is that we begin to formulate a

process, for example, a maturational or learning or situationally adjustive process, as a *difference* across time (t) of such "instantaneous" measures, thus:

$$dij = a_{hijk_{(t^1)}} - a_{hijk_{(t^2)}}$$

(1-2)

where *di* is behavioral difference that could, with further knowledge from other variables in the pattern, be expressed as a development in structure.[2]

1-2.   Bivariate and Multivariate Experimental Advances
beyond the Clinical and Literary Phases

From measures of associations between behaviors (formula 1-1), and changes in behavior (formula 1-2), we are going to build up concepts of traits and states. But this is not the way such concepts have been built up in the past, before experimental psychology was brought to bear on personality. It behooves us to ask what we are going to do about possibilities of integrating concepts from different stages of method that are still presented side by side with little comment in psychological texts. This question calls for a brief historical perspective.

Personality study has gone essentially through three phases, each briefer and more accelerated than its predecessor. From biblical times until the early nineteenth century it was a matter for intuitive insights expressed in the language of literature. These often reached systematic schematization and scholarly intent, however, as in Plutarch, Theophrastus, Bacon, La Rochefoucault, Goethe, Fourier, Bain, and others whom one may study in Roback's (1927) historical evaluation. Then, from the middle of the nineteenth century, the study of pathological behavior by medical men introduced a clinical phase, scientific in general approach, but limited in precision by clinical methodology and concentration on medical, pathological psychology. From the taxonomic beginnings of Kraepelin, Azam, Koch, and others, this clinical advance passed through the more cautious explanatory development of Bleuler (1933), Janet (1900, 1965), Kretschmer (1921), Ribot (1896), and others (projecting their discussions to normals). At the turn of the century this movement flowered in the theoretical developments of Freud, Adler, Jung, and McDougall. Some experimental checking was introduced by the two last-named investigators, but it was not until after the World War I that this basically qualitative clinical-observation phase began to move, under the influence of a new generation, into a truly objective and experimental attack on personality theory.

It is with this third—experimental and quantitative—phase that the present book is concerned. But the phase is itself not a uniform era, for over much of the last 50 years we see it developing in two distinct methodologies, proceeding in parallel, with some unlucky lack of coordination. The first I shall define as *bivariate* (or classical, or brass-instrument) experiment. This methodology is confined to manipulating one specific variable, called, in that context, the *independent* variable, to see what happens (by a plot for curve fitting or analysis of variance) to a second, *dependent* variable. It is curious that although bivariate methods have been pursued mainly by conservative laboratory researchers, who shudder at the methods of clinical psychology, the personality theories they have set out to test have largely been picked up as an inheritance from clinical psychology, for example, from the work of Ericksen on perceptual repression; Murray and Berkan on displacement; Mowrer (1938) on conflict in the rat; Barker, Dembo, and Lewin on frustration and regression; Levine, Chein, and Murphy (1942) on perceptual distortion; and countless others.

By contrast, the approach through the other main type of experimental design—that of *multivariate* experimental psychology— has generated an impressive gallery of entirely new personality concepts, unknown among the products of clinical observation. For, like any really new technical development, multivariate analysis came only slowly to catch the popular mind. Yet, with the inevitability of a rising tide, it has developed a momentum of hypothesis creation and hypothesis testing that has lifted personality almost completely away from its psychoanalytic and other clinical beginnings, as Eysenck and Rachmann (1966), among others, have challengingly pointed out. There are good reasons for this more continuous creativity and broader scope of the multivariate method, which can be clarified by a digressing footnote on the essential nature of methodological schools and movements as such.[3]

The integration in this book is based on a two-handed use, with flexible appropriateness, of both multivariate and bivariate experiment. However, it is a far more rewarding strategy to enter with multivariate methods *first*, in order to generate the hypotheses most relevant to the field. Thereafter, these emerging concepts, viable beyond bivariate gropings and now measurable with sufficient validity, can be used in bivariate and manipulative designs.

Psychology as a science, as distinct from a humanistic, literary, and esthetic study of man, is moving fast into a domain of purely quantitative and experimental methods. In areas technical in quality from the beginning, such as those of perception, this movement is unimpeded by a popular past; but, in personality, advance is constantly and widely thwarted as the manoeuvres of an army might be by a mass of refugees larger than itself. These "refugees" are largely the literary and more speculative clinical writers continuing the "ancient regime" into present times.[4] Both the researcher and the student need explicitly to recognize this reality and to adopt a sure policy toward it. On the one hand, one can totally reject concepts from either of the two preceding phases, literary or clinical, as Eysenck, for example, and probably most members of the Psychonomic Society, do. One can respect this position without necessarily considering it best for the advancement of science. As an alternative, the position I have adopted is one of respecting possible leads from our intellectual ancestry, but subjecting them to independent judgment on the basis of modern methods. Thus, unlike Eysenck's total rejection of psychoanalysis, my attitude is to adopt those concepts, and even the terminology (e.g., *superego, projection*), when such structures or processes are later shown by quantitative, factor-analytic research to have true unitary qualities. Of course, a concept developed from nonquantitative clinical observations changes to some extent under the enrichment and precision brought about by a mathematical model and statistical pruning, and the concept is often brought into new company. For example, factor analysis brings to light the patterns of the self-sentiment structure (Q_3 in the index) alongside the superego as a pattern not previously seen. Unfortunately, in retaining clinical concepts renovated and extended as experimental findings one encounters the danger that discussants will impose the imaginary or unsubstantiated features of the older concept and term on the new theory. But that sort of verbal carelessness can and does happen within the experimental and psychometric approaches themselves, as when some Rip van Winkle treats operant conditioning phenomena as classical Pavlovian conditioning, or assigns to the fluid intelligence factor, g_f, the properties of Spearman's g.

A normal scientific wariness is surely more profitable than automatic or total rejection of the looser concepts from the literary and clinical phases. With concepts, as with commodities, the ancient adage remains: *caveat emptor*. If the psychologist is mature enough not to be hypnotized by the verbal fantasies that spring like luxuriating weeds around the comparatively few empirically persisting and verified concepts that clinical theory propounded, those concepts can well be carried forward, under renewed examination, into their new experimental transformations.[5]

1-3. Describing Personality by Common Surface Traits

With this brief but essential glance at the historical roots and methodological standards of research, let us turn to our first item of technical business, which is developing methods and concepts for defining and describing any personality at a given moment in time. The chief concepts for describing and measuring people, in their behavioral aspects, are *surface traits, source traits, states, processes,* and *types.* We shall deal with them in this chapter in that order. Later chapters will call for a roster of actual, discovered substantive examples of these concepts.

In speaking of individual differences and structures within a species type, the zoologist or botanist first fixes the species itself within genera and wider families. Literature contains a whole spectrum of evaluation of man, from Hamlet's "In face and form how like a god" to some meaner modern views. But the scientist's placing of the human type would require measurement of how much more intelligent it is than the dog, how much slower than the antelope, how much more emotionally stable and foresighted than the rhesus monkey, and so on. To get started, let us bypass the species question and take mankind to that extent, for granted. Statistically, in many cases, all our trait measures are in a framework of *individual differences* among people, and our state or process measures deal even with *differences within one person, over time.*

It is basic methodological truth that to recognize structure, we must have *individual difference* or *movement.* By looking at many people with and without degrees of scarlet fever, physicians arrived at a pattern and a concept for that particular fever. They could do so because when a person differed from normal in having spots, he also tended to have a temperature, and so on. And, as regards process structures, by seeing how the particles of water surge in unison in the sea, I can reach the concept of a wave. By noticing and recording that quickness of understanding, adaptability to new situational demands, capacity to solve problems, and capacity to handle abstract ideas vary together as he compared person with person, Spearman reached a conception of general intelligence, or *g.* And if I notice in myself that a feeling of joy, a tendency to talk, and a willingness to meet strangers vary together from time to time, then I get a conception of a functionally unitary elation-depression axis in feeling states, and can study the process of moving from one to the other.

Human behavior, even in a single culture, is so enormously varied that the question was raised long ago by CORAN methodologists—specifically by those employing factor analysis—whether much behavior could be reduced to unitary patterns common in greater or lesser degree to all people, as, say, size of head, color of eyes, or curliness of hair can be in physical traits. The factor analysts handled this by accepting patterns unique to any specific behavior, and their model was such as to permit a quantitative answer if research could be widely pursued. In the actual outcome, psychologists such as Spearman, Thurstone, and the present writer have been impressed by the magnitude and importance of common trait patterns, while admitting specifics. Others, such as Watson, Michel, and many clinicians have stressed the immense variety of specific conditionings a person acquires in the course of his unique individual history.

A first bit of logic to be made clear is that recognizing the role of common traits does not deny the uniqueness of the individual as an individual. Length, breadth, color, transparency and degree of polish are common traits of a population of jewels, but the uniqueness of each jewel, from the Koh-i-noor diamond to a turquoise in a signet ring, can be fully defined and represented in terms of these common traits. Fully, that is to say, unless one jewel has an initial carved on it. In that case the common trait description has to be completed by reference to a unique trait. But note that even a unique trait has to be defined by reference to common attributes—the common attributes, however, of initials, not jewels. Thus, if a person has a unique trait of obsessively swallowing postage stamps only when they are purple in color, it is defined in common physical attributes, for example, a purple color, but its structure, in the sense of what other behaviors go with it, is unlikely to be found by ordinary cross-person correlation, because no one else has it. But there is still a way, as we shall see below.

Actually, there is no need for the subjective differences of opinion, between enthusiasts respectively for common and unique traits, that all too frequently issue in crass "black or white" assertions overvaluing one or the other. In *The Description and Measurement of Personality* (1946) I recognized and defined both common and unique traits and pointed out that what the factor analyst calls the "communality" (definition in Gorsuch, 1972, p. 294) tells us quantitatively how much of the individual differences on a certain behavior can be accounted for by the discovered common traits and how much must be assigned to unique specifics. "Discovered" is important, for what is called the specific trait variance—that left over when broad common traits are taken out—still need not be unique trait variance, but could be common trait variance of a specific, narrow kind, or part of a broad trait the rest of which has not yet been discovered at that state of research. That is, specific traits (not unique traits) are often undiscovered common traits.

As we proceed we shall see that the term "unique" covers, statistically and psychologically, two rather different concepts, specificity and uniqueness. The confusion arose through statisticians talking about variables and psychologists about people. For the former a common factor was common to all variables in a study (in the matrix) and a unique trait existed in only one variable. We shall alter the labelling to fit the psychologists' meaning and use *specific* for specific to one variable, as opposed to *broad*, covering many. The psychological concepts, on the other hand, we shall continue to call *common* and *unique*, as above. A specific trait is not unique—everyone has some degree of it—but it is peculiar to just one form of behavior. Some of the heat of debate over common traits arises from the previous confusion of terms. Psychometrists were for a time not interested in unique traits, not knowing how to locate them. If the proof of a functionally unitary trait is that a set of measurable behaviors constituting a unique trait really go together (as they should if we are going to call it a unitary trait), how do we know this? We cannot compare measures on other people over these unique behaviors and correlate the scores over a range of people. The only proof now possible of organic connection in some unitary structure arises if the elements can be seen to fluctuate together over time in the life of that individual. (The method of discerning this is later defined as *P-technique*.) For example, I have a desire to revisit a beautiful sea cove among remote cliffs on the South Coast of England. This is a unique trait attachment because probably not one person in a million has landed at that cove, though it is no more unique than countless attachments studied by clinicians.

Presumably some manifestation of my esthetic attachment or interest could be correlated, such as imagery, work associations, choosing of geographical books, that would vary together over time, all being simultaneously high when this interest trait is high and low at other times. Thus the existence and unitary character of a *unique* trait can still be demonstrated, by correlations of elements over a series of occasions and situations, instead of over people, as for a common trait. But though unique unitary traits can thus be demonstrated, there remains still a problem in measuring them. Common traits can be brought to standard scores based on distribution in a population. But if I have a peculiar, unique trait of raising my left eyebrow when the Bible is mentioned, how can one tell, in standard score terms, whether I have this trait strongly or only moderately? Unique traits can be measured only in raw score terms (height of eyebrow lift) or, if they vary over time, in a standard score assigned to a given occasion based on the standard deviation of the individual's range of temporal variation.

This is not all that ultimately needs to be said about unique traits, their location, measurement, and predictive use. But, at an introductory stage, it is enough to make a logical and operational separation of unique from common traits, with which the next three chapters are concerned. In any case, in general psychometric practice, the common trait is decidedly more important, for it can already be shown to account for over two-thirds of the interindividual and much of the intraindividual variance in a wide range of real-life (criterion) behaviors so far measured. The *source* of such a pattern of common variance may differ from trait to trait and comes in for investigation as soon as the taxonomic task is completed. Broadly speaking, it must arise either from genetic or environmental molding forces affecting all individuals in a culture, *but to different degrees.* The reason why people show similar common structure in *innate* temperament patterns, such as hyperthyroidism, emotional instability, and abilities like intelligence, is that they inherit positively contributing genes in different amounts from the same pool of genes. Correspondingly, the origin of what have been called *environmental mold* traits—such as a set of occupational skills, a sentiment for sport, a set of religious values—resides in different degrees of exposure to a pattern of teaching influences representing a particular social institution, such as job, school, family, or church. Our concern at this point, however, is with the principles and products of a *descriptive taxonomy*, and research on origins must wait.

As we proceed with taxonomy it will be necessary to distinguish not only the antithesis of *common* and *unique* traits, but also those of *surface* and *source* traits, *broad* and *specific* traits, and traits in *different media* and *modalities.* But in all these forms the basic conception of a trait as something the behavioral parts of which *vary together* holds, though it is most easily introduced and illustrated by the simplest instance: the *surface trait,* which we shall now examine.

A surface trait is discovered by setting out correlation coefficients among a lot of behaviors when systematic connections are suspected from clinical and general observation. A correlation matrix is then calculated (Table 1-1) and one proceeds to look for clusters of variables that go together. As has been pointed out, although clinicians do not actually compute correlations, it is essentially a search of this kind that they have carried out when they have looked for unitary structures (e.g., medical syndromes, or, in psychology, the superego or the obsessional-compulsive syndrome). The difference

TABLE 1–1.   Clusters (Surface Traits) as Revealed by a Correlation Matrix.

	Variables								
	1	2	3	4	5	6	7	8	9
1	1.0								
2	.1	1.0							
3	-.1	.7	1.0						
4	.3	.2	-.3	1.0					
5	.2	-.3	0	-.1	1.0				
6	.3	-.4	-.6	-.2	.8	1.0			
7	0	.3	0	.3	-.1	0	1.0		
8	.1	-.3	0	.2	-.7	-.6	-.8	1.0	
9	0	.2	-.2	-.2	.6	.5	.4	.9	1.0

Here there are two clusters—(2, 3, and 6(-)) and (5, 6, 8(-)), and 9. The typical problem in locating distinct clusters, namely, that they overlap, is illustrated by variable 6 belonging to both. Variables 6 and 8 belong at their negative poles. Variables 1 and 7 belong to no clusters. The arbitrariness of clusters is also shown by our fiat here that an *r* of 0.4 is the minimum value for acceptance in a cluster.

is that they have depended on shrewd but nonquantified observation and fallible memory, and on a series of patients instead of measured data, IBM records, and computer analysis.

Description by surface trait concepts and measurement by adding scores on the pool (technically the centroid) of the variables were popular in psychology a generation ago, and still have important representation as the formal basis of psychiatric syndromes. Medicine as a whole depends a good deal for its descriptions and diagnoses on common surface traits, as, for example, the correlation clusters observed in diabetes, scarlet fever, or schizophrenia. In psychology, and among normal people, these clusters are not so clear, and bring out the fundamental weakness of this concept, namely, that *clusters*

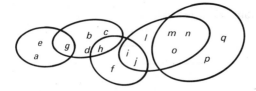

Figure 1-1. Overlap as typically occurring among correlation clusters (surface traits).

rarely have a sharp edge. The correlation sets have a habit of blending into one another as apparently distinct clouds in the sky begin to blend in a storm wrack, as one can see in Figure 1-1. The problem then is that behaviors like *g* and *h* in Figure 1-1 fall in more than one cluster. Such instances are numerous in most real data. The statistician perceives that the correlation cluster or surface trait has had its appeal through a specious simplicity. Today we must reject it from any concept of precision in personality description. True, as later more intensive considerations will show (p. 332), one can seemingly eliminate much of the subjectivity that causes different diagnosticians to settle on different clusters by using an "objective" computer program called Taxonome (Cattell & Coulter, 1966). But any claim for logically reaching an *ultimate* objectivity would be wrong, because Taxonome is a program that has to have certain arbitrary standards plugged into it by the experimenter. This device we shall study in Section 1-7, on "types," because the formal models for types and clusters are almost exactly the same.

1-4.   Source Traits Operationally Discovered and Defined as Uniquely Rotated Factors

As we proceed beyond the surface trait concept to that of the source trait it is appropriate to consolidate some definitions concerning traits in general. In particular, we should recognize from the beginning the involvement of trait definition with situation. A trait may be defined as *that which defines what a person will do when faced with a defined situation.* It might be thought that this also defines a psychological *state;* but to anticipate future developments, for the sake of logical completeness here, we ultimately define a state as the result of the effect of a situation upon a state liability. A situation thus has two effects: that just noted and the effect of a focal stimulus in causing a person to respond through the agency of an inherent trait. This focal stimulus we shall symbolize by h and k would equal the effect of a general surrounding, ambient situation, or set of conditions that can modify the level of the state that certain traits generate. All this will be developed more fully in later chapters, but here we may note that as indicated in equation (1-1) every action, a, needs four subscripts to identify and analyze it: h, the focal stimulus; i, the particular individual; j, the *nature* of the response (the *quantity* is in a); and k, the surrounding total conditions, which we shall call the ambient situation.[6]

Briefly to give concrete illustration, the stimulus h could be an oncoming car on the road, the response j could be a turning of the wheel (measured in degrees of turn), and the ambient situation k could be that of being on a main highway and late for an appointment. In animal research h could be a bar in a Skinner box, j the pressing of it (measured in reaction time), and k the situation of standing on an electrified grill. Now, the basic proposition, regarding a trait as an inherent structure, is that

$$a_{hijk} = (f)b_{hjk}T_{ix} \qquad (1\text{-}3)$$

where (f) means some mathematical function, here involving two terms, T_{ix}, which is individual i's score on the trait x, and b_{hjk} which expresses the impact of the environment hk (focal and ambient) in producing the behavior j. There would in any actual behavior by the total personality be many T's, but introductorily we state the essentials with one. Furthermore, for completeness we must add the state S_y (y being a particular state such as anxiety), omitting for the moment the question of how it is produced by modulating action (to use the correct term) of situation k upon a trait. Thus:

$$a_{hijk} = (f)b_{hjkx}T_{ix} + (f)b_{hjky}S_{iky} \qquad (1\text{-}4)$$

(Again, only one trait and one state where there would normally be many.)

The trait score T has simply the signature of the given individual i, but the emotional state S will be fixed both by the individual and the situation k, because it is his state level *at that moment*. The weights given to T and S are symbolized as b's, for *behavioral indices* (to be defined, but presently seen as representing the environment), and are peculiar to h, j, and k, and to the particular trait t or state s, but not to the individual i. In other words, they are characteristic of a whole population and culture. For economy some subscripts that can be assumed will not always be given in our equations. For example, in some fixed situations b will only have subscripts h, j, and t, as the immediate stimulus and response are the most relevant. Indeed, in most statistical statements of the factor model it is given only j—standing for the whole of h, j, and k—and t, standing for the particular trait it weights. The function sign (f) means that at this point we are not committed to a simple multiplication of a weight b by the individual's score on trait or state.

A second question about traits, and one sometimes debated in philosophical-methodological terms, concerns whether T_x (x being a particular trait) is or is not a structure purely *within the individual*. The answer is that when it is a common trait, it is a pattern fixed and definable only in terms of (1), a total population of people, and (2), the cultural-environmental situation. However, it is a structure carried around with him by the individual in a quantified personal endowment, and "belongs to him" to this extent. As such, it is a structure in him that results in a probability of each of a whole set of responses being made to each of a corresponding set of situations. Doubtless such a structure for potential behaviors usually is "carried around" as a neurological-somatic substrate, but, as stated earlier, we do not lean on physiology before it is appropriate and all we know initially is that it is a concept abstracted from behavior.

With this preparation regarding the character of traits in general we can now concentrate on the definition of a *source trait*. Apart from the ambiguity of culture and identity that dogs surface trait usage, a second objection exists in the statistical fact that a surface trait score in fact can always be resolved into more truly unitary components. These components are source traits. The source trait is operationally a particular kind of factor obtained from factor analysis under certain scientific conditions. Some readers may not be instructed in factor analysis and it is not necessary that they understand its calculations, but they must follow its logic if they are to grasp methodologically the importance and role of the source trait concept in psychology. An attempt will be made here to present the latter in a nutshell, by diagrammatic methods. But if this is not enough, the reader is referred to the excellent brief introductions by Child (1971) and by Lawlis and Chatfield (1973), and to fuller developments by Gorsuch (1974), Harman (1977), Mulaik (1972), and Cattell (1977).

A correlation coefficient, expressing the degree of linear relation between two variables, can be expressed spatially, geometrically, as the angle between two vectors (lines) (Figure 1-2), in which the cosine of the angle is made numerically equal to the correlation coefficient given by the experiment. This convention "follows

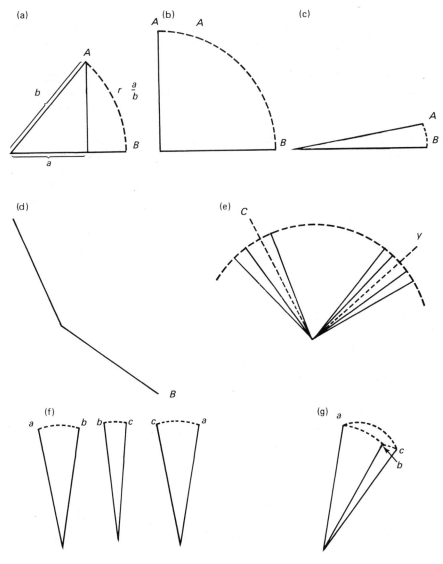

Figure 1-2.   Spatial representation of correlations.

through" in regard to the various properties of correlations. Thus, if the vectors (each drawn at unit length, assuming scores in standard scores) are at right angles as in Figure 1-2(b), there is zero correlation. If they are almost aligned, as in (c), it is nearly +1.0, and if they are nearly diametrically opposite, as in (d), then a correlation close to –1.0 is represented.

It will now become evident that surface traits, as defined by a cluster of variables in a correlation matrix in the last section (Table 1-1), will appear in this geometrical translation as bunches of vectors, visible as if they formed a "quiver of arrows" seen in Figure 1-2(*e*). Sometimes the central vector of each "quiver" will be oblique to— that is, correlated with—the central vector (centroid) of another such bunch. In other psychological experiments the clusters will be mutually orthogonal (uncorrelated, independent), as in the two illustrated at *C* and *y* in Figure 1-2(*e*). However, a moment's reflection will show that our being able to get all the lines (vectors of variables) into the plane of this paper is a special case, because a plane is restricted to representing two dimensions. If the experiment yielded correlations as shown between variables *a*, *b*, and *c* in Figure 1-2(*f*), then the only geometrical model that would represent this cluster is one "in the solid," shown in perspective in (*g*), like a flat cone.

The correlations given by the actual experiment in this last case have forced us to go into three independent dimensions. With more variables and correlations to accommodate, we would frequently find ourselves in four, five, or more spatial dimensions (which do not exist in our physical world), depending on the psychological complexity of the domain from which we take the variables.[7] What the mathematician calls the number of factors (or components) involved (which is fixed by the spatial dimensions demanded), is (when suitable conditions are met) the *number of influences or determiners* required to account for the observed rotations among the variables. It is this equating of factors with determiners, influences, or *sources* of variation that causes a factor in trait elements to be designated a source trait, as explained below.

In practice, the necessary dimensions are not actually obtained by the geometrical plotting process or matrix of correlations (like putting knitting needles into a cork), as illustrated above, but by an algebraic and computational process aimed to determined the *rank* (as it is called) of the given correlation matrix. This statement goes as far as we need go here into factor technicalities as such; the reader may extend his foundations in the recommended literature. Suffice it that the researcher who begins with a matrix of experimentally obtained correlations among *n* variables, as shown in Figure 1-3(*a*), can, by computer processes, get to a factor matrix, as shown in (*b*). This matrix will have columns for the *k* factors required ($k < n$) and *n* rows of variables. The figures down a column in the factor matrix give the loadings of each factor on each variable, that is, the weight to be assigned to the given factor score in contributing to a person's score on the given variable. Thus if one factor were fluid intelligence, g_f, we should expect it to have high loadings on such variables as

(a) Çorrelation matrix of n variables (not completely filled in).

	V_1	V_2	V_3	V_4	...	V_n
V_1	1.0	r_{12}	r_{13}	r_{14}	...	r_{1n}
V_2	r_{12}	1.0	r_{23}	r_{24}	...	r_{2n}
V_3	r_{13}	r_{23}	1.0	r_{34}	...	r_{3n}
V_4	r_{14}	r_{24}	r_{34}	1.0	...	r_{4n}
.	.	.	.	.	.	.
.	.	.	.	.	.	.
.	.	.	.	.	.	.
V_n	r_{1n}	r_{2n}	r_{3n}	r_{4n}	...	1.0

(b) Derived factor matrix: k factors (F's) loading (b's) on n variables.

	F_1	F_2	...	F_k
V_1	b_{11}	b_{12}	...	b_{1k}
V_2	b_{21}	b_{22}	...	b_{2k}
V_3	b_{31}	b_{32}	...	b_{3k}
V_4	b_{41}	b_{42}	...	b_{4k}
.	.	.	.	.
.	.	.	.	.
.	.	.	.	.
V_n	b_{n1}	b_{n2}	...	b_{nk}

Figure 1-3. Transition from experimentally given correlation matrix to factor matrix.

The matrix (b) is set out here only to show the common factors. Later we shall see that for completeness it needs an $n \times n$ square extension to the right to represent the n, specific factors. The diagonal of the correlation does not have unities in it when factors (rather than components) are desired. It would normally be composed of estimate communalities, symbolized as h^2.

of running a mile or ability to sing; it would have near zero correlations with the latter.

The columns of V_{fp} (the symbol for the *factor pattern* matrix), if factors are kept orthogonal, can be set up as coordinates (at right angles) with regard to which the positions of test (behavior) variables can be plotted visibly in space. To get any such plot one takes the columns of V_{fp} two at a time, to constitute a single plane—the graph paper—and using the pairs of numbers for each variable, as shown in Figure 1-4(b), gives it a point in space, as the tip of a vector (arrow).

Geometrically, one can thus look at the factors as coordinates or axes in space, but they are algebraically and statistically the sources of variance contributing to the variance of the variables. The variance contribution is shown by the loadings (squared), which are the projections in Figure 1-4. It is from this plotting from the V_{fp} matrix that one can visualize the variables in space, in the manner in which we began (Figure 1-2). This diagram (Figure 1-4a) enables us to see clearly that the number of surface traits need not be the same as the number of factors, and, indeed, the surface traits will typically be more numerous, each being resolvable, as stated above, into some particular combination of the common, more basic, source traits. In the MMPI, for example, which has scales that are surface traits, it has been shown in various researches that five or six factors suffice to account for a dozen or more of the scales (Cattell, 1973).

This means that any set of surface traits (i.e., the central vectors in the clusters)—or, for that matter, any set of variables—can be represented, estimated, and perhaps explained in terms of the factors,[8] because, as seen above, the latter are the coordinates that give the traits position. For example, any of the several clusters in Figure 1-4(a) in two-space can be represented, analyzed, and located by their projections on each of the two common broad unit-length factors. Thus, in Figure 1-4, the projections for some three variables, C_2, C_3, and C_1, on two factors F_A and F_B, might be extracted from two columns of a matrix like V_{fp} in Figure 1-3(b) and set down separately as:

	F_A	F_B
C_2	.80	.30
C_3	.25	.84
C_1	.46	.75

We can plot them, giving the positions for the variable vectors shown at C_2, C_3, and C_1 in Figure 1-4(b).

Psychologically, this means that we can explain the behaviors in

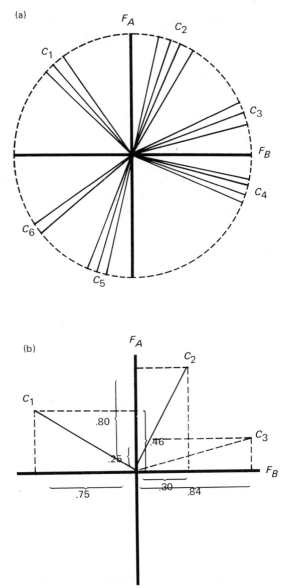

Figure 1-4. The placing of test vectors by their discovered projections on factors.

each of these syndrome clusters in terms of just two broad source traits, operating with different relative influence. Algebraically, in a domain of statistical values, it means that we can estimate an individual's scores on behaviors C_2, C_3, and C_1 by taking his factor scores

F_{Ai}, F_{Bi} and introducing them into the equations that follow, using the factor weights from the V_{fp} above, thus:

$$C_{2i} = .80F_{Ai} + .30F_{Bi}$$

$$C_{3i} = .25F_{Ai} + .84F_{Bi}$$

$$C_{1i} = .46F_{Ai} + .75F_{Bi}$$

Strictly these are not complete equations because they only give *best estimates* of C_2, C_3, and C_1, and for the full *specification equation*, as it will be described below, *all* the common *and* the specific factors we have talked about would have to be included.

Such equations (in their complete form), as generalized in equation (1-5) below, are called *behavioral specification equations* because they specify the observed behavior in terms of underlying factors. Granted certain conditions in the factor analysis (Gorsuch, 1974; Cattell, 1978), we can assume that the factors found are *underlying influences* that build up the surface traits or specific behavior responses and explain a person's endowment in those performances. Thus the specification equation is both a means to estimate a specific person's score, in some particular behavior and environment, from his known factor scores and the V_{fp} loadings, and also a general statement about what the magnitude of different behavior sources is in that particular response for people in general.

Symbolically, in algebraic statements, we shall represent the *loadings* (i.e., .80, .30, -.75, etc.) by *b*'s, to indicate that they are behavior indices, that is, contributions to behavior from the factors. For ease of memorizing and recognizing what an equation means, in this book I have chosen symbols as far as possible as easily remembered mnemonics for the words and retain these symbols as a standard language. Thus in general we write a response *act* as *a*. Subscripts *h*, *j*, and *k*, as stated earlier, indicate that it is response *j* to the focal stimulus *h*, in "ambient situation" *k*; *j* defines the particular character of the act and *a* the aspect or units in which it is measured (it could be distance covered, errors, number of words spoken, etc.). Similarly, we will now write *T* (not *F*, which is only the mathematical *factor*) for any factor experimentally so extracted that it corresponds to a *trait*—a source trait. The subscript *i* is written below both *a* and *T* to indicate a given *individual's* magnitude on the response act and his particular score on the trait. Thus generalized, and extended to *p* factors, the behavioral specification equation can be written:

$$a_{hijk} = b_{hjk(1)}T_{1i} + b_{hjk(2)}T_{2i} + \cdots$$

$$+ b_{hjk(p)}T_{pi} + b_{(hjk)}T_{(hjk)i} \qquad (1\text{-}5)$$

There are p factors instead of one as in the previous equations, because we now move on to recognize the important principle, always respected hereafter, that *human behavior is multiply determined*. To do something solely for one purpose, and to have it affected purely by one ability and one temperament trait is a limiting and highly exceptional action. Parenthetically, the trait number for b is placed in a bracket here to emphasize that the b involvement is peculiar to each factor. Hereafter this separate emphasis will be omitted.

The last term is a specific factor T_{hjk}, specific to the response j, to stimulus h in the ambient (background) situation k. As pointed out above, it should not be confused with a trait unique to an individual. Everybody has it; but it is unique (or *specific*, as we say to avoid confusion) to that bit of behavior. Such factors may play an appreciable part in highly practiced skills. Ability to hit a target when firing an arrow from a bow may depend partly on general dexterity, spatial ability, intelligence, and other general, broad traits, but principally on a specific ability related to years of practice with a bow and arrow. To avoid confusion we shall continue henceforth with the distinct terms developed above: *broad* (not common), as opposed to *specific* factor traits, and *common* (across people), as opposed to *unique* (peculiar to one person) traits.

The use of correlation and factor analysis to structure behavior, though now widespread, successful, and technically greatly developed, has met some spirited objections. The majority are from critics who give painful evidence of not understanding it. (Some counter-critics have said that its technical difficulties have aroused in the critics a desire not to *want* to learn it!) But other analyses of certain defects and limitations are real, relevant, and valuable. For example, one may ask whether it fits the scientific model, that is, our conception of how influences *actually* interact, in that (1) it adds the effects of influences, whereas it is possible that, for example, they multiply one another; and (2) it assumes, as does all representation by correlations, a linear, not a curvilinear, relation between variables and factors. For adequate discussions of these the reader must be referred to a factor analysis text (Cattell, 1978); Gorsuch, 1974; Rummel, 1970). But one point should be clarified here: that source traits are not just factors; but factors with special auxiliary conditions required in their extraction. Principally the factors must be what is called *uniquely rotated.* It will be evident that the factor axes in Figure 1-4 could be rotated to different positions yielding alternative sets of projections (loadings) that would equally well place the *tests* in their correct relative positions, that is, with their correct correlations. Indeed, mathematically the factors can be rotated into an infinite number of equivalent positions. (Imagine F_A and F_B in Figure 1-4 spun like a roulette wheel.) Power of prediction is not altered by their rotations, but the meaning of factors *is*, for we interpret factors by what they do to variables.

The psychologist thus introduces conditions beyond those of the mathematician's factor textbook, namely: simple structure, invariance as shown by proportional profiles (Cattell, 1944, 1976), replicability across experiments, the freedom of factors to go "oblique" (to be themselves mutually correlated), yielding higher-order structures, and so on. The psychologist must have the rotation uniquely determined by conditions outside those of mathematics because he is looking for a relatively small number of underlying real-life influences that his scientific faith in simplicity tells him can account for the bewildering array of correlations among the almost infinite number of variables with which psychologists have to deal. (Just so the chemist sees the immense variety of compounds in nature, for example, in the rocks beneath our feet, as products of scarcely 100 elements.)[9] The principle of simple structure by which a factor is aligned with a real determiner or trait is expressed very briefly in Figure 1-5. (The second available aid—confactor rotation—is more complex. See Cattell, 1978.) The basic argument—the simplicity condition—is that if one takes enough manifestations of behavior, no one trait is likely to affect more than a subset of them. Consequently the position is sought in which *most* variables have only zero projection on most factors, and that position is reached in Figure 1-5(*b*) by moving the mathematical factor *Y* to the position *T*, which is most likely to coincide with a trait.

1-5.   A Taxonomy of Trait Varieties and the Personality Sphere Concept

Our excursion into factor analysis in Section 1-4 may seem a little tough, but it is necessary for later developments. If so condensed a presentation is not sufficiently clear on first reading, the reader can count on help from supplementary clarifications given as we proceed.

Putting together source traits with respect to the action of the total personality upon a single variable performance, as achieved in

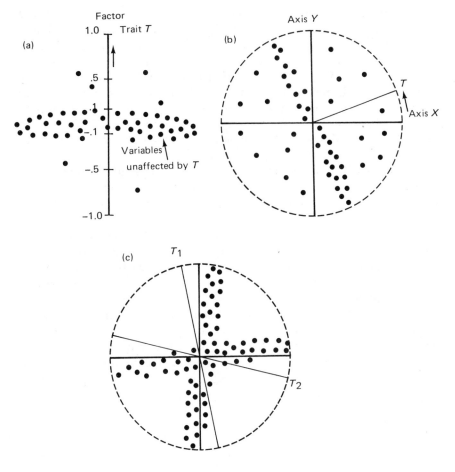

Figure 1-5.   Illustration of unique rotation to simple structure.

the specification equation (1-4) above, was necessary to complete the overall picture of the relations of traits to various specific response performances. It is a fundamental psychological concept, but our concentration in the rest of this chapter will be on the taxonomy of traits and states in *themselves*, which is a prime necessity before proceeding to developmental questions.

We have described the difference between common traits (of which some level of endowment is possessed by everyone, such as intelligence, stature, exvia, anxiety), and unique traits (those peculiar to one person, such as shivering at the sight of a crab apple). It has been added that many seemingly unique traits can be largely resolved into unique combinations of common traits.

A second dichotomy of traits—broad versus specific—has already been distinguished from the first, but it remains now to define it more fully. A broad trait is one that affects a great deal of behavior, as does intelligence, anxiety, or exvia. A narrow—ultimately, a completely specific—trait is one that affects only relatively specific behavior and ultimately a single bit of behavior, for example, power to distinguish two shades of green. Note that this is "orthogonal" to the above common-versus-unique dichotomy and that both common and unique traits can be either broad or specific,[10] as we can be reminded schematically by Table 1-2.

The scientific model—in this case, the psychological model—must therefore be distinguished from the local mathematical usage, in that the terms *broad* and *specific* in psychology have no dependence on any particular correlation matrix. Indeed, to avoid confusion with the mathematician's use of "specific factor," it might be useful to speak of broad and *restricted* source traits, for it is really psychologically unlikely that some skill will be absolutely specific to one behavior, with no transfer at all. However, we shall stick to "specific," with the qualification that it may not be absolute.

By now the reader will have realized that the distinction between broad and specific (restricted) must ultimately have to rest on some conception of *a totality of behavior*, and to this question of choice of a total population of variables in investigating source traits we must now come. Anyone looking back at publications in personality

TABLE 1—2. Essential Types of Source Traits (Operationally, Uniquely Rotated Factors)

| Experimentally Obtained from: | Analytically Separated among Variables as: | |
	Broad* (factors)	Specific (factors)
A group	Common broad trait	Common specific trait
An individual	Unique (personal) broad trait	Unique (personal) specific trait

*This table aims particularly to remove the confusion due to a statistical tradition of using "common" and "unique" only from the point of view of a given matrix of variables. If "broad" is used regarding variables (which is more correct even from the statistical point of view, since rotated factors do not load *all* variables in a matrix) the communication difficulties are resolved.

6346026

research over the last 50 years must recognize that although investigators have rightly been seeking for "significant variables," the search has been conducted very unsystematically. Indeed, the choice of "significant" variables for analysis has largely been dominated by the fads and fashions of each decade. The search for the main dimensions of personality by factor analysis has been seen correctly as the most objective way of finding central, significant concepts, but that search often has been superficial and unsystematic. The initial theories that directed choice of variables for research were frequently hunches from loose popular themes, or at best from clinical observation, instead of arising from careful search of the emerging network of connections—that is, from scanning significant correlations scattered through the quantitative research literature. Sometimes this research even has deserved the label "magpie research," because the researcher has been fixated by the twinkle of some experimental gadget or fine-sounding scholarly term.

Search for the major and ultimately theoretically important source traits can be pursued more systematically than by these undirected and often odd choices, and on a broad front, in two ways. First, new research must carry *marker variables* for factors already known. It necessarily must move by trial-and-error expansion into new areas from the existing boundaries of known areas. An analogy in geography is the expansion of the Roman Empire before the concept of the spherical earth was popularly accepted. The second principle is that one can break loose from the restrictions of one's immediate horizons and abstractly define some totality of behavior. A geographical analogy here would be the argument by Prince Henry the Navigator (and therefore of Columbus) that the earth was a finite sphere over which one could plan systematic exploration. The first principle can be illustrated at its best by Spearman taking out the factor of general intelligence from ability tests, followed by Thurstone's careful extension of findings to new primary abilities by more detailed representation of the new behavior areas involved along with the old. It can also be illustrated in demonstrations by Spearman's students, such as Pinaar, Studman, Bernstein, and others, of factors of speed, rigidity, and fluency, while they kept markers on general intelligence so that it could be partialled out of the later measures.

The proposal for the second principle of research was made in the concept of the *personality sphere* (Cattell, 1946). This notion of staking out a *totality* of human behavior, in a stratified sample, was attempted first by resort to the dictionary. Allport and Odbert (1930) had found 3,000 to 4,000 words in the dictionary describing human behavior; it seemed reasonable to them that after 10,000 years of behavior description by human gossips and playwrights, symbols for most kinds of behavior would have grown into the language. The gains from this new approach to source traits—basing the choice of behavior variables and correlation matrices on a stratified sample from the verbal personality sphere—were at once evident. As the next chapter will show, it raised the number of replicated factors at one stroke from about four or five replicated in researches in arbitrary domains to that date to 15 or 20.

However, it is evident both from certain restrictions in the final results and from logic that human terms for defining humans cannot be considered to complete the definition of the human personality (a sobering thought for "humanistic" psychologists). What an automobile, or a dog, or a bed, "sees" in human beings does not get into human language. One must come in the end, therefore, to the more objective and complete conception of the personality sphere of human behavior variables provided by a more empirical look directly at behavior. The proposed improved source is an actual sampling of what people in our culture are doing over a typical 24-hour period. A stratified sample of, say, 1,000 such measurable behavior response variables has not yet been investigated, but the concept has guided much of the trait research here discussed. Incidentally, even when the sample of 1,000 representative behaviors is made, one is not entirely clear of subjectivity. A closer consideration of measurement shows that a need remains for a rationale of what operational measures to take on these elements. The further refinements of principle needed here are discussed systematically in Cattell and Warburton (1967).

Only with respect to a total *personality sphere* defined in some objective way can the terms *broad* and *restricted (specific)* be given unambiguous meaning. Almost certainly the calling of certain performances "specific traits" from a matrix of, say, 100 variables is only a confession of our ignorance of common, broad traits not yet pulled out of the given specific variance by the presence of requisite variables to show what at first seems a specific. Given more variables to join up with, such specifics often would become part of broad traits. The psychologist cannot go along with certain artificial factor-analytic procedures that artificially give all traits unit communality, that is, account for *all* behavior by broad traits, as in Caffrey and Kaiser's alpha factor analysis (1965), for truly psychologically restricted specific traits undoubtedly exist. On the other hand, and particularly in refutation of what amounts to a theory of total chaos of specifics (see Mischel, 1968, and others), one must point out that specific factor variance gets smaller with every year of substantive research.

For lack of further systematic work on the time-sampled personality sphere, however, some important advances even today are still made by the first approach—trial-and-error expansion from a known area. This is seen in the location of seven missing personality factors and 12 pathological factors by Bolton (1965), Delhees (1971), and Watterson (see Cattell & Watterson, 1978), and in the discovery of new abilities through the exploration of new types of test by Hakstian (1974) and Horn and Anderson (1978).

With broad and restricted thus defined, the summary of the main categorization in the taxonomy of traits in Table 1-2 should be clear. If we take a statistically more refined look at the concept of the common, broad source trait, we must recognize that it will change its pattern somewhat with divisions of the total population, as in special samples by age, sex, social class, and so on. In a manner of speaking, therefore, we can recognize a gradation between a common trait and a unique trait pattern.[11]

1-6.   Processes and States

A famous doctor, Sir William Osler, used to remind his students that "It is important to know not only what sort of disease the patient has, but also what sort of patient has the disease." As it happens, psychologists have been in need of precisely the opposite admonition, because for 50 years they have tried to predict behavior from traits, without any practice or rational theoretical model for handling the *state* in which the individual finds himself. Normally a good deal of the determination of the level of a response will be found to depend on a state measure, for example, whether a man is angry, tired, or fearful, and so on, as well as on scores on his permanent traits.

But how do we discover the basic mood states? Popular language may mislead us. For example, although there is one word "anxiety," there *may* be two or three distinct kinds of anxiety instead of one. Possibly the word "depression" hides the existence of several distinct and independent axes of depression variations. Certainly the descriptive array of moods as we actually experience them is almost infinite, and the novelist uses many words indeed. Yet the probability is that most moods are mixtures that can be resolved into a not-excessive number of primary states, just as the painter gets all the colors of the rainbow out of three primaries.

The way to find the naturally unitary states—which are presumably innately defined autonomic and hypothalamic response patterns— is obviously to take some individual and measure him day after day on an array of variables known to fluctuate a good deal with

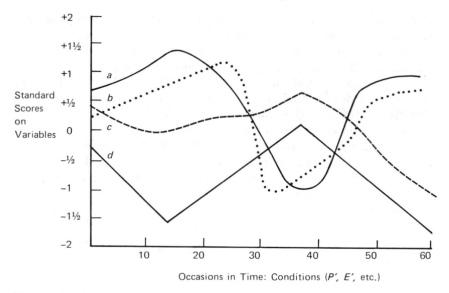

Occasions in Time: Conditions (*P′, E′,* etc.)

Figure 1-6.   Location of unitary state response patterns by covariation over time: basis of *P*-technique correlations.

emotional and other states. Then if we plot the scores over time, as in Figure 1-6, it will be seen that some variables change together and others do not. Correlated over time, certain variables—as *a* and *b* above—would appear as a cluster following one course, while another —*c* and *d*—shows a totally independent course. Actually, as with traits, it is better to seek them as factors rather than clusters. Then we factor a correlation matrix among the manifestations, the correlations being derived from a series of measurements over many occasions. They thus represent distinct axes along which states can vary, and we recognize the nature of the states—say, elation and anxiety— by the variables most consistently affected by (loaded on) the factors.

If we tried to separate by eye such common trends in the plot, it would become very difficult as the number of variables and clusters increased beyond those in the simplified case in Figure 1-6. So we *correlate* the variables *over time*, just as with traits we have correlated them over people. From factor analyzing such a correlation matrix, we get the number and nature of the independent state response patterns necessary to account for mood change in that person. This has been called *P*-technique, because it factors the individual *person*, to contrast with *R*-technique, the term given to the usual over-persons, individual-difference factoring. There is also a differential *R*-technique, written *dR*-technique, which is a cross-check with

P-technique and will be more fully discussed in Chapter 5, devoted entirely to states.

Before experiment got going in this area, one might not have risked giving an a priori answer to the question "Are state patterns the same for all people?" But it turns out that, at least for anxiety, depression, fatigue, and so on, people are highly similar in loading pattern—although not so much in the sources of provocation. One could speculate, as the Laceys (1958) have done, whether different stimuli for, say, anxiety, produce different patterns of anxiety. It will be noted that in ordinary *P*-technique one does not bother to supply the stimuli (life does this) but one does nevertheless get a pattern indicating that whenever anxiety is turned on and turned off it tends to appear with the same response pattern. The differences seen by the Laceys and others would be accounted for, on this supposition of unchanging state factor dimensions, as differences only among *surface* states. Different combinations of the constant source states thus produce different surface patterns. In fact, precisely the same categorization can be made for types of states as was done for types of traits in Table 1-2, and actual state patterns are set out in a factor pattern matrix as in Figure 1-3(*b*).

When states and associated behaviors follow a certain sequence, we have what everyday language calls a *process*. Such a process may be unique, never again repeated; but actually a great deal of our behavior and our development patterns repeat some characteristic sequence and constitute *common* processes. Thus the sequence of yielding to a particular temptation and experiencing remorse afterward may repeat itself in some clinical cases, and the sequences in adolescence are recognizable as a common developmental process across many persons. Again, just as with traits and states, we can recognize once more common and unique *processes*. Naturally the concern of science with generalization and with prediction on as broad a basis as possible leads to most attention being focused on common processes that are also broad processes, in terms of the categories in Table 1-2.

Very little substantive research has been done with a precise model for processes, but it is clear from general principles that any process can be represented, as in Figure 1-7, by a thread of events woven along a time axis orthogonal to a two-or-more-dimensional framework. *P*-technique will supply us with the list of dimensions necessary in such a framework to represent state and other behavior change. The new feature that enters process representation is that environmental stimuli and situations *also* change over time; in later chapters, such as 5 and 7, we shall show how these also are incorporated into the matrix of occasions by rows, and factors by columns.

(a) Directly on Variables as Score Sequence

(1) General Case

(2) When Responses can be Reliably Tied to Particular Stimuli

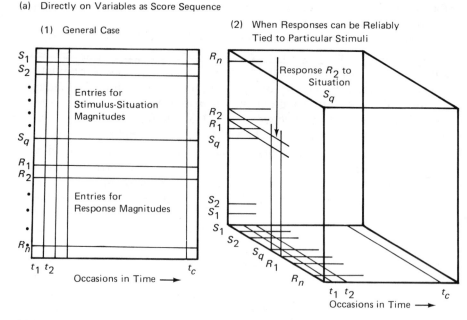

(b) In Fewer Dimensions, from Factoring Variables, and Expressed (For Two Dimensions) Graphically

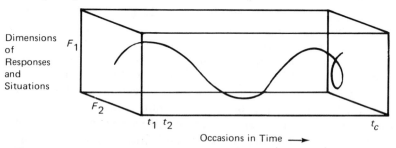

Occasions in Time ⟶

Figure 1-7.   Description of a sequence or specific process.

Beginning with a score matrix of variables over time for one person, as shown at Figure 1-7(a)(1), factoring yields state dimensions. Upon these dimensions the process in the given individual can be plotted as a curve in time, as in Figure 1-7(b). This is also representable digitally as a matrix like (a), except that scores are on factors instead of variables and the things scored are occasions. The next step after thus defining some one instance is to locate *common* processes, and this calls for applying pattern similarity coefficients among many matrices like that just described. The procedure for sorting out the different "types" of process from this matrix is then the same as in Section 1-7 below, on types generally.

As mentioned, because processes include the subject's encountering a prescribed series of stimuli as well as making the series of responses, the full description of a common process ultimately requires both strength of the characteristically encountered stimuli and of the responses to be included in the descriptive matrix, as in Figure 1-7(a)(2). The objective location and measurement of common processes by this (or any other) basic model is practically unrepresented in psychological research at the present time. Psychologists depend on everyday observation to define a process such as courtship, adolescence, onset of schizophrenia; and the statements of what happens are correspondingly imprecise and open to doubt. A fuller account of statistical notions involved can be read in Cattell (1966) and an excellent review of change analysis in general in Harris (1963). Despite this methodological neglect it is obvious that processes, for example, typical processes of learning, maturation, and adjustment, are important structures. They are structures in the sense of recurrent patterns of behavior, but even less than traits are they to be considered as definable entirely in the individual. They are joint structures in the individual and his physical environment. But recognizing, naming, and measuring them are very important parts of the taxonomy of human behavior.

1-7. Types and the Methods for Their Discovery

Psychology in its early and clinical observation stages has been as prone to recognize types by eye as it has processes. But for type the disagreements are compounded by abuse of the term in diverse and ill-defined senses. Few terms are so abused in psychology as "type." There are many arbitrary definitions. The present writer (1946) once collected 45 such, but fortunately most psychologists are interested in much the same two basic uses. The problem is that these two uses are seldom clearly and operationally defined and distinguished. One practice defines a type by a person at an *extreme score*, commonly in a bipolar distribution, as in Figure 1-8. In this sense some define introvert and extrovert, or idiot and genius, as types. For them the "extreme" cases on *any* trait constitute "types." This is a redundant concept, for trait score will handle what is described—and more accurately. A second use, offering much that is needed over and

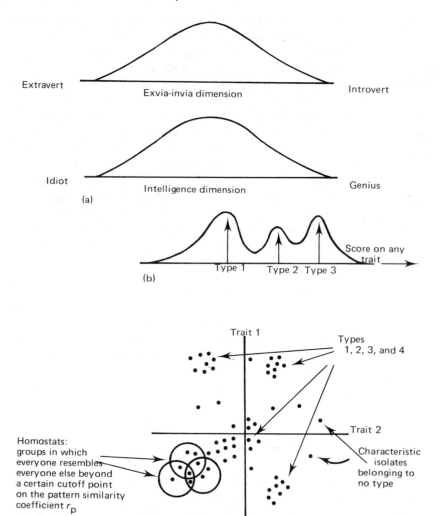

Figure 1-8. Operational meaning of type.

above the trait concept is to define a type as a *mode*, as shown in Figure 1-8(*b*).

More frequently in nature, as we look at such "species types," we recognize that they are at *modes* in the statistical sense, occurring on several trait axes at once. This means, as in Figure 1-8(*c*), that they are clusters of people (or other organisms) that segregate out into groups in special zones of the space marked out by the several trait axes. As in biology, where it seems that certain combinations are just not viable—a serpent with wings, for example—so in human psychology there are blank spaces in the mathematically possible combinations. For example, a man with great rapidity and strength but poor vision cannot become a typical successful boxer; a man with the human insights needed in a diplomat, but hopeless at languages, would not function as a foreign consul.

This is not the place to digress into all Darwin's wise observations about the *origins* of types because our purpose is descriptive, but one can see that by survival rates individuals will present a mode—that is, multiply in combinations of scores that have some happy functional interaction and advantage. Similarly, in the cultural aspect of types, rewarding jobs and other roles will create certain peculiar combinations of skills producing modes in hyperspace at measurable points where those combinations are functional. There may be additional reasons for some combinations being so plentifully represented, beyond survival and cultural fashioning; but our concern at this point is with discovering and defining, not explaining.

The discovery of types was first undertaken using the same methods as for finding clusters of variables (compare Figure 1-8 with 1-4*a*), because the situations are formally similar. The main difference is that in one case we have test variables and, in the other, people, placed by projections on factor axes in a factor hyperspace. A minor difference is that we use a different index of nearness. We have already pointed out that clustering by correlations among variables is a poor procedure (see Burdsal & Cattell, 1974, for the problem in detail), and the correlation coefficient is still poorer for evaluating the similarity of individuals' profiles. The first step in typing a population is to find *homostats*. These are defined as closely similar positions in the space. To locate them it is necessary to make a Q-matrix (like an R-matrix but bounded by people instead of tests) and to enter in each cell the resemblance of the profiles of the two people concerned as measured by the pattern similarity coefficient r_p (instead of correlation r). A cluster in r_p values, like one in r values in Table 1-1, means that the people are close together. They form a homostat, as shown at the lower left of Figure 1-8(*c*). The overlap of several homostats is recognizable by a further calculation and defines technically a *segregate*, which is a scientific definition corresponding to one common use of type.

Typology is a complex field as regards methodology, and in research one must either study it thoroughly or leave it alone. However, a computer program called Taxonome (Cattell & Coulter, 1966) has been invented to sort profiles by basic principles of taxonomy objectively into species types (segregates). Parenthetically, the reader should be warned that the factor-analytic procedure called

Q-technique is *not* a means of finding types, but only of finding dimensions, as pointed out long ago by Burt (1936) and later by Cattell (1951), Ross (1963), and others. As an illustration of Taxonome, it is of behavior-genetic interest to note that it has successfully sorted dogs, *by behavior alone*, into types that prove to be the same as the physically recognized breeds (Cattell, Korth, & Bolz, 1974). The psychologist who would get into this statistically and conceptually complex field should read Bolz (1974); Cattell and Coulter (1966); Cattell, Coulter, and Tsujioka (1966); May (1973); and Sokal and Sneath (1968).

When types have been shown by objective methods to exist, each abstract "type as such" can be represented exactly by the vector of the centroid (mean pattern) of the people in the homostat or segregate, and its members can be still more completely separated from those of other types by applying the multiple discriminant function (Tatsuoka, 1970). Any single individual can then, by r_p, be assigned indices for how true he is to the main pure type to which he belongs and how much he has resemblances to other types. From knowing that an individual belongs to a type, the advantage is that we can predict one part of the type pattern from the rest. "Is he a dog?" Then he will bark. "Is he a mathematician?" Then he will score high on an intelligence test.

The factor analytic definition of trait patterns becomes blurred when a population of mixed types is factored (see Gorsuch, 1974). Good taxonomic principles tell us, therefore, that we should first put people into types (where they exist), and then find trait structures within those species. The definition of an individual is that he or she belongs to a categorical type—a female human, a college graduate—and that he or she possesses such and such source trait score deviations from the known central tendency of that type. In analysis of variance with a single effect, we can break down an individual's score into the mean score of his subgroup and his deviation from that mean. What we are advocating here is analogous to this but in multivariate terms. More variance can indeed be accounted for by common factors if we recognize between-group and within-group factors. Assigning an individual to a type on the between-group variables will tell you a moderate amount about him—for example, if a person is diagnosed as a drug addict or a manic-depressive we can predict much—but individual trait scores from the *mean* of such groups are wanted, too. Finally, there is the special statistical development in which we say an individual is so much of this type and so much of that and so much of yet another, but this distance score from a set of points is more cumbersome and less widely useful than source trait measurement per se. The distance measures are handled, as indicated above, by r_p's between the person's profile and the various pure type profiles.

1-8. Summary

1. The study of personality and personality learning change has gone through three major, very different methodological phases: literary, clinical, and experimental. In the present experimental phase research needs a strategic alternation of multivariate and bivariate experimental methods.

2. The necessary basis for experiment is a sound taxonomy of traits—not an arbitrary concentration on this and that particular bit of behavior from the infinite possible number of such response variables. *Surface* traits are found by locating correlation clusters of variables, while both common and unique *unitary source* traits can be located by a special development of *factor analysis*. The division of either *common* or *unique* traits into *broad* and *restricted* (or specific) traits can be pursued objectively with the aid of the personality sphere concept, which maps a total population of variables.

3. The exact description of an individual at a given moment requires measurements on both traits and states. The structure of states is found by factoring measurements made at a series of occasions in time, as in *P*-technique and *dR*-technique. The unitary state response patterns thus reached as factors we call *state dimensions*. Research indicates that when the environment provokes a shift along one of these dimensions, the state patterns of expression of a state in variables are largely independent of the specific nature of the stimulus that provokes them. (The psychophysiological pattern of fear, for example, is fear regardless of whether it is provoked by a letter, a bull, or a thunderstorm.)

4. A process, common or unique, is representable as a sequence of state behavior *and* stimulation situation level plotted over time against multiple coordinates. This curve can alternatively be expressed by a process *matrix*. One must distinguish between a particular process (one person, one period) and a common process. Common processes are located like types by r_p similarities of many process profiles (each a matrix), for which purpose Taxonome can be used. The value of adding information about processes to measures of traits and states is that the probability of certain sequences is implied, permitting at any moment a stochastic estimate of behavior at various further intervals.

5. Except for a superfluous usage of "type" for extremes of a dis-

tribution on a source trait (which is more precisely statable by a source trait measurement alone, for example, "His IQ is 64" rather than "He is a mental defective"), the useful application of type is for a "species type" (the term comes from biological analogy). This in turn splits technically (see Chapter 5) into a *homostat* and a *segregate*.

6. Objective means of locating species types, where types exist, have been developed in the Taxonome method and program. Using the pattern similarity coefficient in a Q-matrix, the Taxonome program leads to the isolation of a set of groups and to a defining modal set of measurements for each group isolated. Strictly, psychometrics should first define the type to which the individual belongs (which may itself give some prediction of his behavior), and then deal with source traits defined *within* the species, permitting a statement of his source trait deviation measures from the centroid (or mode). There are in fact two sets of trait coordinates, those placing the particular type within the population of types and those placing an individual within his own type.

7. Our concern in this chapter has been primarily to set out the methods whereby the significant trait, state process, and other such structures can be found, conceived, psychometrically defined, and measured for individuals. (Technical psychometric considerations of measurement scaling, such as validity and reliability, will be discussed in later chapters.) However, even though our main concern is descriptively to take the individual to pieces, we should, even at this stage give a glimpse of how he can be put together again. This is done, as far as the role of the total personality and situation in a single act is concerned, by the behavior specification equation (1-5), p. 23 above. Therein the theory predicts the magnitude of a response act, a_{hijk}, from the total trait scores of the individual, each weighted by a behavioral index peculiar to the stimulus situation and the nature of the response behavior. This general model was developed (equations 1-3 and 1-4) without the special development of traits as unitary factors, but is finally shaped with traits and behavioral indices defined in that more precise framework. In this model we shall consistently use the subscripts h for a focal stimulus, i for an individual, j for a particular pattern of response, k for an ambient situation, and a for a quantitatively scaled numerical score on the act j. The source traits are T's, the states S's, and the behavioral indices defining the role of the environment, in perception and act, are b's.

8. The psychological model used at this point represents a linear and additive (summative) action of traits and states—the simplest model that can be supposed. It has error and specific terms for the

part that cannot be scored. Later (Chapter 5) we shall consider possible modifications for a still better fit of the scientific model to the data, though it can be said here and now that the empirical findings studied in the next few chapters show that the simple model works very well.

NOTES

[1] Virtually all sciences have some disreputable episodes in their infancy! Chemists are a bit embarrassed by the philosophers' stone of alchemists, and astronomers do not like to talk about astrology. But psychology has been more wayward than most in its attempt to escape the difficult discipline of a descriptive taxonomy and in its wild addiction to global explanatory theories. Further, it is probably more inconvenienced than any other science—except possibly medicine—by the entanglement of its serious study with popular folklore. Even the shrewdest everyday generalizations, when couched in undefined terms, are of little value to a scientific psychology. At last we are seeing that, just as the medical profession made progress by introducing sober but precise Latin terms (at the risk of charges of pomposity), so we have to start afresh with technical, specialized, operational terms for our descriptions. Only thus can we save our exact ideas and careful research from the continual waste and confusion of discussion that arises when we use popular terms meaning all things to everyone.

[2] Incidentally, as a change over time, a movement, measured as *d*, should really be called a *kinetic* term; but psychology has often invoked "dynamic," to be opposed to "static." Unfortunately, this use of dynamic, which creates two different usages in psychology, again obscures discussion. When used in what is properly the sense of "kinetic," the term "dynamic" means "having to do with change over time." In the other, more established use it refers specifically to the modality of "motivation and drive." It would help if, as here, we consistently referred to the first as the physicist does in "kinetic measures," and "kinetic analysis," reserving "dynamic" for referral to motivational phenomena and theories.

Equally confusing is the way in which the term "genetic" strays into this area of change study, in that some child psychologists use it to describe "developmental psychology." Genetics is today surely best used with the firm associations it now has throughout the life sciences, namely, as the study of inheritance. Psychological genetics, consequently, is the study of *hereditary determination of behavior*. Developmental psychology is strictly that aspect of kinetic psychology that deals with long-term rather than momentary changes.

[3] In the bivariate method the experimenter relates (by mean differences or correlation) two variables only. If their measurement is made successive (sequential) in time he may properly call one the dependent and one (which he may also manipulate) the independent variable (otherwise his choice of which is independent is arbitrary and *statistical*, not causal, and does not really have the same meaning as causal dependence). Each variable in bivariate design is often considered to stand for a whole concept. For example, the bivariate experimenter may relate anxiety to rate of learning, representing the first by skin conductance (known to rise during periods of anxiety) and the second by

rate of conditioning of a GSR response to a visual stimulus (conditioning being equated with learning). It is important—but uncommon—to recognize that the correlation of the single-variable measurement operation with the concept is necessarily poor, because of the large specific, extraneous factors in the variance of any specific variable. Sometimes, moreover, the equating of operation and concept is entirely arbitrary and prefaced by no demonstration of their correlation. For example, one investigator, stating a not-untypical hypothesis that women are more extraverted than men, depends on his own fiat that extraversion is measured by memory for faces.

In the multivariate approach the experimenter adopts a very different strategy. To investigate the above hypothesis he begins by correlating many alleged manifestations of (operations for) anxiety or whatever concept is being used and, by factor analyzing (Section 1-4), sees if anxiety behaves operationally as a *single* entity, influence, or concept. As Chapter 3 indicates, he is likely to find, in most behavior to which the word anxiety is traditionally attached, *two* common factors, quite apart from specifics. These are to be differentiated as *anxiety* and *effort stress*. Similarly, he may examine the second concept above, rate of learning, and find that rate of autonomic conditioning on the one hand and of cognitive learning of say, verbal material, on the other, are distinct factors, practically uncorrelated. Working with a mixture of the two can give us no intelligently usable answer.

For the bivariate approach to use a single concept, rate of learning, as the dependent and to claim to be relating it to a unitary concept, anxiety, as the independent variable is, therefore, an entirely unjustified identification of a single operation with a unitary broad concept. The conductance measure may prove on factoring to represent partly anxiety and partly stress (and, in fact, it does so and also measures partly the excitement or activation level, located and defined as PUI I [Cattell, 1957]). Thus we have yet a third unitary state, distinct from both anxiety and stress, covered by the alleged operational measure.

By contrast with this bivariate design procedure, the multivariate experimenter, having structured each field by the preliminary factoring described above (and, incidentally, having emerged with two entirely new concepts beyond the clinical concept of anxiety—namely, effort stress and PUI I), will now measure anxiety by a weighted collection of variables known to be loaded on the factor and producing a known, calculable degree of validity. For a good state measure, he thus sets up a battery of typically as many as six to eight varied subtests, combining them with weights indicated in the factoring. He next proceeds to relate this factor-proved anxiety measurement to a similarly more refined and broadly anchored concept of, say, "rate of autonomic learning among learning variables," having also shown other learning factors are different. The conclusions from the multivariate experiment are psychometrically more reliable and conceptually more advanced than those from the classical bivariate experiment.

As we are all painfully aware, logically planned advance is one thing and history is another. Consequently the student needs to be wary of the insidious effect on research of many traditional terminologies. One must remember that when Wundt, eager to give scientific status to psychology, overenthusiastically imitated the physical sciences, he took over the traditional physical science bivariate experiment without question as the main tool. Possibly he failed to appreciate that the physical sciences are in a very real sense simpler than the behavioral and life sciences. Mass, time, and distance sufficed to account for the then observed movement of the whole solar system, and these concepts came readily to common-sense thinking. But when Johnny steals the teacher's dog, we have to recognize a larger number of factors—physiological, psychological, social, economic, familial, and so on—contributing at once in complex ways. It is not easy to see *a priori* what the significant concept variables are, and still less easy to hold any constant.

While Wundt and Pavlov were religiously following the methods so far used in physical and physiological sciences, others, notably Galton, Spearman, and (later) Thurstone were shaping a new, more original, multivariate experimental approach capable of simultaneously recording and analyzing the interaction of many influences. These new multivariate methods, born expressly out of the needs of psychology, have since proved very useful also in economics, sociology, political science, and, most recently, in medicine. In short, they show their virtues and potency more especially when *multiple determination* of events is characteristic. The artificial experimental isolation of two variables from their interaction with others, while appealing to a sense of tidiness, is often neither practically nor ethically possible. Galton, Pearson, Spearman, Hotelling, Thurstone, and others consequently developed sensitive statistical analysis to compensate for our incapacity to manipulate and control events and lives. (Astronomy, meteorology, and some other sciences would also be stultified by insistence on classical bivariate experiment, especially in manipulative form.)

The fact that matters of major emotional and characterological importance to human beings cannot be made the subject of manipulative (miscalled "controlled") bivariate experiment has produced some remarkable but insufficiently appreciated biases in the development of psychology. Among those psychologists who remained in classical bivariate traditions and never introduced multivariate designs in their personality research, it has led to two diversions from essential goals. First, there has been diversion from emotionally important to merely cognitive experiments of an increasingly trivial nature, wherein researchers give up the search for laws involving powerful human motivation. Second, it has led to restriction of research on powerful motives to animals *only*, whose lives *can* be manipulated. Unfortunately, the initial scientific exactitude of the animal research is often completely thrown away at the end, when the experimenter insists on carrying his conclusions by the merest analogy into the human field. Here our possession of a culture, not to mention a complexity of personality of a totally higher order, distorts the meaning of animal-derived concepts and conclusions almost beyond recognition.

[4] I was recently invited to contribute a chapter on "Personality Theory Based on Experimental Methods" to a book containing a symposium on *Current Personality Theories*, in which eight of the remaining 11 chapters turned out to be neither quantitative nor experimental in method and origin. Such a ratio, in 1978, is startling.

[5] The clinical phase of personality research has been recognized in these discussions as preexperimental and limited in the precision of its conclusions. Although we use the brief label *clinical*, it includes, of course, all inference from observations made without measurement or sophisticated statistical treatment. Thus the label would include ideas of human nature found in much anthropological and political science writings (Mead and Benedict, but not, say, Rummel, 1974). However, the conceptual conclusions of the clinician, thought looser than those of the bivariate experimenter, have been in a very real sense richer and more fruitful. The reason for this appears when we recognize that clinicians have *implicitly* been devoted to multivariate methods all along. Admittedly they have done so with rough standards, and even without explicit

consciousness of the method and its requirements, but they have recognized that we can hope to reach useful laws and concepts only if a sufficient array of variables are taken into the system.

However, we must recognize that in any fundamental sense there is no such thing as a (scientifically acceptable) separate clinical method of research, although there is a clinical method of diagnosis and therapy. In any ultimate analysis research falls into one of the two main possibilities of design: bivariate or multivariate. The reader may pursue these arguments in more detail elsewhere (Cattell, 1966; Schneewind, 1970, where surveys of possible research design alternatives for checking hypotheses by their fit to facts are offered). The clinician in research is typically multivariate but has to be content with observation only by eye, and relation-eduction only by fallible memory.

By contrast, the multivariate experimentalist on the one hand aids the initial observation by experimental instruments of measurement, and, on the other, pursues his inferential analysis by statistical-mathematical models, the practical testing of which has become widely possible since the advent of the electronic computer. The results of this difference have been that the multivariate experimenter has built a far tighter and more testable structure of theory, and, incidentally, has shocked the clinician by introducing into the latter's fishing pond original new shapes as strange to the clinician as things dredged from the deep ocean might be to a local reservoir fisherman.

[6] The reader may take heart, in facing this and subsequent formulae, from the assurance that I shall keep throughout the book to the same symbol meanings, as stated in the summary to this chapter. Thus the reader is acquiring at this point a standard shorthand for more rapid and precise communications of psychological concepts and relations.

[7] When one deals simply, as here, with variables that are considered in *standard scores*, and therefore all of unit sigma and length geometrically, the correlation as stated is represented by the cosine of the angle drawn. As the reader proceeds to grasp the factor-analytic concepts, he will see that fitting variables together simply, as in Figure 1-2(g), corresponds to the special case when all the variance of the variables is accountable for by three common factors, without specifics.

[8] A practical illustration of the reality of factors as influences or determiners may illuminate these brief abstractions. Dickman (1960) and Cattell and Dickman (1962) took 80 balls of different sizes, weight, elasticity, and length of attached string. They were measured on 32 "behaviors," such as bouncing, swinging on a pendulum, running down an inclined plane, and so on. The factoring to unique simple structure of this 32 x 32 correlation matrix yielded five factors: diameter of ball (size), weight, elasticity, angular inertia, and length of the attached string. These are the concepts that a physicist would know are necessary and sufficient to account for the scores in the 32 kinds of "behavior." But in the biosocial sciences, the complication is such that we cannot formulate the basic influences with such common-sense insight as in physics and so need to unearth them by a procedure like factor analysis.

[9] Perhaps no comment is really necessary here on the simple-minded view that the psychologist can or should "rotate for meaning," that is, spin the axes for the source trait factors to where he *believes* they should go. This is rotation only for personal meaning, undoubtedly different for different psychologists, and does not belong to science! Even if the particular concept that this spurious use of factor analysis attempts to "confirm" were a widespread one, sanctified by tradition, it could still be wrong, as the flat-earth concept was wrong. Such

procedures in any case overlook that the aim of factor analysis is to *discover* hypotheses or to *check* hypotheses, in both cases by statistical tests, not arbitrary notations. Psychology has suffered too long from conflicting, unstable, and altogether too numerous alternative views of what traits exist. These new multivariate methodologies provide a means of ending this bedlam.

To say that it is pointless to rotate to arbitrary subjective positions does not mean that factor analysis cannot be used to check a hypothesis.

The *Procrustes Program* (Cattell, 1978; Hurley & Cattell, 1960), or the procedure called *proofing maximum likelihood* (Jöreskog, 1972), can rotate any experimental results as far as they can go to fit a theoretically prescribed position. Then statistical checks can be applied in the usual way to see if the fit of the patterns supports the hypothesis. At the present stage of psychology, factory analysis probably is still needed more as a *hypothesis-generating* than a *hypothesis-checking* device. Let us, therefore, definitely dismiss most so-called rotations for meaning as rotations rather for some psychologists' specific predilections. Scientifically, it is merely chasing one's tail. To rotate for *general* meaning, in the sense that the resolution must have formal properties we recognize as consistent with the scientifically meaningful set of conditions associated with real influences, is something very different, and this is what simple structure and confactor rotations do.

The first, simple structure, as briefly stated above, argues that if we start with a varied set of personality measures, sampled (randomly or in stratified representation) from all over the behavior sphere, it is highly unlikely that any one factor influence will affect all the measures. For variables to be unaffected by a factor means that it will have zero projection upon them, that is, that they will tend to lie on a line going through the zero point of the axis, at right angles to it, as shown in Figure 1-5(*a*). Consequently, as we plot the tests as points (let us now omit the vector lines) relative to the arbitrary initial axes *x* and *y* with which we come out of the computer, we should expect to detect a "crystallization" in the configuration plot in the form of a line of points, as shown starting across the initial plot in Figure 1-5(*b*). If now we shift the arbitrary axis *X* to the position *T*, at right angles to this flat nebula of points, it presents our best inference as to where the true source trait lies.

In a two-dimensional case the unloaded, unaffected items would form a thickened line, as in the plots in Figure 1-5, but in a three-factor space they form a plane like a wheel at right angles to the axle that constitutes the factor axis. And in the most general, multiple-dimension situation, we speak of these crystallizations or deposits as *hyperplanes*. As shown in Figure 1-5(*c*), the source traits thus revealed need no longer lie at right angles to each other. Commonly they *are* actually somewhat oblique, that is, correlated. This should not surprise us, for surely such traits as, for example, intelligence and emotional stability will not be entirely independent in our culture but will get correlated. This could occur, insofar as they have genetic components, by assortative mating (tendency to marry within one's own social stratum), as R.A. Fisher has shown (1930). His conclusion supposes that intelligence and emotional stability independently favor promotion, so that a more intelligent person will be more likely to meet, in his class, a more emotionally stable person than he would in the population at large. The children of such a pair would be likely to be simultaneously higher on both. In that generation the traits would get positively correlated.

Simple structure has been demonstrated to work effectively. Experience with wide diversities of data has demonstrated that these flat nebulae of hyperplanes exist in most real data, lying like cleavage planes in a feldspar crystal, waiting to be found by trail-and-error search. They are found regularly in all real experimental, organic material; it is important to note that they have also been demonstrated *not* to exist in artificial material made from random correlations or numbers (Cattell & Gorsuch, 1960).

However, finding the unique simple structure rotation is commonly the most prolonged and difficult part of a factor-analytic experiment. Indeed, in considering personality and other factor-analytic studies done in this decade, the psychologist should be warned that the computer seems to have induced individuals with little apprenticeship or perspective in the strategies of this complex method to turn entirely to dependent or automatic program solutions. Misleading conflicting conclusions certainly abound in published rotations and they arise from a variety of technical failings, but particularly from disregarding the experimental precondition: to get simple structure, variables should be sampled widely according to a *personality-sphere* principle. Obviously simple structure will fail if "hyperplane stuff" is not provided, or if both marker variables and hyperplane variables are too few for an unambiguous answer.

If these conditions for simple structure cannot be met satisfactorily, then the second method of resolution—confactor rotation (Cattell & Cattell, 1955; Cattell & Brennan, 1977)—is preferable. In this method we do *two* experiments with exactly the same variables, but in samples and circumstances so chosen that each of the factors might be expected to exert a greater influence in one situation than the other. For example, the loading of the intelligence factor on a set of performances among university students would be expected to be less than in a group of nonstudents of the same age, because the variance of intelligence is greater in the latter. On the other hand, the stress of intense examination competition might bring out a greater emotional instability range in the university group, so that this factor would, now, be larger in the student than in the nonstudent experiment.

Theoretically, when both experimental results (beginning with the orthogonal factor analyses) are rotated to the position where factors correspond to the real influences, there will consequently appear a simple proportionality of loadings on any one factor between the first and second experiment. For example, if we consider the loadings of the general intelligence factor T_g, on two performances x and y in the first experiment as $b_{xg(1)}$ and $b_{yg(1)}$, and the loadings of these in the second experiment as $b_{xg(2)}$ and $b_{yg(2)}$, then, when intelligence has a 50 percent bigger variance (range) in the first, we should expect the parallel relation:

$$b_{xg(1)} = 1.5b_{xg(2)} \qquad b_{yg(1)} = 1.5b_{yg(2)}$$

But, as the variance resulting from emotional stability T_e is reduced in the nonstudent group, $b_{xe(1)} = .6b_{xe(2)}$, and similarly for the loadings of test y and for all other points. Thus the plot for experiment 2 is compressed on the vertical factor and extended on the horizontal relative to that of 1.

Now in support of the idea that this could only occur in the unique rotation corresponding to real influences at work, it has been shown that if any such proportionality of the two influences exists and is located, then no other rotations of either, or both, can be found with this property. It is a unique position—as unique as the position of the two cylinders in a combination lock that alone unlocks the door. Fortunately, the confactor position—the position at which the factors correspond to scientific influences rather than to any mathematician's factor—does not have to be found by trial and error, for with many dimensions such a search would be a lifetime task. It has been demonstrated that it can be found analytically, in a few minutes (Cattell, 1944, 1955; Cattell & Brennan, 1977). However, in the last resort, this confactor approach bristles with technical problems still to be overcome before it can be used readily with oblique factors.

Regardless of whether the unique resolution is found by simple structure or confactor rotation methods, it should have the property, which does not exist for other random positions, that it yields the same factors, that is, factors with essentially the same pattern of loadings, from experiment to experiment. (Confactor rotation, of course, guarantees this for, at any rate, two experiments!) The possession of such "factor invariance" is the hallmark of a scientific concept and is the justification for our arguing that such factors correspond to real influences, which we can call, in the personality domain, source traits.

[10]The confusion among unique, specific, common, and broad terms seems to have arisen historically because terms from mathematical statistics were carried uncritically into the psychological model. Mathematicians call a factor *common* if it is common to all variables in a given correlation matrix (not to all people, as a psychologist would) and they call it a *specific* (or, unfortunately, a "unique") factor if found in only one variable. The mathematical definitions are local to a given analysis because they hold only for the group of variables that happens to come together in a given matrix. Thus factor common to all in one study will cease to be common to all in another. Similarly the meaning of a specific holds only for a given mathematical matrix. Consequently, the term *broad*—meaning spreading over several variables but not necessarily *all*, depending on the matrix—is psychologically more stable and meaningful; and what we call specific must be shown to be specific to one variable only after one has tried to match it up with many variables *in many matrices*. For example, performance on a vocabulary test would probably depend on a broad factor of intelligence and another broad factor of verbal ability, but probably also on a quite specific habit of frequently picking up the dictionary from the shelf. But to the mathematician, verbal ability could be a specific if only one verbal test occurred in the matrix, whereas a habit of consulting the dictionary could be common in a matrix of 10 tests all involving dictionary search!

[11]The notion that even before the form of a common trait is blurred by any widespread, hypothetical, purely individual uniqueness, it is attenuated by difference of form in constituent subpopulations perhaps needs more illustration. For example, the crystallized general ability factor g_c expresses itself by one pattern of loadings in 18-year-olds and a somewhat different pattern in 50-year-olds (yet is the same trait, for repeated annual cross-sectional studies would show a continuous transition between the two patterns). But a factoring of a mixed population of 18- and 50-year-olds will yield an *attenuated* common pattern, that is, it will leave more variance in specifics. The reduced common factor, moreover, will be a blurred composite of two different expressions of the trait.

However, at least in the case of some common source traits, it seem probable that we are nevertheless ultimately dealing with the same influence behind these patterns; that is, the origin is identical for all people. In this case the simple model holds, although the differences of the expression of the factor in different sub-populations still exist. (These last are principally, for statistical reasons, differences in its total variance and the variance and correlations of other factors.) In this case the problem in measuring the trait *comparably* for different groups is only one of finding variables so highly loaded on it that they change less than the first-found set of expressions as one moves across populations and samples. This goal is practicable because, as research progresses, we get to know more about the single influence itself, which is identical with the factor (see Chapters 2 and 7). When an actual variable is located that identifies with the factor we become less dependent on estimating it from many variables in a broad pattern. For example, in temperament research (Chapter 3), a certain pattern of high activity, UI(T)21, may turn out to be determined by metabolic rate and ultimately perhaps by thyroxin concentration in the blood. At present we are deprived of a simple common estimation formula because this pattern of weights alters with age and cultural setting. But if we have located the influence itself, or something that correlates 0.95 with it, the correlation will alter only trivially with setting and we can base our trait measures on this variable—in the above case, thyroxin concentration—over a wide range.

Until we can find these really high markers we do best to avoid measuring the same trait by the same battery over large ranges and population mixtures. Instead, we should assess the same common trait more accurately by a battery based on the pattern peculiar to each well-chosen subgroup. In this way the spurious size of false specific factors will be reduced. Just so in engineering we can calculate the approximate horsepower of an automobile by a formula involving cylinder area, stroke length, and so on, but what we are really after is brake horsepower. For no type of engine will the formula accurately predict the brake horsepower and for certain engine designs the cylinder formula would be better if it were appreciably modified.

A proper pursuit of this and of several related issues will soon require that the student set out to gain more familiarity with the factor-analytic and other multivariate models than we have yet required in this chapter. For example, the problem arises of how best to compare the trait score, for example, for intelligence, of a student aged 18 with that of a business man aged 45, when the pattern of weights for the same test battery has been shown to be different in 18-year-olds and 45-year-olds (note we are not concerned here with age curve differences in typical level but only with *form*). Methods and concepts for handling this have been worked out as the *equipotent* and *isopodic* designs (Cattell, 1970), to which the advanced student may be referred.

However, in the present mathematico-statistical substrate to trait theory we have essentially not required more than high-school algebra, and one can, indeed, proceed with our main models and discussion simply by stating that (1) experiment shows that stable common factors do emerge by applying the standard factor-analytic techniques to correlation matrices among variables; (2) by taking a weighted sum of the loaded test measures (as one does of the subtests of an intelligence test to get a person's general ability score), a person's scores on personality source traits can be tolerably well estimated; and (3) by taking the specification equation for any given performance (which is obtained either by factor analysis or by simply correlating each factor score with the criterion performance) and multiplying each factor score by the appropriate behavioral index b, weight obtained in this way, one can estimate reasonably well what the given individual is likely to do on that particular performance. This simplest approach assumes that the b's represent a *linear* relation of factor size to performance score (despite clinicians and others sometimes arguing for more complex curvilinear formulae) and that the factor acts additively with every other factor (rather than through the products among factors or some other complex function).

With this fuller technical background we can summarize the unique trait problem more precisely. First one must always distinguish among (1) a unique *trait* concept, (2) the uniqueness of a total *personality*, and (3) a unique *way* of making some response performance. The adequacy of a unique *combination* of common traits for (2) has already been described. As to (3), we see that even with absolutely common traits fitting the simple model, theory and computation alike recognize that different people bring different traits to bear to different degrees in performing the same act. Let us take a concrete example of a behavior specification equation for behavior a_j with just three common source traits (factors) as follows:

$$a_{ij} = .4T_{1i} - .6T_{2i} + 2T_{3i}$$

If the trait scores of three people, *A*, *B*, and *S*, are as in the following score matrix:

Individual *(i)*	T_1	T_2	T_3
Albert	0	1	2
Bill	-5	2	6
Sam	2	2	1

then all three will reach the same level of performance on the act a_j in response to the given situation as shown by the following calculations from the specification equation:

$$a_a = .4 \times 0 - .6 \times 1 + .2 \times 2 = -.2$$
$$a_b = .4 \times -.5 - .6 \times 2 + .2 \times 6 = -.2$$
$$a_s = .4 \times 2 - .6 \times 2 + .2 \times 1 = -.2$$

This "equality with difference" we recognize in common-sense terms as the difference in "quality" of a performance, as when two people tie in a game of tennis, but one performs more through vigor and agility "factors" and the other more through factors of intelligence and experience of playing.

To gauge, at the level of present evidence, the extent to which actual psychological evidence fits the simplest common factor model, as described above, it is illuminating to compare what would be expected from the other chief possible models, namely, (1) the remotely possible model of entirely unique broad factors, and (2) the equally remote model of entirely specific factors. If traits were wholly unique in pattern, not centering upon any single common factor central type, the application of the factor-analytic model, that is, the factor analysis of an ordinary correlation matrix, would yield no broad trait structures whatever. The science of individual differences would then have to be couched in entirely different terms, which would be forbiddingly complex and cumbersome. Before any scientific prediction could be made, we should have to do longitudinal studies on each person to locate the unique patterns, as will be discussed in a moment. With this possibility we need not concern ourselves because the results of *R*-technique factor analysis definitely do not show any such chaos. If traits were, according to the second theory, wholly specific, again the results of factor analysis would be an absence of broad factors: there would be no "communality," to use the correct technical term. Personality prediction would then relapse into the disheartening situation in which any particular piece of behavior could be predicted only from having seen that particular piece of behavior before, and even this has the proviso that the behavior would have to be free of any change or function fluctuation!

Although common structure undoubtedly emerges from R-technique, we are suggesting that the ultimate theory we work with may have to admit some degree of uniqueness of individual patterns about the central form of a common trait, which leads to the somewhat paradoxical title, "The uniquely modified common trait theory." We recognize, of course, that much of the individual difference in the expression of trait A can be fully handled by its combination with different endowments in traits B, C, and so on. That is to say, the pure common trait theory is still capable of representing a good deal of apparent variation in form of a common trait. In any particular matrix it can probably give at least as good a representation of the facts, that is, prediction, as any that we would get from our uniquely modified common trait model. It is probably only when we go from one matrix and population to another that the uniquely modified common trait model would prove to have greater applicability, if such greater applicability on any degree is indeed confirmed.

CHAPTER **2**

PERSONALITY STRUCTURE
SEEN IN THE LIFE SETTING

2-1. The Characteristics and Interrelations of the Available Observation Media

In the opening chapter we necessarily concentrated somewhat abstractly on the formal methodological and mathematical problems of structure, defining exactly all subsequent use of trait, state, process, and type. In this chapter we can reward the psychologist who has mastered these concepts by presenting him a rich harvest of psychological findings. For theory and models are not reached merely by abstract and a priori definitions. The vigorous growth of any science depends on a trial-and-error process of alternation in which emergence of results by a rough model is studied. A revised model then is drawn up in new hypotheses and the revision tested by a fresh emergence of results.

Over the last 50 years the basic multivariate and associated bivariate research on structure in the ability and personality fields has greatly enriched and clarified our concepts. We might mention, for example, the refinement of the Jungian notion of extroversion into exvia; the separation of anxiety, stress, and neuroticism; the recognition and valid measurement over various ages of such new primaries as surgency, affectia, parmia, and premsia; and the confirmation and new preciseness of such clinical concepts as ego strength, superego strength, and ergic tension (undischarged "id").

However, because our purpose here is not so much to drill the clinician and the personality student in the substantive anatomy of their subjects as to use this new knowledge to bring out general psychological principles, we are faced with a dilemma. Whole books have been written to cover what goes into this chapter; for example, those of Cartwright (1974), Dreger (1962), Eysenck (1960), Eysenck and Eysenck (1969), French (1953), Guilford (1959), Lindzey and Hall (1965), Pervin (1970), Wiggins (1973), and the present writer's *Personality and Mood by Questionnaire* (1973a) and *Handbook of the 16 Personality Factor Test* (with Eber & Tatsuoka, 1970). The ideal solution would be to assume the reader is familiar with at least one of these. But a design of presentation that may assist one who is not, without trespassing on the time of one who is, is hard to achieve. Our compromise is to attempt very great compression of the substantive findings into about half of this chapter, and to move on in the second half into some new general principles provoked by the results, expanding the technical points covered in footnotes in the preceding chapter.

As we approach actual surface and source results, let us note first that there are three and *only* three ways of observing human behavior, one of which does not extend to animal behavior. Psychologists have become accustomed to designating information from these three *media* as *L*-, *Q*-, and *T*-data, as follows:

L-data. Recordings of behavior in the *natural life situation*, "in situ," as a geologist would say, recorded by observers other than the subject, either by mechanical counts $L(T)$ or by ratings of traits $L(R)$.

Q-data. Information about behavior likewise "in situ," but recorded in a questionnaire, the subject being his own observer.

T-data. Data on behavior recorded in a laboratory test or other controlled objective ("performance") test situation.

Table 2-1 summarizes some important properties of these media. Although they constitute three fundamentally very different sources of information, they are related in various ways, as to type of reliability and validity, and show some distinguishable subdivisions justifying some specialized symbolism.

Let us first look at the properties of these media in terms of their reliabilities.[1] Consistency coefficients can be determined for all, in the three forms of consistency: (1) homogeneity, (2) dependability, and (3) transferability coefficients, except for some $L(T)$-data, because real-life performances sometimes cannot be repeated (liability to fatal accidents, for example). *Conspect dependability,* which is the extent to which two scorers of the same recorded

TABLE 2—1.   The Media and Areas of Observation on Personality

	Area in Which Behavior Occurs	
Medium of Observation	*In situ* (in everday life situations)	*In a test* (in a specially devised cooperative situation)
Objective quantification (by measured response or recorded counts; impersonal, reaching reliability close to 1.0)	Symbol: $L(T)$-data Based on life records, time sampling of concrete behaviors. In testing considered a criterion variable.	Symbol: T-data Objectively measured defined responses to defined situation.
Involving rating by people (a) Ratings by other than subject himself	Symbol: $L(R)$-data Behavior rating by judges. Often considered to give criterion variable, but questionable.	Symbol: LRT Ratings of behavior made in an interview, consulting room, or other defined, structured constant social situation.
(b) Ratings by subject in informal consulting situation	Symbol: $Q(C)$-data Questionnaire type of self-evaluation, but in consulting or interview situation.	
(c) Ratings by subject in precise test situation	Symbol: Q-data Standard inventory or questionnaire test. This can be Q' and Q-data according to whether scoring does or does not assume described behavior to be actual behavior.	

observation agree, can be determined for all except Q-data. For two or more observers cannot look in on the same introspection. L-data, in $L(T)$ and $L(R)$ forms, are commonly called in psychometrics the *criterion* data, for they are concerned with behavior in the world (and generally have at least good conspect reliability, or dependability). But we should note that $L(T)$-data—records of a person's real-life behavior over, perhaps, years—may have the peculiarity of an indeterminate consistency coefficient. At least this is true of the dependability (test-retest) coefficient form of consistency, because life opportunities for some behavior do not get repeated. Knowing and respecting the combinations of properties in Table 2-1 is important for the later inferences one may need to make about possibly conflicting results from the different media of observation. In Chapter 8, on distortions from mode of observation, we will have more to say about the instrument factors—the systematic effects— in these media and their consequences for our trait conceptions. But for the present we shall record the source-trait patterns as they have been discovered, in separate lists for each medium in this and the next chapter.

Within any one of the above media the psychologist has been free to set up chosen variables, to correlate over various sets of variables, and to look for patterns of common or unique source traits. Such search for human source traits may be done either with a prior hypothesis—in which case it happens that most researchers up to recent times have turned to clinical psychology for their ideas—or without one, employing a stratified sample of variables from the personality sphere. The latter approach is possible because factor analysis and cluster analysis are methods for hypothesis creation as well as for hypothesis testing.

Researches by myself and my associates in *Q*- and *L*-data values in the 1930s and 1940s were explicitly planned to be *hypothesis creating*. New hypotheses were needed because it was obvious that clinical theories had by no means avoided the astigmatism inevitable in dealing only with pathological subjects, and, in the case of psycho- analysis, even specifically with middle-class *fin de siècle* Viennese culture. Moreover, existing personality rating factorings as covered in a thorough survey (Cattell, 1946) had not been based on the personality sphere and often even confined their interest to one particular conceived dimension. This was the state of affairs around 1945 as to *L*-data; but as to *Q*-data the situation was if anything worse. The same survey, and another a decade later (Cattell, 1957) showed that questionnaire items had been chosen largely from the clinical field. The factorings confirmed this, for neither in question- naire items nor *L*-data studies existing at that time were there more than a third of the spectrum of dimensions that were obtained soon after, from the introduction of the personality sphere concept and the systematic factoring thereof.

2-2.   *L*-Data Requirements: The Personality Sphere and the Universal Index

Systematic factoring, on the basis of the personality sphere, yielded its first fruits in the late 1940s and early 1950s. It showed at once that personality psychologists needed to address themselves conceptually to some 10 to 20 recognizable unitary source traits, not to the two or three structures on which psychoanalysts and some factor analysts had settled from earlier theoretical predilections.

Appropriately, the first attack was made through the *L*-medium because this domain of observed behavior in everyday life was (and is) the most down-to-earth reality in human behavior (used as the "criterion" in much predictive work), and because it offered, as will soon be explained, the best basis for defining the "personality sphere"—a total population of variables. Moreover, it offered the best basis for linking up the new multivariate experimental approach with past clinical and general concepts of personality structure, because these also had been derived from everyday life behavior.

On the assumption, developed elsewhere (Cattell, 1946) that the English language, at least since the time of Shakespeare, had sufficiently expressed all personality behavior, the first personality sphere of variables was made up from all trait behaviors listed in the dictionary. Fortunately, Allport and Odbert (1936) had already combed standard dictionaries for words applicable to human personality behavior, and emerged with about 4,000 trait variables. By bracketing highly similar terms as synonyms, the number was cut down to 182. By empirical correlational evidence of tight clusters among ratings on these word lists, taken on a typical adult population sample, the number of essential variables was cut down further to 40 (Cattell, 1946). This final condensed list has been slightly amended since to 45 (Cattell, 1957; Cattell, Pierson, et al., 1976). The additions arose from new factor evidence and from such theoretical writings as those of Goldberg (1972) and Norman (1967). This list has fortunately been used by several investigators to provide a standard basis whereby their factor experiments can be brought into an interlocking basis of knowledge. Here one notes particularly the work of Digman (1965), Hammond (1976), Mulaik (1964), Meredith (1967), Norman (1963), Sells, Demaree, and Will (1970), Tupes and Cristal (1961), and others. Because Eysenck (1969) used comparable lists, the fact that he located only three factors—*P*, *E*, and *N*—cannot be explained by a defective basis of variables. As pointed out elsewhere (Cattell, 1964), it is undoubtedly the result of the technical neglect of sound statistical tests for the number of factors. If this number is wrong all that follows—rotations and communalities—are wrong. There exist nowadays adequate technical bases for this and other decisions as documented by Cattell (1946, 1972, 1973a), Vaughan (1974), De Young (1972), Cattell and Vogelmann (1977), and others. The discrepancy of the Eysenck, Howarth, and many other results from those here arises from underfactoring. The lack of congruence can sometimes be resolved by noting that these underfactorings, if severe, have actually reached at the first factoring approximations to second-order factors, but in other instances, for example, that of Comrey and Duffy (1968) in Q-data, the discrepancy clearly results from a lower density of representation of the personality sphere itself. In both sources of initial discrepancies, an agreement with factors here often appears with the emergence of second-order factors.

By density we mean the number of variables per unit of behavioral space. The personality sphere is multidimensional; so its surface is not two-dimensional, but that of a hypersphere. However, if there are 5,000 behavior terms in the surface and we sample only 50, there is some risk that some smaller dimensions will be lost. Indeed, it is easy to see that if we went to the experimental extreme of taking only one variable for each primary dimension of the sphere, the factor analysis would go directly to what will be more fully defined later as second-order factors. (Temporarily, we will define second-order factors as broader, shallower factors reached by factoring the R-matrix of correlated primary factors.) The converse effect on the factor outcome can be produced by reducing density by multiplying closely similar variable names—begetting many trait terms that are virtually synonyms. Thereby, from a specific factor of very small area, we could artificially create a seemingly broad personality factor. This inflation, by producing a "bloated specific," and showing a factor alleged to be of general interest to personality theory, has undoubtedly occurred in some research.[2]

The notion of density of variable representation, necessary to arguments for stratified sampling, cannot, however, be based on indications of distance between variables that is based on correlational evidence. To do so would throw us into a circular argument. It would also abolish the simple structure by which one rotates factors and finds structure. For obtaining evenly spaced samplings of variables on a correlational basis would obliterate the real and natural increases of density at hyperplanes. The only other alternatives to this unacceptable "thinning out" by taking the less correlated variables are: a random sampling of the above verbal list; and a sampling of actual behaviors in our culture through 24 hours, taking behaviors at one-minute, 10-minute, or (say) half-hour intervals, according to the density one wants. In general, it can already be concluded that the density of a total personality sphere of from 36 to 150 variables proves to suffice to surpass some critical lower limit and leads to most or all of the same primaries turning up in different samples of people and situations.

Although L-data are an appropriate beginning, $L(T)$ would be best; that is, behavior scored by actual life behavior counts. But with a few exceptions (Cattell & Peterson, 1958; Koch, 1942), cost has dictated the use of $L(R)$-data. However, it is important to note, regarding $L(R)$-data, that when scores become mediated by the rating behavior of human observers, the door is opened to all kinds of error, notably projection and bias. Unless rating is well done, loss of structures or complete chaos ensues, and even in the uncommon experiments where it is well done, instrument factors can be expected. The following conditions repeatedly have been stated as essential for a sound beginning in rating factoring, but, as the alert reader can check, the surprising fact appears that they have been met in only two or three researches in 30 years, and hopelessly inconsistent results have appeared among the many published researches that ignored them. Largely, this results from investigations succumbing to the convenient approximations demanded in applied psychology. The basic rating requirements are the following.

1. That the rated variables be sufficiently numerous to test for number of factors (hypothesized). Two or three times as many variables as factors is reasonable.
2. That each variable be sharply defined and illustrated by *actual behaviors* that the raters are trained to observe.
3. That the raters not all be in one and the same *role relation* to the ratees, for example, teacher to children, but preferably be peers, or constitute a sampling of roles.
4. That each subject be rated by at least six to eight observers who have plenty of chance to observe the subject. Reliabilities are then to be worked out between the pool of one-half (that is, four observers against the pool of the other four).
5. That the observations not be made in some limited environment, for example, a parade ground or a consulting room, but extend as far as possible to a 24-hour cycle of life behavior.
6. That ratings be made only after reasonably prolonged acquaintance.
7. That in the actual rating procedure the raters deal with one trait at a time over all subjects, not one subject over all traits (to minimize halo effect). Ranking with paired comparisons of people is better than rating by points.
8. That statistical treatment use appropriate transformations to meet the fact that a large number of subjects cannot be rated by one set of observers. If there are, say, 300 subjects they will need to be rated in, say, 30 groups of 10 each and then brought together.

Briefly, it is best to have each judge rank rather than rate, and pool point-scale transformations of the ranks. This will inevitably eliminate some real between-group covariance, but as that is of the same nature as the inter-individual covariance, the factor outcome is not affected. Meanwhile, the gain of eliminating subjectively derived interjudge differences of mean more than compensates for this.

By obtaining measures of the judge's personality, we can, by corrections contributed by trait view theory (Chapter 8), use even a single judge and still escape some of the worst rating evils, but it is far better to average 8 to 12 judges rating each person. When the above conditions are observed, the primary traits found are consistent among different studies and, still more interestingly, between L- and Q-data (Cattell, Pierson, et al., 1976), as are also the second-order factors (Cattell, 1957; Cattell & Vogelmann, 1976). It is this finding that enables us to handle the L- and Q-media concepts as a single set of source traits persistent across both L- and Q-media.

In any searching analysis the far-out possibility must be considered that such L-Q consistency—or even repeat consistency in L-data alone—could possibly arise as mooted by Passini and Norman (1966) from *internal consistency in language itself;* for we are using traits verbally defined, not laboratory measurements. This is unlikely to account for L-Q consistency because the variables in L-data use trait words, even though of narrow traits, whereas the variables in questionnaires, if well designed, refer to specific concrete behaviors to which a subject might often be puzzled to assign a trait term. Actually, this notion that in assigning trait rating people might merely be projecting the correlations among the trait meanings in their own minds—a notion debated in this decade—had already been raised and answered in essence by Cattell and Dickman (1962). Because we do not know beforehand what factors exist in psychological data, the kinds of subjectivities that exist in ratings cannot be tried against an extraneous criterion. But the effect of possible stereotypes and language projections could be tried, as these investigations realized, by taking properties of physical objects and comparing a factoring of them as measured with a factoring of the same variables rated. They took behavior, but of physical objects. There were 32 behaviors—for example, height of bounce, distance of rolling, measured on 80 to 100 balls—and the 32 variables were both rated by observers and actually measured. The number and nature of factors proved to be exactly the same in objective measures and in ratings, and the same in young and old raters. If the structure is in language, therefore, it is because language ("the cognitive map") has—possibly with some exceptions—long adapted itself by trial and error to the physico-psychological realities of the environment.

Factoring of ratings that had been very carefully made according to the above principles led initially to the conclusion that there were rather more than a dozen primaries (see survey of various researchers' findings in Cattell, 1946; 1957); factoring of many hundreds of questionnaire items led initially to 16 to 18. By inspection of psychological meaning, it seemed clear that the same factors were being found, over most of the range, in both media. It is some reflection on the keenness of research strategy, however, that a check on these alignments has only recently been carried out by factoring in both media together (Cattell, Pierson, et al., 1966). One says "over most of the range" in regard to the early matching, because certain factors present in ratings—those indexed as J and K—were not at first found in Q-data, and certain factors in Q-data, indexed as Q_1 (radicalism), Q_2 (self-sufficiency), Q_3 (self-sentiment), and Q_4 (ergic tension) reciprocally could not be matched in L-data. These gaps in matching apparently resulted from gaps in variables, and as certain areas in L- and Q-variables have been progressively filled by more sensitively designed variables, the matches have increasingly appeared. Possibly up to 20 primary and 6 secondary (second-order) personality factors might be considered matched across the L-Q media, though a conservative estimate would be 14 or 15, and the field calls for more complete studies with the refined rating methods above and some extensions to new rating variables (Q variables already subtend 35 primaries).

Finally, a word is needed about nomenclature and indexing. Francis Bacon pointed out three centuries ago the danger to science, or indeed to any reasoning, of premature and popular naming. A premature theoretical interpretive name may fool both the person who gives it and the person who uses it. Indeed, the false implications of a rash theoretical title can bias for years the research of those who use it—as, say, phlogiston did in chemistry, or pangenesis in genetics. Use of a popular name, per se, drags in all the vagueness or trailing false connotations deep in folklore that the untrained mind has long given to it. I therefore proposed in the 1930s certain standards for naming and indexing in this growing domain. First, I suggested that because nothing but error could come from calling truly new things by old and contaminated name concepts, new technical language—derived or acronymic—should be applied. Second, I suggested that any well-replicated factor pattern should receive a new symbol or index number to hold it firmly identified while further work was being done to interpret it. However, because most people find it easier to say sulfuric acid than H_2SO_4, so that names need to be used, I suggested that names should be relatively restricted to *description* of the pattern unless interpretation should happen to be far advanced.

Accordingly, in the *L-Q* media, letters of the alphabet were assigned to factors in order of their decreasing mean variance contribution to the totality of variables in the personality sphere. This "size" of source trait, measured as mean variance contribution, will naturally vary somewhat with population, and the goodness of the stratified sample of variables from the personality sphere used in the study. Not surprisingly, the order of their discovery and of their confirmation turns out to be much the same as that of their size, larger factors like *A* (affectia–cyclothymia), *B* (intelligence), and *C* (ego strength) tending to be found first. However, there are exceptions, and in any case the size differs between, for example, adults and children. (Factor I, for example, would have come earlier in the alphabet than *I*, if its rank order of size in the child, rather than the adult groups, had been the basis.)

The names assigned to the factors and symbols will be explained as the factors are met. Meanwhile, in the objective, laboratory test series (*T*-data), which for long showed no easy one-to-one relation to the *L-Q* factors, a numbering system was used instead, called the Universal Index system; hence the symbols UI 1, UI 2, UI 3, and so on, as described in the next chapter, on *T*-data research.[3]

Every time a new instrument—be it a physical one like Galileo's telescope or Herz's oscillator, or a methodological one, like Pasteur's inoculations or Curie's measurement of radioactivity—has broken open a new nest of concepts, there have been objections by an old guard to innovative terms. This happened also with factor-analytic findings, but after the usual lag the above new terms and indexing were so obviously proving their worth that scholars increasingly adopted them. The system has proved extremely valuable in eliminating confusion in cross-reference among exact researches. The fact that the Institute for Personality and Ability Testing has backed up theoretical findings by steadily providing solid operational test measures—in the form of scales and batteries—for each of these concepts has facilitated the growth of criterion associations for them in applied psychology and advanced our grasp of their meaning. Nevertheless, rough popular synonyms are retained in these chapters (and, incidentally, in IPAT handbooks) alongside the technical terms, mainly for the use of the professional psychologist who has to communicate in popular terms with patients, parents, and teachers. Medicine, of course, has the same need for a technical-popular duality; for example, several Latin-derived terms for distinct kinds of arthritis are popularly lumped into the collective term "rheumatism." But the precise new terms are the most important, because scientific work would be crippled without accepted, precise technical usage. The objections to new technical terms in theory by humanistic psychologists, and in practice by some clinicians and social workers who must communicate popularly, must be met in some other way than by abandoning technical labels.

2-3. The Larger Primary Source Traits
in the *L*- and *Q*-Media

Because this book has to be compressed in its psychological content, the whole series of known personality primaries, covering 40 years of work by dozens of experts in the field, is condensed to a mere description listing in this and the next section. And because the most important can be matched across *L*- and *Q*-media, and the tabular presentation of questionnaire items loaded on each would be prohibitive, we shall describe their characters largely by the loaded variables in the rating medium. It is possible to sort the dimensions to some extent into normal and pathological source traits, and the main pathological factors in fact are placed last in the next section. But the division is naturally not sharp because factors like *C*(-), low ego strength, and *O*, guilt proneness, although powerfully discriminative of neurotics and psychotics, fall in the first 16 normal factors.

At present, the full number of primary personality factors (excluding pathological and depressive factors, which are dealt with exhaustively in Chapter 3 in Cattell, 1973a) arising in the personality sphere of behavior as it is recordable on normal people is 23, according to the work of Harman and Dermen (1976). This agrees closely with the several analyses of Cattell (1973a, 1973b) and Delhees (1972). About the clearest and largest 16 of these primaries much has been discovered in the last 25 years concerning their nature, age curves, heritability, and so on. (See Cattell, Eber, & Tatsuoka, 1970; Cattell, 1973.) It was the publication of the 16 personality factors in 1949 that made possible the discovery of so many valuable criterion associations. Meanwhile, systematic factor analysis began to be extended into substantially pathological items—largely defined by the MMPI and by the numerous depression-related questionnaire studies (Beck, 1967; Becker, 1974; Cattell & Bjerstedt, 1967; Friedman & Katz, 1975). In this domain some 12 factors now have been confirmed. They have been checked as true unitary traits by Cattell and Delhees (1973), Kameoka (1979), Krug and Laughlin (1977) and others, and as being independent of the 23 normal dimensions.

In setting out these 35 primaries in Q-data (a majority also known in $L(R)$-data), the source traits are almost always defined in bipolar form, with labels for the opposite ends. Psychologists ask whether this is a verbal convention to aid definition or whether it means that in some sense the trait itself ranges from positive to negative extremes of expression rather than from zero to a positive extreme. In the case of ability traits, they have almost invariably presented at the measurement and factor-analytic levels what the mathematician calls a *positive manifold*. That is, if all *variables* are scored in the direction of few errors or high performance, the loadings on verbal, numerical, spatial, and other *factors* are all positive. With personality-temperament factors, on the other hand, it was soon apparent that tests distribute themselves about equally over positive and negative loadings. We could say that this merely means that initially we did not know which way to score the tests, but there is more to it than that, for there was an unconscious tendency of experimenters to score tests in what they felt to be a psychologically positive direction. The new finding means, therefore, that some "desirable" life performances are aided by one extreme of temperament whereas others belong to persons at the opposite end of the temperamental tendency. There is rarely a "good" end to a temperament dimension as such, in the sense that there is a "capable" end to an ability factor or a "powerful" pole to a dynamic trait such as a drive. However, it is still conceivable that just as darkness is the absence of light, and mental deficiency the absence of brain capacity, so, in personality, a trait like desurgency could be the absence of some positive quality that causes surgency (say, level of cortical acetylcholine).

The issue of the possible direction on which some real influence is acting along these dimensions must be left open to research on interpretation of the primary source traits, which is only just beginning. However, we should be logically clear that the fact that the behavioral loadings on temperament (general personality) factors are distributed evenly over positive and negative values does *not* preclude such factors being entities that start at zero and increase only in one direction. What this rough balance of positive and negative loadings points to is that there are advantages and disadvantages at both ends, and, as will be suggested later, a possible inference is that natural selection favors a medium position. Thus there are advantages and disadvantages at the extreme scores of the physical factor we call body stature, but the balance nature has maintained somewhere between five and seven feet over many thousands of years suggests that a middle range gives the best equilibrium of these advantages and disadvantages. In any case the bipolar labels used here are neutral in "value" and at a descriptive level in most. But not all factors have this property (intelligence and superego are examples of exceptions). The bipolar *labelling* is thus simply a desire to help tie down meaning, just as the direction of a stick is best fixed by nailing it down at both ends.

List of Primary Source Traits[4]

FACTOR *A*(UI(L)1): SIZIA-AFFECTIA. It is a historically and methodologically interesting comment on the convergence of statistical experimental and clinical methods that the largest $L(R)$ factor yet found turns out to be the same as that first defined in pathology, by Bleuler (1920), as "schizophrenic-vs.-manic depressive," and developed by Kretschmer (1928), in abstraction from the pathological (just as our factor is) as schizothymic-vs.-cyclothymic temperament. Here affectia (Table 2-2) simply means *prone to affect* and sizia (same root as size in painting, meaning flat) means a *flatness of affect*, with feeling kept out of thought and action. Neither pole is itself pathological, but the theory is that if psychotic disease occurs, one pole of this temperament dimension is prone to manic-depressive and the other to schizoid behavior.

TABLE 2–2.   Factor *A* (UI(L)1)

Sizia *A*− *(Reserved, detached, critical, aloof, stiff)*	Affectia *A*+ *(Warmhearted, outgoing, easygoing, parti-cipating)*
Critical	Good-natured, easygoing
Stands by own ideas	Ready to cooperate, likes to participate
Cool, aloof	Attentive to people
Precise, objective	Softhearted, casual
Distrustful, skeptical	Trustful
Rigid	Adaptable, careless, goes along
Cold	Warmhearted
Prone to sulk	Laughs readily

FACTOR *B* (UI(L)2): INTELLIGENCE. Again, what could be called the second largest concern of the guidance clinician—mental retardation—proves to be the second largest statistical factor. Also we note some "personality" variables moderately affected by (loaded on) intelligence.[5]

TABLE 2—3.   Factor B (UI(L)2)

Low Intelligence B— *(Crystallized, power measure, dull)*	High Intelligence B+ *(Crystallized, power measure, bright)*
Low mental capacity Unable to handle abstract problems Not intelligently organized Poor judgment Low morale Quitting	High mental capacity Insightful, fast-learning, intellectually adaptable Intellectual interests Good judgment High morale Persevering

FACTOR C (UI(L)3): EGO STRENGTH.   Among the many associations found to scores on factor C that give strong support to its interpretive label given here are (1) the abnormally low score on it found both in all forms of neurosis and all forms of psychosis, (2) its increase in level steadily with maturation after adolescence (also with experiences such as getting married!), and (3) its higher level in people in responsible and crisis-facing occupations (administrators, airline pilots), and so on (see as background reading Cattell, Eber, & Tatsuoka, 1970).

TABLE 2—4.   Factor C (UI(L)3)

Low Ego Strength C— *(Affected by feelings, emotionally less stable, easily upset, changeable)*	High Ego Strength C+ *(Emotionally stable, mature, faces reality, calm)*
Emotional when frustrated Changeable attitudes, interests Easily perturbed Evades responsibilities, tends to give up Worrying Gets into fights and problem situations	Emotionally mature Stable, constant in interests Calm Does not let emotional needs obscure realities of a situation, adjusts to facts Unruffled Shows restraint by avoiding difficulties

FACTOR D (UI(L)4): PHLEGMATIC TEMPERAMENT-EX-CITABILITY.   Excitability in factor D (Table 2-5) must not be confused with high general emotionality. It does have association with conduct disorders such as enuresis or dropping out of school. But it has more the character of a cognitive excitability and insecurity and shows no noticeable association with personality disorders and general pathology.

TABLE 2—5.   Factor *D* (UI(L)4)

Phlegmatic Temperament *D*— (*Undemonstrative, deliberate, inactive, stodgy*)	Excitability *D*+ (*Excitable, impatient, demanding, overactive, unrestrained*)
Stoic	Demanding, impatient
Complacent	Attention-getting, shows off
Deliberate	Excitable, overactive
Not easily jealous	Prone to jealousy
Self-effacing	Self-assertive, egotistic
Constant	Distractible
Not restless	Many nervous symptoms

FACTOR *E* (UI(L)5): SUBMISSIVENESS–DOMINANCE. Factor *E* is high in creative and adventurous people and is associated with sexual aggressiveness and somewhat with psychopathic behavior (Table 2-6). It appears to be very similar to what has been studied as dominance in mammals and the primates.

TABLE 2—6.   Factor *E* (UI(L)5)

Submissiveness *E*— (*Obedient, mild, easily led, docile, accommodating*)	Dominance or Ascendance *E*+ (*Assertive, aggressive, competitive, stubborn*)
Submissive	Assertive
Dependent	Independent-minded
Considerate, diplomatic	Stern, hostile
Expressive	Solemn
Conventional, conforming	Unconventional, rebellious
Easily upset by authority	Headstrong
Humble	Demands admiration

FACTOR *F* (UI(L)6): DESURGENCY–SURGENCY. In *F* we meet one of the first of the entirely new source-trait concepts due to factor-analytic research (Table 2-7). It was named surgency from experimental evidence of a ready "rising up" (Latin *surgere*) of ideas in persons who score highly on ratings. It has a stronger hereditary determination than most other personality traits except intelligence.

FACTOR *G* (UI(L)7): SUPEREGO STRENGTH. The concept of conscience is at least as old as the Hebrew prophets and Greek dramatists, but current research shows two factors operating in the

TABLE 2–7.   Factor *F* (UI(L)6)

Desurgency *F*–	Surgency *F*+
(Sober, taciturn, serious)	(Enthusiastic, heedless, happy-go-lucky)
Silent, introspective	Talkative
Full of cares	Cheerful
Concerned, reflective	Happy-go-lucky
Incommunicative, relies on inner values	Frank, expressive, reflects group
Slow, cautious	Quick, alert

general area of right behavior and control of antisocial tendencies, namely, factors *G* (Table 2-8) and Q_3 below. The pattern of *G* seems to support the particular description of the psychoanalytic *superego;* Q_3 corresponds to the less fundamental and more socially oriented *self-sentiment.* Guilt and shame have been terms used to distinguish them, and also concern for what is right as distinct from maintaining personal honor and reputation, the former in each case being *G* and the latter Q_3. *G* is a strong predictor of school achievement (with intelligence constant). It increases with experience of responsibilities and with marriage, and is abnormally low in psychopaths.

TABLE 2–8.   Factor *G* (UI(L)7)

Low Superego Strength *G*–	High Superego Strength *G*+
(Disregards rules and group moral standards, expedient)	(Conscientious, persistent, moralistic, staid)
Quitting, fickle	Persevering, determined
Frivolous	Responsible
Self-indulgent	Emotionally disciplined
Slack, indolent	Consistently ordered
Undependable	Conscientious, motivated by duty
Ignores obligations to people	Concerned about moral standards, rules

FACTOR *H* (UI(L)8): THRECTIA-PARMIA.   Factor *H* (Table 2-9) would be called boldness-vs.-timidity in popular language. It is temperamental and has a number of physiological associations. Because of the sociability and talkativeness that go with it, it has long been confused at the clinical observation level with *A* and with *F*, and, indeed, it joins with these in producing the broad shallow second-order extraversion factor. We should note that this primary is a pivot or point of overlap of the second-order factors of anxiety and of introversion. For (in its negative direction, threctia, that is, susceptibility to threat) it loads highly in both of these second orders. This has accounted for some confusion over the seeming tendency of anxiety and introversion to act similarly in some situations. What actually acts similarly and produces some common features is *H*, which loads strongly on invia and on anxiety. One kind of explanation would be that there are two different possible adjustments to high threctia (*H*−), namely being anxious or being withdrawing.

TABLE 2−9. Factor *H* (UI(L)8)

Threctia *H*− *(Shy, timid, restrained, threat-sensitive)*	Parmia *H*+ *(Adventurous, "thick-skinned," socially bold)*
Shy, withdrawn	Adventurous, likes meeting people
Retires in face of opposite sex	Active, overt interest in opposite sex
Emotionally cautious	Responsive, genial
Sometimes embittered	Friendly
Restrained, rule-bound	Impulsive
Restricted interests	Emotional and artistic interests
Considerate, quick to see dangers	Carefree, does not see dangers

FACTOR *I* (UI(L)9): HARRIA-PREMSIA. This source trait was never noted in clinical theory, yet factor-analytically Factor *I* (Table 2-10) is of substantial variance, especially among children. Furthermore, this overprotected, emotional sensitivity (for which

TABLE 2−10. Factor *I* (UI(L)9)

Harria *I*− *(Tough-minded, rejects illusions)*	Premsia *I*+ *(Tender-minded, sensitive, dependent, overprotected)*
Unsentimental, expects little	Fidgety, expects affection and attention
Self-reliant, takes responsibility	Clinging, insecure, seeks help and sympathy
Hard (to point of cynicism)	Gentle, indulgent to self and others
Few artistic responses (but not lacking in taste)	Artistically fastidious, affected, theatrical
Unaffected by fancies	Imaginative inner life and conversation
Acts on practical evidence	Acts on sensitive intuition
Keeps to the point	Seeks attention, flighty
Does not dwell on physical disabilities	Hypochondriacal, anxious about self

pr-em-sia—protected emotional sensitivity—is an acronym) is a powerful contributor to neuroticism, beyond anxiety and other factors in classical neurotic theory. Girls are significantly more premsic than boys, and some cultures are more harric than others. It also has some genetic determination. The age plots show this overprotected dependence dropping sharply between 6 (the earliest measured) and 20 years of age.

FACTOR *J* (UI(L)10): ZEPPIA-COASTHENIA.   This is an interesting, because still somewhat elusive, factor, first located in children. Coasthenia (Table 2-11) represents a high capacity for independence of thought and emotional life, combined with a certain lack of energy—at least in group enterprises. It has, along with surgency, the highest heritability among personality factors, and is definitely temperamental. Indeed, *F* and *J* account for most of the inheritance in the second-order exvia-invia factor, in which they participate.

TABLE 2–11.   Factor *J* (UI(L)10)

Zeppia *J*— *(Zestful, liking group action)*	Coasthenia *J*+ *(Circumspect individualism, reflective,* *internally restrained)*
Likes to go with group	Individualistic
Likes attention	Guarded, wrapped in self
Sinks personality into group	Fastidiously obstructive
Vigorous	Neurasthenically fatigued
Accepts common enthusiasms	Evaluates coldly

FACTOR *K* (UI(L)11): SOCIAL CONCERN.   This factor, which could alternatively be called mature socialization, has only recently been found among questionnaire factors, in studies on the "seven missing factors" (Cattell, Cattell, & Watterson, 1979; Cattell, 1973). It loads such items as preferring plays on socially apt themes to exciting plays, preferring learning by interaction with people, and so on. The obvious problem is obtaining conceptual distinction of *K* from Q_3, which it resembles. However, Q_3 is a broader and larger factor involving the whole self-concept and the sustenance thereof, whereas *K* seems very much a cultural development in "polite society." Most likely it is the result of being brought up in a more sophisticated and also socially responsible home and class environment.

TABLE 2—12. Factor *K* (UI(L)11)

Social Unconcern *K*— (Socially untutored, unconcerned)	Social-Role Concern *K*+ (Socially mature, alert)
Boorish	Gentlemanly
Ignorant of social requirements	Alert to social responsibilities
Awkward, unprepared for social expectations	Polished
Does what he wants	Self-disciplined
Does not overrate people	Concern to show respect for personalities

FACTOR *L* (UI(L)12): ALAXIA-PROTENSION. Protension (Table 2-13) has sometimes been called a "paranoid" tendency, but in the pathological realm we find quite another factor for that disease process as such. More likely, it is an instance of a much more general use of a particular defense dynamism (mechanism) constituting a definite personality source trait—in this case, the defense of *handling tension by projection* (hence the name pro-tension). It seems to be high in individualists and creative scientists (Roe, 1953; Drevdahl, 1956).

TABLE 2—13. Factor *L* (UI(L)12)

Alaxia *L*— (Trusting, accepting conditions)	Protension *L*+ (Suspecting, jealous)
Accepts personal unimportance	Jealous
Pliant to changes	Dogmatic
Unsuspecting of hostility	Suspicious of interference
Ready to forget difficulties	Dwells on frustrations
Understanding, tolerant	Tyrannical
Lax about correcting people	Demands people accept responsibility for
Conciliatory	errors
	Irritable

FACTOR *M* (UI(L)13): PRAXERNIA-AUTIA. Autia is the "Bohemian" factor of vivid internal mental life with disregard of the external world (Table 2-14). High-*M* individuals have greater creativity and greater accident proneness. It decreases after marriage, and increases in those sheltered from practical demands, for example, those who go to college after school compared with those who go to a job (Barton, Cattell, & Vaughan, 1973). As its name suggests, it may be a more active form of that autism that becomes excessive in the autistic child, but is primarily a more intense inner life.

TABLE 2—14.   Factor *M* (UI(L)13)

Praxernia *M—* *(Practical, has "down to earth" concerns)*	Autia *M+* *(Imaginative, bohemian, absent-minded)*

Conventional, alert to practical needs
Concerned with immediate interests
Prosaic, avoids far-fetched ideas
Guided by objective reality, dependable
    practical judgment
Earnest or worried but steady
	Unconventional, absorbed in ideas
	Interested in art, theory, basic beliefs
	Enthralled by inner creations
	Fanciful, easily seduced from practical
	    judgment
	Enthused but occasional hysterical swings
	    of giving up

2-4.   Primary-Source Traits of Lesser Variance in the Normal *L-Q* Domain

As stated above, there is no sharp line between source traits in the last section and this one. We simply proceed here from the first 12 larger primary-source traits to those of lesser variance and ultimately to those found in purely pathological behavior.

FACTOR *N* (UI(L)14): NAIVETE-SHREWDNESS. This source trait (Table 2-15) has always been hard to define, both in *L(R)*- and in *Q*-data, and its existence has been questioned by some because of an unstable loading pattern. (Adcock & Adcock, 1976, could not find it in a New Zealand population.) However, the next few years should, by progressive rectification (Cattell, 1973) clarify its expressions. For undoubtedly a dimension exists here, and its concrete criterion predictions, for example, in business success and in separating nonpsychotics from psychotics, are substantial. In addition to terms like polished and shrewd given in the table, high-*N* people have been reported to show behavior such as watching other people and being realistic; at low *N* we find reports of simple, natural in feelings, unguarded, gauche, and undiplomatic. Darwin, for example, and his wife, recognized him as decidedly low in *N* characteristics. The *N* factor expresses what is probably a largely acquired pattern, learned in the *N+* direction, and most probably is based on a childhood situation of competitive insecurity or hostility, and having to fend for oneself.

FACTOR *O* (UI(L)15): GUILT PRONENESS. In Table 2-16 we encounter a source trait of profound importance in clinical psychology. Best labelled guilt proneness, it also includes a general

TABLE 2—15. Factor *N* (UI(L)14)

Naivete *N*— (Forthright, unpretentious)	Shrewdness *N*+ (Astute, worldly)
Genuine but socially clumsy	Polished, socially aware
Vague, injudicious mind	Exact, calculating mind
Gregarious, warmly involved	Emotionally detached, disciplined
Spontaneous, natural	Artful, devious
Simple tastes	Esthetically fastidious
Lacks self-insight	Has self-insight
Unskilled in analyzing motives	Insightful regarding others
Content with status quo	Ambitious, possibly insecure
Blind trust in human nature	Smart, cuts corners

sense of unworthiness and inadequacy, along with sudden swings of depressive mood. It is significantly high in alcoholics, criminals, neurotics, attempted suicides, and psychotics. It increases with such events as instability of job, chronic illness, and disability, and declines with job promotion and a larger circle of friends (Barton & Cattell, 1972).

TABLE 2—16. Factor *O* (UI(L)15)

Untroubled Adequacy *O*— (Self-assured, placid, secure, complacent)	Guilt Proneness *O*+ (Apprehensive, self-reproaching, insecure, worrying, troubled)
Self-confident	Worrying, anxious
Cheerful, resilient	Depressed, cries easily
Impenitent, placid	Easily touched, overcome by moods
Expedient, insensitive to approval or disapproval	Strong sense of obligation, sensitive to approval and disapproval
Does not care	Scrupulous, fussy
Rudely vigorous	Hypochondriacal, inadequate
No fears	Phobic symptoms
Given to simple action	Lonely, brooding

FACTOR *P* (UI(L)16): CAUTIOUS INACTIVITY-SANGUINE CASUALNESS. Factor *P* (Table 2-17) has shown itself primarily in *Q*-data, the positive pole being there shown in more detail by self-assurance, casualness, lack of realistic organization of time, goodwill, speculative mind, and hypomanic diversification of interests.

TABLE 2–17.   Factor *P* (UI(L)16)

Cautious Inactivity *P*–	Sanguine Casualness *P*+
Melancholy	Sanguine
Cautious	Speculative
Takes no risks	Independent

FACTOR Q_1 (UI(L)17): CONSERVATISM-RADICALISM.   In this and the remaining factors, all of which were first discovered in questionnaire material, the replication in the rating area $L(R)$ medium is either slender or still unexplored. To emphasize this, the ratings terms have been put in parentheses. Factor Q_1 (Table 2-18) was first defined by Thurstone and his co-workers, largely in political and religious attitudes. Cattell and co-workers tested the hypothesis that it is not entirely a sentiment among socio-intellectual values, but a temperamental, or at least an early acquired, tendency to be experimental and fond of the new, rather than fixated on the old. As to the values for specific institutional elements in this pattern, they have changed so fast in a generation as to be poorly measured by older scales. For example "liberal" today has more of an autistic than an analytical-rationalist emphasis, and because Q_1 has analytic, tough-minded, and adventurous rather than stress-avoiding qualities, liberal may no longer be a good term for Q_1. However, Q_1 *does* have value elements and an attempt to measure it purely through a shift to items expressing a more generalized "tendency to experiment" has not been too successful either. Q_1 therefore remains difficult to measure with high cross-cultural transferability.

TABLE 2–18.   Factor Q_1 (UI(L)17)

Conservatism Q_1 –	Radicalism Q_1 +
(Disinclined to change)	(Experimenting)
(Respects traditional values)	(Analytic)
(Tolerant of inconveniences or old methods)	(Free thinking)

FACTOR Q_2 (UI(L)18): GROUP DEPENDENCY-SELF-SUF-FICIENCY.   The heritability coefficient shows Factor Q_2 (Table 2-19) to be, unlike *J*, an acquired rather than a genetic pattern of self-sufficiency. Q_2+ is predictive positively of school achievement, especially at later ages, and is markedly higher in creative scientists and artists than in the general population (Cattell & Drevdahl, 1960).

TABLE 2–19.   Factor Q_2 (UI(L)18)

Group Dependency Q_2-	Self-Sufficiency Q_3+
(Sociably group dependent)	(Self-sufficient)
(A "joiner")	(Resourceful)
(Sound follower)	(Prefers own decisions)

FACTOR Q_3 (UI(L)19): SELF-SENTIMENT. The importance of this source trait both for psychological theory and effective practice is great, and its firmer appearance in observer rating is shown by removal of parentheses from subtraits. Factor Q_3 (Table 2-20) is the set of attitudes concerned with maintenance of the self-concept and, as such, it shows itself firmly also as a factor in objective dynamic measurements (Chapter 4). It is higher in individuals who achieve better in job or school, low in neurotics (Cattell, Eber, & Tatsuoka, 1970). It increases with college education, higher job responsibilities, and such challenges as an unhappy love affair, parental illness, and so on. It declines with alcoholism. It has to do with maintenance of the individual's self-respect, honor, and social reputation and is probably one of the two main factors in the "need for achievement" (McClelland, Atkinson, et al., 1953), as discussed in Chapter 4.

TABLE 2–20.   Factor Q_3 (UI(L)19)

Low Self-Sentiment Q_3-	High Self-Sentiment Q_3+
Uncontrolled	Controlled
Lax	Exacting will power
Follows own urges	Socially precise
Unintegrated	Compulsive
Careless of social rules	Follows self-image

FACTOR Q_4 (UI(L)20): ERGIC TENSION.   Factor Q_4 (Table 2-21) can be related to the psychoanalytic concept of unexpressed libido, because, among other things, it contributes powerfully to anxiety. It increases into adolescence and after age 21 declines into middle life. It is low in airline pilots and school counsellors, and high in journalists, supermarket personnel, and others under speed pressures. It is characteristically above normal in persons who manifest most pathological syndromes, neurotics, alcoholics, manics, in unstable compared to happy marriages, and in people who have "had a run of bad luck." It is increased by an unhappy love affair, absence of promotion, and by chronic illness, but reduced by participation in religious activities (Barton, Cattell, & Vaughan, 1973; Cattell, 1973). It is physically associated with high blood pressure and other indicators of stress (Cattell, Eber, & Tatsuoka, 1970).

TABLE 2–21.   Factor Q_4 (UI(L)20)

Low Ergic Tension Q_4-	High Ergic Tension Q_4+
Relaxed	Tense
Tranquil	Frustrated
Torpid	Driven
Unfrustrated	Overwrought
Composed	Fretful

FACTOR Q_5 (UI(L)21): LACK OF SOCIAL CONCERN-GROUP DEDICATION.   This source trait (Table 2-22) has not been demonstrated properly as yet in rating analyses. It is one of the "seven missing factors" recently found by Delhees and Watterson in Q-analysis (see Cattell, 1973 and Cattell, Cattell, & Watterson, 1979).

TABLE 2–22.   Factor Q_5 (UI(L)21)

Lack of Social Concern Q_5- Tough	Group Dedication with Sensed Inadequacy Q_5+
(Does not volunteer for social service)	(Concerns self with social good works)
(Experiences no obligation)	(Has a certain feeling of inadequacy: not
(Is self-sufficient)	doing enough)
	(Likes to join up in social endeavors)

FACTOR Q_6 (UI(L)22): SELF-EFFACEMENT-SOCIAL PANACHE.   Like most other factors indexed as Q, factor Q_6 (Table 2-23) has no rating support as yet and may be a relatively narrow form of behavior.

TABLE 2–23.   Factor Q_6 (UI(L)22)

Self Effacement Q_6-	Social Panache Q_6+
(Quiet, self-effacing)	(Feels unfairly treated by society)
	(Makes abrupt antisocial remarks)
	(Has no hesitation about self-expression
	in groups)

FACTOR Q_7 (UI(L)23): EXPLICIT SELF-EXPRESSION. With factor Q_7 (Table 2-24), we come to the end of the 23 factors in "normal" behavior, both as rated and as appearing in normal questionnaire items. There are a few more "fringe" factors, but the above have been replicated sufficiently to justify the conclusion that there exist no fewer than 23 normal primaries. There are now at least two equivalent standardized questionnaire scales available to mark each of these 23 factors, and no fewer than five for each of the first 16. An excellent discussion of the role of most of these factors in clinical and broader behavior is available in Karson and O'Dell (1976).

TABLE 2–24.   Factor Q_7 (UI(L)23)

Lacks Explicit Self-Expression $Q_7 -$	Explicit Self-Expression $Q_7 +$
(Is not garrulous in conversation)	(Enjoys verbal-social expression)
	(Likes dramatic entertainment)
	(Follows fashionable ideas)

2-5.   The 12 Factors Found Among Pathological Abnormal Behavior

The 12 further primaries now to be designated are mainly established in Q-data, although equivalent patterns in L-data are generally known (Cattell, 1957; 1975), but not checked by cross-correlation. They are all patterns that arise from factoring descriptions of behavior that is abnormal or borders on the abnormal, for example, as in MMPI items.

In view of the two distinct prevalent clinical positions (1) that the abnormal is statistically only an extreme degree of normal behavior and (2) that it is a totally different product of disease process, what is our hypothesis about abnormal factors? Note that accepting the second position does not mean that the same basic behavioral laws do not apply, but only that variance on the pattern is likely to be small in normal subjects and that ulterior evidence of a disease process exists. The answer is that our purpose at present is purely descriptive and that, although the behavior is "odd," we shall leave its interpretation to later research with the obtained factor scores.

Deliberately, in this new domain, we enter with behavior items that are regarded as biologically and socially maladaptive, and statistically uncommon and deviant, and research generally uses a population for factoring that has at least as many psychiatrically judged abnormal as normal. We then find, as will be shown below, that new dimensions appear that have been either absent or too small to register easily on normal groups. A sharp issue that arises in this work is whether the search for abnormal dimensions should be made wholly in a mental-hospital population or in the intermediate zone where normal processes give way to abnormal. We have chosen the latter kind of sample because (1) the line is not sharp anyway—there are as many neurotics and possibly psychotics out of as in clinics or mental hospitals—and (2) for practical diagnostic purposes, the psychiatrist *needs* to measure dimensions most clearly at the *frontiers* of abnormality, that is those on which the normal-abnormal continuum will be most stretched out and expressed.

Now in abnormal as in normal behavior, we need a personality-sphere concept of representative behaviors (variables). The MMPI was so put together by its authors as to constitute a good beginning in spanning pathological behavior. To this, between 1960 and 1970, our co-workers Bjerstedt, Delhees, Specht, and others added collec-, tions of new aspects of abnormal behavior, notably in the area of the depressions, judiciously including behaviors with some claim to being marker variables in the existing factorings by Grinker, Nunnally, et al. (1961); Weckowicz, Cropley, and Muir (1971), and others. When this "enriched MMPI" pool of extension items was factored on joint normal and abnormal subjects, some 12 dimensions appeared that were demonstrably new because the old dimensions appeared alongside them. In fact, the 16 PF normal dimensions were discernible in MMPI type "abnormal" items, though clothed somewhat in pathological expressions. This illustrates the wise clinical injunction that one should know not only the severity of the disease processes, but also the scores on the patient's essential prepsychotic or epipsychotic underlying normal personality traits.

Among these 12 factors, the last five are very steady in replications. They have been given names that might seem to place them as *type-syndrome* designations (for example, schizophrenia) rather than pure *dimensions.* But, regardless of how we later construe the type-dimension relations in this field, these factor scales are operationally definitely *dimensions;* that is, source traits. It is in regard to the first seven factors—mainly in the depression area—that some puzzling difficulties still face us. Their correlations become very high in mixed normal and abnormal groups, and though this is legitimately explicable (see below) by a large second-order depression factor, the primaries in themselves come near to collapse in certain population samples. And, unlike the last five, these first seven among the "abnormal" factors can be found, in attenuated condition, in purely normal groups. In any case, the distinction of psychological meaning *among* these depression primaries fits clinical sense, and further psychometric research will almost certainly separate them more clearly as scales.

Table 2-25 offers a brief description of these primaries, which may be followed up readily in extended discussions elsewhere (Cattell & Sells, 1974; Cattell, 1973, p. 84).

2-6. Origin and Nature of 15 Second-Stratum Source Traits

When simple structure fixes the positions of primary factors, it is found that they are usually mutually correlated, moderately but significantly, and with consistent values from sample to sample. This should not surprise us, for most factor influences are themselves in turn worked upon by other influences, and when a higher-order influence affects two primaries, they become correlated. For example, in the more obvious physical world, across a sample of weather stations, if we took several variables, rate of evaporation, growth of trees, rate of rusting of iron, and others that are effects of temperature, humidity, and air pressure, we should get separate primaries for these three last. But temperature and air pressure would be correlated because both would tend to be lower at stations of higher altitude; that is, altitude would appear as a second-order factor. Carrying an inappropriate mathematical concept into a scientific model, some investigators, like Guilford, have insisted that factors should be kept orthogonal (uncorrelated) or even as principal components. But orthogonality has been shown in countless studies to be incompatible with maximum simple structure characteristic of truly located influences, as well as with invariance of influence pattern (V_{fp}) from population to population. Furthermore, leaving factors orthogonal denies us any possibility of exploring higher-order factors.

Second-order factors are found by taking the correlations among primary factors and factoring them just as we did initially the correlations among single behavioral variables. Consistently with the general principle in first orders, the factors so reached are rotated to simple structure, on the assumption that they are broader influences operating on the lower-order primaries.

Eight second-orders have appeared with great consistency from the first 16 primaries, both across ages and across cultures. Insufficient research has yet been done on the remainder of the 23 normal

TABLE 2–25. Description of the 12 Pathological Source Traits With Their Index Symbols[a]

Factor	Low Score Description	High Score Description
D_1	Is happy, mind works well, does not find ill health frightening LOW HYPOCHONDRIASIS	Shows overconcern with bodily functions, health, or disabilities HIGH HYPOCHONDRIASIS
D_2	Is contented about life and surroundings, has no death wishes ZESTFULNESS	Is disgusted with life, harbors thoughts or acts of self-destruction SUICIDAL DISGUST
D_3	Avoids dangerous and adventurous undertakings, has little need for excitement LOW BROODING DISCONTENT	Seeks excitement, is restless, takes risks, tries new things HIGH BROODING DISCONTENT
D_4	Is calm in emergency, confident about surroundings, poised LOW ANXIOUS DEPRESSION	Has disturbing dreams, is clumsy in handling things, tense, easily upset HIGH ANXIOUS DEPRESSION
D_5	Shows enthusiasm for work, is energetic, sleeps soundly HIGH ENERGY EUPHORIA	Has feelings of weariness, worries, lacks energy to cope LOW ENERGY DEPRESSION
D_6	Is not troubled by guilt feelings, can sleep no matter what is left undone LOW GUILT AND RESENTMENT	Has feelings of guilt, blames himself for everything that goes wrong, is critical of himself HIGH GUILT AND RESENTMENT

D_7	Is relaxed, considerate, cheerful with people LOW BORED DEPRESSION	Avoids contact and involvement with people, seeks isolation, shows discomfort with people HIGH BORED DEPRESSION
Pa	Is trusting, not bothered by jealousy or envy LOW PARANOIA	Believes he is being persecuted, poisoned, controlled, spied on, mistreated HIGH PARANOIA
Pp	Avoids engagement in illegal acts or breaking rules, sensitive LOW PSYCHOPATHIC DEVIATION	Has complacent attitude towards own or others' anti-social behavior, is not hurt by criticism, likes crowds HIGH PSYCHOPATHIC DEVIATION
Sc	Makes realistic appraisals of himself and others, shows emotional harmony and absence of regressive behavior LOW SCHIZOPHRENIA	Hears voices or sounds without apparent source outside himself, retreats from reality, has uncontrolled and sudden impulses HIGH SCHIZOPHRENIA
As	Is not bothered by unwelcome thoughts and ideas or compulsive habits LOW PSYCHASTHENIA	Suffers insistent, repetitive ideas and impulses to perform certain acts HIGH PSYCHASTHENIA
Ps	Considers himself as good, dependable, and smart as most others LOW GENERAL PSYCHOSIS	Has feelings of inferiority and unworthiness, timid, loses his head easily HIGH GENERAL PSYCHOSIS

[a]By permission of IPAT and the authors of the CAQ. Copyright IPAT 1976.

primaries or on the 12 abnormal primaries to give so dependable a basis, but the loading patterns in Table 2-26 show both the first eight, summed from 14 studies and cross-validated over nine researches, and the later second-order factors, as yet replicated only over two studies, covering the full 35 primaries.

There has been little difficulty among psychologists in recognizing the earlier and larger of these second-order factors in Table 2-26. The first is extraversion, or exvia, as it may now better be called to separate it from what has long since degenerated into a popular journalistic and vague term. Exvia-invia loads affectia, surgency, and parmia positively and coasthenia and self-sufficiency negatively.

Incidentally, the term *stratum* is better than *order* in referring to factors beyond the primaries, because a higher order simply defines an operation—a factoring of the present order—whereas the idea of strata is that of a definite structural position. Just as the position of a chemical element in the periodic table eventually has more meaning than that given only by atomic weight, and takes valency and other issues into account, so the stratum level of a factor is located not only by order in a particular factor analysis but also by evidence of general breadth of influence, relation to physiological and sociological influences, and so on. The expanding findings of research may shift stratum rank. Spearman's "*g*," for example, was treated initially as a primary factor, but later was clearly shown to be a second-stratum factor among Thurstone's primary abilities. The present theoretical status of second-stratum factors is one that accepts two possibilities: (1) That each is some kind of underlying influence that acts directly on several different primaries (but *not* directly on the variables the primaries themselves influence); and (2), that each is a new emergent from mutual interaction of a set of primaries, namely, the set on which the second order is found, statistically, to have loadings. This latter has sometimes been called the *spiral interaction model.* Although, by (1), a secondary is an independent influence uncorrelated with the primaries before it acts on them, statistical expressions can be worked out (the Schmid-Leiman and the Cattell-White formulae) to express the extent of the indirect influence of the secondaries on variables.

A second very clear second-stratum factor is QII (note Roman numerals for second-stratum factors), which is undoubtedly the precise core of what is popularly called anxiety. It fits, incidentally, the psychoanalytic formula of weak ego strength ($C-$), guilt (O), and undischarged libido—general ergic tension (Q_4)—though it adds new entities unknown to psychoanalysis, such as threctia (H), poor self-sentiment development (Q_3-), social panache (Q_6), hypochondria (D_1), and, among the abnormal factors, avoidance of challenging excitement (D_3-), and asthenia (As). Note D_1, D_2, etc. have come to mean the seven first-order depression factors and should not be confused with simple D in the alphabetical series, which is *excitability:* Table 2-5 above.) Countless criterion-relation studies show this QII measure behaving as anxiety should.

Beyond the readily "clinically" recognizable traits like QI (exvia-invia), and QII (anxiety), however, are other secondaries that are quite new. Thus $QIII$ (cortertia-vs.-pathemia) seems to be a predominance of cortical over hypothalamic excitability; QIV (independence), is a temperament factor apparently underlying Witkin's "field independence"; and $QVIII$ is a factor of "good upbringing," now named *control*, which simultaneously raises the superego, G; the self-sentiment, Q_3; and probably ego strength, C; while inhibiting high surgency, F.

Among the pathological primaries is a general psychosis factor, XIV—a concept also supported by work of Eysenck and Eysenck (1968). The nearest approach to a truly general depression factor is XIII, which hits D_2, D_5, and D_6 strongly, but D_1, D_3, and D_7 only lightly. In fact, as shown elsewhere, there are probably three second orders in depression and the two later ones are nonpathological, namely, invia (QI-) and subduedness (QIV-), but the first is commonly called *general depression* (Krug, 1978).

Although several of the 15 second-stratum factors now tolerably defined, in terms of their primaries loadings are still not interpreted, there is little doubt about their existence and only moderate uncertainty about certain loadings in the case of the last seven (Cattell, 1979). Consequently, theoretical interpretation can proceed as psychologists apply the scales for them, such as the Barton *Core Trait and State Battery—CTS* (1978), to determine clinical and other criterion relations. Already something is known about their heritability and age courses (see Cattell, 1973; Eysenck, 1970; Eysenck & Prell, 1951). For example, anxiety (QII) falls after adolescence, rises slightly again after middle age; cortertia rises for 6 to 16 and then falls slightly through adulthood, and so on.

Four third-stratum factors have been replicated on a basis of correlations among nine secondaries. Hypotheses that make them out as intelligible, *very broad* influences on personality are discussed elsewhere (Cattell, 1973).

TABLE 2–26. Secondaries Derived From the Full Series of Known Primaries, Normal and Abnormal

Table 2–26a: Thoroughly Replicated Over First 16 Primaries

Primary	Sym-bol	Pattern							
		I	II	III	IV	V	VI	VII	VIII
Affectia	A	58	01	-25	01	28	00	-00	-01
Intelligence	B	-00	-02	00	-01	-01	00	67	-01
Ego strength	C	07	-66	10	-01	-02	-00	04	05
Dominance	E	-07	-00	01	56	-03	08	01	-18
Surgency	F	51	-03	01	30	-02	-04	02	-27
Superego	G	06	-03	01	-03	00	-05	05	67
Parmia	H	50	-38	-14	34	05	-01	-02	-00
Premsia	I	07	00	-73	-03	01	04	01	02
Protension	L	05	54	06	40	02	-01	-06	04
Autia	M	12	03	-47	20	-05	14	-02	-08
Shrewdness	N	-00	-02	00	03	63	00	-01	03
Guilt proneness	O	-02	78	-06	-05	-00	00	-04	03
Radicalism	Q_1	-02	-06	-01	07	06	56	05	-02
Self-sufficiency	Q_2	-65	-01	-04	03	02	07	01	01
Self-sentiment	Q_3	-05	-43	01	02	01	03	-02	47
Ergic tension	Q_4	-00	80	-05	10	-02	-03	09	-02

This table represents the mean pattern loadings from 14 studies originally presented in 9 summarizing matrices. The goodness of hyperplanes and the magnitudes of congruences of patterns across the studies were high, as can be studied elsewhere (Cattell, 1973). The mean congruences across these studies were:

QI	QII	$QIII$	QIV	QV	QVI	$QVII$	$QVIII$
.93	.98	.92	.84	.92	.70	.77	.86

Table 2–26b: Recently Obtained Secondaries From the Totality of 35 Primaries

Secondary

Primary	Symbol	I	II	III	IV	V	VI	VII	VIII	XI[c]	X[c]	IX[c]	XII[c]	XIII[a]	XIV[b]	XV[c]
Normal behavior source traits, long checked																
Affectia	A	47	-27	-29		19	-26									
Intelligence	B							65								
Ego strength	C		-66						-25							24
Dominance	E				62											
Surgency	F	42			27										-30	
Superego	G							21	60						-30	
Parmia	H	47	33		30	28	24									
Premsia	I			-62												
Protension	L		29		37											
Autia	M			-13	28		27							26		
Shrewdness	N					-27										
Guilt proneness	O		52													
Radicalism	Q₁	73			25		50	23							25	
Self-sufficiency	Q₂		47				15									
Self-sentiment	Q₃		59						44							-38
Ergic tension	Q₄															
Normal behavior source traits, new																
Excitability	D		24								-60					
Coasthenia	J	-22				22						66				

[a]Values in parentheses in column XIII are from a third research. Secondary XIII is the main *general depression* factor, with (-)IV as a second.

[b]Secondary XIV is the *general psychosis* factor.

[c]Factors IX, X, XI, and XII are not yet sufficiently checked and expanded to be given any interpretation.

TABLE 2–26b (continued)

Primary	Sym-bol	I	II	III	IV	V	VI	VII	VIII	IX[c]	X[c]	XI[c]	XII[c]	XIII[a]	XIV[b]	XV[c]
Normal behavior source traits, new (cont.)																
Socialization	K															
Sanguineness	P									74						
Group dedication	Q₅				-48								-64			
Panache	Q₆		73				21	30	33	-18	-32					
Expressiveness	Q₇					70										
Abnormal behavior factors																
Hypochondriasis	D₁		55											(35)	50	
Suicidal disgust	D₂					45								60		
Brooding discontent	D₃		-37	47										(20)		
Anxious depression	D₄				-42									(30)	36	
Low-energy depression	D₅				-34									39		
Guilt and resentment	D₆													55		
Bored withdrawal	D₇							-41								
Paranoia	Pa					*46*									64	
Psychopathic deviation	Pp														39	-65
Schizophrenia	Sc				-26		-28	-36							14	
Psychasthenia	As		47												47	
General psychosis	Ps													43	53	

[a]Values in parentheses in column XIII are from a third research. Secondary XIII is the main *general depression* factor, with (–)IV as a second.

[b]Secondary XIV is the *general psychosis* factor.

[c]Factors IX, X, XI, and XII are not yet sufficiently checked and expanded to be given any interpretation.

2-7. Summary

1. Human behavior may be observed and quantified through three main media of observation: (a) L-data, behavior in the life situation reported, by outside observers; (b) Q-data, behavior in the life situation as seen by the subject himself; and (c) T-data, objectively measured behavioral response in a defined test situation. Various combinations of medium and method are possible; for example, L-data, can be quantified from records ($L(T)$-data) or *rated* by human judges $(L(R)$-data), yielding various properties in terms of consistency and validity coefficients, and the likelihood of instrument factors.

2. To be sure that the personality structures found by correlational, factor-analytic, and other multivariate experimental methods really span personality, omitting no important area and avoiding exaggeration and distortions of perspective through uneven density of variables, the concept òf the *personality sphere* and of *density* are introduced. Two methods for reaching these, sampling the *language pool* and *behavior time sampling*, are set up. It is recognized that the last still leaves freedom for differences in style of measurement, but a sampling principle for style described elsewhere (Cattell & Warburton, 1967).

3. This chapter is concerned simply with the *formal psychometric evidence* for the nature of some 35 primary- and 15 second-stratum personality source traits in $L-Q$ data. Interpretations and calculations about them are reserved for later chapters.

4. The sheer evidence for their existence, and for taking them more seriously than alleged traits or types "pulled out of a hat" by amateur or even clinical observation, takes the student inevitably into relatively refined technical penetrations. These technical penetrations include:

   a. Factor-analytic tests for numbers of factors, and other technical standards, for recognizing the crystallization of hyperplanes in graphic plots are essential for unique resolutions. As Cattell and Burdsal (1974; 1975) have recently shown, the requisite precision of unique resolution of factors as independent influences also requires, in $Q-data$, factoring of radial parcels not single questionnaire items.

   b. When these factors have their scores estimated (according to the obtained factor pattern V_{fp} and the factor estimation matrix V_{fe}) and plotted for age, sex, and hereditary evidence, each shows a definitely idiosyncratic and characteristic life course.

c. They show a continuity of appearance in cross-sectional researches at different age levels. That is to say, statistically significant congruence coefficients are obtained between the patterns from factoring different age populations.

d. They turn up with considerable constancy also across cultures, as more basic traits should. This is true both of the Q patterns here in the 16 PF and of the objective test factors in the next chapter.

e. When these source traits are scored, each proves to respond in its characteristic fashion to experimental manipulation and to life influences such as success in career, marriage, illness, and so on (Cattell & Barton, Cattell & Vaughan, 1973; Barton & Cattell, 1975).

f. They show widely different nature-nurture ratios; some, such as surgency (F), intelligence (B), and coasthenia (J) showing marked hereditary determination and others, such as radicalism (Q_1) and ergic tension (Q_4), being largely determined by environment.

g. They predict real-life criteria—clinical, educational, industrial— to a substantial degree. For example, the accuracy of school achievement prediction is doubled by adding personality measures.

h. They show the above relationships and changes in relation to life criteria in a way consistent with the meanings initially hypothetically given to them from their intrinsic loading patterns.

5.   These statements, covering the rapid progress of the last 30 years in identifying source traits comprehensively across the personality sphere, and in exploring their properties and criterion relations, do not mean that the exploration-definition stage is complete, still less that really high psychometric validities are yet reached in the constructed batteries for all source traits. Especially in the later factors we do not yet have in all countries scale validities and reliabilities (of the questionnaires, or the ratings) at levels we would ideally desire. The validities of the 8- to 10-item single-form questionnaire scales in the 16 PF, HSPQ, and CPQ tests, for example, are around 0.7 and the equivalences (inter-form reliabilities) around 0.5. However, these have been kept to very short scales, and the validities and reliabilities are entirely adequate when compared with those for well-established ability and other factors that psychologists are accustomed to measure. For the latter are rarely as brief as 10-item scales, and, if we correct the questionnaire personality source-trait reliabilities by the Spearman-Brown formula to lengths of 40 to 60 items as in most intelligence tests, the results in personality turn

out already to be comparable to those in abilities. The important advance is that unique factorial definition has been given in Q-data to some 35 normal and abnormal personality primary source traits effectively spanning the personality sphere. It is now a relatively mechanical, if laborious, matter to build up items to bring scales for them to suitable lengths and validities. This has in fact been done in producing the five equivalent forms of measurement for each factor in the 16 PF (and its extension to 23 traits in all) and the two equivalent forms of the Clinical Analysis Questionnaire, while in the rating field Dreger's lists provide access to many of the same source traits.

6. Despite some "instrument factor" intrusions (Chapter 8), a one-to-one alignment of primaries found in *L*– and *Q*–media can in general be demonstrated. The failure to recognize this simplifying result earlier arose from failure in most rating studies to meet even limited basic requirements for unbiased ratings and good psychometric properties in the ratings used. Arising from a personality sphere of some 50 rating variables and over 2,000 questionnaire items, some 23 normal personality primaries emerge, and another 12 appear in pathological or borderline-abnormal items. These are probably not exhaustive and will be further expanded, but they already account for between half and three-quarters of the variance of most concrete variables and criterion measures used.

7. Primary factors, when they are truly at unique simple structure positions, naturally, like all influences interacting in a common universe, have moderate mutual correlations. Orthogonal factors, adopted for the immediate, short-view convenience of mathematicians and for computing simplicity are merely artificial entities from the standpoint of a psychological understanding of personality. Their use ultimately produces confusion because, as physical examples show, it is the oblique factors that retain invariance and identity of pattern across studies in which correlations among factors naturally vary. It can already be shown, by this and other considerations, that the model that science requires in almost all behavioral phenomena is one of oblique factors.

8. The resulting correlation matrix of primaries can be factored to discover second-order factors (secondaries). These, if taken to simple structure, consistently with what is done with primaries, may be regarded, by the same arguments, as real influences operating on real influences (see Chapter 8). Strictly we should speak of first, second, and higher *strata*, not just *orders*, for the strata model fixes factor statuses with regard to more than a single factor analysis.

9. Some 15 secondaries already have been replicated and 11 or 12 of them are recognized as having definite theoretical meaning, which

is opened to further experiment by their being rendered measurable in new scales recently constructed. Among these are QI, exvia-invia; QII, anxiety, $QIII$, cortertia; QIV, independence; $QVII$, fluid intelligence; $QVIII$, good upbringing or control; $QXIII-$, general depression; and $QXIV$, general psychoticism.

10. Because the above secondaries are also oblique, they can be factored to tertiaries (third-order personality factors). In fact, such analyses have been done and replicated, leading to five tertiaries tentatively identified by Q_α, Q_β, Q_γ, Q_δ, and Q_ϵ. In principle, this regression can be continued "indefinitely," but there are indications that already by the third order some of the shaping influences are sociological and physiological organizers rather than psychological traits.

11. The personality factors found on the basis of general behavior in the personality sphere are called *general personality* source traits, to distinguish them from *abilities*, found specifically in right and wrong performances, and from traits of *dynamic modality*, as studied later (Chapter 4) deriving from motivation-interest variables only. At this stage we recognize only that these *general* personality traits are likely to be of diverse origins and natures—some temperament traits largely arising from genetic action, some produced by learning-reinforcement schedules in social institutions, and so on. Answers on questions of origin and nature are now open to research through the measurement basis provided by research on taxonomy and measurement.

NOTES

[1] The use of both consistency (reliability) and validity coefficient concepts in this book follow the modern treatment in Cattell and Butcher (1968) and Cattell and Warburton (1967). Thus test consistency has three forms—homogeneity, dependability or retest reliability, and transferability; validity is concrete or abstract, direct or indirect. Conspect reliability refers purely to reliability of *scoring*, distinguishing tests with keys from others.

[2] For example, a single variable of "animosity to the sergeant major" might normally load on a broad factor of pugnacity and an antimilitary sentiment structure. But if we make separate variables out of "I do not like the way the SM talks," "I do not like the way the SM walks," and so on, to, say, 10 variables, a new apparently broad factor will emerge to impress us as a common broad personality factor *as seen in such a matrix*. Yet when brought into a more carefully chosen personality sphere matrix it is seen to be only a specific.

[3] Although the present author's "principle of indifference of indicator" and "instrument-transcending personality source trait" concepts have postulated that in the end the various factors found in L, Q, and T media will prove to be the same personality traits in "different dress," it is only recently that four or five

instances of matching between L and Q on the one hand and T on the other have been found. (L matches with Q, on the other hand, now down the whole series).

For completeness the L and Q traits were given UI numbers as well as alphabetic identities, in the order of their size and/or date of discovery. These UI's are the same for L and Q but different in identity (when matching is known) from T (for example, UI(Q)II is the same as UI(T)24). Strictly, therefore, all UI numbers should have L, Q, or T attached to show the medium of observation in which the given factor is established. As cross-media matchings are achieved in years to come it will be possible to use simply a UI number for the trait that can be made the same across L, Q, and T media.

[4] The technical terms for source traits and their index numbers are those in standard use in both L- and Q-data (see also Table 4, Chapter 2 in Cattell, 1973). There is a double system: the familiar use of alphabetical identification from A through P, and the more formal universal index (UI) with L- or Q-data numbers such as UI(L)19. The high pole in scoring is always the name on the right of tables given here. If we are prepared to base rating-factor identification on a single research, then the recent research of Cattell, Pierson, and Finkbeiner (1976) points to more rating factors than here, extending closer to the 23 found in normal Q-data. The subtitles given directly below the factor names are an attempt to define in about four words the essence of the given pole of the trait. The list of terms below the line is constituted by ratings used in actual researches, from standard rating variables (Cattell, 1957), and found to have significant loadings, higher for those higher in the list.

[5] The measurement of intelligence has been shown to carry with it, as a factor in the personality realm, some other ratings besides those shown here; the correlations, however, are very low.

CHAPTER 3

SOURCE-TRAIT STRUCTURE
SEEN IN LABORATORY MEASUREMENTS: *T*-DATA

3-1. A Systematic Taxonomy for a Personality Sphere in Objective Test Performances

No one sensitive to the history of theory and method in psychology can escape the impression that doubt, and even disgust, characterized the attitude of experimental psychologists toward the areas of personality and social psychology during the first half of this century. Moreover, we must admit that this attitude was justified by verbal pretentiousness and operational flimsiness in the theory, for example, entire dependence on rating and clinical observations—if on anything. The way out, as argued in Chapter 1, was not, however, to succumb to a slavish imitation of bivariate "brass instrument" traditions, concentrating on bits of specific nongeneralizable behaviors, but to develop the considerable latent power of multivariate experiment.

Although the potency of multivariate analytical methods has surely been confirmed amply by the structuring demonstrated in Chapter 2, an experimentalist may yet not be entirely happy about the firmness of rating and questionnaire foundations. Questionnaires are vulnerable to motivational distortion and most rating are generally poor things, too tied to the personality of the rater and the local role situation to give a real measurement quality. (For instance, we cannot compare ratings of A by X with those of A by Y three years later, for purposes of developmental study.) Questionnaire distortion, as will be discussed in Chapter 8 (Section 8–5), extends all the way from poor self awareness to deliberate faking.

As we shall see later, various corrections can be made for distortions in original data in the L- and Q-media. Nevertheless, the experimentalist does not feel really happy until the original data are obtained in the controlled form of most laboratory measures of actual behavior; that is, in what we have called T-data. In passing let us note for verbal clarity that in the past the term "objective test" was often used for a test that is objective only in *scoring*. We use, here and in other books, the word *conspective* (looked at together) to mean objective only in scoring. A conspective test is either a multiple-choice test (with key) or an open index (with key); but a test that is open ended *without* a key is a *subjectively scored* test—and often a crystal ball. The conspect reliability, as indicated below (p. 123), is the coefficient of agreement between scorers of the same test result and is 1.0 for a fully conspective test.

The real hurdle in this research domain, of which the present writer has been acutely aware throughout 40 years of research with close to 100 research associates, is that the invention of actual test situations that are at once *objective* and potently *diagnostic of individual differences in personality* requires psychological insights and creative capacities that scarcely one psychologist in twenty possesses. This being so it is not surprising that before the mid-forties, the creation of such objective tests came in the merest trickle. The roster could just about be completed by listing Hartshorne and May's honesty tests; the Rorschach; Spearman's disposition-rigidity measures; McDougall's use of fluctuating perspective and spot-dotting; Brogden's persistence measures; Ryan's endurance-of-discomfort tests; Allport, Vernon, and Rimoldi's suggestions for "tempo measures"; the Szondi; the present writer's "fluctuation-of-attitudes" test; Darrow and Wenger's use of GSR-response situations; the Blacky Test; the Downey test of inhibition in writing; Hull's sway-suggestibility test; Cattell and Luborsky's "reaction to humor" test; the Kretschmer tests; Jaensch's eidetic imagery test; ergograph curve patterns; the cursive miniature situation (moving ribbon) test; and a few others (Cattell, 1943). The above are not individually referenced here, being listed and briefly described in a broad survey up to 1945 (Cattell, 1946). The TAT, of course, belongs to motivation, considered in Chapter 5, not to general personality factors.

The major advance in trait taxonomy during the 30 years after this 1946 survey has been considered by some to be the novelty of systematically applying factor-analytic methods—previously used only with abilities—to personality and (later) to motivation domains. But, although this application was basically important, and required and brought about remarkable developments in models, in precision of results, and in flexibility of application in the factor method itself, it was not really the main achievement. The real *tour de force* was the invention, across a really broad spectrum of human behavior, of some 500 miniature situations and response possibilities (*T*-data) capable of catching vital behavior. (See the compendium survey in Cattell & Warburton, 1967, and articles during the following decade.) Just as astrophysicists had the calculations necessary to send a rocket to the moon in 1930, but could not send the rocket for more than 30 years, so psychologists had factor analysis in 1930 but no sufficiently experimental devices to stake out the 20 or so personality dimensions for most of another 30 years.[1]

The rarity of fundamental creativity in this area meant that until the late forties and the fifties of this century there was not a wide enough repertoire of laboratory-measurable behaviors into which the full dimensions of personality could begin to be projected. Moreover, creation of tests and interpretation of factors faced a difficulty here that does not exist in *L*- and *Q*-media, namely, that in the latter, as Pawlik has pointed out, we know "where we are" by the familiar landmarks of language. A factor pattern on *L*- and *Q*-data bears its meaning on its face, so that the use of such variables always permits a personality sphere to be readily "blocked out." By contrast, in the behavior caught in objective tests, we embark on a new and strange ocean. Not until the factor experiments begin to show the systematic groupings of behaviors do we get an insight into what certain behaviors in a miniature situation really mean, despite our a priori intentions in design.

Despite these differences in the medium, the basic objectives of research remain the same here as in *L*- and *Q*-data, namely, to map out the independent functional unities in behavior, without prejudice from the pre-experimental concepts existing in the forties and fifties of this century. That is to say, researchers followed the explicit concept of a total *personality sphere* population of behaviors, from which stratified samples could be taken. Considerable advantages, for example, stable rotation against multidimensional hyperplanes, accrue to a strategy of factor analysis that attempts to embrace this whole spectrum in each research, as contrasted with one (reminiscent of bivariate design) that proceeds in bit-by-bit factorings in particular corners.

The objectives of *T*-data factoring are consonant in this and other aspects of design with those of *L*- and *Q*-data in a still more important sense, namely, in that *L*-, *Q*-, and *T*-data are expected to cover the same sphere and to converge on the same personality structure. That the structure will be the same is a hypothesis rather than a postulate, but it is a very basic hypothesis. It supposes that the personality structure is a real entity, out there in the individual and society, regardless of the medium of observation used. Parallel factors should therefore be found in the three media, representing the same structure in a "different dress" of observations. This principle of *medium-transcending personality factors*, or of *indifference of indicator*, is examined more fully and is empirically tested in Chapters 7 and 8. If such parallelism of trait expressions exists, it sanctions the aim of covering a personality sphere with *T*-data, even though it is difficult to see our way immediately to the meaning of behavioral data in this medium. The time sampling of behavior, as contrasted with the sampling of human vocabulary, *would* provide such a model (p. 218) but no one has yet carried it out. Such researchers as Barker (1968) and Sells (1963) have given thought to this objective sampling of environmental stimuli and responses, and Sells developed an excellent research proposal along these lines following his book on situational determiners of behavior (1963). Actually, the devising of objective tests has been guided not only by a personality-sphere concept directly but also by the major factor areas systematically indicated by the prior work with the *L-Q* domain. However, we should be clear that this does not mean, as some critics have argued, that such inclusion of areas commits or predisposes analyses of *T*-data to finding the same factors. Common data commit studies to the same pie, but in no sense to slicing it in the same way.

A last point needing to be clarified regarding the nature and status of *T*-data concerns the separation of genuine *T*-data as described above from that use of *Q*-data designated in Chapter 2 as *Q*-data above. The use of questionnaire data in the *Q'* sense takes response simply as behavior in the test situation, *not* as a reliable statement about the person's behavior, as described in the item content of the response. In a purely logical sense this makes *Q'*-data a form of *T*-data, though there are important qualitative differences still remaining. Some 20 years ago it was proposed (Cattell, 1955), as above, to distinguish *Q'*- and *Q*-data on the basis of whether the subject's introspections on himself in responding to questionnaire items were accepted at face value or treated simply as behavior. For example, the response "Yes" to the question "Are you shy in meeting strangers?" has undoubtedly been taken in much personality research to permit the conclusion that the individual is shy. This has been called *Q*-data use of questionnaires, yielding what may be called statements describing "mental interiors." But a distinct *Q'*-data usage is possible, in which "Yes" is simply a test-behavioral response, and it might represent, say, hostility or arrogance, not shyness.[2] Then, as is more clear if we imagine both question and answer couched in a language foreign to the experimenter, the experimenter simply *treats the test response as something the meaning of which has still to be found by correlation with actual life criterion behavior.*

Most truly behaviorist investigators—and we would want to stand and be counted among them—will in the last analysis of postulates use questionnaires only in this *Q'*-data sense of data interpretation. Nevertheless it is legitimate to get some help on the way to pure behavior inference from contingent and partial trust in the picture given by the mental interiors of *Q*-data. If *Q*-data are treated purely behavioristically, that is, as *Q'* data, then someone may object that the label *Q'* is superfluous, in that the distinction between *Q*- and *T*-data vanishes, for both are behavioral. In a generic and logical sense it does vanish, but inspection of Table 2-1 (p. 51) will show that we never supposed *Q*-data to be defined simply and solely by resting on the subject's introspection. (Many objective tests rest on introspective processes.) Questionnaires differ and have the *Q*-data quality only if we permit the introspectible meaning of the items to guide us to the meaning of the factors. If the psychologist treats the questionnaire as if written in some language the subject understands but he does not—say, Swahili—then he is using it as *Q'*-data. That is to say he will interpret the factor only by the way the marks on paper correlate with some observed, for example, criterion, behavior. Even so such use is properly treated as a definitely distinct subspecies within *T* in the general domain of tests. For even so treated there is so much that is peculiar to the questionnaire, compared to the broader variety of other objective tests.

Some confusion might be expected to arise in an evaluation of a taxonomy of personality test data from unavoidable subtleties like the above, but much poor communication among test users springs from far more superficial causes. For example, there is the use of the term "objective" (especially among educational psychologists) to designate tests in which, as noted with respect to "conspective" above, scoring is objective, by a key or its equivalent, but which are still rating or self-rating inventories.[3] An objective test is best defined as one in which *the subject agrees to respond to a standard situation (perhaps with an instruction that suggests how the test will be scored), without actually knowing reliably how his or her response will be interpreted.* In the questionnaire, of course, the subject is keenly conscious of and responsive to the manner in which a choice will be interpreted and probably evaluated as to desirability.

Now, although objective tests essentially have been equated with laboratory tests and though their initial invention came largely as such individual and laboratory tests, this did not prevent the gradual successful transformation of most of them into group-administrable tests. Both research and practice required that the situations and responses be conveniently shifted into pencil-and-paper form. Several tests, in fact, actually involve answering questions as if in questionnaires, and might be misperceived as questionnaires, though in fact the real measure taken is some contrast of, say, answering questions with and without strong suggestion from authority, or involves simply a scoring on *extremity* of response regardless of content.

In the programmatic work by Baggaley, Barton, Bolz, Butcher, Coan, Damarin, Dielman, Gruen, Finkbeiner, Horowitz, Howarth, Hundleby, Klein, Knapp, Horn, Nesselroade, Pawlik, Rickels, Saunders, Scheier, Schuerger, Tatro, Warburton, and many others between 1946 and 1975 (see references in Cattell & Schuerger, 1976), the strategic aim of working from a personality sphere defined in a true population of subtests was kept in mind as much as in *L-Q* data. However, as pointed out above, the lack of a time-sampled behavior-personality sphere compelled achievement of the strategy by more diverse tactics, as follows:

1. By making the types of invented test as diverse as possible from the standpoint of observed everyday life behavior. Whenever one of the investigators saw in everyday life some personality-relevant behavior that might conceivably be caught in an objective test device, he attempted to devise a trap to catch it.

2. By pondering on the theoretical interpretations of the *L-Q* factors, the investigators tried to spread their inventions over the 35 or so primary trait concepts involved.

3. Relatively late in the second decade, Cattell and Warburton (1967) came up with some explicit dimensions of objective-test design in connection with the taxonomy used in publishing their test encyclopedia.

Cattell and Warburton's dimensions of tests per se took account of (a) type of instruction, (b) use of situation or material, and (c) the responses and their mode of scoring. The parameters of instruction-situation (a and b together) were: (1) scoring as reacting or not reacting, (2) restricted versus unrestricted variety of responses, (3) inventive versus selective answers, (4) single versus repetitive responses, (5) ordered versus unordered responses, (6) homogeneous versus patterned reactions, (7) natural or utmost willed performance limit; and so on to 10 polar parameters permitting 2^{10} = 2024 types of test. Parallel with this, six parameters were recognized in the ways a given response can be scored: (1) objective versus distortable, (2) overt versus physiological, (3) parametric versus nonparametric, (4) normative versus ipsative, and so on (see Cattell & Warburton, 1967, for technical treatment).

The domain of objective tests opened up by this taxonomy has proved both more complex and more extensive than sporadic previous test invention, for example, the Rorschach or the Downey, might lead us to expect. Some intriguing vistas of hypotheses for further imaginative invention have been opened, but for the moment the above glimpse must be left to take the reader to the original work (Cattell & Warburton, 1967). Suffice it that with further attention this taxonomy is likely to provide both a systematic basis for a personality sphere, that is, a population of variables avoiding neglect of some areas and any rank overproliferation in others, as well as a means of recognizing which "area" we are in. However, it has already achieved its main aim: that of providing an operational grip, in replicable behavioral situations and measures, on about as many dimensions of personality as have been found in the other two media.

3-2. Strategy of Research in the *T*-Domain and the Resulting Universal Index of Traits

In reviews of research in the area of *T*-data particular attention has been given to the question of correct factor-analytic, experimental, and general statistical treatments in the foundations. Such careful attention to principles and standards of factorial and general analysis is still rare, and yet indispensable to reliable discovery of source traits. But, as mentioned above, the greater contribution in this area, and harder to command, has been the sheer psychological creativeness, finally issuing in some 500 subtests. Sound trigonometry is vital to mountain map making, but it cannot fix the height of mountains that are not seen. The years of invention of radically new subtests for factor batteries provided the quantification of variables over broad areas of behavior without which no statistical structural analysis could have reaped source-trait structures.

Briefly viewed, the history of growth of the strategy developed in this area of research since 1940 can be summarized by the following points.

1. Preservation of regard for the personality sphere sampling concept.

2. Inclusion in factoring of new tests of the above few existing tests of an objective, *T*-data type. (None of these had previously been factored.)

3. Designing experiments with quite large matrices of variables in order, (a) to keep overlap as new areas are explored, and (b) to ensure good simple-structure rotation and avoidance of confusion of similar factors. Such design involved long subject time (4 to 8 hours was not unusual) and short subtests (5 to 10 minutes each). To perceive tests having promising factor loadings through the haze of the resulting low reliabilities of short tests required use of correction for attenuation.

4. Proceeding with interlocking successive experiments, in *programmatic* research.

5. Carrying proved marker variables along with new test invention based on the inductive-hypothetico-deductive (IHS) spiral (Cattell, 1966). By the latter we mean that the first emergence of new factors is followed by hypotheses about the nature of each, followed in turn, deductively, by invention of new tests deemed likely to prove better markers for that factor than any yet known.

6. Broadening the personality sphere by spotting new factors of small variance, and aiming especially at higher-loaded variables on these.

7. As soon as a factor is replicated at one age, seeking equivalent tests adapted to younger or older ages, thus checking on the continued existence of the source-trait structure over the age range, and also across cultures.

No serious attempt was made in the first 20 years to cross-identify *T*-data factors with the *L-Q* factors; to proceed to the next step of plotting age curves and nature-nurture ratios; or to develop any theories more elaborate than were necessary to guide new test construction. Every effort was concentrated simply on *establishing empirically the nature of the factor pattern for each of the 20 or more primary factors* that eventually appeared. Second-order structures, however, were intermittently explored. These tasks alone presented an enormous undertaking in terms of a reliable accountancy of loadings for numerous tests, the choice of a balance of markers and new tests as research progressed, and the use of many large samples of subjects for long testing periods. As far as the development of theoretical meaning was concerned, it followed the path from *empirical constructs*, derived from examining what does and does not load in the factor pattern, and from initial evidence on criterion associations, age curves, and so on, into a later stage of importation of *theoretical constructs*, as the work progressed. For example, the pattern indexed as UI(T)16 was later considered ego strength; UI(T)24 quickly turned out to be identifiable with anxiety; and UI(T)23, matching Eysenck's "neuroticism" (in his *T*-data, which does not match his *Q*-data), was theorized to be mobilization *versus* regression of interests.

Two features of this whole research plan that have not been widely understood are the use, as described in (1) above, of very *short* tests, necessarily of low reliability, and the basic "faith" that the traits found by factor analysis on this personality sphere basis will turn out to be clinically and socially important source traits. As to the first, if the vital aim of covering the whole personality sphere with up to 100 tests (the effective best from the 500) were to be achieved (putting together many "patchwork" factor studies, each tied to a very limited area of tests is, as pointed out above, technically impossible), the tests had to be short (even with the generosity we encountered when we asked for 5 to 10 hours of the subjects' time). For inferential purposes, as indicated above, the *possible* level and promise of the actually obtained loadings could be found by correction for attenuation, according to the discovered reliabilities. Once the principal factors were stabilized—a stage that began in the 1960s—the usual psychometric steps were followed in proceeding to adequate batteries, namely, item analysis, trial of various modifications instruction, and analysis of effects of different scoring rules applied to the best subtests discovered.

The question may be asked, however, whether batteries for objective measurement of personality factors can ever be cut down to as few subtests per factor battery as are used, for example, for intelligence and the primary abilities. Here we face the evidence that most behavior seems intrinsically complex as far as personality factors are concerned. Any specific objective behavior, in test or criterion, usually proves to be loaded by several factors, and therefore no more than moderately by any one. This fact, together with the unavoidable brevity of tests, resulted in studies over the first decade having such low loadings on the factors—.25 to .35—as to cause impatient critics to doubt either that the factor existed or that one could ever hope to measure it with the factor-concept validities customary in the ability field. This stage of doubt has now been dispelled; but it remains true, evidenced in development of the recently appearing batteries (Cattell & Schuerger's O-A

Battery, 1978; Hundleby's Clinical Battery, 1979; Schmidt & Haecker's German O-A 1976), that six to eight subtests (and close to half an hour of testing) are needed. They are needed to accumulate enough common factor variance among them, that is, enough concept validity, and to ensure that no specific becomes too prominent in the score for that factor.

Practical psychologists who wish to avail themselves of the new tests at the earliest opportunity, should recognize that their services are still needed in perfecting the instruments. The task of preparing a thoroughly item-validated and broadly standardized battery for, say, the most important 12 of the 21 UI indexed personality factors is obviously about 12 times as great as that involved when psychologists required a good battery for the general intelligence factor, which took a decade after Spearman's discovery and definition of *g*. Substantial further help from research sources is required if it is to be accomplished to most psychologists' satisfaction.

As to the more theoretical issue in debate—whether factor analysis locates real influences and structures and is capable of presenting us with new source-trait measures that are able to predict important life criteria—the answers are already with us over a sufficient number of instances to be convincing. The traits *exist* as determiners of behavior both in and out of test patterns, and the evidence that has accumulated since the HSOA and OA batteries were first used against criteria has shown that (1) each trait has a characteristic age curve and a characteristic nature-nurture ratio; (2) solid predictions are obtained from them on real-life criteria, such as success as an air pilot, achievement in school, and so on; and (3) that, in the clinical field, diagnostic separations are obtainable exceeding in statistical significance those from any other testing procedures (Eysenck, 1950, 1960, 1970; Cattell, Schmidt, & Bjersted, 1972; Cattell, Cattell, & Killian, 1967; Tatro, 1965; Price, Cattell, & Patrick, 1979). Whether clinicians can recognize and give meaning to these unitary traits in their thinking and practice depends only on their grasp of the source-trait concept and their enterprise.

As to the naming and interpretation of these source traits, essentially the same policy was followed for indexing and other procedures as with *Q*- and *L*-factors. Here, however, in contrast to *L*- and *Q*- patterns, which present us with a meaningful face validity immediately, the *T*-data pattern typically presents an intriguing puzzle. Any single test could be tapping several alternatives. For example, inability to name many friends in one minute could spring, hypothetically, from several sources, and it is only when the whole context of unwillingness to take risks in a maze, restrained choice of books to read, guilt over inadequacies, rigidity, and incapability is studied that we come to the concept of anxiety (Table 3-6, p. 109). In some cases the face of a factor, as a pattern, is suddenly recognized as a familiar trait, but in others it remains new. The names in such cases become attempts to describe more abstract processes, as in tensidia (originally tensinflexia) for an inflexibility of performance that seems to arise from tension, as seen across subtests in UI(T)25; or the term somindence, which is derived as an acronym for a somnolent phlegmatic independence that runs through all the tests loaded on the factor pattern indexed as UI(T)30. Nevertheless, about half of the factors, such as UI(T)17, UI(T)18, UI(T)24, and UI(T)32, were recognized, from an early stage, as fitting pre-existing clinical or experimental concepts, namely, general inhibition or control, hypomania, anxiety, and extraversion.

The universal index, numbers—UI's—are followed by a T for objective tests, a Q for questionnaire factors, and an L for life rating, although the UIQ and UIL's also have designations A, B, C, D, and so on, as in the 16 PF. In the case of T-factors the decision had to be made whether to start a fresh series or to continue immediately beyond the UI(T)1 through UI(T)15 list of ability factors (which are certainly T-factors) already begun by French (1951). It was decided, as the line between ability and personality factors is not considered a sharp one by many investigators, to continue the French series, starting the largest personality factor, ego strength or assertiveness, as UI(T)16 and continuing through UI(T)36. Hakstian and Cattell (1974) and Horn (1972) have since continued abilities beyond 15, beginning again at UI(T)37.

3-3. The Measurement Foundation of Factor Interpretations and Identifications in the Test Encyclopedia and the Master Index of Variables

Because a general agreement on the interpretation of T-data factors, as distinct from the L-Q series, is likely to take at least a generation, the use of an index system, as above, to hold their identities precise while they wait in limbo is especially important for T-data source traits. Only thus can integration of findings by various investigators proceed. But a pattern, identified by the UI number, is both an indexed dimension and a set of variables, and the identification is firm, therefore, only if the nature of the variables is also held in a reliable index system. Even a comparatively simple test such as sway suggestibility can be given in different ways that appreciably alter its factor loadings and value as a marker. It is important, therefore, to preserve the tests under a test-indexing system. Parenthetically, the completion of the record stipulating a factor requires also an adequate record of the *population* sample from which its pattern emerged.

As to *L*- and *Q*-data test markers, several sources of the index of *L*-data rating variables have been mentioned (Cattell, 1957; Cattell, Pierson, & Finkbeiner, 1976), and the *Q*-factor variables are available in published subscales in the 16 PF, the 16 PF Extension, the CAQ, and so on. To preserve a similar foundation for *T*-data, Warburton, with the present writer, put together an encyclopedia of all objective tests, factored and unfactored, as used at some time or other in correlational studies (Cattell & Warburton, 1967). There proved to be over 400 such tests, some individual, some group, but all indexed together up to UI(T)412. (There have appeared about 80 since then.) A test is a defined situation and a defined set of instructions for responding; however, the *response* often permits scoring in three or four different ways (for example, by speed, by errors, by repetitions of a previous response, by a number of threatening objects named per total number of objects named). The real variables are the responses, but as scored in one particular way, so that there are, with different ways, more variables than tests. In fact no fewer than 2,366 proved to have been tried in the personality sphere in relation to the 412 tests at the time Warburton completed his survey. Each of these response variables as a test score is given an MI or Master Index number and remains, along with the test from which it is derived, the real element in the foundation of factor identification.

Experience shows, it must be explicitly pointed out, that comparatively trifling changes in instructions, especially those involving motivation in doing the test, can produce a fairly marked change in factor loadings. It is therefore not enough to define a test as "pulse change under shock," "cancellation performance under distraction," or "memory for threatening versus nonthreatening pictures," but the shock must be the same, the time interval to permit the pulse change must be the same, and so on. The test encyclopedia gives these particulars, and though the designs of most tests can almost certainly be improved upon, some tests must always be held absolutely the same, to mark and identify the given factor reliably, while other tests can be more freely modified, as new measurement situations, to fit the emerging factor meaning better, thus giving better loadings.

The purpose of this book is to develop the best models for personality structure and its changes, and some readers may feel that the present chapter has gone rather too far into technical particulars of test design research as such. However, our perspective is that theoretical models must grow from close association with the data, and the general concepts of personality structure would lack "body" if we had not come close to the behavioral expressions in these subtests. Nevertheless, at this point we must cease from any attempt at comprehensive substantive treatment and return to cardinal illustrations of a few main types of source trait. The student who wishes to penetrate further into the intellectual game of test creation and factor interpretation as such is advised to become familiar with, on the one hand, the test encylopedia (Cattell & Warburton, 1967), and, on the other, the evidence on factor-matching researches (Hundleby, Pawlik, & Cattell, 1965, for adults; Hudson, in press, for children). To illustrate factor identification and test performances we shall now take just 6 out of some 20 factors, but to illustrate their hardiness as real influences across diverse populations we shall also consider evidence of cross-cultural pattern matching.

3-4. The Psychological Nature of Eight of the Larger *T*-Data Primary Source Traits

In the tables that follow it should be understood that the variables listed are only those that load at least significantly and sometimes highly. At least three times as many variables as those shown in these lists have been entered experimentally into the factor-analytic researches concerned. However, consistently with simple structure, most of them have essentially zero loading when not shown in the table of salients for a given factor. These variables have defined the *hyperplane* through the position of which the salients are located, the latter naturally being recognized as the identifying expressors of the factor.

UI(T)16: Ego Standards

In Table 3-1 it will be seen, first, that the variables marked with an x, which have been put in as markers from 20 years of previous research, have crystallized out in this factor at the top of some 70 diverse variables in the study, as theory would require. The confirmation of pattern may here be rated excellent. Alone among the 20 or so personality factors, we might be tempted to call this one an ability factor, for it loads several performance commonly loaded by the general speed factor g_s. However, we notice that some are tempo, that is, natural speed rather than top speed, and that several have

TABLE 3—1.   Pattern Across Three National Cultures of the UI(T)16: Assertive Ego[a]

MI No.	Marker	Short Description	USA	Japan	Austria	Mean
			| Loadings			
307a	x	Faster speed of letter comparison	50	75	68	64.3
282	x	Greater number of objects seen	44	58	50	50.6
309	x	Faster line length judgment	37	56	59	50.6
199	x	Higher numerical ability	25	80	44	49.7
171	x	More hidden objects seen	26	56	44	42.0
271		Higher fluency on topics	28	40	48	38.7
6a		Faster ideomotor speed	24	40	31	31.7
143	x	Higher total score in CMS	52	(09)	25	28.6
474		More acquaintances recalled	24	63	(–06)	27.0
167a		Better immediate memory	29	33	12	24.7
13a		More oscillation of performance	13	(–15)	67	21.7
473		More friends recalled	47	(15)	(02)	21.3
278	x	Faster tempo of reading	27	28	(07)	19.7
773		Greater standing height	43	(04)	(–08)	13.0
33		Larger gross size of myokinesis	(05)	34	(00)	13.0

[a]Data from Cattell, Schmidt & Powlik (1973).
[b]x indicates that the variable is known as a marker variable from former studies.
[c]All the loadings without parentheses are significant at least at the 5% level, following the Harris test. Such loadings are given to provide the possibility to check the goodness of the matching, and to permit calculating the average. Note that decimal points, on the two-place decimal correlation values, are omitted in this and all subsequent tables.

nothing whatever to do with speed, for example, number of acquaintances, numerical ability, accuracy in mazes. Consequently, we can better interpret this factor as taking up much of that unknown variance in speed tests that does *not* have to do with the speed of cognitive operations as such. Indeed, our final present hypothessis is that this influence is a personality factor expressing an ego striving for excellence in *any* performance and showing itself in competitive speed. Because its concrete life-criteria predictions include a decidedly low proneness to neuroticism, a strong tendency to excel in school and other achievements (for a given intelligence), and a tendency to demand one's rights (Knapp, 1962; Knapp & Most, 1960), we must see it as having several qualities of the ego-strength concept. On the other hand, clinically, some behavior here looks like overcompensation and assertive narcissism. Consequently, pending further evidence, we are compelled to "sit on the fence" concerning whether this source trait is squarely in the area of the ego-strength concept or presents some previously unknown variant thereof. This

TABLE 3–2.   UI(T)18: Hypomanic Temperament

MI No.	Marker	Short Description	Loadings			
			USA	Japan	Austria	Mean
24a	x	Higher ratio of final to initial performance	64	56	54	58.0
282		Fewer objects seen in unstructured drawings	-22	(00)	-56	-26.0
—		More cheating	(04)	36	26	22.0
143	x	Higher total score in CMS	(07)	52	(05)	21.3
199		Less numerical ability	-19	-25	(00)	-14.7
309[a]		Faster speed of line length judgment	(-10)	25	(11)	13.0
		Q Factor O, Guilt Proneness (CPQ)	06	08	26	13.3
		Q Factor F, Surgency (CPQ)	-03	31	04	10.7
		Q Factor A, Affectothymia (CPQ)[b]	03	09	18	10.0
120[a]		Ratio of accuracy to speed	01	-23	00	- 7.3
264[a]		Faster speed of tapping	33	—	(11)	22.0
—[a]		Less desire to hear completion of stories	-26	—	(-08)	-13.0

[a]The last four variables are inserted, though not significant on all three studies, because of their theoretical interest to the hypomania interpretation.
[b]CPQ means Child Personality Questionnaire.

position on the UI(T)16 hypotheses has been held by calling the factor, descriptively, Assertive or Competitive Ego, rather than committing ourselves entirely to ego strength.

UI(T)18: Hypomanic Temperament

As with the symbols *A*, *B*, *C*, *D*, for the *L-Q* factors, the UI numbers here were originally assigned in descending order of size (mean variance) found for the factors. But because the personality-sphere sampling in *T*-data has necessarily been decidedly more "chancy" than in the *L*- and *Q*-media, the size order has tended to vary somewhat in successive researches. UI(T)17 (control) and UI(T)18 (hypomanic tendency) originally came right after the large and influential UI(T)16 (the first personality factor following French and Hakstian's primary abilities in *T*-data). But later results put them around the eighth or ninth personality factors, and indeed we omit UI(T)17 from discussion of large factors here and place UI(T)18 by the relatively low loadings of a recent high-school-age-level research across cultures (Table 3-2). The two main markers,

TABLE 3–3.   UI(T)19: Independence–Subduedness

MI No.	Marker	Short Description	Loadings			
			USA	Japan	Austria	Mean
–	x	E+ (Dominance)	22	56	40	39.3
100		Greater pessimism over doing good	25	29	33	29.0
125a		Higher personal than institutional values	(08)	49	28	28.3
21		Fewer questionable reading preferences	–15	–44	(04)	–18.3
473		Fewer friends recalled	(–06)	–36	(–10)	–17.3
–		I– (Harria)	(–06)	–38	(–04)	–16.0
–	x	Greater accuracy in searching task	19	20	(07)	15.3
199	x	Higher numerical ability	(10)	27	(07)	14.7
108		More confidence in untried skills	(01)	28	(13)	14.0
321	x	More restrained book preferences	(–05)	34	(11)	13.0
53		Less criticism of self vs. appreciation	–	–	–56	–56.0
30		Less criticism of self relative to others	–	–	–46	–46.0

put in as checks on the hypothesis appear clearly in the prominent loadings and others are consistent with fast, impatient, and impulsive behavior. A really substantial depiction of this factor, bringing out the hypomanic qualities, is Tatro's study (1967) on a mental-hospital population, where variances (loadings) are much greater and where all the psychiatric ratings of manic behavior fall clearly on this factor along with the same objective tests as here. Note the inclusion here of personality factors *O*, *F*, and *A*, which fit the "cyclic pathology" temperament.

UI(T)19: Independence–Subduedness

An interesting feature of factor UI(T)19 (Independence) is that it represents support for the wisdom of the original personality sphere approach (Table 3-3). For the UI(T)19 trait has located in a fuller perspective what has been reached in only partial and narrow perspective by following a "stylistic theory" approach, notably in Witkin's (1960) search for associations to field independence in perception tests. An interesting insight on research strategy can be gained here by those who take a historical glance. Through the fifties a fashionable approach to personality was through the "stylistic" concepts of Allport (1961) and others. Psychologists working with the traditionally sanctioned ability and cognitive measures began to squeeze out of their observations on them, as a by-product, some information on personality. The "new look in perception" discovered, for example, that Freudian dynamic projection had been overlooked in classical perception study. The word "styles" became fashionable, though no one had been able to demonstrate that a style persisted across diverse behaviors—for example, that a man exact in handwriting would be exact in ethics, or that a man bouncy in his style of walking would be so in his social approaches. Indeed, since Thorndike debunked transfer of training, it seemed unlikely that these operationally too-vaguely defined "styles" would carry very far.

In strategic terms this approach was really an attempt to sidle into personality measurement from the respectable ground of cognitive tests, without making the radical restructuring of ideas necessary for a clean plunge into objective personality research (and, one may add, without the creative pains of designing entirely new tests based on personality concepts per se). Tactically, the stylistic approach has led to an ignoring or slowing down of test development in the areas of broader expression of factor source traits and to virtually no discovery of new factors. Thus in UI(T)19, perceptual-field-independence behavior has proved only a fragmentary segment of the general concept, which is here shown to lie in a general *temperamental* independence.

The application, soon after this factor's discovery, of planned nature-nurture investigation, revealed that independence is substantially an inherited trait, and also sex-linked, in that boys are significantly higher than girls (Cattell, Stice, & Kristy, 1957; Witkin, et al., 1962). Its concrete criterion associations, for example, with low neurosis proneness, high creativity, school achievement, and leadership, fit the interpretation of personal independence and aggressiveness, as gathered from looking at the variables themselves, that is, from contrasting the nature of those variables that do and do not load. In the cross-cultural comparison, we note incidentally that the Japanese factoring does a better job than the American or Austrian of picking up variables 19, 24, 25, and 38, which have previously marked the factor with American subjects—a tribute to the constancy of human nature across cultures, in the primary personality source traits!

UI(T)20: Evasiveness

The pattern for this factor is not set out as it has shown modifications with subcultures. It is, however, in any group, for example,

adolescents, well replicated and has considerable criterion associations, notably, as Cartwright's studies show, with delinquency. It
has appreciable genetic determination and looks very like the
emotional impulsivity described by Burt in *The Young Delinquent*.

UI(T)21: Exuberance–Suppressibility

For UI(T)20, first called sociable, emotional evasiveness, and
now shortened to *evasiveness*, the reader is referred to Hundleby et
al. (1965), who show it significantly associated with development
psychopathy. We proceed to UI(T)21. As shown in Table 3-4, it
could be thought to have some association with an ability factor,
namely g_r, retrieval capacity (Cattell, 1971), the second-order
cognitive factor perhaps more frequently called general fluency. But
again, as in the cognitive associations of UI 16, the indications are
that it is picking up a different and supplementary part of the total
fluency variance to which g_r contributes as only one component.

Again, the traditional pattern of markers for this factor stands
out well across all three cultures. The theoretical problem here is
whether it represents high vitality of output or low inhibition of
expression. The quite high genetic determination—one of the two
highest among personality traits—inclines some psychologists to the
former. However, strong heritability could also exist for ability or
inability to acquire normal environmentally imposed inhibition. The
term *exuberance-suppressibility* best expresses, by straddling both
possibilities, the caution that present theory should have.

TABLE 3–4.   UI(T)21: Exuberance—Suppressibility

MI No.	Marker	Short Description	Loadings			
			USA	Japan	Austria	Mean
278	x	Faster tempo of reading	58	20	40	39.3
271	x	Higher fluency on topics	18	44	48	37.3
106	x	Less acceptance of unqualified statements	-43	-26	-12	-27.0
167a	x	Better immediate memory	20	(12)	43	25.0
13a	x	More oscillation of performance	(07)	70	-05	24.0
206		Greater accuracy in Gottschaldt figures	20	56	-05	23.7
219		More common frailties admitted	18	(13)	29	20.0
—		Greater accuracy in searching task	35	(-03)	21	17.7

UI(T)22: Cortertia

UI(T)22, cortertia, represents quickness and alertness and absence of distortive emotional infusions into cognitive activity. It has been hypothesized to be the typical level of cortical arousal or activation at which a given individual settles down for most of his daily life; for Nesselroade's research (1967) shows that, even if it has some state qualities, each person tends to stay consistently at one level. A modification of activation theory would be that the score represents the equilibrium position an individual reaches between cortical and hypothalamic activity. Its pattern may be seen elsewhere (Hundleby, Pawlik, & Cattell, 1965).

UI(T)23: Capacity to Mobilize–Regression

UI(T)23 is of especial clinical interest in that when the present writer and Eysenck independently and simultaneously isolated and confirmed its pattern in the late 1940s, Eysenck interpreted it as *the* neuroticism factor. There has been theoretical debate since between Eysenck's interpretation as "neuroticism" and the present writer's interpretation as regression of interest, that is, dynamic regression of motivation, as in long-term fatigue. In any case the "neuroticism" label had to be rejected as soon as the demonstration appeared (Cattell & Scheier, 1961) that at least five *other* of the 20 known *T*-data personality factors were equally or more strongly associated statistically with neuroticism. The alternative hypothesis that the factor represents *regression*—a *component* in neurosis, can be regarded as having some relation to Freud's concept of regression, though it primarily means here a regression of interest and energy from more complex and integrative performances. This shows in decreased will power and persistence, increased motor-perceptual rigidity, and greater error when compelled to hurry. This is implied also in the title "capacity to mobilize" for the *positive* direction of scoring. The factor is of smaller variance in children and healthy adults, and comes out most clearly in mixed normal and clinical groups, suggesting a "disease process" nature. However, it is sufficiently identified and invariant to appear for the normal school children in Table 3-5.

UI(T)23– has many concrete criterion correlations. Besides neurosis, it is associated with poorer school performance, psychoticism, chronic debility, and inability to stand stress in the program of selection for astronauts.

TABLE 3—5.   UI(T)23: Capacity to Mobilize—Regression

MI No.	Marker	Short Description	USA	Japan	Austria	Mean
			Loadings			
120	x	Higher ratio accuracy to speed	53	56	44	51.0
609	x	More accuracy in spatial judgment	73	36	19	42.7
2a	x	Less rigidity	–19	–58	–27	–34.7
206		Greater accuracy Gottschaldt figures	38	32	30	33.3
6a	x	Faster ideomotor speed	62	(12)	(06)	26.7
—		Greater accuracy in searching	41	(16)	(03)	20.0
106		Less acceptance of unqualified statements	(–05)	–41	(–04)	–16.7
13a		Less oscillation of performance	–21	(02)	–26	–15.0
167a	x	Better immediate memory	(13)	25	(02)	13.3
113		Less acceptance of reality principle	(–09)	(04)	–32	–12.3
—		Slower speed of tapping	–25	·—	–28	–26.5

3-5.   The Nature of Anxiety and Some Lesser *T*-Data Source Traits

UI(T)24: Anxiety–Adjustment

The factoring of anxiety manifestation has repeatedly led to a *single* general factor, unlike, for example, the complication of finding seven or eight factors in the depression area. However, there *is* some complication regarding separation of *state* and *trait*, which we shall deal with in Chapter 5. Actually the factoring of anxiety and clinical manifestations per se merely confirmed the extent and nature of a factor, UI(T)24, already deemed to be anxiety, found in the general advance of factoring in the total personality sphere. Indeed, it was the broader strategic procedure rather than clinical ties that gave the basic proofs in 1965 (1) that a factor exists loading largely anxiety behaviors, and (2) that no other factors than this loaded markedly on any anxiety variables. In this same year of successful replication of the pattern the proof was also given that the *T*-data factor fully aligns with the second-order "introspective" anxiety factor, that is, that found in *Q*-data (see Section 3-6). The pattern has been well replicated across normals and patients and also stands up across cultures, as shown in Table 3-6. (The congruence coefficient r_c, calculated between the American and the Japanese patterns, here is +.54. Between the American and the Austrian, it is +.65, and between the Austrian and the Japanese +.68. All these values are significant at the $p < .001$ level.) It will be noted that the second-order questionnaire markers, mentioned in the "proof by introspection" above (Q-data) are here again present, and prominently. At the same time the usual objective-test markers, such as admitting frailties, annoyability, restrained preferences (and, more moderately, concreteness of drawing, rigidity, and lower severity of judgment), are also present. Physiological measures such as high ketosteroid excretion and low electrical skin resistance consistently appear in the anxiety factor when individual tests are added to the experiment.

As mentioned under tactics above, the trend in test development, for good practical-application reasons, has been toward inventing ways of transforming valid individual tests to valid group administrable forms, and because most replicating studies have used group tests, the individual tests tend to get less chance of replication. For administrative, organizational reasons they had to be omitted from the cross-cultural research tabulated here, but several important laboratory and physiological variables in the anxiety factor can be seen elsewhere (Cattell, 1957; Hundleby, Pawlik, & Cattell, 1965).

This glance at the anxiety source trait offers a good moment at which to turn to the help obtainable in source-trait interpretation from criterion relations—here the relations of UI(T)24 to the concrete validation of source-trait batteries against clinical categories and outcomes of treatment, etcetera. A whole book was devoted to

TABLE 3–6. UI(T)24: Anxiety—Adjustment

MI No.	Marker	Short Description	Loadings USA	Japan	Austria	Mean
—	x	Factor $Q+$ (Guilt Proneness)	35	80	50	55.0
—	x	Factor Q_4+ (High Ergic Tension)	66	48	46	53.3
219	x	More common frailties admitted	45	60	34	46.3
—	x	Factor $H-$ (Threctia)	-39	-72	(01)	-36.7
—	x	Factor Q_3- (Low self-sentiment Integration)	-25	-37	-37	-33.0
—		Factor $G-$ (Low Superego Strength)	-20	-51	-23	-31.3
211a	x	Greater susceptibility to annoyance	19	43	(11)	24.3
—		Factor $F+$ (Surgency)	(-06)	49	(02)	15.0
2a		Higher rigidity	(04)	(14)	27	15.0
321	x	More restrained book preferences	(01)	25	18	14.7
—	x	Factor $C-$ (Ego Weakness)	(-10)	-1.00	-25	-12.0

this by Cattell and Scheier (1961), and many articles on changes of T-data scores on UI(T)24 with therapy, by Rickels, et al. (1966, 1968), DiMascio, et al (1960), Cattell, Rickels, et al. (1966) and others have appeared. Cattell, Schmidt, and Bjersted (1972) and Tatro (1967) have returned to extend and check the Scheier work in a recent monograph taking a variety of psychotic categories, too.

Regarding "validations" (strictly relevances) against clinical criteria, the evidence is that UI(T)19 (low), UI(T)21 (low), UI(T)23 (low), and UI(T)25 (low) are particularly potent in distinguishing all varieties of psychotics. UI(T)23 (low) and UI(T)25 (low) especially distinguish schizophrenics. To the reasons already given for rejecting Eysenck's interpretation of UI(T)23 as "*the* neuroticism factor" is now added the evidence that UI(T)23 is extreme also in major types of psychosis. Actually, as Scheier found and Schmidt confirmed, neurotics are distinguished from normals by statistically very significant ($p < .01$ or better) differences on UI(T)16 (low), UI(T)19 (low), UI(T)21 (low), UI(T)22 (low), UI(T)23 (low), UI(T)24 (high), UI(T)25 (low), UI(T)28 (high), and UI(T)29 (low). As regards the much-discussed distinction of neurotics from psychotics, Schmidt has recently confirmed, by discriminant function, that (in the neurotic direction) UI(T)16 (low), UI(T)24 (high), UI(T)28 (high), and UI(T)30 (high) are statistically valid in this separation. Deviations on such other dimensions as UI(T)19, UI(T)21, UI(T)23, UI(T)25 are thus characteristic of neurotic as of psychotic pathology, and neurotics are distinguished from psychotics mainly by much higher anxiety (UI(T)24), lower assertive ego (UI(T)16), higher asthenia (UI(T)28), and higher somindence (UI(T)30).

A matter for ironical comments by posterity will be that the altogether better level of diagnostic separation obtained by the O-A batteries (around 80 to 90 percent correct separation in both Scheier's and Schmidt's published analyses) has been virtually completely neglected by this generation of clinicians. Whereas practical preliterate cultures will adopt air travel or a washing machine because they work, and medical men did not take long to adopt the x-ray machine, clinical psychologists tied to theories of a pre-experimental nature have not availed themselves, in any numbers, of the unquestionably better diagnosis from the T-data measures. This may be because diagnosis per se is temporarily unfashionable, or because the batteries are at present cumbersome, or, if we give weight to theoretical considerations, because the source traits are alien to psychoanalytic and other past theories. As the structures are undoubtedly real and replicable, the remedy would seem to be to measure them and enrich them with new and genuine theoretical meaning derived from clinical criterion findings.

UI(T)25: Realism–Tensidia

Meanwhile let us look at another pattern with strong clinical associations: UI(T)25 (Table 3-7). This pattern, like anxiety, is one that has been discovered independently in America (Cattell, Dubin, & Saunders, 1954; Gruen, 1955) and in Britain (S. B. G. Eysenck, 1956). Again there is a difference of interpretation, however, in that Eysenck considers it *the* psychoticism factor, whereas our results show it is also very deviant in neurotics, though somewhat more so in schizophrenics than, say, anxiety neurotics. Pursuant to this and other evidence it has been called realism-tensinflexia (or simply tensidia), implying that the lack of realistic response to factual input found at the negative psychotic pole is for some yet unexplained reason associated with tension and inflexibility.

UI(T)28: Asthenia

Source traits UI(T)26 and 27, being less known as to associations, are left to the main textbooks, and we pass here to UI(T)28, asthenia (Table 3-8).

This is psychologically a subtle pattern of explicit rejection of authority, along with, paradoxically, a higher "tendency to agree" and to modify attitudes under suggestion! It has been interpreted as the product of a too-early imposition of superego standards, followed by later revolt and partial rejection, along with the asthenia and the irritability accompanying a persisting conflict. By contrast, UI(T)29, not tabulated here, appears a straightforward superego or even compulsive pattern.

TABLE 3–7. UI(T)25: Realism—Tensidia

MI No.	Marker	Short Description	USA	Japan	Austria	Mean
				Loadings		
246	x	Higher respect for authority	28	57	33	39.3
125a	x	Fewer personal relative to institutional values	-67	-24	-21	-37.3
100	x	Greater pessimism over doing good	16	29	57	34.0
277		Higher age	(12)	37	(06)	18.3
609		More accuracy in spatial judgment	(09)	27	(05)	14.0
206	x	Greater accuracy Gottschaldt figures	(11)	(00)	31	14.0
106		Less unreflective acceptance of unqualified statements	(-07)	(03)	-38	-14.0
39		Higher ratio of color to form in sorting	33	—	33	33.0

TABLE 3–8.   UI(T)28: Asthenia—Self-Assuredness

MI No.	Marker	Short Description	Loadings			
			USA	Japan	Austria	Mean
116a	x	Greater severity of judgment	55	28	45	42.7
211a		Greater susceptibility to annoyance	39	66	(07)	37.3
38	x	Less suggestibility to authorities	-44	(-10)	-43	-32.3
100		Greater pessimism over doing good	45	33	(-02)	25.3
—		D (excitable temperament)	21	39	(12)	24.0
146b	x	Less correct Gestalt completion	(-12)	(-12)	-47	-23.7
—		More cheating	(03)	21	28	17.7
206		Less accuracy Gottschaldt figures	-27	(-02)	-23	-17.3
609		Lesser accuracy spatial judgment	(-10)	(-09)	-23	-14.0
34		More shifting of attitudes following additional information	(09)	22	(07)	12.7

UI(T)30 is a depressive factor, important clinically and briefly reproduced here from Schmidt's and Dubin and Saunders' clinical factorings instead of the cross-cultural studies. Recent work by Patrick and Price also shows the "stolid" pole tied to neurotic depression. UI(T)31 will be passed over, but UI(T)32 (Table 3-10) is of great theoretical importance—or, at least, central to much psychological discussion—as the extraversion-introversion factor.

UI(T)32: Exvia–Invia

The challenging paradox about the UI(T)32 pattern is that despite extraversion standing, since Jung, in the forefront of all discussions about temperament dimensions, it stands 17th (counting UI(T)16 as number 1 in personality factors) in order of size, in terms of mean variance contribution of each factor to all objective tests. The original (1955) demonstration that this *T*-data factor is extraversion as rated and self-rated in *L*- and *Q*-data is borne out by the present loadings on *A*, *F*, *H*, and *J*-, the second order (*QI*) exvia factor. If *Q*-data were included in the variance, the rank position of UI(T)32 would, of course, march much higher, but we are concerned in *T*-data with loadings on actual behavior. Incidentally, as mentioned in the previous chapter, the designation *exvia-invia* has been introduced for UI(T)32 to escape all the surplus and erroneous meanings sticking like burrs to the bedraggled popular and journalistic usages of "extraversion-introversion."

TABLE 3–9.   UI(T)30: Stolidity–Dissofrustance[a]

MI		Loadings	
No.	Short Description	I[b]	II[c]
1730	More faces judged cheerful than depressive	—	63
109	Fewer pleasant associations to events	-45	-51
269	Slower tempo of leg circling	-44	-36
155	Large variability of flicker-fusion speeds	48	—

[a]The term dissofrustance defines the theory that lower scorers on UI(T)30 are prone to *disso*ciation of memory and dynamic systems when meeting strong *frust*ration.
[b]Cattell's research with normals, 1957.
[c]Cattell and Schmidt's study of patients, 1972.

In addition to the objective tests shown loading exvia cross-culturally here, the tests entitled "more fluency about people's characteristics" (MI 763), "more objects found in unstructured drawings" (MI 282), "more self-confidence in untried performances" (MI 108), "higher proportion of total fluency in relating dreams" (MI 283), and "more rapid alternating perspective" (MI 8) have been confirmed as characteristic of the exviant individual. As a methodological issue it should be pointed out that once a battery for a source trait has been made available the more is it possible for numerous bivariate experimenters to come forward and relate the

TABLE 3–10.   UI(T)32: Exvia–Invia (Extraversion–Introversion)

MI			Loadings			
No.	Marker	Short Description	USA	Japan	Austria	Mean
—	x	F+ (Surgency)	46	69	42	52.3
—	x	H+ (Parmia)	32	33	42	35.7
—		Q₃- (Low Self-sentiment Integration)	(01)	-47	-38	-28
—	x	A+ (Cyclothymia)	17	47	(12)	25.3
—		J- (Zeppia)	-41	-20	(05)	-18.7
219		More common frailties admitted	(09)	31	(13)	17.7
309	x	Faster speed of line length judgment	(04)	29	(03)	12.0
106		Less acceptance of unqualified statements	(-11)	(05)	-29	-11.7
116a		Lower severity of judgment	(-06)	(-02)	-21	- 9.7
64		Male sex	(11)	—	38	24.5
—		Faster speed of tapping	22	—	(13)	17.5
178		More agreement with majority	22	—	(00)	11.0

trait to this or that particular performance that has been the center of their work in theoretical terms. Thus Horowitz (Cattell & Horowitz, 1952), for example, specifically found exvia related to degree of hostility toward annoying people, and Eysenck to rate of tapping. We should be aware, however, that such relatings of some single variable to a factor battery, although very significant by ANOVA tests examining mean differences of exviants and inviants, often do not correlate *enough* with the factor to be useful factor definers or scale contributors.

The character of exvia in objective tests fits well the rating, *L*, and the questionnaire, *Q*, picture of this factor, in that the former depicts the exviant as more careless, more confident, more openly aggressive, more fluent, less inhibited, more sociable. The concrete criterion validities found, though as yet few and more often based on *Q*-data, also agree with the general conception, showing schizophrenics low on exvia, that is, inviant, and showing somewhat better scholastic performance for inviants, better salesman performance for exviants, and so on.

UI(T)33: Dismay–Sanguineness

The remaining *T*-data source traits are UI(T)33 through UI(T)36. Of these, UI(T)33, dismay-sanguineness, is one of the several completely new concepts factor analysis has brought to personality. It has commanded importance through powerful clinical predictions. Schmidt (1976) finds it more weighted than other factors in separating schizophrenics (high "dismay") from affective psychotics. These undescribed factors—as well, of course, as the 10 already described—may be studied fully in the books by Hundleby et al. (1965), Hudson (in press), Cattell and Schuerger (1978), and others.

3-6.   The Interpretation of First- and Second-Stratum Traits and of Cross-media Relations

Three problems have especially confronted further advance in understanding of personality structure through *T*-data: (1) the relative difficulty of interpreting factors from their "content" of loaded tests, because of the obscurity of meaning of some of the behaviors themselves; (2) some slowness of less statistically trained psychologists to provide a supplement to such "internal" interpretation by external evidence on the meaning of the total factor score, in terms of life-criterion associations, nature-nurture ratios, age curves, and other natural history. This lack is probably a consequence of greater time and skill required to administer the O-A than for questionnaires such as the 16 PF; and (3) the central riddle of the relation of trait patterns in *T*-data to those in *L-Q* data.

As to the first problem, the path to interpretation has not been an easy one. In some cases an abstraction from the nature of variables positively loaded, negatively loaded, and absent has led to a tolerably clear conception. Thus the subtests in UI(T)24 clearly gave it a character of low self-confidence, insecurity, and so on, which soon led to the interpretation as anxiety. Those in UI(T)21 were immediately recognizable as expressing exuberance and unrestraint. Such common meaning across the loaded subtests could be recognized in perhaps half the factors. The researcher who would pursue this approach further to hypotheses is advised (1) to familiarize himself far more thoroughly than has often been done with the actual test situations, as listed in the 2,000 MI descriptions in the Cattell and Warburton encyclopedia of test creations (1967); (2) to watch, with a clinical eye, the performances of subjects on the factors; and (3) to accustom himself to think in terms of division in any variable into *components* of behavior variance, recognizing that as many as, say, four different factors can each and all be involved to the extent of an appreciable correlation—0.5—*with one and the same performance.* We recognize then that some *one aspect or ingredient* of this performance *only,* derives from one factor. The nature of that factor can then be divined only by an act of psychological abstraction, through considering the *other* behavioral measures similarly associated in part with that factor. The scope for skill in wedding psychological insights to statistical reasoning is here very great. The researcher is further advised (4) to remember that the path toward interpreting a factor trait is also a process of convergence on a concept by successive approximations. In the inductive-hypothetico-deductive spiral, the deduction phase requires inventive capacity to create a new subtest that will permit a crucial experiment on the validity of the hypotheses reached at that stage. Several instances of such a spiral could be given. The history of test invention in testing the two alternative hypotheses of Eysenck (reactive inhibition) and the present writer (social inhibition) as to exvia, UI(T)32, and of factoring afresh with new test insertions is an interesting instance. Such research leads to helpful modifications both of tests and factor interpretations in the light of the new obtained loadings.

As to evidence from (2) in the opening paragraph in this section—natural history and criterion relations—though slow, it has not been lacking. Age curves have been plotted for most factors from 10 to

18 years. Nature-nurture ratios have been determined as a strategic first step, showing, for example, UI(T)19, UI(T)20, and UI(T)21 to be more genetic and UI(T)16, UI(T)24, and many others more environmental in origin (see Volume 2, Chapter 1). As shown above, powerful relations have been found to clinical and educational (though scarcely as yet to occupational) performances, which have helped to show UI(T)16 and UI(T)23 as very positive contributors to adjustment and achievement, and have clarified the nature of anxiety, UI(T)24. Useful criterion relations have also been found to UI(T)22, UI(T)25, UI(T)30, and UI(T)33, and several others. The broad and intensive attack on the criterion associations of UI(T)23 and UI(T)24 by Scheier, by Rickels and associates, and by Schmidt, Hacker, and others, was particularly successful in leading to a firm grasp of the nature of these particular source traits. Theoretical articles on specific factors have been published by Cattell (1964, 1966, 1972b), Meredith (1967), Pawlik and Cattell (1965), Scheier (1958, 1959), Wilkins (1962), and others.

Finally, as to (3) in our opening paragraph, namely, the relation to L-Q factors—the attempt to handle this at first by factoring a pool of variables simultaneously brought in from all three media, L-, Q-, and T-, resulted in chaos. Moreover, as Hundleby, Pawlik, and Cattell (1965) reported, the correlation of T-data factors directly with questionnaire factors in general yielded low correlations not easily interpreted as showing any one-to-one relation of T-factors on the one hand and of the mutually aligned L-Q factors on the other. Does this mean that the "principle of indifference of medium" has broken down and that the concept of an "instrument-free general personality factor" back of several media of manifestations has failed? Before approaching perspective on the relations, we must remember that the early results to which reference has just been made came at a time when the T-batteries and Q-scales thus thrown together were still of distinctly low validity in themselves. Moreover, there was no theory then, such as perturbation theory since (see Chapter 8), that could suggest any rationale for better analysis of results.

The breakthrough, throwing a shaft of light at least over part of the scene, came suddenly in 1955 by the discovery, through a joint factoring of Q- and T-data (checked across two substantial, adequate samples), that UI(T)24 and UI(T)32 showed a beautiful alignment with the second-order questionnaire factors for anxiety (QII) and exvia (QI). The finding is confirmed in three more samples, at a different age and in three different countries, in Tables 3-6 and 3-10 above. Indications have been found in two researches that two other T-factors may align with second-order L-Q factors: UI(T)22, cortertia, with QIII, tentatively named cortertia in the Q-series, and UI(T)19, independence, with QIV, definitely deserving the term independence by content, in the Q series. Recently Wardell and Yeudall (1975) have brought evidence for a fifth second-order alignment: that of UI(T)17, control, with QVIII, at one time called "good upbringing" but now *Inhibitory control.*

Naturally theory leaps to the attractive simplification that the riddle of L-Q and T-media alignments could be universally solved by the formula that all T-data source traits *stand at the second order* relative to the primaries of the L-Q media. Some recent work by Vaughan, at the child level, gives some encouragement by indicating one or two further possible instances. Certainly one hopes that experimenters competent in factor analysis will now hasten to a systematic search of possible alignments of other T-data factors with second-order Q-data factors. A somewhat disconcerting thought, however, is that only some 10 to 15 second-strata L-Q factors (Chapter 2, p. 80) have been produced from a wide search over the personality sphere, whereas 20 T-data factors are already known, and the trial-and-error character of the coverage of the domain has been such that extension can be expected.

Time for cumulative enrichment of experimental data, as well as improved grasp of the technical issues in instrument factors, are needed before more definite answers can be given. Possibly there are indeed domains of behavior caught in T-data of which the human observer is too unaware to permit them to appear in L- and Q-data.

Meanwhile, in the instances, perhaps four or five in number, where clear alignment has appeared, the question remains, "Why do we go to primaries in the L-Q media, before secondaries, but *directly* in T to what are ranked as secondaries in Q?" Turning to the concept of "density of representation" of variables in the personality sphere as developed above we ask "Are questionnaire items more 'dense' in personality space than objective tests?" For example, the H primary spans questions like "Do you startle easily on a quiet street at night?" "Do you blush easily if made prominent at a party?" In laboratory T-data, however, a single measure of autonomic response to threat, say by GSR, might, shorn of local social expressions, represent the whole threat susceptibility of the H factor. If the other primaries in anxiety, C, L, O, Q_3, and Q_4, were similarly essentially each represented only by one variable in T-data, then T factoring would proceed directly to the second-stratum factor of anxiety among them.

There are other possibilities, and although the question is too complex to handle definitely in this space, one more can be mentioned. This is the theory that inverts (as a special case in psychology) the *general* factor-analytic model assumption that second-order factors are influences acting upon first orders. It supposes—in the *spiral action theory*—that the first orders by mutual interaction generate a fresh dimension, which is the second order. Simple structure persists because only a subset of all primaries have this power of interaction. Thus in the case of QI, exvia, high A causes an individual to seek more society, and being more in society increases his social skills in F, and success in shining socially increases his dominance, E, while high H also makes him immune to the inevitable social snubs to a pushy person that would cause a more threctic (threat-susceptible) person to withdraw.

A similar spiral of interaction could occur in anxiety, QII. Indeed in this case the process has already been described in Freud's theory that weak ego strength, $C-$, makes the individual more susceptible to the generation of anxiety from high ergic tension, Q_4, as well as from guilt proneness, O. If this is the nature of the generation of at least some secondaries, then the T-data factor could be *a measure of the single end product of interaction of several primaries.* It would be the end product we might call social approach (social interest) in the case of exvia, QI (UI(T)32), and anxiety per se in the case of QII (UI(T)24). The T-data factor is in that case not necessarily sampling at a lower density, but is primarily taking its variables from a different area of manifestation, namely from the manifestations of the single product formed from interaction of the questionnaire primaries.

This concept may need for its fuller clarification the discussion of higher-order structure as such in Chapter 7. Meanwhile we can be sure taxonomically that factoring of the oblique T-data primaries leads, just as in Q-data, to a definite and replicable higher strata structure. In fact seven second-order and three third-order factors have been found among some 15 of the T-data primaries, the former being shown in Table 3-11. Work in progress shows some changes in the structure here with different populations.

According to the "one-stratum difference" between L-Q and T-factors, we would expect the five or six *tertiaries* in Q to be found among these seven secondaries and the three third-order Ts to correspond to fourth orders yet to be structured on the Q-data foundation. No research has yet penetrated these domains with sufficient breadth and accuracy to inform us about the truth of these speculations. Pawlik (see Pawlick & Cattell, 1964) was inclined to interpret the three ultimate factors in T-data as Freud's three main structural components, but equally cogent arguments can be made for their being influences beyond psychology, for example, in sociology and physiology, which produce correlations among traits. For example, a range of social status produces a social-status factor loading intelligence, surgency, self-sentiment, dominance, and other primaries and secondaries correlated with social status. The *T*-data secondaries could be of this type.

3-7. Summary

1. The extension of personality structure investigation to laboratory-type, objective-behavior-measurement tests has been a long-desired advance both in providing links with much that has been traditionally measured in bivariate "classical" experiment (for example, reaction time, GSR, style of perception) and in rescuing personality research from the distortions and experimental error more prevalent in a foundation of ratings and questionnaires.

2. The scientific requirement that one should proceed from a comprehensive personality sphere of measured variables is as urgent here as in *L*- and *Q*-domains, but not so easily met. Lacking time sampling of daily behavior, research sought guidance from the span covered by *L-Q* data, from Cattell and Warburton's taxonomy of objective test features (1967), and from sheer pursuit of behavioral diversity.

3. The primary demand of the *T*-data domain on researchers (as competent factor methods per se are well within our reach) has been for psychological creativity and insight in producing individual-test and, by further invention, group-test designs really capable of involving personality behavior. Some 400 diverse tests (indexed by *T*-numbers), with over 2,000 measurable derived performances, defined and indexed by Master Index (MI) numbers for performance measures were created by a programmatically directed group of researchers over 30 years. The tests cover a sufficiently broad personality sphere, as evidenced by their covering initially as many factors as are found in *L*- and *Q*-data, and ultimately more.

4. The identification and preliminary description and interpretations of factors rest first upon insightful abstractions from common content (what they load and do not load); from their predictions of concrete everyday life criteria; from their alignments with *L-Q* media factors; from their natural history (age curves, inheritance ratios); and from their positions in higher-order structures. To hold the patterns firmly identified, during many years of interaction of researchers in interpretation and integrated research, they are primarily identified and indexed by Universal Index (UI) numbers, beginning at UI(T)16, following the 15 objective-test abilities primaries. Because firm identification of experimental measures of behavior is also essential to the identification of the patterns in

TABLE 3–11.   Nature of Second-Order Objective Test Factors: Average Loadings in Five Studies

F(T)I   Tied Socialization or Superego Development — Absence of Cultural Introjection

First-Order Factor (in direction of scoring)		Loading
UI 20+,	Evasiveness	+.36
UI 1–,	Low intelligence	–.34
UI 25+,	Realism	+.33
UI 35+,	Long-circuited dynamics	+.44[a]
UI 28+,	Rigid superego	+.21
UI 19–,	Subduedness or resignation	–.20
UI 32–,	Exvia or extraversion	–.19

F(T)III   Temperamental Ardor — Low Dynamic Involvement, with Sublimatory Capacity

First-Order Factor (in direction of scoring)		Loading
UI 21+,	Exuberance	+.31
UI 1–,	Low intelligence	–.28
UI 20+,	Evasiveness	+.27
UI 19+,	Independence	+.21
UI 27–,	Keen involvement	–.19

F(T)II   Expansive Ego — History of Difficulty in Emotional Problem-Solving

First-Order Factor (in direction of scoring)		Loading
UI 16+,	Assertive ego	+.34
UI 23–,	Regression	–.29
UI 1+,	Intelligence	+.28
UI 19+,	Promethean will	+.23
UI 36+,	Self-sentiment development	+.29[a]
UI 18–,	Naive self-obliviousness	–.15

F(T)IV   Educated Self-consciousness — Inexplicitness and Unrealism of Self-sentiment

First-Order Factor (in direction of scoring)		Loading
UI 22+,	Cortertia	+.31
UI 18+,	Hypomanic temperament	+.28
UI 36+,	Self-sentiment development	+.51[a]
UI 25–,	Tensidia	–.17
UI 30–,	Dissofrustance	–.16
UI 29–,	Low adaptation energy	–.15
UI 33,	Dourness	+.20[a]

TABLE 3-11 *(continued)*

F(T)VI   Narcistic Development — Responsiveness to Environmental Disciplines

First-Order Factor (in direction of scoring)		Loading
UI 26+,	Narcistic self-will	+.33
UI 27+,	Apathy-fatigue, lack of keen involvement	+.30
UI 34+,	Autia, bohemian non-conformity	+.51[a]

F(T)V   History of Inhibiting, Restraining Environment — Possibly Bound Anxiety

First-Order Factor (in direction of scoring)		Loading
UI 17+,	Inhibit	+.36
UI 23+,	Mobilization	+.18
UI 31+,	Wary realism	+.15

F(T)VII   Tension to Achieve or Controlled Drive Tension Level

First-Order Factor (in direction of scoring)		Loading
UI 24+,	High general level of free anxiety	+.40
UI 18+,	Hypomanic temperament	+.23
UI 30-,	Dissofrustance	-.19
UI 25-,	Tensidia	-.18
UI 19+,	Promethean will	+.16
UI 33+,	Dourness	+.21[a]

Note: the T's are omitted after UI throughout this table.
[a]This variable (first-order factor) appeared in only one study and thus has not been replicated.

successive experiments, the variables have also been indexed themselves by Master Index (MI) numbers in all publications and have finally been made generally available (Cattell & Schuerger, 1978) in their Objective Analytic (OA) Battery.

5. The patterns and tentative interpretations for most of the *T*-primaries have been set out here. It is seen that some—such as UI(T)16, assertive ego strength, UI(T)18, hypomanic temperament, UI(T)24, anxiety, UI(T)32, exvia—correspond to concepts already familiar in clinical psychology. But more than half are concepts entirely new to most texts on clinical and personality psychology and require new, apt terms for their introduction into personality theory, along with theoretical recognition of their predictive power.

6. These source-trait patterns are demonstrated here to have un-

mistakable, and generally high, stability across cultures, and the same has been demonstrated elsewhere about their continuity with gradual change across ages. Practical matters of scoring and battery psychometrics do not concern us here, but it has also been demonstrated elsewhere that the concept validity, that is, the battery score against the pure factor, of a 20- to 30-minute, 6- to 8-subtest battery for each source trait is about 0.85 (see Cattell & Schuerger, 1978).

7. The concrete (life-criterion) validity or "relevance" of the *T*-data source traits has been examined so far most thoroughly in the clinical area, though lately there is evidence also that they substantially predict educational achievement and occupational competence. In the clinical area diagnostic potencies claiming to exceed those of any other known measures have been shown both with respect to separating patients from normals and to distinguishing among various diagnostic categories. For example, UI(T)24, anxiety, is very high in neurotics but not at all in most categories of psychotics. Discriminant functions can be set up producing good separation of psychotic types on other *T*-data source traits, notably UI(T)19, UI(T)21, UI(T)23, UI(T)25, UI(T)28, UI(T)30 and UI(T)33. In industry, criterion research has just begun, and in education such factors as UI(T)16 and UI(T)19 have been shown to predict achievement significantly beyond what is predictable from intelligence alone. The reasonable concern of some critics of factor analysis that these factors might be some specific, narrow behavior generated among artificial laboratory tests is therefore fully dispelled. The creative insights of the test designers have proved able to catch basic personality behaviors and the factor analyses have structured the behaviors in ways consistent with results from other media.

8. The process of developing structural theory, and of building up sufficiently valid, practicable batteries, requires a strategy of carrying markers systematically over years of research and of converging on more and more highly loaded variables in a programmatic series of factor analyses. At each new round of findings and interpretations new tests are constructed to provide crucial experiments deciding between alternative hypotheses that have emerged from highly loaded tests at the round before.

9. Early experiments attempting to identify the same traits across media by factoring variables together from all three kinds of data failed because markers were not good enough and validities in all media were then too low. Since 1955 it has been demonstrated, however, that second-order factors as recognized in the *Q*- and *L*-media align excellently (within expected error measurement) with certain primary *T*-data factors, notably UI(T)24, anxiety, UI(T)32, exvia-invia, and possibly UI(T)17, control, UI(T)22, cortertia, and

UI(T)19, independence. At this stage, though more remains to be aligned than has yet been brought into alignment, we nevertheless are prepared to state the "principle of indifference of indicator" (or of the existence of "medium-transcending source-trait patterns"), which says that a source trait exists as a real structure in the personality that will appear in parallel across factors in all three media of observation. By factoring them together and setting aside instrument factors, we can obtain a pattern simultaneously across all media that is thus independent of the restrictions of any one medium. (This is more fully handled in Chapter 8.)

10. Source traits in T-data fit the model of a linear and additive specification equation with about the same degree of closeness as do those in L- and Q-data. In short, the exploration of the third domain has presented no demand for any significant change of the source-trait model and the specification equation, in the prediction of concrete particular behaviors.

NOTES

[1] Seen in other terms, we may say that even the finest sculptor has first to be provided with his block of marble. Many years and many psychologists were necessary to produce the meaningful, precise, and replicable test behaviors across the spectrum of behavior. As an aside on research history and research realities, I would record that only one Ph.D. in 10 in our research teams had sufficient insight, ingenuity, and persistence to produce new objective (T-data) instruments. The rest, offered some clearly designated trait, for example, social aggressiveness, honesty, dependability, or capacity to empathize, would invariably gravitate from observing real behavior to asking the subject questions. The road from T- to Q-data was a regular, predictable descent.

[2] An actual instance is the reply "yes" to the Q-item, "Do you feel faint at the sight of blood?" This loads the superego factor G, though, taken at its "face validity," it might be expected to load ego weakness, C-, or threctia (susceptibility to threat), H. The reason could be that most subjects should answer yes, but that only higher-G individuals are truthful enough to admit it.

[3] It may be desirable here to point up a little further what was said in the test above. It was suggested that a test "objective" in scoring, contrasted with an essay test or other open-ended test in which the examiners rate from a general impression, is better called a fully *conspective* test. Most but not all conspective tests are multiple choice. The *conspective coefficient*, which is one aspect of the reliability of a test, is the correlation of scores of subjects for *two psychologists scoring the same series* of subjects, and it is simple to designate all tests in which this normally reaches 1 as *fully conspective*.

CHAPTER **4**

DYNAMIC STRUCTURE:
ERGS AND SENTIMENTS; *U* and *I* COMPONENTS

4-1. Objective Motivation Measurement: The Attitude Stimulus-Response Unit

For many personality theorists, especially in the clinical phase of research, personality essentially began and ended with motivation and motivation structure. One looks in vain in Freud, Janet, and Adler, for example, for any reference to the role of abilities or even, until Jung, for some systematic regard for the role of temperament traits such as have been the object of our intensive study in the preceding chapters. A book on personality theory could be distinguished from an exciting novel of intriguing motives within motives only by some academic attempt to conclude with generalizations adopting a scientific stance. The hard-boiled experimentalist was often inclined to attach to these writings the novelist's disclaimer that "all characters in this story are purely fictitious." Nevertheless, upon a broad and unprejudiced examination of the attempts at prediction, the recognition of need for some internal theoretical consistency, and other tests of scientific intent, some of the central concepts in such clinical, dynamic psychology possessed a genuine if operationally shaky scientific character. There is no doubt that the clinical and the classical-experimental approaches could benefit by mutual criticism and mutual linking of concepts. As to criticism of the clinician's airy, subjective treatment of data, a counter-criticism would be that the classical experimentalist, when not lost in animal experiment, had done little in human psychology to devise quantitative experiments to check the clinical theories.

However, much of the thrust of the present book is that the issue is not between clinical and classical-experimental schools, but that the future lies more in multivariate experimental methods of investigation. It is not a question of testing clinical theories by bivariate experiment, but of generating entirely new theories through multivariate attacks. If results on this experimental-statistical basis generate some precise concepts to which clinical theories were a rough approach, all well and good; and if bivariate experimenters take the "significant" variables provided by multivariate methods, and work intensively on them, so much the better.[1]

It requires special initiatives and experimental ingenuity to develop multivariate experiments in the subtle dynamic area hitherto left so completely to the clinicians. However, it is evident to any multivariate experimentalist who has thought about the fundamental nature of clinical developments, in relation to general psychological observation and inference, that clinicians were actually, at an early stage, *implicitly* using a multivariate approach. Unfortunately, because the latter are unaware of their relation to this mathematical methodological model—and perhaps also because of the general human reluctance to labor at recording and measurement—they failed to give their theories testability. On the other flank of psychology, many experimentalists have shown, by inaction, their lack of faith or understanding that multivariate and factor-analytic methods could grasp the intangibles of motivation as successfully as those methods had revealed the structure of abilities. Fortunately, others viewed the success in the ability field as evidence that, with improved experimental method and more flexible, technically developed use of factor-analytic and pattern-analytic procedures, substantial gains *could* result. This insight has been vindicated by results. With wide perception of the break-through, multivariate experimental and psychometric psychology began to expand in the fifties from the domain of abilities and temperament dimensions, hitherto relatively static in treatment, into the domain of motivation and dynamics. In doing so it at last produced that balance—that focus on the complete personality—that the clinician's preoccupation with dynamic elements only had obscured. (How many psychoanalysts give the client an intelligence test? How many school psychologists use the School Motivational Analysis Test (SMAT) to discover the backward child's interest and motivation system?) Yet the interaction of dynamic and ability traits in a common specification equation is vital to any prediction.

As anyone who knows the history of science might have anticipated, the advance into the motivational area had to begin with good measurement operations as such. In fact it began (Table 4-1) with exploration of the validity of a wide array of devices for objectively measuring motivation and interest strength. To approach this we must first get a perspective on the ways in which this kind of measurement is likely to differ from that used in relation to personality (including ability) factors above.

Psychologists have long recognized what are currently called three *modalities* of traits, stemming from the affective, orectic, and cognitive categories of experience discussed by Plato and Aristotle. The *ability*, or cognitive, modality is well known. The temperament modality is also reasonably defined. However, it should be pointed out that what we have contingently called the general personality trait category in the last three chapters does include not *only* temperament traits but also some generalized dynamic traits fished up in the multivariate net. (Incidentally the terms *ability, temperament* and *dynamic* for these modalities are better than cognitive, affective and conative which carry over a purely introspective and even medieval scholastic flavor.) Ultimately, in Chapter 7, it will become desirable to give a precise and operational distinction of measurement forms in the three modalities, but at this point, in proceeding from largely temperamental to specifically dynamic structures, we shall be content to follow a less explicit—but still widely accepted—current consensus on what the dynamic area as such covers.

Assuming that we are sufficiently agreed, at a common-sense level, on distinguishing the dynamic modality, covering interests, motives, impulses, and drives, from the modalities of temperament and ability, our main aim in this chapter will be simply to ask what is known about the major dynamic structures. (A more advanced analysis of conflict, adjustment, integration, will be made in Volume 2.) Dynamic structure is usually conceived as covering drives, propensities (or *ergs*, as we shall call them), and the sentiments, attitudes, or "secondary drives," or other acquired attitude structures learned from culture. In studying this area we shall start with no bias from pre-existing speculations—they are little more than that—about the number and nature of human drives, but begin, as for temperament traits, with the principle of basing investigation on the broadest possible personality-sphere-like domain of dynamic behavior. On that broad theoryless basis we shall then see for the first time what covariation methods and simple structure resolution produce in the way of replicable structures. This, of course, will be only a beginning. There will remain the task of integrating this clinician's view of personality with the structures already stably located in ability and temperament modalities. Perhaps, after all, this dynamic region, approached last of all by the experimentalist, will prove to be, as clinicians have implied, the first in importance. But the total scene as we eventually see it will be a richer one than the clinician's, embracing a reliably broadened spectrum of normal and abnormal trait structures and recognizing new laws for their integration in actual behavior integrations.

Again, condensation must be great, but fortunately there are many extended discussions and illustrations now available; for example, Cattell and Child (1974), Cattell and Kline (1977), Cartwright (1973), Cartwright and Cartwright (1972), Horn (1966), Sweney (1967, 1975), Pervin (1975), Dreger (1962), Cattell and Dreger (1970), Lindzey and Hall (1965), and others. With this help those presently unfamiliar with the evidence will be able fully to follow the final model below.

The new developments, which began around 1950 and have earned the name of the *dynamic calculus*, seriously attacked first the task of shifting the measurement of the dynamic strength of interest to the basis of objective methods. Self-report (*Q*-data) was then the sole approach in general: the Strong Interest Blank, the Kuder Preference Test, and many other interest inventories, as well as measures of Murray's supposed drives in the Edwards PPI or the Jackson PRI. The judgment of psychologists today must surely be, as in such recent, broad, and intensive studies of questionnaire methods as those of Wiggins (1972) and Cattell (1973), that despite "desirability" and other observer distortion, the questionnaire yields relatively faithful pictures of temperament structure. On the other hand, in the motivation realm and in the ability modality, the distortion becomes so great in self-evaluation methods that it becomes a strategically ill-chosen approach, doomed to require so many props, corrections, and allowances that it is scarcely worth pursuing. That is why, in surveying the questionnaire method as a valid personality investigation procedure, we omitted its use in motivational investigation, as in the Edwards and Jackson questionnaires aimed at Murray's arbitrary list of dynamic needs (Cattell, 1973).

No one would think of using self-report *Q*-data rather than *T*-data to determine a person's IQ or his centile rank on spatial ability. It is time we became equally critical of using *Q*-data to measure motives. In no domain is the subject so likely to be unaware as in regard to his real motives, and nowhere is he so likely in a real test situation, for example, job seeking, to distort his self-evaluations.

Such tests as the Kuder, Jackson's PRI and the EPPI have excellent psychometric properties in the narrower traditional sense of high homegeneity coefficients of scale items. What is lacking is the relation of the scales to factorially established dynamic trait structures. (Both of the latter orient themselves to nothing more substantial than Murray's arbitrary list of needs—differing from William James', McDougall's, Freud's, and Drever's equally mutually-disagreeing lists.) Because in this chapter we proceed to a constructive solution by a totally new objective approach, it is not our purpose at this point to examine the perturbation and bias that might be corrected in inventory approaches to motives. It has long been known to every novelist or shrewd observer that we are unable to gauge the strength of our own desires, are unwilling to parade socially our deepest desires, and are in fact even unconscious of that nine-tenths of the iceberg of drives that psychoanalysis reliably tells us is below the surface of verbalization. Interest inventories and check lists are at best a temporary and inherently superficial approach to understanding human dynamics.

The term objective tests is defined in precisely the same way here as in general personality *T*-data. It covers all methods of assessment by measuring performance, without resting on self-evaluation of trait strengths. So we are simply dealing here with *T*-data in the dynamic modality instead of the temperament or ability-trait modalities as in Chapter 3.

The central, opening question is: "How do we validly measure the strength of motivation in any given response or intention to respond?" First, we have to agree on the element of behavior to be observed and measured. The unit of behavior that is observed and measured here is still kept strictly in stimulus-response, behavioristic psychology. It is a measured response to a defined situation, as in measures in ability and temperament modalities, though obviously we are out to measure a different *aspect* of the response. Now S-O-R units can be of different sizes—from the eye-blink reflex or pecking at a grain of corn, such as the Pavlovian or Skinnerian has typically measured, to the complexly organized course of action when a student responds to news of a poor grade by getting more library books and putting in more hours of study. The personality researcher, still using the stimulus-response model, has to take larger units of response than the animal experimenter *if he is to keep contact with relevant personality structure and everyday life behavior.* He needs, nevertheless, to work at some middle level that permits behavior to be caught in precise operations. The middling-size situation-response unit that is conveniently small and specific enough to measure, yet large enough to be "visible," as part of the subject's general life behavior, we shall call an *attitude*. It is defined verbally by the following paradigm.

"In this situation   I   want so much to do this with that"
     Stimulus   Organism   Response

The response is a *course of action*, almost invariably conceivable as taking place with reference to some object—"that." But the response course of action is "to do this with" and "that." The "want so much" is the strength of interest in the defined course of action, which it is our object to measure. Parenthetically, whether the person actually carries out the action or merely wants to carry it out is irrelevant to the immediate measurement of strength. In place of "want to" we could easily and properly substitute "do," "do" being measured by frequency and intensity of response, the number of obstructions overcome, punishment faced, and so on, to carry out the course of behavior. However, "want to" is used because circumstances or internal inhibitions often prevent the actual behavior from emerging in humans, for long periods at a time, and meanwhile in these periods we measure the strength by signs of autonomic tension, memory effects, and so on, which have been empirically shown to correlate with the strength of the actual behavior when it appears.

At the moment there is no need to concern ourselves with the nature of the inhibiting forces or the secondary conditions that decide there will be action or inaction. However, there are other aspects of this definition that, if pursued to behavioral observations, require one or two qualifying additions. For example, "this situation," if we deal with a habitual attitude, has to be a *steady* situation, and it is assumed that carrying out the action will usually temporarily reduce, by satisfying it, the strength of interest, though the latter will resume a more or less steady state in the intervals between satisfactions and the various stimulus trigger releases. Furthermore, we could extend consideration to certain taxonomic varieties of attitudes that need consideration in a more specialized, refined definition.[2] Parenthetically this whole definition and manner of approach is very different from that used in sociology and in certain traditional cognitive uses of *attitude* in psychology. In these latter, derived largely from polling, an attitude is a verbal statement *pro or con some object or idea*. The dynamic definition concerns a course of action or response, (1) to which any object is purely incidental, and (2) which is much *richer emotionally*, as will be seen, than merely "for" or "against."

4-2.   The Nature of Motivation Components

The purpose of measuring the strength of an attitude is to permit correlations to be made among sampled arrays or chosen sets of attitudes from the dynamic personality sphere. The attitude is the suitable brick or unit variable, out of which the house of dynamic structure is to be built. By applying factor analysis to the correlations of this type of variable, just as has been done with ability and personality-temperament variables, research aims to uncover some definite, steady underlying structure. Parenthetically, this strategy calls in principle for correlating *response strength* over many attitudes while holding the stimulus-situation strengths as constant as possible. Only later do we move out of this steady environment and supplement the generalizations with the supplementary methodological approach of correlating *response strengths* with *changing stimulus (and gratification) strengths.*

Before seeking to relate attitudes from a "dynamic sphere," representative of life attitudes, we must know, as suggested above, how to measure the strength of interest by objective devices in any *single* attitude. Between 1945 and 1965 more than 100 diverse signs of strength of interest, as advocated in the writings of scores of psychologists of repute in the field, were taken (see Table 4-1) as defining the semantically and conceptually general domain of "strength of motivation" and were intercorrelated systematically to examine test validity. Naturally this intercorrelation had to be carried out afresh for each of several diverse types of attitude to see how far the same validities would hold regardless of content. Furthermore, instead of assuming that the pool (sum) of these physiological, clinical, learning, and life-criteria manifestations of motive was *the* criterion of validity for the separate tests, an open mind was maintained as to whether a single dimension would in fact fit the data in the first place. Perhaps there would be several kinds of strength of motive. Psychometrically, this means rejecting any simple-minded "testing of validity by homogeneity with the pool." Instead, we first ask critically and analytically, whether the pool represents a single concept or several.

Actually, there proved to be no fewer than seven or eight primary motivation components, which are given symbols $\alpha, \beta, \gamma, \delta,$ $\epsilon, \xi,$ and η. The wide spectrum of motivation manifestations used and the replication of these primary patterns in motivation expression can be most quickly seen in Table 4-1, though detailed accounts of these and other devices must be seen elsewhere (Cattell, Radcliffe & Sweney, 1963; Cattell, Horn, Sweney, & Radcliffe, 1964). After an interval of over ten years the seven primaries above

TABLE 4–1.   The Nature of Primary Motivation Components Expressed in Objective Measurement Devices

Devices	Average Loadings							Number of Studies
	Alpha α	Beta β	Gamma γ	Delta δ	Epsilon ϵ	Zeta ζ	Eta η	
Distortion of reasoning	41							8
Autism[a]	43		30					9
Preferences	48		49					11
Fantasy: topics to explain	44		30					3
Fantasy: books to read	48							2
Decision time	33							4
Perceptual closure	37							2
Naive projection	36							2
True projection	–45							1
Id projection	38							1
Defensive fluency on good consequences	27							2
Information[a]		29						11
Learning a language		40						5
Perception integration		37						1
Availability: free association speed		50						2
Auditory distraction		41						2
Warm-up speed		31						1
Fantasy: time spent ruminating		39						2
Availability: free association[a]			38					5
Perseveration: low perceptual integration			32					2
Superego projection			28					1
Availability: oriented association			54					2

[a]Devices used in the construction of MAT and SMAT.

TABLE 4–1   *(continued)*

Devices	Average Loadings							Number of Studies
	Alpha α	Beta β	Gamma γ	Delta δ	Epsilon ϵ	Zeta ζ	Eta η	
Selective perception			38					2
Expectancy: effort to be expended			23					2
Physiological involvement: Systolic blood pressure change				−48				4
Diastolic blood pressure change				−44				3
Psychogalvanic response deflection				39				3
Decision speed				42				2
Retroactive inhibition				31				1
Physiological threat activity: Deflection of PGR to threat					34			2
Memory for cues					−40			3
Interference: reminiscence by recall					−54			5
Utilities (time and money spent)[a]					36			2
Impulsiveness: decision speed						54		2
Impulsiveness: agreement speed						49		2
Decision strength						42		2
Fluency on cues							33	2
Persistence: perceptual task							−44	2

[a] Devices used in the construction of MAT and SMAT.

have been re-confirmed by Cattell, Lawlis, McGill, and McGraw (1979) with slight modifications of the alpha pattern.

Although no psychoanalytic theory was favored by these investigators, some of the primaries, by pattern, fitted far more readily to psychoanalytic theory than to other theories then available, notably ability-theory, concepts. Tentative titles for them have contingently been used for a decade, namely, alpha as id, beta as ego, gamma as super ego, delta for autonomic component, epsilon for unconscious complex and zeta for bodily tension. However, an alternative conceptualization in terms of stimulation, deprivation, and learning characteristics is now being proposed for consideration, as discussed below.

The discovery that it is psychometrically absurd to give one single score (except in the sense of an admitted conglomerate sum) for the strength of an attitude opens up new complexities in attitude study and incidentally casts major doubts on the conclusions from much sociological attitude work proceeding with purely verbal self-estimates. Henceforth, the strength of an attitude has to be stated in seven or eight distinct scores. As an additional complication these components might have proved different for different interest content areas, but fortunately for the retention of some simplicity, it was soon found that no matter what the "content" of the attitude might be—sports, politics, family—the 50 or more devices used always grouped themselves in the same seven or eight components. (The list of devices, and the evidence for factor structure can be seen in Cattell, 1957; Cattell, Horn, Radcliffe, & Sweney, 1964; Horn, 1966; and Sweney, 1975.)

The life criteria—such as hours of effort or money spent on the given course of action—are loaded upon and predicted in various degrees from most of these primaries, so they are all motivation relevant and criterion valid in the broadest sense, as indeed the original staking out of the motivation manifestation domain would suggest. Also, it may be noted that the most hallowed traditional device for interest measurement—the preference statement or self-conscious motivation estimation in verbal terms in an inventory— loads largely on *only one* factor, α, and to a value that indicates it is defining only about one-ninth of the motivation strength vouched for by the totality of indicators of strength. Such an approach is thus revealing only a visible fraction of the whole iceberg, as we anticipated, and supports our argument that inventories are invalid in the motivation and interest measurement area, especially when the situation is likely to involve embarrassment or faking.

Further discussion of the tentative interpretive labels just mentioned as newly given to the primary motivation components, alpha, beta, gamma, etc., is best deferred until we bridge to learning theory in Volume 2 of this work. Initially the interpretations above—in covering at least three by psychoanalytic terms—were based simply on the content in terms of high-loaded performances. This gives, for example, an "I want, I wish" character to α (called id component) and a more realistically integrated and cognitively invested expression (knowledge about, rapid word association, rate of learning about) for β, the ego component, and so on. As soon as more motivation investigators see scope for research here, interpretive steps regarding the different components can be shifted to depend more upon observations of differences in the "natural history" and life criteria relations of these different components, measured in familiar interest area. How does the strength of each of the various components relate, for example, to the age of the interest, the strength of current stimulation, the amount of deprivation of gratification, and the degree of conflict, for instance? Such research data are urgently needed. At present we lack information even on the relative stability of the component levels over time, such as would tell us which are more traitlike and which may be states.

The practical sociological or political-science-attitude measurer, dismayed by being asked to state results in seven components instead of the simple—but specious—single score to which he or she has been accustomed, has asked if second-order factoring might not obligingly show a *single* secondary factor covering all of these seven or eight primaries. Not for the sake of this expediency, but to know exactly what the higher-order structure is, the oblique (correlated) simple-structure primaries have themselves been factored. In doing so a check was made also on the constancy of the second-order patterns over diverse attitudes and subjects. The result has uniformly been that three to four second orders appear, but two have been so small relative to the other two that investigators have for the present concentrated on two. What they load, and how well the loadings agree for children and adults, is most readily shown by a plot, as in Figure 4-1. The results from longitudinal factoring in a single individual (over a hundred days) (Birkett & Cattell, 1979) of several different devices measuring interest expression, agree only in a general way with this second-order structure, suggesting that some features of m.c.'s may be traitlike.

It will be seen (though simple structure rotation on so few points needs more replication than usual) that the grouping certainly fits psychological meaning well. The id, the physiological, and the complex-indicating primaries—α, δ, and ϵ—load a factor obviously having to do with unintegrated or unconscious aspects of interest, while the primaries tentatively interpreted as ego and superego

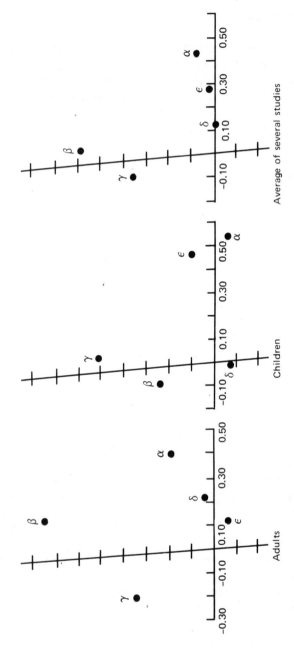

Figure 4-1. The structure of second-order motivation components: U (horizontally) and I (vertically).

sources of motive—β and γ— load a distinct factor. It appears that the first factor is defined not so well by the line between unconscious and conscious (as is customary in psychoanalysis), but by the character of being *unintegrated*, which includes, but is not alone concerned with, unconscious roots. Contrasted with this unintegrated component—henceforth U—is the *integrated* component, seemingly concerned with that part of interests tested and tried in behavior and stably expressed in the individual's life. This is the integrated, or I, component. This is our *present* theory to fit these new motivation component discoveries, but, as will be evident later, we can also entertain other theories.

What has been gained to this point can be summarized by two specification equations. If d is a particular objective measuring *device* used on some attitude j, and I_{jd} is the strength of interest in response course of action j as measured through expression d, then (omitting subscripts for the individual)

$$I_{jd} = b_{jd\alpha}\, F_\alpha + b_{jd\beta}\, F_\beta + \cdots + b_{jd\eta}\, F_\eta + b_{jd}\, F_{jd} \qquad (4\text{-}1)$$

when F_α, F_β, and so on are the individual's degrees of endowment in factors that are the motivation primaries—and the b's are behavioral indices as usual. Alternatively, in secondaries only:

$$I_{jd} = b_{jkU}\, F_U + b_{jdI}\, F_I + b_{JD}\, F_{JD} \qquad (4\text{-}2)$$

Capitals (U, I) are used for subscripts for secondaries and (D) on the specific term—in the latter also to distinguish specific variance on secondaries from that on primaries—as in the primary d in equation (4-1) above.

This formulation permits us to assign validity coefficients to any given complex device d, calculated as its correlation coefficients with each of the primaries or secondaries. And because our evidence is that these remain much the same regardless of the nature of j—the particular attitude content—an average across several js gives a stable statement of the validity of a given device as a measurer of motive strength (see the recent check by Cattell, Lawlis, McGill, & McGraw, 1979).

4-3. The Evidence for Ergs and Sentiments as the Main Dynamic Structures

Armed at last with a means of objectively assessing the strength of an individual's interest in responding with a given course of action within an attitude, researchers were ready by the early 1950s to begin structuring the "interest space" for the typical member of our culture. As with the personality sphere, so here it was important to avoid the bias of subjective and passing fashions in theory, for example, that there are just so many drives (3 in Freud or 30 in Murray), or that, as animal experimenters have presumed, such and such are "primary" and others only "secondary" drives. Instead, with this more potent method, it was most desirable to begin completely afresh. Work was begun with humans and a foundation was laid for later work with animals (Cattell & Dielman, 1974), which showed curiously enough that there are seven primaries also in animals. (This favors our shift from a psychoanalytic to a learning theory explanation of the primaries.)

Such a mapping effort in regard to the major areas of human interest and motivation required that research should begin with a stratified sample of attitudes from the typical total interest spectrum of the average person. The ultimate and ideal method of achieving this would be by time sampling of acts through the day, as in general personality variables. But a sufficiently substantial advance over the narrowness of past work could be made by a stratified sampling of human-interest topics. The nearest basis for objectivity here seemed to be page space in American and British encyclopedias or newspapers. A first approximate foundation, on the encyclopedia, was laid by Cattell in quantitatively defining an *interest sphere* in 1935. However, it should not be difficult today to improve on that by the human-interest and activity surveys of the environment by Barker (1968), Sells (1963), and some recent sociological examinations of newspaper content.

Beginning at first with 30 such interest-area-derived attitudes and then extending to 50 or more attitudes, measuring each by a battery of the best six to eight objective devices, several factor analyses, programmatically sequenced (surveyed in Cattell & Child, 1975), finally gave evidence of about 15 *dynamic structure* factors. ("Dynamic structure" distinguishes these from "motivation component" factors.) At once it was evident that at least half of these corresponded to drives—such as hunger, sex, curiosity, gregariousness, and parental protectiveness—recognized by ethologists in the primates, though not so broadly recognized by experimenters with rats. Several of these patterns had also been posited by such writers on drives or propensities as Freud, McDougall, James, Drever, Murray, and others. Actually, the list of objectively discovered patterns (see Table 4-4, p. 143) corresponded best with that of McDougall, which also was based on good ethological study, though his list of innate propensities was less extensive than those of Tinbergen and

Lorenz. No one of the previous "armchair" lists fitted the new empirical findings as a whole, though it is interesting that Freud's split of sexual interest into heterosexual, object-libido and a narcissistic, self-oriented component was supported, as was McDougall's (1937) clear conception of pugnacity (somewhat ambiguously since named aggression) as a drive deriving its energy solely in a parasitic way from that of the appetitive drives that happen to be thwarted.

This mapping work by Horn, Miller, Radcliffe, Sweney, and others was the first substantial, experimentally based reentry of drives into human psychology since they were banished under a pall of largely verbal and *a priori* criticism by Watson and the sociologists in the 1920s. The common-sense observation of psychologists had nevertheless quietly stood firm in this period of exile of "propensities," and the drives came back under other names. For the drive concept remained a functional and indispensable concept hiding under no matter what name. However, it was not until the advent of multivariate experimental methods, with their quantitative means of firmly demonstrating these latent, underlying patterns in man, that they could come back with some solid scientific respectability into psychology. Bivariate experiment meanwhile permitted only animal-research psychologists to retain and use the concept of instinct or drive, man being beyond experiment, ethically and by his complexity, by the controlled methods of animal research. Because of the importance of the turning point brought about by the restoration of drives to human dynamics, it becomes important to examine more closely just what the evidence means.

In the early researches in the fifties the factoring of, say, 40 attitudes over, say, 200 persons, was conducted on the summed U and I components for the "total" strength of each attitude. But later the second-order U and I measures—and even primary α, β, or γ measures and single valid devices (as in the Guilford et al., 1954, factoring of preference measures)—were factored separately for these attitudes. All devices proved to yield the same dynamic structure patterns among the 40 attitudes. In all of these methods the correlations bunched variables for each drive together, and ultimately were revealed to be influenced by one simple structure factor for each drive. These patterns, moreover, proved to be a set of attitudes within which *a common ultimate biological goal* was clearly visible. Table 4-2 shows two instances of such factor loading patterns. In looking at Table 4-2 we must not forget that although the attitudes are written as verbal statements, consistent with the form of the paradigm above (page 130), they are *not* measured by mere verbal self-report, but by the summed score of the same battery of objective devices (autism, word association, projection, knowledge, reaction

TABLE 4—2.   Two Dynamic Structure Factors Interpretable as Drives: The Fear and Sex Ergs

Attitudes loading and defining the security-seeking (fear, escape) erg

	Loadings
I want my country to get more protection against the terror of the atom bomb	.5
I want to see any formidable militaristic power that actively threatens us attacked and destroyed	.5
I want to see the danger of death by accident and disease reduced	.4
I want to see those responsible for inflation punished	.4
I want never to be an insane patient in a mental hospital	.4
I want to see a reduction of income tax for those in my bracket	.3
I want to take out more insurance against illness	.3
I want to become proficient in my career	.3
I want my country to have power and influence in the world	.3
I like to take part in political arguments	.3

Attitudes defining the sex erg

	Loadings
I want to fall in love with a beautiful woman	.5
I want to satisfy my sexual needs	.5
I like sexual attractiveness in a woman	.5
I like to see a good movie now and then	.4
I like a novel with love interest and a ravishing heroine	.4
I like to enjoy smoking and drinking	.4
I want to see more good restaurants serving attractive food	.3
I want to listen to music	.3
I want to travel and explore the world	.3

time, and so on) in all attitudes, adapted only in *content* to each attitude concerned.

In a series of factorial researches in which, programmatically, most major human-interest areas were eventually covered and various new attitudes were introduced to test crucial hypotheses, such dynamic structure factors were replicated again and again. From inspection of the loaded compared with the unloaded (the remaining) attitudes, it could readily be seen that all attitudes on one-factor lead toward a particular "instinctual" goal (if we may for the moment continue to use a rather uncertain popular term). That is, today the loaded variables can be seen to be sustained by the same emotion and concerned with the same ultimate biological satisfaction.

But in every such research the simple structure resolution produced also an initially puzzling set of dynamic structure factors that did not fit this same formula. Soon, however, it became apparent that the psychological "formula" for these new patterns was precisely the inverse of that recognizable for what appeared to be innate drives. Whereas each drive pattern loaded some 6 to 10 (out of 30 to 50) attitudes that came from *different* cultural areas but had the *same* common emotional goal, the new dynamic traits showed attitudes offering *diverse* emotional goal satisfactions but centered on one and the same common *cultural* institution. For example, the fear drive ("instinct of escape from danger" in the case of lower animals) in Table 4-2 has attitudes couched in such diverse cultural areas as medicine (freedom from disease), economics (concern over one's bank account), freedom from accident, and escape from war (not to mention fear of what the internal revenue service can do!). But all have "fear-sight": foresight and concern about dangers. Conversely, in such a dynamic factor as that labelled "job" in Table 4-3, *different* emotional satisfaction qualities are involved, such as love of flying, interest in a safe pension, liking to command and lead men, and even the excitement of combat. But all have in common the adaptations and values that fit one to an *institution*—the American Air Force in this case—and the courses of behavior learnt therein.

Between 6 and 12 (depending on degree of confirmation) patterns of the first type (drives) have been discovered in adults and in children, and rather more than that of the second type. From evidence of various kinds, most yet to be presented, the theory we have developed is that the first represent innate predispositions, sometimes called drives but here designated *ergs*, and the second represent learned patterns, acquired through the culture, which, in conformity with some previous usage, we shall call *engrams*, or *sentiments*. Regarding the term ergs, let us recognize that so much conflict and misunderstanding has arisen from using the term "instinct" in regard to man that it, and its clinging train of biases, are best dropped. In considering alternative terms it might yet be said in favor of "instinct"

TABLE 4—3.   Sentiment to Job (Air Force)[a]

	Loadings
I want to make my career in the Air Force	.70
I like the excitement and adventure of combat flying	.63
I want to get technical education such as the Air Force provides	.58
I enjoy commanding men and taking the responsibilities of a military leader	.44
I do not want to take more time to enjoy rest and to sleep later in the mornings	-.41
I like being up in an airplane	.41
I want to satisfy my sense of duty to my country by enlisting in its most important defense arm in threatening times	.39
I want to become first-rate at my Air Force job	.36
I do not want to spend more time at home puttering around	-.36

[a]Here, as in other tables setting out factors, the signs of the loadings are given as they occur for all the positively directed ("I want") attitudes in the original list of variables. For the reader's convenience in reading the list of salients, the qualifying "not" is inserted whenever the loading has gone negative. The attitudes thus read consistently as they stand and need no change.

and "propensity" that they have at least been sharply, even if too arbitrarily, defined, whereas "drive" has been used in both human and animal psychology in so many ill-defined ways that it is unsuitable on grounds of a history of vagueness for effective use in the new domain of exact dynamics now appearing.

Accordingly, in company with several leading experimenters in this new field, we have adopted here and elsewhere the term *erg* (rhymes with berg) for this class of factor patterns. It is apt here for the same reason that it is apt in physics: derived from the Greek word for work, it implies energy. If our conception of dynamic traits is correct, these ergs in man are the source of all response action and of energy in the generally accepted sense. For they are the source of all initial reactivity to stimuli and if they could in some way be abstracted the organism would be inert. Erg also has the grammatically useful property (which drive has not) of leading to a convenient adjective, ergic (rhymes with allergic), and an adverb, ergically.

It is not our purpose here exhaustively to assemble evidence for all presently known ergs and sentiments, such as a psychologist would ultimately want for his complete taxonomy of human nature, but rather to proceed through examples only to the extent necessary for ensuring understanding of their general character. Consequently we leave to Tables 4-4 and 4-5 (p. 145) the listing of those ergs and sentiments for which there already seems reasonable evidence.

Among ergic patterns of more borderline or special character are (1) adjustment mechanisms so specific or physiological that they might be in a different class, such as avoiding excessive heat and cold (see lists by Murray, animal psychologists such as P. T. Young, 1970, and so on); (2) ergs with unusual stimuli, such as pugnacity (frustration of another erg) and sleep (absence of stimuli); (3) ergs seen in mammals but seemingly tied to modes of living with which mankind has not had much to do for a million years, and which are not well-evidenced yet in attitude analysis in humans. Conversely, we see very disproportionate development in man of patterns, such as curiosity, not so strongly developed in higher mammals. An important instance of a pattern strong in mammals is Ardrey's (1960) territorial defence pattern, which in man is possibly merged with the broader self-assertive erg. On the other hand, a pattern of amusement and laughter present in man (though not yet well replicated in present methods) is scarcely present in mammals. The principal debate in regard to (2) has centered on pugnacity.

In this connection, it seems desirable to substitute pugnacity for

TABLE 4–4. List of Human Ergs

Goal Title	Emotion	Status of Evidence
Food-seeking	Hunger	Replicated factor; measurement battery exists
Mating	Sex	Replicated factor; measurement battery exists
Gregariousness	Loneliness	Replicated factor; measurement battery exists
Parental	Pity	Replicated factor; measurement battery exists
Exploration	Curiosity	Replicated factor; measurement battery exists
Escape to security	Fear	Replicated factor; measurement battery exists
Self-assertion	Pride	Replicated factor; measurement battery exists
Narcistic sex	Sensuousness	Replicated factor; measurement battery exists
Pugnacity	Anger	Replicated factor; measurement battery exists
Acquisitiveness	Greed	Replicated factor; measurement battery exists
Appeal	Despair	Factor, once replicated; battery exists
Rest-seeking	Sleepiness	Factor, but of uncertain independence
Constructiveness	Creativity	Factor, but of uncertain independence
Self-abasement	Humility	Factor, but of uncertain independence
Disgust	Disgust	Factor absent for lack of markers
Laughter	Amusement	Factor absent for lack of markers

the term aggression. The latter has led to endless psychological confusion (whatever it may mean politically) because it fails to distinguish self-assertion, with the goal of competitive excellence or mastery over nature and fellow man, from pugnacity, the emotion of which is anger and the goal of which is destruction of an obstacle. The latter is not particularly tied to assertive achievement but appears at frustration by *any* obstacle, in the way of *any* ergic process.[3]

Actually, there is still much to be done at the experimental level in refining the concept of pugnacity. The earlier factor-analytic patterns of the erg by Cattell and Baggaley (1958) loaded some fear and one or two self-assertive attitudes as well as those attitudes best fitting the hypothesis, that is, directed to annihilation of a thwarting situation or enemy, or to sadism, or to smashing obstructions to impulsive self-expression. The tentative explanation offered is that threats to security and self-expression are now the commonest frustrations in our present culture (in which few people indeed are frustrated, say, in hunger or thirst). Accordingly, Baggaley introduced more crucial markers, and found, for example, that sadism, or "giving people hell," were also characteristic of pugnacity, whereas the fear markers fell away. However, the close physiological similarity of the expressions of fear and rage (Cannon, 1929) may constitute an unusual type of link here. In any case, there is plenty of room for research today applying multivariate experiment toward a nicer delineation of the existing and latent expressions of human ergs.

The evidence begins to pile up that, unlike ergs, which come out as dynamic structure factors roughly constant in number, equal in variance, and covering about the same number of attitudes, sentiments may vary greatly in number and size, notably between child and adult years. Some, like that for home, school, job, or religion, tend to be massive. Others go down to fragmentary conditionings, for example, of a child for his bicycle, or an adult for a comfortable pair of shoes, which pass with no sharp division into what we shall later call mental sets. They seem to vary most markedly, however, as just stated, between children and adults, as might indeed be expected developmentally.

A sentiment of especial importance structurally, to which a lot of attention will be given later, is the self-sentiment—the set of dynamic attitudes centering upon the cognitive entity we call the self-concept. Its peculiarity belongs to its central position in integrating other sentiments. Apart from this, it is no different in essential quality and origin from the others, so no special discussion is accorded to it at this point (see, however, Volume 2, Chapter 3).

TABLE 4—5.   List of Human Sentiments

Symbol Title	Symbol Title
S_1 *Profession* (1)	S_{15} *Theoretical-logical.* Thinking,
S_2 *Parental family, home* (1)	precision (2) (8) (10)
S_3 *Wife, sweetheart* (1)	S_{16} *Philosophical-historical.* Language,
S_4 *The self-sentiment* (1). Physical	civics, sociocultural, esthetic
and psychological self	rather than economic (2) (3) (6)
S_5 *Superego* (1)	(7)
S_6 *Religion.* This has emphasis on	S_{17} Patriotic-political (1) (7)
doctrine and practice, on high	S_{18} *Sedentary-social games.* Diversion,
social and low esthetic values (1)	play, club and pub sociability;
(4) (7) (8)	cards (2) (10)
S_7 *Sports and fitness.* Games,	S_{19} *Travel-geography.* Possibly
physical activity, hunting, military	Guildford's autism here
activity (1) (2) (3)	S_{20} *Education-school attachment*
S_8 *Mechanical interests* (1) (2) (5)	S_{21} *Physical-home-decoration-*
S_9 *Scientific interests.* High theoretical,	*furnishing*
low political; math. (2) (3) (4)	S_{22} *Household-cooking*
(5) (6) (7) (9)	S_{23} *News-communication.* Newspaper,
S_{10} *Business-economic.* Money	radio, TV
administrative (2) (3) (4) (5)	S_{24} Clothes, self-adornment
S_{11} *Clerical interests* (2) (4)	S_{25} Animal pets
S_{12} *Esthetic expressions* (2) (10)	S_{26} Alcohol
S_{13} *Esthetic-literary appreciation.* Drama	S_{27} Hobbies not already specified
S_{14} *Outdoor-manual.* Rural, nature-	
loving, gardening, averse to	
business and "cerebration" (2)	
(5) (6)	

[a]Numbers in parentheses are references, as follows.

(1) Cattell et al. (4 studies)	(9) Strong (1949)
(2) Guildford et al. (1954)	(10) Thorndike (1935)
(3) Thurstone (1935)	*See also*
(4) Gundlach and Gerum (1931)	(11) Cottie (1950)
(5) Torr (1953)	(12) Hammond (1945)
(6) Carter, Pyles, Bretnall (1935)	(13) Crissy and Daniel (1939)
(7) Ferguson, Humphreys, Strong (1941)	(14) Vernon (1950)
(8) Lurie (1937)	(15) Miller (1968)

For any of these references not in the present book see Cattell and Child (1975).

4-4.   Do Components and Dynamic Structures also Have Unity Functionally, by *P*-Technique?

The evidence for the dynamic structures we call ergs and sentiments has been stated so far in *R*-technique, that is, operating on individual differences, which makes them common traits—broad traits in the main instances but sometimes also specific. Knowing what we do about the general character of ergs in animals and men, it is not surprising that the fact of belonging to a common species and a common culture should produce emphatic common patterns. But in the domain of acquired sentiments, as novelists, biographers, and our own personal experiences remind us, interest patterns could be very diverse, and unique traits very frequent. Indeed, those who approach personality from a reflexological point of view have a priori told students to expect complete uniqueness of structure—and not in the more acceptable sense, from research evidence, of a "unique combination of common traits."

The objection to the structural chaos theory explicit in, for example, Mischel (1970), and several lesser writers, but implicit in many reflexological accounts of personality is simply that it does not come anywhere near to fitting the known facts. Common traits—communalities in factor matrices—are substantial and even the a priori reasoning that would seem to require "structural chaos" is faulty. For it has failed to envisage the tremendous amount of common conditioning of persons to a broad pattern set up in any culture.

However, variations in pattern are probably more frequent in dynamic trait than in ability or temperament modalities. Thus we should expect (1) that even ergs would have somewhat different common factor patterns in different cultures and (2) that sentiments would have such idiosyncracies that even within the same culture many sentiment structures unique to individuals should be expected. As to (1) the courses of action that are picked up as attitudes having the highest loading in ergs are generally close to the consummatory goal, but nevertheless each culture can favor some expression more than others even close to the goal. Few individuals have the same sentiments as that of Macbeth for Burnham Wood or Rupert Brooke for Grantchester (at least if we consider statistically a population of poets rather than the population of Grantchester!).

Now statistically, there is no great mystery, nor any practical research problem about locating unique trait patterns—if our method carefully fits the logic of our definition. As for common traits, if there are relatively extensive uniquenesses of pattern, existing in a common area of variables in which most people have *some* attachments, the correlations that yield common patterns will be reduced. In fact, the common trait patterns will be blurred "averages" of appreciably different patterns, and the statistical predictions from such factors as are found will be relatively poor.

There exist technical ways of handling such problems into which we will not digress here, but leave for Chapter 7. One way is to throw moderately divergent patterns together as a "type" of pattern, and to find one or two variables that load all of them with a sufficiently representative high loading to act as a dependable measure. Some such statistical solution is particularly necessary in the area of sentiments here being discussed. If we wish to score the strength of sentiment of husbands to wives in a comparative fashion, we run into the difficulty forthwith that all wives are different—in personality, appearance, and life history. Yet by choosing some features of the "sentiment object" common to all wives—their abilities, their out-of-home concerns, their beauty, their areas of conversation—we may find a very similar sentiment-to-wife pattern in all men. As this psychometric technique is extended to more diversified sentiment objects, for example, those to different jobs or hobbies, to concern for relatively specific bodily ailments, dynamic psychologists become more alert to the problem of detecting, naming, and scoring common traits in comparable ways. But, knowing the problem, they can achieve some acceptable degrees of success.

Although the common-trait system is that in which most measurement has to be carried if applied psychology is to proceed with reasonable convenience, it is in the dynamic modality that psychologists ultimately are forced to develop techniques for handling what was defined in Chapter 1 as the unique-trait system. For it is in this area of dynamics, interest, attachments, and sentiments that the individual's history is likely to be most singular and his structure most replete with unique-trait patterns. In Chapter 1 the research method known as *P*-techniqe was briefly mentioned as the main avenue to unique-trait exploration. However, it is a somewhat complex technique, which will be studied relatively fully in Chapter 5, so its discussion here, as the basis for recognizing the full properties of ergs and sentiments in their unique forms, must be brief. In *P*-technique (single-person factoring), perhaps 30 to 50 variables are measured on one and the same person every day over perhaps 100 occasions. Naturally, the devices—in the case of motivation measurement, too—must be of a kind that can be repeated without practice effects becoming too intrusive. Thus the experimenter will favor variables such as GSR response, reaction time, or fluency, or, alternatively, resort to constructing new equivalently standardized forms of test each day. The time series of measurements on every variable, matched occasion for occasion, are then correlated for each possible pair of variables and the resulting square *R*-matrix factored. One recognizes that, logically, this is calculated to yield the unitary sources or *dimensions of change* (as simple-structure factors).

P-technique introduces the student to a relatively new and wide world of factorial experiment beyond the ordinary individual-difference "correlation over people." The latter, which is the only technique the student is likely to have is called, in the perspective of other methods, *R*-technique. It is one of several extensions of multivariate experiment at which we should glance even at this early stage of structural analysis. To see *P*- and *R*- (and other) techniques in perspective requires familiarity with the concept of the *basic data relation matrix*, or *data box*, about which the student should do some reading elsewhere (Cattell, 1966) if he or she has not met it in methods courses. The data box is shown in Figure 4-2, in which there are three Cartesian coordinates, labelled "people," "attitudes," and "occasions," in 4-2(*a*). Each coordinate is marked by a series of ids, that is, individual objects (each a pattern), all belonging to one species. Thus people, occasions, responses, and so on, are the ids, bounding the data box. In Figure 4-2(*a*), illustrating *P*-techniques, we have a series of different attitudes (vertical coordinate), people

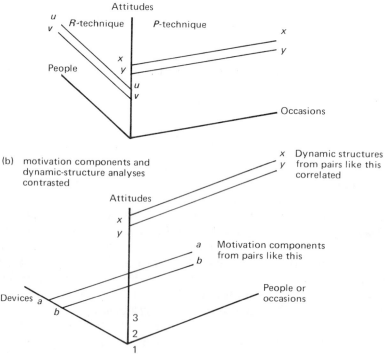

(a) *R*- and *P*- techniques contrasted

(b) motivation components and dynamic-structure analyses contrasted

Figure 4-2.   Most relevant excerpts (3-dimensional) from the 5-dimensional data box showing *R*- and *P*-techniques and motivation vs. dynamic-factor distinctions.

(coordinate to the left), and occasions of measurement (coordinate to the right). No coordinate is given in this diagram for *devices* or for *observers*, though these would actually complete what is typically in the last resort a five-dimensional data box. In three dimensions, which is what we can depict here, we shall suppose that on the remaining two dimensions all is held constant at one value—one particular observer and one test stimulus for each response. The typical pairs of score series that are correlated in *P*-technique are shown by the parallel lines in the Attitudes-Occasion facet, and those for the typical *R*-technique in the Attitudes-People facet. (A facet is one slice parallel to some face of the box and constitutes the usual score matrix, for example, people by tests.)

Correlating two attitudes, *x* and *y* in Figure 4-2, on one device over a series of occasions, as shown by the facet to the right in Figure 4-2(*a*), can be altered to correlating a sum of devices as we usually do, by collapsing the devices dimension (a fourth dimension to these, not shown, of course) and running all devices together. (Such a summation over several facets in the fourth dimension is then called a *face* instead of a *facet*.) Most *P*-technique studies have used a short balanced battery of four to six subtest devices to give a single attitude-strength score, just as have most *R*-technique studies.

Figure 4-2(*a*) is introduced primarily to show how the score series correlated in *P*-technique differs from the score series correlated in *R*-technique. The clusters or factors emerging from such correlations show *what interests vary together, from some common cause, over time and circumstance.* Another grid from the data box, in Figure 4-2(*b*), will help to bring out the difference we have already recognized between correlations of devices (all on one attitude) to yield *motivation components* (m.c.'s) and correlations of attitudes (all measures on one device or device battery) to yield *dynamic-structure* (d.s.) factors. The present writer's experience of discussion groups in this area unfortunately shows that students often trip over this difference between m.c. and d.s. factors, failing to notice its real nature; yet for what now follows it is essential that we have it clear. Figure 4-2(*b*) shows that the typical analysis for m.c.'s correlates a pair of devices over a series of people (or occasions) and factors a matrix of correlations from all such pairs. The analysis for dynamic structure (d.s.) factors proceeds by factoring the correlations among *attitudes*. Each attitude may be scored, for the series of persons, either on some single device or on the summed subset that represent a primary m.c., such as α, β, etc., or even a secondary m.c., such as U or I. This distinction in the source of m.c.'s and d.s.'s, whereby they depend respectively on devices of measurement and on attitude elements holds regardless of whether the measures are made over people (*R*-technique) or over occasions (*P*-technique), and that is why the axis to the right in Figure 4-2(*b*) is marked "People or Occasions."

In brief, the alternative of seeking motivation component (m.c.) factors or dynamic structure (d.s.) factors exists both in ordinary *R*-technique and in longitudinal *P*-technique, and which we get will depend only on our choice of variables: devices or attitudes. Incidentally, in neither setting could it at first be taken for granted, a priori, that the same components among motivation-strength measurement devices would appear regardless of the *particular* attitude to which they were applied. Nor, reciprocally, could it be assumed that the same d.s. factors would appear among sets of correlated attitudes regardless of the device or battery by which each was measured. From over 20 years of experiment it has become evident, however, that the same motivation components will appear regardless of the attitude to which the objective devices are applied, and that the same dynamic-structure factors appear regardless of the devices used -provided they are valid at all. Thus Guildford's factors from a conscious-preference measure of interest (though we know it to be not highly valid) still turn out, with cooperative subjects, much the same as those from more objective batteries (Cattell, 1957).

With this preamble we can turn to our next main concern, which is how to locate trait patterns unique to an individual, for example, a clinical patient, in the dynamic modality. Since the only way to discover structure in an individual is to watch covariation of manifestations over times and situations we become involved in the general psychometric problems of studying change scores. These problems arise not only in *P*-technique but in what is described later (Chapter 5) as *dR*-technique, and they concern both the statistical and the experimental difficulties in repeating measures of the same test.

Dynamic structure involves both the motivation component foundation in the actual objective devices used and the structure among attitudes. Doubt was expressed a priori as to whether the devices would remain valid with frequently repeated serial measures. Some could not be adapted to repetition but others could, and a recent factoring (Birkett & Cattell, 1978) over 100 days appears to show that the same motivational components can be recognized in longitudinal (*P*-technique) as in *R*-technique experiments. At the moment, then, experiment is "thinner" here than in older domains of the dynamic calculus and needs extending and checking in theoretically interesting ways. But enough has been done to check this logical necessary principle in making the comparisons.

The question that more immediately excites the interest of the dynamic psychologist is whether (granted that this continued validity of devices against m.c. factor criteria persists into *P*-technique) the attitudes within the individual factor into the same d.s. factors. That is to say, do dynamic structures assume different levels at different times in *P*-technique as, in *R*-technique, they assume different levels among people? The answer is an unequivocal affirmative. In any individual yet examined the same ergic patterns appear as in *P*-technique on another individual and in *R*-technique among people generally. The unique-trait patterns center upon the common pattern. Techniques are not exact enough yet to say whether the slight-to-moderate divergences of pattern usually seen among people express some real individuality of pattern or merely variation due to experimental error. And although the results suggest that there is somewhat more personal uniqueness in the sentiment patterns than the ergic patterns, such sentiment patterns as those for sport, religion, the self-sentiment, and so on, do come out unmistakably in *P*-technique.

As Chapter 5, which develops the theory of states, will argue, this means that the unity initially indicated for ergs and sentiments by *R*-technique now proves to extend to the additional functional unity that derives from their behaving like states as well as traits. This tendency to wax and wane as functional, organic unities has implications, when considered along with other evidence, for understanding the basic nature of ergs and sentiments. It leads to the notion of ergic *tensions* and sentiment *excitations*, and their relation to structures corresponding to and generating them.

4-5. Broader Questions about the Nature of Ergs and Engrams

The firm delineation of the outlines of ergic and sentiment structures by quantitative, objective, and multivariate methods is the strategically indispensable opening campaign for research on human motivation. It ends the more speculative listing of human drives by McDougall, Murray, Freud, and others and offers us a list of ergic tensions checkable by experimental operations. But it is still only the beginning of a scientific dynamics. The dynamic-structure concepts, as we shall develop them and as the reader probably has begun already to relate them to other knowledge, have a greater richness of connotation than is yet given by simple description of the individual-difference and fluctuation patterns discovered.

Questions spring to mind such as: What evidence is there that the ergs are the same in nature and number as those that appear in other mammals? In what way can we consider the ergs to represent innate structures when the attitudes through which we recognize them are obviously acquired? In animal ethology and also in clinical accounts of human "instincts," the definition includes a temporally unfolding *process.* Where is the evidence of such a process here? Is the connection between the ergic tension level in an erg and scores on these varied manifestations in devices as closely demonstrated as we are assuming? Why do *sentiment* structures fluctuate, if they are learned traits rather than physiological appetitive tensions such as ergs may be? Would one perhaps expect sentiments to express themselves more through some m.c.'s, and ergs to express themselves more through m.c.'s of a different nature, instead of about equally, as seems so far implied? Where is the nature-nurture or heritability evidence confirming that the ergic patterns are more innate, or showing, as would be expected, that there is virtually no inheritance for the sentiments?

Regarding the first question, it is methodologically evident that multivariate experiment with animals, showing that what animal experimenters recognize as drives do indeed appear as factors when approached by the factor methods, would strongly support the drive interpretation given to these factors in humans. A step in this direction was made 40 years ago in a remarkably early experiment by E. E. Anderson (1938), who measured a variety of dynamic behavior expressions in rats and showed that they did, indeed, factor to well-known unities of sex, hunger, fear, etcetera (see Cattell, 1930). Haverland (1954) did the same in rats for hunger and thirst. They did not, however, get to examining in animals the equivalent of what we have called motivation components in man. This was left to Cattell, Rican, Schneewind, and Dielman, as part of the general development of the dynamic calculus. In that work (see Cattell & Dielman, 1974) rats were run through a variety of mazes on a variety of ergic deprivations. Correlations were investigated for a variety of dynamic structures because it was necessary to check, as with humans, that motivation components were the same despite changes of ergic goal.

Measuring the traditionally used indicators in animal experiment of motivation strength, for example, speed of running, strength of pushing on goal box door, frequency of lever pressing, and many others, the investigators found 13 primary factors among the motivation indicators, most of which replicated well from maze to maze and motive to motive, for example, for hunger and electric shock. However, by the nature of the content, some five of these were considered to be measures of abilities and only seven showed properties of motivation strength. Three of these were reproduced, for illustration and to show the obtained degree of constancy across mazes, in Table 4-6. It is interesting that seven primaries appear here, as in humans, and a preliminary analysis actually indicates similarly three second orders among them. But it would be premature to speculate on any alignment with the human primaries and secondaries, because virtually none of the actual variables can at present be equated, animal to man, identically. The main conclusion must simply be that the strength of motivation, in rats as in man, is complex, requiring seven primary components and some three secondaries.

Studies on dynamic structure factors in rats were pursued by Weiffenbach on earlier data, and Dielman and the present writer on the above, but because of insufficient support for such novel multivariate approaches from the animal learning grant agencies, these studies have not reached publication stage. Many animal experimenters seem content to indicate by fiat which drive they are testing, and to use measures, such as hours of deprivation of food, that have only moderate validity against the total hunger factor when psychometrically validated. The recent incomplete studies, however, strongly support, as far as they go, the clearer earlier verdict of Anderson that in rats the ergic factors found do correspond to drives as named by animal experimenters and, still better, by ethologists. The gap between the accustomed methods of animal behavior researchers and the new multivariate experimental methods has sadly delayed a thorough demonstration of dynamic, ergic structure in animals, but the pioneer studies above leave little doubt that unitary factors, based on objective m.c. measures of "interest" strength, would yield in mammals the same ergic patterns as are found in humans, and thus support the "instinctual" nature of the latter patterns.

Proof that the ergic factors in man are relatively innate, and that the sentiment patterns are relatively acquired, has not yet been sought by the familiar methods for investigating nature-nurture ratios and heritabilities in human traits. Moreover, we need to clarify hypotheses before such research, because the usual trait model does not apply in its simple form. Whereas with intelligence, for example, we deal with a relatively constant trait measurement, the inheritance of which we seek to investigate, it turns out that ergic tension levels are varying with circumstances all the time from day to day. If we proceed on the assumption from common observation that some people have a stronger sex drive, or are more timid, or more gregarious, than others, then we imply a personal trait level, presumably

TABLE 4—6.   Typical Motivation Components in Motivation-Strength Measures Used in Rats

Variable Number	Variable Description	Loadings in Mazes		
		1	2	3
1.	Urgency-Distractability[a](factor II, maze 1; factor XI, maze 2; factor XII, maze 3)			
5	Faster pushing time	0.81	0.23	–[b]
4	Less susceptibility to distraction	0.58	0.46	0.62
2	Faster running time in long alley	0.36	0.52	0.04
22	Greater temporal efficiency with which intended action is performed	0.57	–0.01	–0.03
24	Greater excess of presses on bar	–0.21	–0.09	–0.15
25	More pushing and shifting activity in delayed response period	–0.28	–0.09	–0.07
6	Less dallying before paper barrier	0.08	0.49	0.67
1	More pushing against door	–0.08	–0.39	–0.04
31	Less total grooming	0.03	0.31	0.10
13	Less time in double bar press chamber	0.07	0.28	–[b]
35	Greater fraternizing in goal box	–0.11	–0.25	–0.09
2.	Goal-box activity (factor V, maze 1; factor II, maze 2; factor VI, maze 3)			
27	More activity in goal box	0.37	0.59	0.04
1	Less pushing against start box door	–0.33	–0.23	–0.07
25	Greater pushing and shifting activity in delayed response period	0.76	0.02	–0.04
34	Greater force on door to goal box	0.56	0.18	0.29
33	Greater force on door in long alley	0.03	0.38	–[b]
28	Less backtracking in door choice compartment	–0.12	–0.55	–0.32
21	More entirely premature pushes on goal box door	0.06	0.30	0.36
26	More fiddling on last door push	–0.14	–0.20	0.09
3.	Purposefulness (factor III, maze 1; factor X, maze 2; factor IV, maze 3)			
32	Smaller total number of turnbacks	–0.35	–0.68	–[b]
35	Greater fraternizing in goal box	0.29	0.27	0.04
31	Less total grooming	–0.21	–0.34	–0.08
8	Less dallying after paper barrier	–0.67	–0.18	–0.13
4	Less susceptibility to distraction	–0.31	–0.10	0.11
26	Less fiddling on last door push	–0.30	–0.01	0.04
30	Less backtracking in single bar press	–0.19	–0.35	0.00
19	Smaller number of premature door pushes	0.07	0.31	–0.11
6	Fewer wrong pushes in multiple door choice compartment	–0.08	–0.26	–0.69

[a]Note that in relation to the original article (Cattell & Dielman, 1974) the direction of labels in this factor has been reflected to read correctly for urgency rather than for distractability.

[b]This indicates that this given measure was not used in the particular research listed.

to be obtained by averaging for each person the ergic tension scores on the given erg over many occasions. It is to these averaged scores that heritability analysis would have to be applied. There is the further difficulty that because some of the same attitudes contribute to both sentiment and erg scores, and, indeed, *every* attitude has both genetic (ergic) and acquired components, no sum of ergically well-loaded attitude scores will deliver an ergic measure free of environmentally acquired variance. Summing many attitudes with an erg in common will make trivial the contamination with any one sentiment; but it will not make trivial the contribution of the acquired element in every attitude. The ordinary nature-nurture variance analysis on this measurement basis would therefore not be expected to show measured ergs as wholly genetic or measured sentiments as wholly environmental.

The usual MAVA (Multiple Abstract Variance Analysis) or other trait-heritability-determining methods thus need supplementation by other modes of observation and reasoning. One such supplement here is cross-cultural research. According to our hypothesis, this should show, in factoring the same (translated) set of attitude variables, that the ergic patterns remain much the same in number and content, whereas the sentiment patterns should alter substantially with cultures and in ways that can be shown to be consistent with the differences in institutional patterns, as mapped by the sociologist. Another source of evidence would be the typical age curves of growth of ergic and sentiment scores, which in one case should correlate more with physiological signs, for example, the sex hormone, and in the other with cumulative learning-situation experiences. Yet another approach, though only a fragmentary treatment of what is proposed holistically above, would be to see if attitudes with higher loadings on an erg show higher heritabilities than those with lower (and reciprocally for sentiments).

At the present moment it must be confessed that the main argument for ergic patterns being relatively innate is that the patterns as psychologically interpreted align in number and content with the instincts that ethologists, from McDougal to Lorenz and Tinbergen, name in the higher mammals. The attitudes that load substantially on an erg are those that we know from everyday observation lead to satisfaction of a biological or innate goal. Yet we recognize that these particular attitude paths to an ergic goal differ somewhat in different cultures; such sociological variations are still wholly compatible with the goal itself being innate. That is to say, the consummatory behaviors by which we recognize and define a goal satisfaction remain constant but are led up to by different rituals and role behaviors in different cultures. The multivariate experimental evidence favoring this conclusion is that attitudes (representing courses of action) that are more highly loaded on the ergic factor are those *closer to the ergic goal consummatory behavior.* On the other hand, especially in samples of peoples mixed in their subcultures, the more distal attitudes, that is, those more remote from the biological goal, are comparatively low in loadings on the ergic factor concerned. These phenomena can be more precisely discussed when the concepts of *subsidiation* and the *dynamic lattice* have been reached in Volume 2.

While dealing with the difference of ergs and sentiments it is appropriate to examine two concepts fairly common in the literature, which have a vaguely intermediate status between ergs and sentiments and which have never been adequately defined operationally: complexes and secondary drives. Clinicians have defined a *complex* essentially as a set of attitudes (which includes symptoms) organized about some object, but differing from a sentiment in that the subject is not consciously aware of the logical connections and subsidiations (the latter will be described shortly) between the courses of action and the goal. Though commonly described as unique to the individual, the patterns of some complexes, such as Oedipus and inferiority complexes, would be expected, statistically, to be common (as also would be Jung's archetypes). If complexes are of this nature, we should expect the factoring of objective attitude and symptom-strength measures nevertheless, to reveal their presence. For *consciousness* of connection is not necessary to the establishment of connection by correlation evidence. Consequently, we can logically expect that unique complexes should be revealed by *P*-technique and common complexes by *R*-technique just as with any other dynamic structure. They should be revealed, at least, if unconsciousness of the purposeful connections does not *essentially* interfere with the functional covariation of strengths that the factor analysis normally detects in the particular motivation component measures used for the behavioral elements, as just argued. However there could be some differences in emphasis of the m.c.'s in the dynamic structure measurement. For instance, it is just conceivable, if the tentative naming of β, γ, and α as ego, superego, and id is correct, that structures of complexes would appear among attitudes measured by alpha, delta and epsilon devices, but not by batteries using only β and γ devices.

Because only a few leading research clinicians have as yet caught hold of dynamic calculus methods, evidence is scant, but instances have appeared that seem to justify the conclusion that, in *P*-technique at least, patterns emerge that can be set aside from sentiments as a different species of acquired trait from a straightforward sentiment.

If there are thus two species of acquired traits, sentiments and complexes, then a term is needed for the genus. For some years Gross's term *engram* has been adopted for this in our writings. Thus, just as ergic tension factors will be represented in equations by E, so the acquired patterns, representing either sentiments or complexes, will be represented by M for engram (see equation 4-3 below).

The term "secondary drives," on the other hand is an ambiguous and unfortunate one. As sometimes used, it corresponds to the secondary reinforcement offered by an acquired incentive. About this use, as referring to an operationally definable and existing entity, there can be no doubt. But it is also used to refer to ergs such as gregariousness, curiosity, and even fear, and to denote other nonviscerogenic drives, on the assumption that they are derived from more primary (primary patently meaning only *viscerogenic*) drives such as hunger, thirst, and pain avoidance, by operant conditioning. If such existed, we should for one thing expect them, through the haphazardness of daily life conditionings, to be very poorly defined as common traits, whereas in fact these alleged "secondary drives" emerge factor analytically as clearly as the more viscerogenic and even appetitive "primary" patterns. Thus, since as revealed either factor analytically or in other ways, their nature as "secondary" drives has not been demonstrated, we conclude that in any fundamental sense secondary drive is a superfluous concept.

The "secondary" idea seems to have developed as part of the reluctance of the physiological psychologist to regard as tangible or real any innate drive for which he or she could not demonstrate (at this early stage!) a gross physiological substrate. There is, however, no real evidence that such ergs as curiosity, gregariousness, or self-assertion are less innate and less built into the physiology of the central nervous system than hunger or sex, in which the physiology is visceral and more evident. On the other hand, if we want to sketch a preliminary taxonomy of ergs, the classification into *viscerogenic* and *nonviscerogenic* ergs advanced by both Murray and the present writer is a meaningful first step, though the line is not sharp. A so-called secondary drive is thus actually a primary that happens to be nonviscerogenic. Another useful dichotomy, not entirely to be aligned with the first, is that between *appetitive* and *nonappetitive* ergs. An appetitive erg is simply defined as one that if not used shows an increasing reactivity ("demand to be used"), whereas a nonappetitive erg has its tension level altered only by external stimulation. Appetitive ergs are most obvious among viscerogenic ergs, but it is conceivable that such a nonviscerogenic erg as fear is nevertheless appetitive, as shown by the danger seeking we see in mountaineers, surf riders, and others. In short, the two classifications make a fourfold table.

4-6. The Analysis of Attitude Response Potential into Defined Ergic and Engram Contributions

The discovery by multivariate experiment that any wide array of interests, measured objectively by response potential in various forms, resolve into two types of underlying unitary structures, needs to be expressed in a precise model for any particular interest. That model should allow us both to predict the interest on any occasion and understand the ways in which it is likely to change. Pending further research we take the simplest mathematical formulation, namely, a linear additive equation such as factor analysis has used for abilities and personality traits. Since the use of the symbol I for interest strength might get confused with I for integrated component we will use d, meaning dynamic strength (in whatever composite of components may be indicated). This is lower case to distinguish from a broad dynamic interest. Indeed, if

$$d_{ij} = b_{je1} E_{1i} + \cdots + b_{jep} E_{pi} + b_{je} E_{ji} + b_{jm1} M_{1i} + \cdots \\ + b_{jmq} M_{qi} + b_{jm} M_{ji} + b_{jx} X_i \tag{4-3}$$

the extreme reflexologist were right *all* our interests would be largely specifics—the response potentials from quite particular, isolated reinforcements. The size and importance of specifics has yet to be accurately evaluated, but results to this point suggest they are no larger than with abilities and personality variables, that is, less important than the latter by about 2 to 1 in variance contribution. *Unique* factors are, of course, conceptually different (p. 26), and X, error, is different from the specifics, E_j and M_j.

The assignment of a specific to the ergic modality, by E_j, indicates an openness to experiment on this; but it seems likely that these are few. Possibly an innate tendency to fear of, say, black spiders or snakes or the dark, could have some independence of the natural strength of the fear erg, and in the sex erg some putatively innate specificities are said to exist. If so, we may anticipate ultimately that our ergic primary factors have various d's under them in a factorial hierarchy. Statistically, of course, the d's initially found may be expectedly with wider search to aggregate to further common factors trait D (an erg E, or a sentiment, M), since it is a narrow attitude. Like any response behavior it could have subscripts h

(the stimulus), i (the individual), j (the nature of the attitude course of action) and k (the ambient situation) but initially we give it only j and i. The E's here $(E_1, E_2, \ldots, E_p)$ represent the ergic tension levels of the p human ergs that enter most behavior in greater or less degree where the E's represent a series of particular ergic tensions, of which there are p in number. The M's as before represent the individual's strength of development of q different sentiments. X is a broad error of measurement factor. The b's are, of course, the behavioral indices or loadings. They have m or e subscripts according to whether they apply to engrams (sentiments, etc.) or ergs, and also numbers (1 through p for ergs and 1 through q for the q sentiments).

Like most specification equations this admits specific factors, written M_j for the engram, and E_j for the erg. There is no question about the need for M_j terms for the various j's. For the average person an interest in the folk songs of Khatmandu would play a small and narrow and negligible part among his broader sentiments.

As we go deeper, in Volume 2, into motivation and structured learning theory it will be necessary to recognize that the b's (which define the situation) are composites of what the situation does to *provoke* this and that dynamic trait and also of what scope it habitually gives to the given response path to satisfaction. For the present, however, there are concepts needing priority, and we shall treat the behavioral index values (the b's) as loadings or correlations of the ergic tension with the level of the given d_j expression.

More immediately important, in general personality theory, is to realize that the D terms (E's and M's) have to play their part along with traits of ability and temperament modality in estimating the score on the given response by the specification equation above. What the relative b weights will be will depend on the way in which the given performance j is measured, for example, how well he does it (ability), how strongly he does it (dynamic), and how steadily or frequently he does it (personality). (See Cattell & Warburton 1967.) In the present chapter, however, we have agreed to concentrate on d_j's, that is, on how much he *wants* to do so and so. Consistently with this it is reasonable to simplify the specification equation in abstraction to the E and M terms as in equation (4-3) above.

Even at this early stage one should note that the E's, if not the M's, are not to be expected to be as unchanging as traits already dealt with. The P-technique results below, in fact, show that ergic tension levels do alter considerably with time and circumstance (Cattell & Cross, 1952; Birkett & Cattell, 1979).

Although d, the strength of interest in the attitude course, could be measured by some aspects of the actual overt everyday life behavior, it has been measured here mainly by test scores on motivation-strength components, which in any case would cover the former. Now we know in fact that the battery of, say, half a dozen devices used to get an objective measure of d is typically not homogeneous, but consists of distinctly measurable U and I components, or is even separable into the seven primaries α, β, γ, and so on. The theoretical possibility strikes one at this point that the distinct motivational components might correspond to the E and M contributions. Specifically E's might appear largely in U component measures and M's in I components. Thus in examining further the nature of E's and M's we may be returning, in a new way, to consideration of the nature of motivation components. However, up to the limits of precision of present experiment, the evidence forces us to conclude that even if the d measure is by a single device, both E's and M's still appear, though of course our measurements may at present be insufficiently pure. But regardless of whether the d measurement is a single device, for example, a GSR response, or a group of devices constituting a primary m.c., or, yet again, a second-order m.c., that is, a U- or I-component battery, it would not, with the present level of technical advance, constitute a "pure" U or I, or α, β, or γ, measure and so could not be reliable used to test the above theory. Consequently the *possibility* still exists either that only an E or an M term would appear, respectively, from a pure U or I measure or that each E and M itself has two parts: a U and an I part. For caution, it seems desirable, in refined work, to add α, β, etcetera, or U, I, etcetera, subscripts to the d, the E's, and the M's as obtained from any experiment to show that all the motivation and dynamic structures involved are being measured through the particular set of devices chosen in that experiment. (Equation 4-3 is not so written at the moment.)

Indeed, in formulating hypotheses about the nature of E's and M's, U's and I's, it is desirable always to scrutinize more closely the nature of the actual motivation strength measures used. In rats (Table 4-6) the motivation-component measures are virtually all *behavior measures in the actual situation.* In initial validating research with humans, some actual behaviors *in situ,* such as time and money spent on a course of action, were included as criteria. Both there and in more recent work (Cattell, Lawlis, McGill, & McGraw 1978) they proved to occupy the same factor space as the laboratory measures. However, the majority of later experiments have dealt only with the subset of laboratory responses, for example, word association, fluency, and physiological responses, such as GSR and muscle tension. These are measured as responses of the subject to stimuli symbolically representing the live stimulus and the course of action attached to it. For example, measuring an interest in playing football, the experimenter presents a picture of a player scoring a touchdown; an interest in photography is measured by memory for features of a series of cameras. What we have defined as "interest in a course of action," therefore, rests on measures of reactivity that might be called response *potential*. There is in fact at this stage no reason why this concept should not be equated with Hull's response potential. Certain difficulties in building a simple bridge to the experiments and concepts in the reflexological models largely based on animal research will be handled in a later, qualifying discussion in Volume 2.

One such difficulty in conceptual alignment with reflex findings lies in the sheer difference of scale between our macroscopic measurement of whole attitudes, on the one hand, later put together in ergs and sentiments, and the microscopic single-reflex act, on the other, in much of the Hull-Spence and Skinnerian formulations. Any attitude as we have defined it is a whole set of organized stimuli and responses of the kind used by reflexologists. Even some of our smallest operational units, taken separately, for example, changing the lens of a camera, going to the store to buy such and such film, are, as elements, still at a higher organizational level than the reflex response on which the great bulk of laboratory learning theory has been built. Moreover, an attitude is not just a unified aggregate of stimuli and a related collection of responses, but a set of built-in *sequences* of stimuli and responses. Nevertheless, there is no reason to suppose that this macro-micro difference of scale should affect the principles of measurement and prediction involved.

What might cause some problems is the proper sampling of the smaller stimulus-response units in what is a sequential and hierarchical structure in the typical attitude. As far as the attitude units themselves are concerned the dynamic lattice (see Volume 2) presents a rational model for their relations. Perhaps we need not worry about the part-whole relations in attitudes themselves because the consistency of the empirical results encourages the conclusion that the intrinsic nature of the devices that prove validly to measure an attitude is such that they directly or indirectly record *response potential for the attitude as a whole*. That is, they indicate the level of readiness of the individual, under smaller or larger symbolic stimuli representing the total situation, to reach the threshold of response in the given course of action (or, under constant stimuli, the speed and strength with which the individual will respond in overcoming obstacles).

From this point on we shall proceed on the tentative theory that there does exist some relation between U and I motivation components on the one hand and E and M dynamic traits on the other, in the sense that ergs would contribute largely U components to d and sentiments largely I. On existing data this could only be tested on the assumption that, in U measures of a collection of attitudes, the E factor variance would be larger and the M smaller, and vice versa for I measures. Strictly, the mean magnitudes, not the variances, should be compared, but the practical restriction in the ordinary factor model (as contrasted with *real base true zero factoring*, Cattell, 1972) compelled us to examine the question by assuming the higher mean would usually produce the higher variance. Although higher U-component variance was found associated with higher E contribution to attitude variance, the result did not reach a convincing statistical significance. In any case, our hypothesis is not one calling for complete alignment, because in dealing later with the phenomena of arousal we shall hypothesize a difference of U and I components between the need strength and the arousal strength. The relation of U to E and of I to M is one of the most crucial experimental issues awaiting research in the dynamic calculus.

Another expectation by most psychologists who have thought over the problem is that the dynamic-structure factors that are ergs should show more function fluctuation from day to day than the scores on sentiments. Again, there is a tendency this way in the data so far available (including P- and dR-studies), but it certainly does not show sentiments as having a trait-like constancy to the degree found in ability or temperament traits. Indeed, in the theory that follows, we have abandoned the expectation of such a degree of constancy. Finally, it must be added that attempts to understand E and M contribution differences in terms of certain of the primaries (α, β, γ, δ, etc.), rather than of the secondaries (U and I), have also not yet given clear results, though sentiments *do* seem rather more validly measured by the β component. Incidentally, before concluding that any of these theories are untenable, we should recognize that experiment in this area is complex conceptually and psychometrically. For example, it is not always meaningful, as in many areas, to use standard scores. Reasons of space at this point prevent us from clarifying further those complexities, which we will approach later.

Meanwhile, the correctness of the concepts in differentiating ergs and sentiments can also be evaluated in relatively broad terms. Notably, we would ask whether the ergic tension levels scored at a given moment stand where we would expect in terms of the stimuli impinging on subjects and the reduction of tension by the degree of gratification the subjects are currently experiencing. Similarly, we would ask whether sentiment levels stand where we would expect in relation to the length and intensity of learning that the individuals concerned have experienced. For the existence of a correlated set of variables defining a sentiment must be due to a reinforcement schedule that, on each occasion of reward, tends to reward *all* attitude variables in the sentiment about equally; and no others. Thus individuals simultaneously high on frequency and intensity of reward will have acquired *all* the attitudes to a greater degree, which is what produces the observed correlations among these attitudes across the range of the population.

The initial multivariate attack on structure was a nonmanipulative one, leaving variation to be produced by existing environmental events, that is, the difference of stimulation and learning among subjects and over occasions. But as soon as the unitary traits were revealed on this basis, multivariate experiment turned at that strategic point to manipulative experiment. For the good methodologist will have noted that manipulative procedures are not limited to bivariate classical experiment. The results of experiments by Adelson (1952) on thirst manipulation; Kawash, Dielman, and Cattell (1972) on fear arousal; De Young, Cattell, and Kawash (1978) on hunger (coeds fasting for two days); and Cattell, Kawash, and De Young (1972) on sex stimuli have shown definitely that some or most of the ergs behave as would be expected from the theory that what we measure at any moment is an ergic tension simultaneously present in all attitudes loaded on the erg.

At this point we hypothesize that the measure of ergic tension (E) is not just appetite and arousal but is mixed with contributions from the learning history, that is, the frequency and magnitude of reward in the given particular attitudes. A developed statement of the model, however, is left to the second volume, on learning theory, since clarifying structure is the first concern here. In some studies, that is, those of Adelson on thirst and Kawash and Dielman on fear stimuli, the results are not always as clear as one would hope, because the main measuring instruments (The Motivational Analysis Test, MAT and the School Motivational Analysis test, SMAT) have the insensitiveness of all new and short instruments, and because human subjects cannot be exposed to stimuli and deprivations as strong as those in animal experiments. One result is reasonably clear, that manipulation of gratification produces changes in ergic-tension level somewhat more strongly in the U, unintegrated, component of measurement, and that past practice and present cognitive stimulation connected with the past practice, at least in some cases, produces relatively strong changes in the integrated component, I, of the dynamic trait.

The remaining evidence that ergs and sentiments found by factor analysis are what they are conceived to be in the present theory comes from quite different sources than factor-analytic ones, namely, from criterion associations in the industrial, educational, and clinical use of the MAT and the SMAT. These tests designed as measures of specific ergs and sentiments for manipulative and other experiment are indeed the first factored and standardized batteries using objective tests. They measure some five ergs and five sentiments, yielding separate U and I component scores for each. The criterion relations can be studied in detail where they are published (Sweney, 1969; Lawlis, 1968, 1971; Cattell & Child, 1975). But such findings as that executives are high on career and self sentiments; that military cadets are high on the assertive and low on the fear erg; and that the chronically unemployed are high on the fear (insecurity) erg and low on integrated but high on unintegrated career sentiment give further support from the grosser criteria of everyday life for the theories developed around the discovery of the dynamic-structure factors.

4-7. Summary

1. The exploration of dynamic structure by multivariate experiment—which is alone capable of revealing complex pattern structures—has been described. Such research, to avoid the quagmire of evaluation by inventories, and to be comparable and integrate with laboratory research on motivation, (a) must be based on *objective* behavioral devices for measuring the strength of whatever stimulus-response unit is chosen, and (b) must settle on definite situation-response units of suitable size within the hierarchy of everyday life behavior the structure of which is to be mapped. The *attitude*, defined afresh in stimulus-response terms, is chosen as the ideal unit brick in building the form of the dynamic structure.

2. The reflex as measured in the laboratory is a unit of altogether too small a size for human-dynamic-structure investigation. The *attitude* is more appropriate, somewhat refined from the everyday meaning; its definition here is different from the specialized "ballot box—for-or-against" attitude stereotyped by sociologists and some social psychologists. An attitude is defined by an explicit paradigm as containing: a stimulus situation in the life space; a desire to respond (act or perform) with a given strength of interest (or an actual response) in a given course of action of given strength, usually involving, as means to an end, some object (but not a "for-or-against" object).

3. An extensive experimental survey of a wide array of psycho-

logically accepted measurable manifestations of the strength of an individual's interest in a course of action shows that some seven or eight primary motivation components (α, β, δ, etc.) suffice to account for the observed covariance. These primaries factor again to two, or possible three, second-order factors. These motivation component (m.c.) factors are the same in nature regardless of the dynamic area content of the attitude interest involved. The two larger second-orders have been named unintegrated (U) and integrated (I) because of the relative emphasis on physiological and "I want" expressions in the former and cognitive, controlled, and experienced expressions in the latter.

4. Once definition of these objective (m.c.) factors was achieved, the validity of any given device as an objective interest measure could be evaluated against any or all of the components (concept validy), and measures of known validity thus set up for any single attitude. By factoring a wide sample of attitudes covering the interest space of the typical member of our culture, some 20 dynamic structures have been located. Dynamic-structure factors can clearly be distinguished from motivation-component factors because they derive from a facet of the data box orthogonal to the facets that yield m.c. factors.

5. By the common content of the loaded attitudes in any dynamic-structure factor it is seen that the factors fall into two types, which have been defined as *ergs* and *sentiments*. The former have the number and nature of mammalian instincts; the latter correspond to patterns learned from cultural institutions. The acquired patterns are generically called *engrams*—to cover both sentiments and complexes and because there are clinical reasons for considering the latter a different species of engram, although they should show up in factoring among other engrams in dynamic-structure factors.

6. Like the other source traits studied, dynamic-structure traits can be either common or unique. The longitudinal study of attitude strengths by P-technique—or, for that matter change-score analysis by dR-technique—shows essentially the same patterns as study by R-technique. P-technique should be ideal for studying the structure of unique complexes as well as unique sentiments.

7. If the ergic factors are what they are believed to be—the human equivalents of animal instinctual patterns—factoring of animal motivational behavior should yield factors corresponding to their instinct patterns. Factoring of animal motivation components but not of dynamic structures has been thoroughly done in rats and reveals indubitably some seven primary and two or three secondary components—the same number as in humans. An equally thorough analysis of dynamic structures still remains to be done. On the

existing evidence, by Anderson, Dielman, Schneewind, and others, as yet not completely published, the argument is very strong that the factors found in rats *do* correspond to hunger, sex, fear, and so on. Proof of innateness of the patterns in humans is not easily given, however, by the usual nature-nurture analysis by MAVA and other procedures, because ergic tensions fluctuate. The inference that these factors are expressions of innate structures rests more on circumstantial evidence. This includes the similarity of the number and nature of the patterns to those in the primates, the tendency of high loadings to fall on more innate and consummatory behaviors, and the cross-cultural persistence of the patterns.

8.   No evidence is found for a class of "secondary drives" derived by learning from primary drives. The notion of "secondary drives" may arise from a misperception of the distinct nature of sentiments or an assumption that nonviscerogenic primary drives are not innate. In engrams (including sentiments), a common reinforcement schedule probably accounts for the unity of the factor. Each element of the pattern is "secondary" to some drive or other, as an acquired expression thereof, but a sentiment is not a single drive.

9.   In spite of the difference of scale, whereby an attitude is a sequential integration of the small stimulus-response reflex units studied by the reflexologist, there is every reason to believe that the mode of measurement is essentially the same for attitudes as for conditioned reflexes and that the strength of an attitude corresponds to the response-potential concept of Hull and others. This response potential is a function of the present momentary excitation strength of the underlying need, which a psychologist would expect to be measured largely in the U component measures and of the frequencies of past reinforcement. The latter would be expected to be largely represented by the sentiment strength and presumably best measured by I-component measures. The measures of E's and M's seem not to be totally composed, respectively, of U and I components, as theory might require. The reason probably is that each of the attitudes of which an E or an M is a weighted sum unavoidably has both components, so that a sum of such attitudes, whether for an E or an M, has mixed U and I contributions.

10.   Manipulative studies with humans, in which stimulation is increased or current gratification reduced, show that each ergic-tension factor acts as a unitary whole and rises and falls—with some exceptions—as theory would require it to do with such stimulation and gratification.

11.   The fact that a unitary ergic-tension state, as a general response-potential pattern, exists for each of the ergs corresponding to mammalian and primate instincts strengthens the theory that there

exist innate predispositions in man to reactivities of certain kinds. The actual attitude elements in the factor patterns, however, are couched in expressions that take the form provided by the culture. The fact that the loadings of behaviors on these factors become higher as one moves closer to consummatory behaviors such as eating, necessarily much the same in all cultures, supports the theory that these ergic-tension unities are themselves innately given.

12. Nonmanipulative experiment relating dynamic-structure factor scores on the MAT and SMAT to job, school achievement, clinical treatment, and life situations shows virtually complete agreement with what would be inferred from the hypotheses interpreting these factors as ergs and sentiments, that is, as having the specific natures inductively reached from factor-pattern content.

NOTES

[1] As often demonstrated in the history of science, progress does not come about mainly through the victory of one side of an ancient debate, as in some Hegelian thesis and antithesis, but through an entirely new alternative. So here, choice is not traditional clinical versus traditional bivariate "brass instrument" experiment, but opens into the new avenue of multivariate experiment, fitted to analyzing influences in multiply determined behavior by quantitative methods. Furthermore, the most fruitful direction is not that of checking clinical theories by experimental methods, which, as Eysenck implies, may be shaping chemical tests to test theories from alchemy, but in building new theories from multivariate research per se. Parenthetically, the clinician has some justification for criticism of the bivariate, manipulative experimentalist's fixation on sensory perception, cognitive and reflexological animal learning, and of the psychometrist's arrest at the boundaries of the ability field. The latter impotence is evident in the last decade in the tendency to try to get personality as "style" in familiar ability tests, instead of inventing true personality T-data—measures.

[2] Doubtless there are differences in various parameters between old attitudes versus recent attitudes; attitudes conscious and explicit versus attitudes logically present but of which the subject has never been aware; conscious attitudes versus attitudes that are blocked from consciousness; and attitudes frequently expressed and exercised versus those kept under constant inhibition. These differences have not been investigated in the immediate dynamic calculus framework, but are more adequately discussed in Volume 2.

[3] Even before experimental work, McDougall did a far more penetrating analysis of the frustration-pugnacity hypothesis than, for example, Dollard and Doob and others who wrote of McDougall's original (1932) theory afresh under the title of frustration-aggression. However, it is symptomatic of the remarkable number of errors in psychology in crediting original concepts (perhaps because of lack of historical depth), of which Schoenemann has recently complained, that the exponents of the coarser, more confused, aggression concepts seem to have received, popularly, the credit for the more subtly conceived pugnacity theory.

CHAPTER **5**

STATES AND PROCESSES:
MODULATION THEORY

5-1. Primary Source States by *P*-Technique

Every practicing psychologist—indeed every intelligent observer of human nature and human history—realizes that the *state* of a person at a given moment determines his or her behavior as much as do his or her traits. [1] In spite of this, it is only in the last 20 years that a theoretical model for investigating moods and dynamic states has been worked out in psychology. And it is only in the very last decade that research on a clear model and methodology has provided the means—in the form of valid scales and batteries—to measure states and their changes. Under states we initially include emotional states, dynamic states of desire, states of fatigue, moods of depression and elation, and so on. And psychophysiological research tells us that in most cases some physiological variables will be part of the psychological state response pattern, that is, the unity of response pattern will generally be at once behavioral, introspective and physiological.

An introduction to the problem of states and a brief sketch of the model to handle them have been given in the general perspective on taxonomy in Chapter 1. Some slight repetition is necessary here. *States* such as anxiety, depression, fatigue, and guilt, which are at first of interest mainly to clinicians, and *processes*, which are of interest to learning theorists, ethologists, and developmental psychologists, are part of the same model, a definition of the first being a precondition for defining the second, which is in general terms a *state sequence*. Here we begin, therefore, with states. [2]

If we take as the first operational definition of a state dimension—to be refined later—that it exists as *a direction of common variation over time* in a number of variables, then *P*-technique and *dR*-technique are the initially indispensable methods for finding a state. Later we may add to the definition that the expressions of the state not only *covary over time* but that they *have other characteristics of a single response pattern*, that is, that they arise from a single external or internal stimulus and *may be associated with hormonal, autonomic, or other physiological covariants*.

In the purely psychological aspects of state study, experiments with humans have been more important and relevant than those with animals because the latter obviously must omit all introspective evidence on feelings. However, the definition of states is rooted in behavioral reactivities, with the introspection as associated epiphenomena. As far as the initial recognition of state-change dimensional directions is concerned, it has not been necessary with humans to begin with the manipulative type of experiment, that is, aiming to *stimulate* state responses, because everyday life provides plenty of stimuli that change a person's moods naturally and over a wide spectrum. Instead, the first aim has properly been a taxonomic one—to find out what the totality of dimensions of mood change may be—and this is best done by taking natural change in the varieties of everyday life situations. *After* the unitary reaction patterns are recognized, listed, and measured, research strategy suggests it will then be strategic to begin finding the stimuli in various cultures that characteristically trigger these internal response patterns.

Indeed, to begin with, psychologists do not even have to commit themselves to that part of the conception that says emotional states are internally preset or innate psychophysiological patterns. We simply can be descriptive and say that certain behaviors, feelings, and physiological changes for some reason go together. The appearance of such a pattern must have a cause, but a response to an external stimulus is, after all, only one kind of causal effect. Nevertheless, it does actually turn out that many states have the character of a built-in response of the organism at the hypothalamic and autonomic level. The procedure in finding and simply describing what things go together requires only measurement and recording over time, as shown in Figure 5-1. Figure 5-1 is deliberately made rather more complicated than the introductory figure on p. 30 in Chapter 1 in order to show the hopelessness of trying to disentangle such a twisted skein by eye alone!

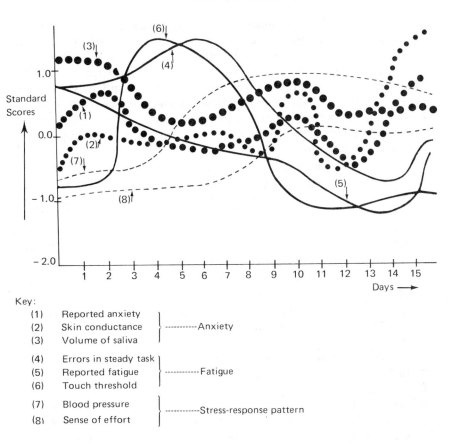

Figure 5-1. Basis of the *P*-technique method locating independent dimensions of state variations.

Following by eye the common curves in plots is indeed an initially attractive and simple way of recognizing covariation, but it turns out to be ultimately confusing and technically inadequate. The new development known as *P*-technique (single person factoring) begins in practice by taking, say, 30 state-expressing variables and measuring them every day (or hour) on one person for, say, 200 occasions. Then the experimenter calculates the correlation co-efficients over this series of 200 occasions for the 30 variables, in all possible pairs. From this 30 × 30 correlation matrix, just as with the corresponding symmetrical triangular matrix when 30 variables are correlated in *R*-technique over 200 people, we can find underlying functional unities in either of two ways: First, we look for correlation clusters, each one of which we can call a *surface state* because it is the analogue of a surface trait in *R*-technique.

Second, we can factor analyze the matrix and find the number of independent dimensions of change—states as defined above— necessary to account for all the observed covariations. The second way—which seeks the *source state*—is more scientifically attractive because, as stated in Chapter 1 and shown abundantly elsewhere (Cattell, 1946, 1966), correlation clusters cannot be uniquely sorted by objective, nonarbitrary methods, whereas factors that meet simple-structure or confactor[3] criteria can be regarded as corresponding to functional unities.

Although by analogy with traits these unique *dimensions* should be called *source states*, we shall henceforth speak simply of *states*— unitary "source" being implied. Strictly, and whenever ambiguity might arise, we shall speak of state *axes or dimensions*, for any particular state is a *point* in time fixed by projections on such axes. Furthermore, any particular complex mood or surface state can now be stated as a particular composite of these source states. Technically, the state definition will be a vector, expressed either geometrically, as in Figure 5-2, or as a series of numbers each corresponding to a projection on a defined state axis. In fact, what McDougall and others described as "secondary or derived emotions," relative to primary ergic emotions, can be expressed precisely in all their subtlety and complexity as mixtures of these primaries. An enormous variety of psychological states thus can be accounted for, just as the full spectrum of the artist's palette can be derived from only three primaries. However, if our research toward understanding the particular "natural history" of each state dimension is to be fruitful, it is extemely important that the factor-analytic procedures pull out the correct patterns, by *P*- and *dR*-techniques, as discussed in Section 5-2.

5-2.   The Relations of States as Found by *P*-, *dR*-, and Chain *P*-techniques

It will be seen that *P*-technique permits no trait variance to be confounded with state variance, because all measures are on the same person and over too short a period, normally, for his traits to change. It offers a clean slate for uncontaminated measures of state change. As to the state dimensions actually discovered by this technique, it is methodologically to be note that the observational data base has been as broadly conceived and pursued as in the personality sphere that was used for traits. Thus the observations rest on ratings (*L*-data), questionnaires (*Q*-data), and objective

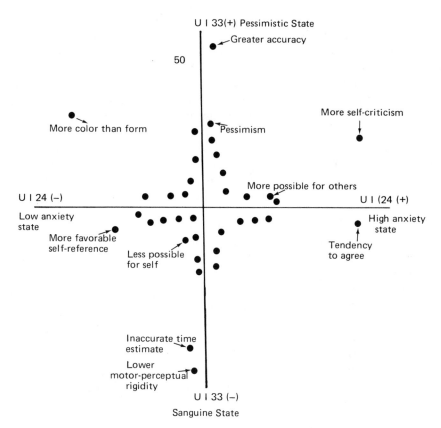

Figure 5-2. The representation of source-state dimensions by factor axes and derived emotional states by vectors.

tests (*T*-data). They have produced evidence on both general states, as we may call them, such as depression, anxiety, joy, fatigue, and on ergic states, which involve dynamic desires and emotions, such as fear, lust, anger, curiosity, pity. These latter common emotions are considered in our theory, as in McDougall (1932), William James (1910), Tinbergen (1947), and others, to accompany the dynamic ergic "instinctual" expressions of primates and higher mammals. Such emotions are probably normal accompaniments of what we have called ergic tension, and, at any rate, have a one-to-one parallelism with various specific needs of a dozen or more distinct ergs.

After initial research confirmed the psychological meaningfulness of the patterns of state change obtained by *P*-technique the next conceptual issue concerned what degree of constancy of pattern was to be expected across people and across methods. Would the loading pattern of, say, anxiety or fatigue come out the *same* from a *P*-technique on Jones as a *P*-technique on Smith? The experimental answer was given in the early replications a decade ago, to the effect that these patterns are indeed very similar and converge on the same central pattern for different people. This supports the hypothesis of innate reaction patterns, physiologically and experientially similar from person to person. The contrary theory—that everyone's emotional patterns are peculiar to himself—has been put forward as a hypothesis at various times, notably by the Lacey's (1959) in their physiological experiments. They and others claim patterns have a different quality according to the stimulus stituation that provoked them.

Some debate here arises from sheer confusion of what surface traits and source traits mean. It could well be that a particular person habitually reacts to a particular stimulus situation with a pattern of response, for example, mixed anxiety and depression, unique to that person and situation. But this pattern defines a surface trait (cluster of variables, tightly homogeneous) in the *P*-technique correlations for that person. It does not in the least contradict the notion that the source traits (common factors) could themselves be non-unique, that is, that essentially the same contributing common trait response patterns, namely, distinct anxiety and depression source states, could occur for all persons and all triggering situations. For we have recognized that a surface state is typically a composite pattern of underlying source states, just as a surface trait is of source traits. Furthermore, if the model is parallel for states and traits, we may expect *some* degree of uniqueness to a sample or person in the form of the source states and, therefore, even more in the surface states. Refined research will soon show us what small variations between persons are real (rather than due to error) in *P*-technique, but the main initial conclusion is that the state axes and the source-state variable patterns thereon are essentially the same for different people.

P-technique is the most easily understandable attack on the basic problem of discovering and defining states, but it can be and should be checked by a strategic combination with a second approach—*dR*-technique (differential *R-technique*). The latter is like *R*-technique in that it correlates over people, and like *P*-technique in that it deals only with change scores and thus eliminates trait patterns. It does so by taking a difference score—the difference on every person's responses between the two occasions on which that person is measured. (Again it is assumed—safely—that manipulation of the stimulus situation is unnecessary because daily life will provide enough emotionally stimulating situations to produce the required variation for most people on most variables.)

The relation of *P*-technique to *dR*-technique—and indeed to several other techniques—can be most quickly and clearly seen in Figure 5-3. This constitutes a further penetration into the Basic Data Relation Matrix (Cattell, 1966)--BDRM, or data box—which was begun in Figure 1-7 and will be brought to completion in Chapters 7 and 8.

The correlatable series in *P*-technique are lines in the facet made by one person, in which facet a variable runs over a series of occasions, as in the score matrix constituted by any one of the three separate "slabs" in Figure 5-3. The *dR*-technique matrix facet, on the other hand, is bounded, like an *R*-matrix, by variables along one edge

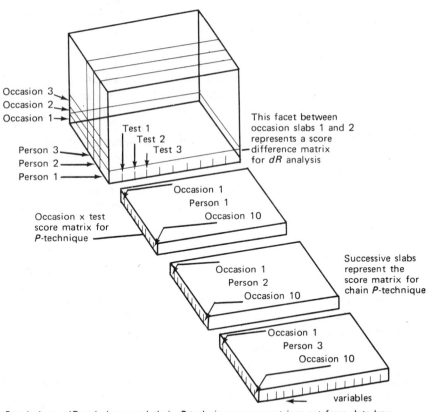

P-technique, *dR*-technique, and chain *P*-technique score matrices cut from data box.

Figure 5-3. Comparison of the scope of *P*-technique, *dR*-technique, and chain *P*-technique in the basic data relation matrix.

and people along the other, as in the floor facet of the box in Figure 5-3. It differs from R-technique in that the scores entered are the *differences* between two occasions, instead of the score on one occasion. The score is how much Bill Smith changed, say, on the variable of electrical skin conductance between Monday and Thursday. The conductance-change score is correlated (over all people) with the change score on every other variable so that, as in P-technique, we get proof of what things change together.

It is readily seen that if we factor the correlations of change scores on all variables, we will get the dimensions of change, free of the individual differences on fixed traits. It also follows mathematically that the patterns of states we get by dR-technique will represent the *average* P-technique response patterns of anxiety, depression, sex erg tension and so on. If the anxiety state pattern were calculated separately by P-technique for each of many people and averaged, it should converge on the dR- pattern. Thus P-technique will actually give unique state patterns, showing what is peculiar to a given individual. Reciprocally, dR-technique will give whatever is peculiar to the given stimulus occasion (what differentiates specifically Wednesday-to-Thursday covariance of changes from Sunday-to-Monday). By contrast, P-technique restricted to one person will pick out the pattern of, say, anxiety, as it rises and falls across many occasions, averaging out any peculiarity of stimulus that might exist in dR-technique through its being restricted to one difference of occasions. Thus, by comparing these two techniques, we can examine the extent of person specificity and stimulus specificity. The main initial finding is that neither kind of sampling effect can be very large, because we get essentially the same number and nature of state dimensions from both.

Tactically, it is worth noticing that when one subject cannot be retained long enough in P-technique to get a sufficient sample of occasions to give a stable correlation (in regard to a whole population of occasions and conditions), we can use what is called *chain P-technique*. This is shown by the series of three facets in Figure 5-3. In chain P-technique, we bring each subject's P-technique scores to standard scores across *his* occasions—thus eliminating any individual differences of level among the subjects—and build one long score matrix in which the variable scores run continuously over the same occasions (or even different calendar occasions) as experienced by Smith, Jones, and Kelley, their score matrices being put end to end. The result of this comprehensive chain P-technique is that we achieve a set of state-dimension patterns that, as in dR-technique, are common across people and, also, as in P-technique, are common across occasions. In the technical language of the data box, we have started with a three-dimensional *grid* of scores, instead of a *facet*. To complete the picture, let it be noted that we can also get state results by factoring a *face*. An $N \times n$ face is an average of scores over several $N \times n$ facets. Thus, we could correlate a set of variables over a set of occasions on which we take the average score of several subjects on each occasion on each variable. This will reduce the variance but also the "error" (whatever is unique and peculiar) in individual measurement, though it would not lose the covariance patterns. However, it would be good tactics only when we use manipulation designs and bring the same state uniformly high on everyone on a given occasion by the same stimuli .

5-3. The Scope of and Necessary Sequences in State Research: Response Patterns and Cultural Stimuli

The above *P*- and *dR*- techniques have been applied experimentally to questionnaire data ("Respond as you feel at this moment"), to objective-test (*T*) data, to physiological data, and to motivation objectively measured. From this there have emerged many patterns, which can be taxonomically classified (at present rather loosely) as states of two kinds: (1) general states and (2) dynamic-emotional states. In the first class belong states unconnected with any single specific ergic tension, and known to us by such examples as anxiety, depression, arousal, and fatigue. Their relation to ergic tensions as such remains an intriguing future problem (see hypotheses in Volume 2). In the second are those dynamic-structure patterns—fear, sex, assertiveness, curiosity—we have already described and already indicated, through *P*-technique results, to have state-like properties in the dynamic field as ergic tensions.

Among the encouraging results supportive of the model, over and above the replication of patterns, is that the same unitary "response" factors appear *simultaneously* in pyschological and physiological data; that is, the patterns fall on the same axes. Cattell and Scheier compiled evidence of this in 1961, and the delineation of the pyschophysiological state patterns has proceeded to a further level of clarity and confidence in the work of Bartlett (see Cattell & Bartlett, 1971), Cattell and Williams (1953), Cattell and Rickels (1968), and especially Conner (1972) and Van Egeren (1973, 1977). Exploration specifically of the dynamic states, across ergs, has continued in the work of Bartsch, Barton, and Cattell (1973), Cattell, De Young, and Horn (1974), and in relation to Pavlov's concepts and arousal (Cattell, 1972). A wide variety of clinical and controlled experimental work on the general states has continued, as instanced in Cattell and Barton (1974), Cattell, Shrader, and Barton (1974), Cattell and Nesselroade (1976), Nesselroade and Bartsch (1977), and summarized in Spielberger (1966, 1973). Consistent alignment is also beginning to be established between questionnaire and *T*-data (behavioral, not physiological) factors, starting with the demonstration by Cattell and Scheier (1961) and continuing to the construction of actual batteries by Curran (1976) and by Nesselroade (1960).

Although we were content initially to suppose no more than that certain groups of individual state expressions go together, additional evidence and argument justify including in the model a statement that a given ergic (emotional) need or general state pattern is a unitary *response* pattern triggered by a stimulus that operates through some autonomic neurological center or some hormone action. That is to say, the model assumes an innately organized pattern either neurally, as in anxiety or arousal, or through some physiological agent pervading the organism, as in fatigue. Even with this theory, behavioral research follows the best and firmest strategy if it first, and without bias, locates and defines these response patterns factor analytically and only *then* begins to identify the neurophysiological mechanism, on the one hand, and the customary physiocultural stimuli for the particular response, on the other. The alternative procedure, to *decide* that this and this and this must go together as a fear response, and to name it "the fear response" because it comes as response to what a psychologist assumes should be a fear-provoking stimulus, is arbitrary and circular in argument. Such a procedure would throw many diverse patterns together because it ignores the idiosyncrasy of personal emotional attachments and the great diversity among cultures of attachments of human responses to particular cultural stimuli. By contrast, the theoretical and methodological approach here says: (1) first find the unique functional response pattern and, when it is well replicated factor analytically, (2) start a fresh phase of research, for example, manipulative experiment and "human ethology," to identify the stimulus situations that typically trigger the response for the given individual. We postulate that these attachments of the response to a given situation are learned, in many cases by classical Pavlovian conditioning (CRI), and can therefore be either peculiar to the individual or culturally common. Regardless whether the structure is idiosyncratic or one of the standard provokers in the given culture, the psychophysiological response expression seems much the same. It is highly probable, of course, that even the connections are not entirely learned and that, from the existence of some innate structure, some are learned more easily than others. The course of action after the emotion appears is, of course, again determined by cultural learning.

It follows that if two primary emotional, ergic states can be conditioned to the same stimulus, a fusion of these in a particular derived emotion (in James' or McDougall's sense) will result that may be peculiar to the individual. A blend such as anger and fear, giving the derived emotion of hate, or of fear and self-abasement, giving the derived emotion of awe, may be called *common derived emotions* and should appear as common *surface states*, not *source states*, in *P*- and *dR* experiments, but other blends might be peculiar and show up as surface states only in a given *P*-technique study. Whether the coincidence on several occasions of primary *A* with primary *B* creates any tendency to a joint response when *A* (or *B*) is stimulated by its own natural stimulus remains to be investigated experimentally, and for this the above multivariate basis of method will be necessary.

Once more, let it be emphasized that it is the source state that is unitary and essentially characteristic and common to all people's emotional responses, but that particular persons may react each with his own characteristic composite of basic source states in the complex feelings (derived emotions) evoked by any given stimulus. For example, one person may habitually respond to a bank account in the red with depression, another with a mixture of anxiety and depression, another with anger, depending on past conditionings. Likewise, as just argued, *all* people may characteristically respond to one defined stimulus with a complex composite of source-state primaries, as children might react to a strange visitor with a mixture of fear, excitement, and curiosity. Let us note that any mixed, derived emotion can be represented as a vector quantity (a vector centroid to the surface trait variables) in what, at the present stage, can be mapped out already as a 9- or 10-dimensional space. The composite form could result either from the composite form of the stimulus in relation to innate responsive paths or, as speculated above, to linkage of response elements themselves through past conditionings.

The question of just what dimensionality is needed, that is, how many basic source-state pattern reactions exist in man, has to be answered, as in traits, by finding some basis for sampling variables from a total population of manifestations, in this case, state manifestations. Corresponding to the *personality sphere*, there must be a *state sphere* of variables. Conceivably, we could search the dictionary for terms dealing with emotional and other states, just as Allport and Odbert (1936) did for traits. But the time-sampling basis, that is, sampling behavior around the clock, appeals as methodologically superior to a verbal basis. Note, however, that such a survey aimed at states would yield the same actual *behaviors* as have already been covered in the personality-trait domain. The state patterns would therefore rest for evidence on the same behaviors and the differentiation from personality traits would follow from the way the behavioral, or self-report, or physiological measures, as the case might be, behave in the subsequent analysis. That is, do they form patterns with other behaviors that yield big change scores *or* do they stay put? Essentially, if a pattern varied greatly with time, it would be considered largely a state manifestation, and if it did not, it would be a manifestation of some trait. But over-simple logical distinctions do not always fit the structure of nature, so before considering this to be the last work on the model, let us browse among some further findings.

5-4.   The Model for Discriminating Traits, States, and Trait-Change Patterns

The search for states actually began not with a behavior-sphere sample but with the variables that common sense and psychological theories have thought of as manifestations of states, namely, the introspective (*Q*-data) statements about mood and the physiological and behavioral (*T*-data) signs of states for which our language has words such as anxiety, excitement, depression, remorse, elation, and fatigue. But, in accordance with the concept above that the time-sampled state sphere would cover the same realm as the trait sphere, an extension was soon built upon earlier "verbal state" research by including a stratified sample of what had been located as primary *trait* measures, as represented in the 16 PF and HSPQ questionnaires or the O-A battery of performance measures, and other personality tests, that is, in principle we *do* revert to the general behavior sphere span.

The remarkable finding then emerged (initially in Cattell & Scheier, 1961; later, in a series culminating in Nesselroade & Cable, 1974) that for virtually every known trait investigated there exists a state-like factor that we may call a *trait-change factor*. That is to say, the factoring of change scores by both *P*- and *dR*- techniques yielded, in addition to what were obviously state patterns, patterns of loadings that closely followed the outlines of those already found as traits in *R*-technique. Horn even found, in a *dR*-technique on cognitive performances, two change factors corresponding to distinct·

diurnal variations in patterns recognizable as the fluid and crystallized intelligence factors recently discovered by R-technique. This remains to be checked. The present writer has pointed out (1966) that there are two merely statistical artifacts in dR-technique that *could* account for the mimicking by change factor patterns of the existing trait factor patterns: (1) a great difference in the standard deviation of all measures between the two occasions (assuming raw score differences are used); and (2) a substantial difference in reliability of the same measures between the two occasions. (Other creators of artifacts may possibly exist but no one has proposed more than these.) It has been shown, however, that these defects do not exist in the main dR- studies examined here. Moreover, the P-technique findings would, in any case, be immune to them; yet the same trait-change patterns are found in P- as in dR-experiment, so we must assume that such trait-change "pulsations" of trait level really exist.

It is not really strange that they exist, for, as Shakespeare said (Sonnet 18) "every fair from fair sometime declines" and most organic objects in some sense wax and wane. When they do so, the correlations of the change scores—unless we use some ill-chosen system of scale scoring or encounter some uneven sequence of growth—would be expected to take the same structural form as the objects themselves. If, for example, we took a series of rubber balloons of different sizes, measured certain variables—diameter, the width of a face painted on the balloon, temperature, pressure, and weight of air inside—and factored individual differences by R-technique, we should probably get one general size factor loading diameter, temperature, pressure, and weight. If we now blew air (at some higher temperature) into all, making each a little bigger, and factored the *increments* by dR-technique, we should again expect to get a general factor spanning the same four variables.

Later, in studying growth (Volume 2), we shall have to recognize *two* kinds of growth—uniform and phased—that bring additions to the present concept, but as an introduction to the main principle, and in the context of the trait-state concepts, the above is sufficient illustration of the principle that R- and dR-factors should tend to be isomorphic. The upshot is that in both dR- and P-techniques, we may expect to find—as indeed we do find—a second class of change patterns that are apparently different from the states that came to recognition as the first class (Cattell & Nesselroade, 1975; Cattell, 1974). Whereas the states are *new* patterns, different from anything found in R-technique, these other patterns obviously mimic the old traits. To distinguish them from states, we shall call them *trait-change patterns*.

There are a number of technical issues in regard to state and trait-change measurement, the discussion of which is not essential to understanding the main model above. The reader pursuing research in this area more intensively, however, would do well to follow the contributions in Harris (1963), in Nesselroade and Reese (1974), and the purely methodological analyses by the present writer (1963, 1966, 1972). As regards the last distinction—between states and trait-change factors—the obvious first taxonomic separation lies in the fact that trait-change factors will be of smaller variance magnitude, more inclined to steady progression, quite closely similar in pattern to known traits, and starting off from different levels in different individuals.

Although for clarity, trait-change and state factors have initially been explained by their appearance in P- and dR-techniques, we have next to recognize that they must have been present all the time in ordinary R-technique, unseen by investigators of traits, or mistaken for traits! The reason for this is, of course, that at any given instant the time covariance of their elements will be picked up along with the individual-difference trait covariance. Very probably *trait-change*, as distinct from *state* factors, will not have stood out as separate new factors, because great similarity of the covariance patterns means that they will be readily confounded—the trait change "state" with the corresponding traits. The trait and its temporal increment will then be picked up as a single factor, at its contemporary stage of growth unless extremely fine estimates are made of number of factors. *Phasic* trait-change factors (defined below), which are more different from the traits, as well as all states, should, however, appear in R-technique. R-technique can pick up a state pattern on a single occasion (moment) of measurement because people usually are scattered at various positions on the dimension of any state, such as anxiety. Thus these measures, frozen at an instant, though actually representing a changing state, give a factor among the traits that would be mistaken for a trait. Just so a person who had never seen the ocean, being shown a snapshot of mountainous waves against a mountainous coast, might assume that the waves were also mountains. Our only method of separating out the states from the totality of R-technique factors is by a second experimental measurement, as in dR-technique, or a series of measurements, as in P-technique, and by looking at the differences. We can set aside the true traits in R-technique by subtracting from their ranks those patterns that clearly correspond to state patterns known in P- or dR-technique. Or if we already know how to get valid unitary measures, by a good battery, of *all* the R-technique factors, we simply *retest* each person on all factor scores after a sufficient time lapse. Thereupon the traits must show high *dependability* (test-retest reliability) co-efficients, whereas the states do not.

The model of states, however, has already been carried beyond its initial definition in factor-analytic operations. For example, states have the further property that their changes will coincide regularly with stimuli of the right kind applied to manipulative experimental designs. Evidence that measures of the anxiety state, for example, change significantly, as we would expect them to do, has appeared from use of the factored IPAT anxiety scales by Scheier (Cattell & Scheier, 1961), with such stimuli as approaching examinations. Substantial changes on these state-factor scores have also been shown by Tsushima (1957) to occur with threats of loss of status; by Rickels (see Cattell, Rickels, Weise, et al., 1966) and Hunt, et al. (1959) with psychotherapy and tranquilizers; and by Curran (1976), Krug (1977), Kawash, Barton, and Cattell (1972), and De Young, Cattell, Gaborit, and Barton (1973), Brennan and Cattell (1979) with a variety of situations over a variety of states.

The model is also enriched by the concept—admittedly not yet adequately checked experimentally—that states will follow a short-term oscillatory course over time, changing within hours, whereas trait-change factors should be more likely to follow either a slower course of development or deterioration, giving a trend over weeks and months, or else a relatively *slow* fluctuation. The rough definition that traits are "fixed" entities obviously has to give way, through the discovery of trait-change factors, to the concept that they are only *relatively* fixed. In this connection we must remember that in the case of dynamic-structure traits—both ergs and sentiments—we already know that there is fluctuation, that is, a non-trend type of change. In the E's and M's we know that the fluctuation is of sub-stantial size, and that it occurs as a response to situations and internal appetitive changes. In psychodynamics, indeed, the problem of defining and separating a trait-change factor as distinct from a state factor is no longer an academic exercise in logic and refined measure-ment, but a new conceptual and experimental problem. In short, is it possible that in this case there *is* no state factor in the ordinary sense of everyone oscillating about essentially the same zero, but only a trait which is so fluctuant that an individual difference value can be assigned to it, though only after measuring across many occasions?

The existence of "traits" of this type might seem to destroy any possible operational distinction between a trait and a state. But this is not actually the case. Even with such large fluctuations in what is apparently a trait, it is quite possible that an operational index can be found that will not form a continuum and will permit a categorical trait-state distinction. Let us call the ratio of variance among people to variance within people the *trait-state index* T-S. This would be calculated for a given trait or state by averaging the within-person variance over a suitable sample of people and dividing it into the variance among the means (one for each person) derived when the within-person scores over time are averaged. This is the principle, as shown in equation (5-1), but as a calculation we might prefer to consider that the variance of n people over o occasions is the sum of within- and between-person variables (each person a group in the ANOVA sense), and proceed from there. Let:

$$\text{T-S} = \frac{\text{Variance of means of } n \text{ individuals (each mean over } o \text{ occasions) about their grand mean}}{\text{Mean, over all individuals, of variance of each about his mean over } o \text{ occasions}}$$

In terms of a statistician's formula this can be stated:

$$= \frac{\sum\limits_{i=n}^{} \left(\sum\limits_{x=o}^{} a_{ix}/o - \sum\limits_{i=n}^{} \sum\limits_{x=o}^{} a_{ix}/no \right)^2}{\sum\limits_{i=n}^{} \sum\limits_{x=o}^{} \left(a_{ix} - \sum\limits_{x=o}^{} a_{ix}/o \right)^2/n} \tag{5-1}$$

where a_{ix} is the score of i on occasion x; n is the number of individuals, and o of occasions.

It would be easy to define a state arbitrarily as a position whose T-S value falls below a fixed value, and a trait as one the successive scores on which fall above a certain T-S value. This, incidentally, could be translated from the T-S index to an intraclass correlation, or on ordinary dependability coefficient over two occasions. However, although this could be done temporarily, as an initial means of separation, the proper conceptualization in the trait, state, and trait-change domain can be developed only by further research on the real "natural history" of these entities.

The first question we must ask regarding natural history is whether all people have the same mean over daily occasions on a given state, regardless of the magnitude of their personal variations over occasions. The second is whether the sigma of one person over occasions is the same as another's. If the answer to both were affirmative, the statistical handling of these questions would be decidedly simpler and, among other things, the T-S index would be zero for states and nonzero for traits. But common observation and existing state measurement answer "no" to both of these simple possibilities. If individuals' mean levels on anxiety, depression, arousal, and other state dimensions are different, are we to call those mean levels of an individual on a state a trait characteristic? The answer could be more complex than present concepts fit. For example, shall we find in the first place that factoring of mean levels of variables—which defines traits—will yield the *same patterns* as factoring of the daily deviations in the same variables which should define state patterns. As far as anxiety is concerned, the answer seems to be that the patterns are recognizably very similar, but contain some significant differences (Cattell & Scheier, 1961).

A clearer view of the necessary concepts here will be reached only by experimenters with the fortitude to gather data for a complete grid score matrix. That is to say their experiments must measure many people on the same days, over many occasions and also many variables (covering both markers assumed to be for traits and for states). And for additional control there should be different manipulations ("effects") over occasions.

Meanwhile, we can at least make headway with the state and trait-change factor distinction, for we can anticipate that the T-S scores for factors obtained in dR-technique will not distribute themselves normally but bimodally. This expectation is based on the reasonably good assumption that the trait change scores will take off from a decidedly different absolute level for each person, whereas the state scores would probably show only small differences in their steady means.

Because there is no question that virtually all traits fluctuate, and because in these circumstances the only stable meaning that can be given to a trait is *as a mean derived from measures over a defined stratified sample of occasions*, we must face the conclusion that existing research on traits, most of which is based only on a single occasion of measurement, has given us a distorted conception of psychological realities. Fortunately, it is a distortion mainly of a simple kind, namely a general attenuation of the true correlation of personality factors with life criteria, or between personality factors measured in different media. Thus in general we have underestimated the magnitudes of intercorrelation of trait factors, or factors with criteria, and of the dependability coefficients of traits—if traits are defined as the steady core of several measures. More accurate research in the future, both on trait patterns and on relations of trait scores to criteria, thus will require that measures be repeated and averaged over many occasions. Even then there will be some confounding of intraindividual with interindividual (trait) score variance, according to the size of the occasion sample; but allowance can be made for this by the rules of variance analysis. Absence of recognition of this confounding of fluctuation with individual differences—or, at least, of adjusting psychometric practice to it—means that most conclusions about trait patterns, criterion relations, age trends, standardizations, and so on, over the last half-century have an element of inaccuracy over and above that of experimental error of measurement. The expensive corrections will have to be left by the basic researcher to large applied psychology services, for example, military and other institutions with resources for such standards.

Meanwhile, the most likely quantitative model to adopt is that most traits possess associated *trait-change* factors (appearing in P and dR) of noticeably smaller variance than themselves but essentially of the same pattern. And since averaging just a few occasions will not fully remove state variance most states will continue to appear as factors extractable from these person means. The former may or may not be of the same pattern as the states, since their variance is so small relative to the states as to be at present only uncertainly perceived. The effective differentiation of state and trait-change factors is thus likely to be established largely through their T-S's lying in a different range. Secondly, in the domain of psychometric evidence, we can use, as stated above, the observation that the difference in loading pattern is relatively rather small between the trait-change and the trait patterns, compared to that between a state and any trait with which it might be paired. Additionally, however, we assume in the broader psychological aspects of the model that the trait-change factors will be found to have more steady trends, of a slow nature, that is, to be less given to rapid fluctuations in both directions, and to be less relatable in their change magnitudes to passing specific internal or external stimuli.

Parenthetically, it is probable that the best psychological model will additionally include recognition of the existence in many states of some definitely cyclical, periodic properties absent in trait-change factors. This possibility has indeed fascinated almost as many psychologists as business cycles have economists. But, in any case, it cannot be reliable investigated until the functionally unitary state dimensions are exhaustively found, identified by patterns, and rendered validly measurable. Probably the only well-established instances of cycles are diurnal rhythms, that is, in fatigue, surgency, arousal, regression, and menstrual and possibly monthly (Smithson, 1970) or weekly work-associated rhythms in normal persons, and elation-depression cycles in clinical cases. These phenomena we take up under the topic of lead and lag analyses below.

The above attempt at a state-trait-change discriminating model will, however, have a lot of new facts and discovered relations to digest if systematic experiment, such as that of Nesselroade (1978), goes ahead as present findings and models encourage it to do. For instance, it seems likely that there are hybrids among the three concepts above. An example arises in connection with the second-order trait of "extraversion" (exvia, *QI*, to be exact). This turns out to have a pattern very close indeed to *P*- and *dR*- findings on the same primaries, which constitute a state by the definition above. It is of considerable variance and fluctuates without a trend, yet in pattern is so close to the trait that but for its great variance we would otherwise call it a trait-change factor. Incidentally, this exvia "state" concept has come as a considerable shock to those resting on a Jungian concept of "extraversion" as a pure temperament trait. A fair amount of experimental work done on the basis of theories of exvia-as-a-trait, for example, Eysenck's theory that "extraversion" is low reactive inhibition, may be invalidated by the assumption that administration of an exvia scale on a single occasion amounts to measuring a pure trait when in fact considerable state variance is involved in measures of the extraversion trait (Cattell & Scheier, 1961; Curran & Cattell, 1976).

Pursuit of a more formal statement of trait and state and trait-change variance interactions, as well as of higher-order relations in states, is taken up in the next chapter, but, meanwhile, the concept of a state axis may be considered operationally well-founded and defined.

5-5. Modulation Theory and State-Liability Traits

With the advance of psychology into clear delineation of particular states, and of psychometry into effective *Q*- and *T*- media measures for them, a substantial part of what was previously left as error of estimate in the specification equation can now be removed and replaced by meaningful predictors—namely *states*—as in equation (5-2). The question of where the unspecified variance lurked before we introduced states is not of major importance; but it was partly in that reservoir of ignorance we call the specific factor and partly in error. For although *R*-technique can pick up states, they would be scored as if they were traits and so be largely error in any repeated use of the specification equation.

$$a_{hijk} = b_{hj1}\, T_{1i} + \cdots + b_{hjp}\, T_{pi} + b_{hjs1}\, S_{1ki} + \cdots$$
$$+ b_{hjsq}\, S_{qki} + \text{uniqueness} \tag{5-2}$$

Here, we suppose *p* common traits and *q* common states to be operating, plus uniqueness. The trait part—T_1 through R_p—is the same as the reader already knows in the usual trait-specification equation (2-1). The state part has a new subscript, k, which defines the state provocation situation or "ambient situation" at this moment. This must be written under a, also, because we are now describing behavior not only to a particular stimulus, h, but on a particular occasion. The k will go under all the states, because they are all on the particular occasion. Thus although equation (5-2) is superior to equation (2-1) in the added precision with which it estimates behavior (amount of variance accounted for), it is more demanding on the practical psychometrist because it requires that he know just what the strength of the state is at the moment of prediction. Indeed, in the everyday sense, he can hardly be said to be *predicting* at all though psychometrically he is *estimating*. For whereas he usually takes the person's trait scores for the specification equation out of some storage file of past battery scores, and makes an estimate of a_{ij} for today, tomorrow, or later, assuming steady traits, here he can make his "prediction" only if he can somehow *instantly* measure the state level at the moment of estimation.

There is fortunately a way out of this impasse, which restores the practical psychologist's capacity to predict before the event happens; but it requires that we reconstruct and extend the first form of the specification equation model to accommodate new concepts. The main step is that already implied, analyzing the total global situation, as we shall henceforth call it, into two parts: a *focal stimulus*, h, to which j is the response; and an *ambient situation* or background conditon, k, which affects the state of the organism making the response. Thus what was first roughly designated a_{ij} becomes a_{hijk}. In defense of using j instead of hj, it may be said that j already contained h. For, at least in such psychological tests as most psychometrists have used as their main variables, h and j are inextricably tied together. When a person is presented, for example, with an intelligence test that includes a list of possible synonyms for a word, the stimulus is the word plus the instructions, and the response is to check synonyms. The stimulus and response are wedded in a single performance concept—"a synonyms test"—and it is reasonable to represent it by a single j.

In everyday life, however, the stimulus, h, and the response, j, must at least be free to conjugate differently, according to over-all purposes and mental sets. The response to a ring at the doorbell may be to open the door or to hide in a closet, and so on; that is, h may be bound to j_1 or j_2. However, even in life, stimulus and response frequently are tied indissolubly by conditioning, and there are limits to what response can be tied to what stimulus; one can eat an egg, but not an egg cup. Nevertheless, in fairly wide limits, different h's and j's can become associated; so what we have written in the past as the simplified behavioral index b_j must henceforth, except in moments of economy, be written b_{hj}, and hj will similarly replace j under the observed behavior variable a. Parenthetically, the behavioral index will be of the same type for a state as a trait, stating how much the trait, or state-as-it-stands-at-k, are involved in producing the behavior a_{hjk}. And b_{hjx}, when x is a given trait or state, will be obtained similarly as a loading from the factor-pattern matrix of a factor analysis.

The state will differ from the trait, however, in having the additional subscript k, as in equation (5-2), for the state is a thing of the moment taken at occasion k, and, indeed, k typically decides at just what level it will be standing. The focal stimulus, h, might be an intelligence test and the ambient situation, k, an hour at the end of a long day, inducing a high state of fatigue. Or h might be a telephone, with a j score representing the length of time one talks to convey a message, and the ambient situation k could be a house on fire, generating a particular state of panic.

This splitting of the environmental situation into two parts requires a special conception of the psychological environment and of the laws that relate it to the organism and the response. The step we are thus taking in the theoretical model will have wide ramifications in later developments, notably in learning theory, and therefore deserves a little more discussion.

As regards the environmental situation in which a response is made we are saying, formally,

Global situation = focal stimulus + ambient situation

It would not add any accuracy to write this in an equation with algebraic properties as $e = h + k$ (where e is environment) for the "plus" does not necessarily mean simple summation, and in any case we are yet far from having appropriate scaling units.

As regards the behavioral specification equation, it will be recognized that the definition of terms has accordingly now evolved and differentiated to four subscripts: h, the focal stimulus to which the person attends; i, the person responding; j, the nature of the response; and k, the nature of the ambient situation. Consistently with this we shall next show an evolution from the mere loading, b_j, of the factor analyst, to a more evolved set of coefficients to be applied to the person's traits. It is illuminating to pause and consider these coefficient subscripts in the full setting of the data box, from which in fact their specialization logically derives. The data box, it will be remembered, has five coordinates. The fifth arises from the often reluctant recognition of an inescapable psychological reality in regard to all experimental data and scoring procedures, namely, that every act has to have an observer in the process of its incorporation into any scientific analysis. Thus the measure becomes a_{hijko}, where o is some particular observer. In Figure 5-3, we took only a three-dimensional box for simplicity, but strictly speaking, there are five basic Cartesian coordinates in the behavior-embracing data box: stimuli, responses, people, ambient conditions, and observers. Note that along these coordinates themselves all points entered are *entities* (people, stimuli, etc.) arranged in a series, not points on dimensional continua in the more usual use. Actually all of these entities are patterns (expressible as vectors or profiles in the simpler cases), not single values. As a shorter term to cover *all* these five types of entity-pattern, we use the word *ids*. A further view of the implications of the data box will be presented later. The important thing initially is to recognize that all the behavior that psychology studies is contained in this data box, and that the full identification of any behavioral concept requires five subscripts referring to five particular ids. That is to say, the response measure applies to a person, a stimulus, an ambient situation, a type of response, and an observer. However, for most of the chapters here (except Chapter 8) we can avoid the complication of the observer, o, and simply deal with h, i, j, and k.

Armed with the order produced by these conceptions, we can now advantageously return to the new specification equation in which we have added states to traits (equation 5-2). Empirical findings already show that behavior prediction is stepped up to a new level of efficiency when state measures are included (Cattell & Rickels, 1968; Curran, and Cattell, 1976; Barton, 1974; Cattell & Nesselroade, 1976; Nesselroade & Cable, 1974). But in applied psychology this conquest of the new domain of states could easily turn out to be a hollow victory. For, in most practical circumstances, how can we measure state levels simultaneously with (or at least immediately before) the criterion prediction situation in which they need to be used? We may know that anxiety does things to examination performance, so that knowing the candidate's intelligence and various relevant personality trait scores is not enough. We know that a measure of this anxiety state (and possibly others) would help the estimation of the examination performance, and permit us to correct his examination performance for the disturbing effect of anxiety. But the trait scores can be kept in a file, whereas the state scores, being last-minute effects of unmeasured ambient stimuli, cannot be obtained and brought beforehand into the weighted predictors. The way out of this dilemma, in the model proposed by the present writer (1963), has been called *modulation theory*. This hypothesizes that every individual has a particular, characteristic *susceptibility*, *proneness*, or *liability* to react with a particular emotion. (We shall use the term *liability* because it gives us a clear new symbol, L, whereas S or P would be confused with other uses.) Further, we hypothesize that any given ambient situation k has a particular provocative power, which we shall call its *modulating index* or *modulator*, s_{kx}, to bring out some particular emotion x in *everyone*. For example, sitting in a deck chair on a peaceful verandah may have a very low modulating action on fear, whereas being in a house on fire would have a very high modulating action requiring a large s_k term to be applied to everyone's fear liability value. Our modulator model supposes that, of the two possible actions—additive or multiplicative—the modulator *multiplies* the liability, though later research may produce some more complex compromise. But at present, let us write:

$$\hat{S}_{xki} = s_{kx}\, L_{xi} \tag{5-3}$$

That is to say, individual i's state level on state x in ambient situation k can be estimated as the product of the modulating power of k on x, and the individual's liability to get excited on emotion x. The estimation "hat" on S_{xki} is meant to indicate that there may be other, additional determiners, forbidding a straight equation for state factor S_x. However, in the more complex relations to other determiners, we shall at this stage drop this caution and assume simply that S_{xki} can be written in equation (5-3). It follows now that we can rewrite the extended specification equation (5-2) in the full form (recognizing, too, the above splitting of the "test" into stimulus and response, and using p traits and q states):

$$a_{hijk} = b_{hj1}\, T_{1i} + \cdots + b_{hjp}\, T_{pi} + \cdots + b_{hjs1}\, s_{k1}\, L_{1i} \tag{5-4}$$
$$+ \cdots + b_{hjsq}\, s_{kq}\, L_{qi} + \text{uniqueness}$$

The modulator index s_{kx} will be, as indicated, peculiar to the trait x and to the ambient situation k, but not special to the individual. It thus has the properties of a general law about how *all* human beings tend to react with a particular emotion in some particular situation. For the moment we shall set aside questions of the technical and experimental methods of calculating this modulator index, to take it up in the more statistical context of

Chapter 6. Meanwhile it will be seen that equation (5-4) has brought prediction once more to a useful form. For, on the one hand, a file of ambient situation indices, the s's, can be built up by research for the most common life situations, and, similarly, a personnel file of individual liabilities, the L's, can be preserved from previous testing, just like a set of trait scores. For a liability to this and that emotion is once more a *trait characteristic* of the individual—whether constitutional or acquired, we do not yet know—and can be measured and recorded in a personality profile file, like any other trait.

Although equation (5-4) has been clarified in its psychological meaning, there are mathematico-statistical aspects that need to be made more precise. In the first place, it must be noted that the product of s and L will result in the state factor S (equations 5-2 and 5-3) having a different variance from one ambient situation to another, according to the s_k value. In the ordinary specification equation all factors normally keep unit variance. This new effect on variance can be shown most readily in Figure 5-4. Statistically, the application of a particular modulator, as a multiplier of an L-score already in standard scores, will obviously (if we suppose that the given occasion calls for an s greater than 1.0) change the sigma of the sL values to something greater than a standard-score range. It will also, if the original mean is above zero, raise the mean of the group as a whole, as shown in Figure 5-4, and the change in mean will hold a constant ratio to the change in sigma, over any range of occasions, with their varied s's.

One important gain from this model—if it proves to fit more experimental data well—is an ability to fit state scale measures to a true zero, that is, to progress from an equal interval to a ratio scale. Along the base of Figure 5-4 we have the modulating strength of situations k_1, k_2, and k_n. (The last we will take as a value of unity that is as our scale unit.) Vertically there are the strength of actual (x) states, shown on the three curves for the person at the mean L_x (state liability) value and the persons ½ sigma above and below the mean. Initially we do not know either the zero state level or the zero modulation strength level. If both the S and s_k measures were taken from their true zeros then it will be evident from Figure 5-4 that:

$$\frac{\bar{S}_{k1}}{s_{k1}} = \frac{\bar{S}_{k2}}{s_{k2}} \qquad (5\text{-}5)$$

where $\bar{S}_{k1}$ is the mean score of people at k_1, and so on.

The s_k's can be given equal interval properties if we assume our *state* has equal interval properties, since the above supposes a linear

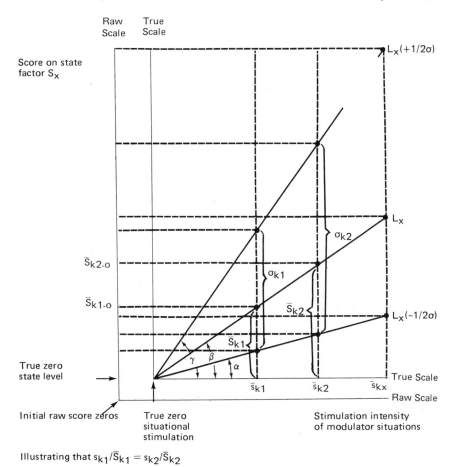

Illustrating that $s_{k1}/\bar{S}_{k1} = s_{k2}/\bar{S}_{k2}$

Figure 5-4. Effect of modulation on the mean and sigma of a state factor.

relation of S's and s's. However, neither the state continuum nor the situational continuum yet has a true zero. Thus any true value such as $\bar{S}_{k1}$ above needs a constant S_d to be added to it to make it an observed value, $S_{k1 \cdot o}$, and similarly s_{k1} needs s_d to be added. Thus (5-5) above, in terms of observed scores $S_{k1 \cdot o}$ and $S_{k2 \cdot o}$ becomes

$$\frac{\bar{S}_{k1 \cdot o} - S_d}{s_{k1o} - s_d} = \frac{\bar{S}_{k2 \cdot o} - S_d}{s_{k2 \cdot o} - s_d} \tag{5-6}$$

$\bar{S}_k$'s have values on this raw score that "scale" directly, but we must begin by giving some arbitrary numerical scale value to s_{k1o} (which can be modified to convenient size later). In addition to (5-6) we have an equation for the sigmas of states, and these are base-free, so we express it:

$$\frac{\sigma_{Sk1}}{s_{k1 \cdot o} - s_d} = \frac{\sigma_{Sk2}}{s_{k2 \cdot o} - s_d} \tag{5-7}$$

By (5-7) a value can be given to s_{k2} from that for s_{k1}. Thus in (5-6) and (5-7) our only unknowns are S_d and s_d for which solutions can then be obtained for making both the S and s scales operate with true zeros as ratio scales. If the state liability trait, L, is to have, like all traits in the factor specification equation, a sigma of one, and S's are also to have a sigma of one, then the highest s_k value must not exceed one. Thus empirical research will give us the necessary re-scaling quotient for the initially adopted numerical value to s_{k1}. However, the future of modulation calculations probably lies in real base factor models, where the scaling would be somewhat different.

So much for the necessary mathematical-statistical framework. What is being simultaneously said psychologically is simple enough. If an anxiety provoking situation, k_1 hits a group of people, the rise for each individual will be proportional to his anxiety proneness or liability, $L_{a \cdot j}$. Both the mean and the standard deviation of the group will rise, and, if the state scale is a ratio scale measured from a true zero the sigma will retain the regular proportion to the mean. It is of further psychological interest that if the model holds we have a means of saying when anxiety (or any other state) is *absolutely absent*, and also have making a list of life situations that are absolutely not anxiety provoking, that is, that have zero s_k values (or $-2\frac{1}{2}$ values if we scale 0 as "average").

Reverting to a necessarily brief glance at the required statistical treatments surrounding modulation we should note that when we use s's, and yet stay within the standard factor specification equation, we are breaking down the empirically given loadings—the b's or behavioral indices—into two parts. At this point we shall introduce a new term, v, the state or trait *involvement* index, such that

$$b_{hjkx} = v_{hjx} s_{kx} \tag{5-8}$$

This says the *total action* of some state liability, L_x, or ergic tension, expressed by b, is the result of how much the situation stimulates the erg, x, namely, s_{kx}, and how much people are accustomed to express the tension through response j when stimulus h occurs, that is, how much x is *involved* in j. Thus the total modulation term, of which there will be several in the specification equation will appear as

$$a_{hijk} = v_{hjx} \, s_{kx} \, L_{xi} \quad \text{(plus several similar terms)} \quad (5\text{-}9)$$

The alternative statistical treatment of modulation in the specification equation is to go to covariance factor analysis, as described in the present writer's *Real Base True Zero Factor Analysis* (1971), which permits different factors to be of different sizes (sigmas) and the same factor to be of different sizes on different occasions.[4] The real base model fits the condition that the rate of change of a behavior score with a trait score should ideally be so calculated as to be constant. That is to say, v denotes a tangent in the plot of any trait or state factor against any variable and which remains the same regardless of the company of other factors. This corresponds to the type of law we seek in science generally and find in the older sciences, such as that the increase of an iron meter rule will be so many millimeters for so many degrees rise in the factor of temperature.

In any case, from now on the term *behavioral index* will be retained for b, in the specification equation as basically calculated, so that it *will be literally a factor loading*. Where modulation occurs, the new *involvement index*, v, will be introduced, acting along with the s index, so that $vs = b$ (in real base). Psychologically, the difference of v and s is important, because s_k describes how the state-liability trait L_x, is transformed into a corresponding state level S_{xk}, under the impact of the ambient situation k, while v_{hjx} describes the rate at which the increasing x state as such increases the given stimulus-response behavior, a_{hjk}. Later v itself will be broken down into two psychologically meaningful components, p and e.

Modulation action is a mechanism that plays so indispensable a role in further developments of personality and learning theory that some basic implications, as well as the evidence for its action, should be clarified before proceeding. The research of De Young, as yet unpublished, showed the expected increase of sigma with mean on two state measures, but Brennan's results (in press) with the Curran State Battery were ambiguous. One feature of the results was that the sigma increased much less rapidly with increase in mean than would be expected, suggesting the zero of environmental stimulation is much further from the levels of experiment, that is, more to the left in Figure 5-4, than was anticipated. In Brennan's case it appeared that there was too low a ceiling (shown by a skewed distribution) in some state scales to permit the expected increase in sigma. This finding calls attention to the vital issue of measurement and scaling discussed in connection with Figure 5-4.

To illustrate the theoretical basis of the modulator scaling problem we referred to only two points in Figure 5-4; but as empirical investigation proceeds to fix the modulating powers of many life situations for many kinds of state and ergic tension liabilities, three, four and more points will need to be taken for greater accuracy. The values settled on will be the averages of the several estimations. Furthermore all such scaling will need to apply auxiliary methodological checks, such as are available in the two major *general* scaling principles of *pan-normalization* and the *relational simplex* (Cattell, 1962, 1973, 1977b). In more extended and precise modulator scaling one will need to keep in mind the two assumptions in the equation around Figure 5-4, namely, (1) that the equal interval properties in the modulation strength scale are dependent on equal interval properties existing in the state measurement scale, and (2) that the initial statement assumes that all subjects in the sample stand at the same situational provocations, k. Actually each person will be simultaneously in several provocation situations. However, if we can assume these average out and only the given manipulated situation is uniform to all persons the general laws indicated should hold. However, the "blurring" effect means in practice that the lowest stimulation point is harder to fix. It is of historical interest that an answer to the seemingly insuperable difficulty of producing absolute scales in psychology, that is, ratio scales with a true zero, should appear first in states rather than traits, and as a by-product from modulation theory.

5-6.   The Discovery and Quantification of Processes

A surprisingly wide range of concepts pursued by psychologists—and economists, biologists, and historians—can be integrated under the concept and model of a *process*. Thus, in psychology, there are processes of perception, processes of learning, pathological processes, developmental processes such as adolescence, ergic processes in the unfolding of the behavior of an erg, and so on. What they all have in common is some characteristic relation of behavior to the dimension of time and a sequence of encounters with the environment. In introducing the definition and model of process in Chapter 1, we have shown that the essentials can be reduced to a graph represented by a line weaving its way in a path across psychologically definable dimensions along a time axis (Figure 1-6). However, that was only the first rough draft of a model, with insufficient detail about the incorporation of stimuli and situation (h's and k's), the manner of representing the graph in a matrix, and the mode of calculation for recognizing *common* processes from the actual data of particular processes.

So long as the dimensionality of a process is derived from the correlations among various *responses* measured simultaneously on a series of occasions—just as the dimensionality of states is derived— there is an incompleteness in the description of a process. A process may be so represented, with comparative completeness, it is true, if each stimulus for the next phase is an *internal* condition resulting from the previous phase. It is then close to what the learning theorist recognizes, in more bivariate perspective, as a chain of reflex responses mediated by internalized stimuli constituted by the effect of each response. But more frequently a process, even at the simple level of a chain reflex, has appropriately to recognize the intrusions of *external* stimuli, too, at particular points.

Without restricting ourselves to the microscopic and trivial (in personality terms) chain reflex, and with major regard for the macroscopic processes of the kind mentioned above, let us consider what has to be recorded and explained. Illustration of the needs of the model typically can be seen in the unfolding of animal instinctive behavior as recorded by ethologists. In courtship behavior the sequence of readinesses in one partner has to be matched by appropriate stimuli presented by the other if all is to go well. Often it does not, as any observer knows, when the female response to the male courtship displays is interrupted by her sighting some good morsel of food! And even if the "partner" is inanimate in nature rather than a partner that has appropriate built-in sequences, the presence, availability, or dependability of external conditions is essential to the process and therefore a part of its description. The process of taking a shower cannot follow its usual largely automatic course if the water won't come on, the soap is missing, or the towel is not in its usual place. The process of returning each day from business by car would also fail—indeed become a nightmare—if the traffic lights displayed strange colors and the familiar landmarks did not appear at accustomed turning points, or the car's automatic gear did not work.

All this may seem to make a process a pretty chancy and inconstant pattern because of its dependence on conditions at special times. But it is realistic to note that any survey of daily process behavior would indeed show a typically substantial proportion of processes that "turn awry and lose the name of action" as Hamlet expressed it. In World War II a standard military communication was SNAFU—"situation normal; all fouled up," but the "normality" of such events was naturally the business of the enemy, which was to upset processes. But this reminds us that the description of a process simply as a familiar succession of scores on dimensions of *behavior*, for example, state behaviors, unmindful of situational terms, is an ideal and unreal abstraction, likely to be inadequate in further use. The matrix for describing a process—and it is indeed a matrix—must contain descriptions of the intensities of the stimuli as well. The vertical columns that express the factors recognizing independent dimensions of change will have to contain loadings for the involvement (v terms) of environmental as well as behavior response variables. The R-matrix from which this factor V_{fp} matrix is derived will be a correlation of variables over a sample of occasions in time, either for a single person, or, if we think we have a common process, synchronized over people, as average response scores over people.

Another problem that will occur to the reader if we describe a process by a P-technique analysis (taking this as the essence and basic form of process analysis), followed by plot-estimated factor scores over time, is that in ordinary P-technique we *simultaneously* measure on each occasion, for example, on each day, a person's response on several variables, whereas in many processes only a single response may be made at any given occasion so that the majority of variables would have zero entries. The initial P-technique procedure and model thus fit process analysis, description, and measurement only in a general way, and require development if they are to become a potent way of experimenting on process.

This does not mean, as far as response recording is concerned, that we can retreat from the economy and meaningfulness for process analysis of using the theoretically significant dimensions factor analysis gives us in place of a bewildering multitude of bit-response variables. This would mean that the psychometrist would get lost in the jungle of descriptive detail covering every trivial act, stimulus, and sequential side chain with which a naturalistic ethological surface-trait description would at once enrich and burden us. (Actually, a good ethologist in the end does his or her "mental factor analysis" to reduce to essential trends.)

As far as the matrix representation of a process is concerned there are two main possibilities: the P-technique model of variables, reduced to factors, changing their structural relations over time; and the stochastic model expressing probabilities of one event following another, or a series and combinations of others.

The P-technique model is already familiar from the earlier part of this chapter. It resolves variables—in this case a set including both stimulus situations and responses—into factors and finishes with a matrix of factor scores changing over time. By reason of the factor matrix (V_{fp}) these can, of course, be expressed in the change of variables over time, and the V_{fp} shows the way in which the variables are determined (Table 5-1).

There are some further features of this representation, depending on the difference between a single process occuring once in a single person, as in the ordinary *P*-technique matrix and (1) a repeating process that occurs over and over again in one person, and has to be located and averaged, and (2) a common process that occurs over many people and similarly needs an experimental-statistical exploration to locate it and put it in a standard average form.

Only brief and unpublished studies have yet been done to locate repeating and common *P*-technique patterns. The undoubtedly substantial capacity of this model to reduce the bewildering complexity of real-life processes to matrix form has yet to be fully tested. We would expect that a section of factors will be largely among stimuli and another among responses. Thus, in driving a car, a road might present factors of right and left, up and down, broad and narrow, among stimuli; among responses there will be response factors in the individual which, over the sequence of occasions of measurement, will show characteristic relations, with a short lag, to these stimuli factors.

The stochastic model is equally attractive and useful except that it usually employs no reduction of variables as in *P*-technique. It employs essentially a matrix, as shown in Table 5-2, in which the rows represent a series of events (again both stimuli and responses) and the columns represent succeeding events (stimuli and responses). The entries are the probability of the event at the head of the column following the event designated at the end of the row. The full matrix is three dimensional, for it needs to repeat the columns at various intervals of time after the rows, or to set out fresh matrices of pre and post events at each moment of time.

Examining Table 5-2 in more detail we see that at time one (t_1) there are m stimuli that could be encountered and q responses that could occur. At time two (t_2) there are n stimuli that might be encountered and p responses that might be made. It would be possible to link stimuli and responses in pairs, but we are assuming the wider possibilities of a given response occurring to any stimulus.

The entries in the cells—x's, of which only four are shown—are probabilities. Thus x_1 is a statement purely about the objective, environmental aspects of the process, saying that the likelihood of h_{11} being followed by the appearance of h_{12} is x_1. The psychological fact that a response, a_{12}, can next produce an encounter with a certain stimulus, h_{22}, is expressed on the right by a probability x_2. In x_3 we have the less common feature in a process in which a

TABLE 5–1.　Steps in Economically Describing a Particular (P-technique) Process by Meaningful Stimulus-Response Factors[a]

(A)　Process matrix in terms of variables:　scores on stimuli and responses

	Stimulus 1	Response 2	Stimulus 3	Response 4	Response 5	Stimulus 6
Occasion 1	10	3			6	
2		6				5
3			8	8		
4	5	6				6
5			4	5		
6	4					6
7			3	6		
8			3	6		
9						10
10			8			

(B)　Factor dimensions of process (P-technique, simultaneously covering stimuli and response variables)

	F_1	F_2	F_3
Stimulus 1	.5		
Response 2	.4		
Stimulus 3		.6	
Response 4		.6	.5
Response 5		.4	-.5
Stimulus 6	-.2	.2	
Response 7	-.3	.2	.6
Stimulus 8			.7
Response 9			.7

(C)　Process matrix of factor scores on occasions

	F_1	F_2	F_3
Occasion 1	.4		.1
" 2			.1
" 3		.5	
" 4	.2	.2	
" 5		.3	
" 6	.3		
" 7		.7	.3
" 8		.6	.3
" 9			
" 10			.2

[a]The first matrix (A) is a statement in raw scores of the intensities of stimuli and responses for a given person on 10 consecutive occasions. (100 might normally be required as a sample.) A P-technique factoring indicates in (B) that three factors are sufficient to describe the changes on the 10 variables. In (C) the factors are scored over time and could yield a diagram as in Figure 1–1 (p. 14). The values here are merely for illustration, they are imaginary and not calculated as for a real example.

TABLE 5–2.   Stochastic Process Model

		Time t_1		
		Stimuli	Responses	
		h_{11} h_{12} ... h_m	a_{11} a_{12} ... a_{1q}	
	h_{21}	x_1		
	h_{22}		x_2	
Stimuli	.			
	.			
	.			
	h_{2n}			
Time t_2				
	a_{21}		x_4	
	a_{22}			
Responses	.			
	.			
	.			
	a_{2p}	x_3		

stimulus, h_{12}, at time 1 will be connected with a significant probability of a response, a_{2p}, appearing at time 2. Finally, x_4 expresses the probability that a response act a_{1q} at time t_1 will be followed by a response act a_{21} at time t_2. This would usually express some motivation state in the organism itself that favors both a_{1q} and a_{21}, requiring only the right stimulus for each. Initially a Markhov chain statement of this kind is purely descriptive, and for completeness would require a full time series of such matrices as that above,

and probabilities connecting t_1 not only with t_2, but t_{31}, t_5, . . .,
t_z. However, such a matrix is ultimately more than descriptive in
purpose, being subject to various calculations about the inner laws
of the process which is being described. As far as we know no substantive psychological process has yet been studied by this model.

This is no place to go further into the complexities of stochastic-
process calculations and the use of Markhov chains. The latter
consider, in the probability of reinstatement of a particular behavior,
not only the calculation from the immediately preceding event, but
from a whole chain of preceding events. An excellent account of
developments in stochastic process, in games theory (which is
related), and in the uses of Bayes' theorem in relation to degree of
knowledge of the environment is given by Brand (1966).

It is easy to set up processes in the laboratory, for example, in
animal runs in a maze, where the stimuli and responses are so few,
and occur in such isolation, that factoring is unnecessary and, in fact,
impossible, because there are insufficient correlatable variables. In
that case the matrix (A) in Table 5-1 is an adequate statement of the
process matrix. But in rich cognitive-emotional-conative processes
in humans, and in virtually all everday life situations, a large number
of variables, behavioral and physiological, are assuming changing
values on each occasion of successive measurement, and the expression of the process matrix in stimulus and response factors, as
in Table 5-1(C), may then be more intelligible.

As in all taxonomic research we must distinguish between describing an individual case and describing a type or common
process. Among the innumerable processes by which the course
of our lives is describable there must be some that repeat themselves and, if so, there will be conveniences in studying them
intensively as a particular important class. Just as psychologists
have not hesitated to classify *personality* into types by the naked
eye—until they got into a jungle of conflicting subjective typologies—
so they have not hesitated to concentrate on typical *processes*, as
G. Stanley Hall did on adolescence, Freud on the neurotic process,
ethologists on courtship sequences, and so on. But a more objective
procedure is necessary here, as with personality typing, if imaginary
types are not to be created and subtle types not missed. The research
approach is actually closely analogous to that for locating personality
types—application of a pattern-similarity coefficient in a Q-matrix
bounded by ids, which are process matrices instead of person vectors.
Each matrix will be the account of a process in a single person over a
single set of k occasions and n behaviors, and r_p will measure the
similarity of such person matrices over all terms in the matrix, that
is, $n \times k$ numbers in a profile.

We then ask if such sequences of experiences "cluster" in various types. There is a special problem of insightfully "cutting the tapes" so that possibly similar parts are temporally next to one another in the two series. To follow the technicalities of these modified steps in discovering "typical" (common) processes, the reader is referred to Cattell and Coulter (1966) and Cattell and Dreger (1977).

A fairly extensive further development in models for the taxonomy of processes as such is possible and needed. A taxonomy must cover, for example, first the above distinctions among (1) a *unique* once-occurring process, (2) a *person-common-recurring* process peculiar to one person, and (3) a *common-type process*, which recurs frequently in everyone. Next, the taxonomy must recognize a pair of process concepts paralleling that of surface and source traits in traits. There are methodological problems also, as just mentioned, of recognizing the beginning and end of a process. These must be decided in experiment before the process matrices in Table 5-1(C) can be set side by side to test, by the pattern similarity coefficient, r_p, and Taxonome, whether they belong to a number of types of common recurrent processes. It is as if we had several sound recordings of an organ playing a fugue, each recording beginning at different points, and we wished to pick up the existence of the fugue and structure. These methodological questions must be pursued elsewhere in the references just cited, for it must suffice here to define the models and show that a process is representable by an occasion matrix. The concepts will be developed somewhat further as we meet an appropriate concrete instance—the learning process—in Volume 2, Chapter 5.

5-7. Summary

1. A *state axis* is an independent, simple-structure dimension of common variation of a number of variables over time. It commonly covers behavioral, introspective, and physiological variables; in fact, the same L-, Q-, and T-data media of observation as in trait study. However the psychometric weaknesses of L-data have resulted in their playing a much smaller part than Q and T so far in defining state factors. A state is a given position on such a state axis. Most actual moods, however, are complex, *derived emotions* involving projections on several dimensions at once.

2. The methods available for discovering state axes are P-, dR-, and chain P-technique, which can yield both unique states and common states, analogous to the trait traxonomy. The distinction of states

from traits rests basically on the fact that trait factors cannot appear in P- and dR-technique, though states can appear in R-technique. The last fact is frequently overlooked, as also is the fact that trait research should strictly be based on factoring measures averaged over several occasions. Possible production of the presently known change factors by mere statistical or experimental artifacts has been examined and rejected. It is possible to state definitely what the expected relative variance of traits and change factors should be from the results of the three factor-analytic approaches, which help in separating them. More formal treatment of these relations is deferred to Chapter 7, p. 316.

3. The initial definition of a state is as a loading pattern, showing behaviors covarying over time, as stated above; but the known facts justify further development explaining the covariation as a genetically built-in psychophysiological response pattern. However, research needs to identify the response pattern of the single process per se, first, and then proceed to find the stimuli in a given culture that provoke it, as these may vary from culture to culture.

4. In states as in traits we recognize the existence of both surface and source patterns, the former resolving into the latter. A surface state, either common or unique, may appear in only one case or may be a habit of responding to some situation with a particular mixture of source states. So far no evidence has been found that the source states themselves differ according to the stimuli that trigger them. Apparent instances thereof turn out to be different *combinations* of source states appropriate to a particualr complex stimulus.

5. Some 12 source-state axes have so far been located, covering anxiety, seven kinds of depression, arousal, fatigue, stress, regression, and so on, and they are measurable both by questionnaires (for example, the Curran-Cattell IPAT state scales) and by objective-test physiological measures. Just as there is demonstrable alignment of Q- and T-factor source *traits*, so there is of Q and T *state* axes, though confirmed instances are only about half a dozen in number. Substantial loadings of physiological variables along with T-data variables have been found on factors initially defined by introspective Q data items. This finding gives added support to the theory that a state axis represents a biological reaction pattern, the coherence of elements in which is largely genetically given.

6. Second-stratum, and presumably higher-stratum, factors are to be found in states as in traits. Furthermore, one finds as in traits that a second order in one medium may correspond to a first order in the other. For example, the second-stratum state QII aligns with

the first-stratum state UI(T) 24, in objective tests. However, in higher orders, the factor may sometimes apparently represent the unitary consequences of *a structure in the provoking situation* rather than a biological response pattern. Research should be alert to both possibilities. Among the seven primary depression state factors, demarcated for example in the CAQ, there are one large and two smaller second order depressions (Cattell, 1973; Kameoka, in press). The large second order is in the Cattell-Curran 8-state scales, and probably a physiological condition common to the primary depressions associated with dynamic frustrations. But the third order analysis (second order to the Cattell-Curran 8 state) by Brennan (1979) and others shows an association of depression with anxiety and stress which is more likely due to a single life situation being likely to provoke all three. Some preliminary data on higher order states among objective state measures is represented in Figure 5-5 suggesting that approach to a frustrating problem tends simultaneously to evoke both stress and other frustration states.

7. It seems likely that experiments aimed at stimulating and reducing states, for example, by drugs, disturbing situations, etcetera, may show that the factor patterns of the same state may be somewhat different when waxing and when waning. It is also suggested that lead and lag *P*-technique be applied because some expressions of a state that are really equally loaded may have different delays in appearance, reducing the apparent loading of one relative to the other. This misleading indication reaches its fullest expression in Yule's case of correlating cyclic variations in sine curves with a lag on one causing it to be half a wave length out of phase, which results in the correlation falling to zero despite the obvious systematic connection (Cattell, 1966).

8. A discovery that may call for far-reaching revisions of current concepts of traits, and perhaps of states, appears in the *P*- and *dR*-technique finding that pure change factors sometimes turn out to have patterns that are virtually identical with those of well-known traits, for example, exvia. It seems necessary, therefore, to recognize three concepts: traits, states, and trait-change patterns. Trait-change factors can be part of growth trends or of fluctuations. Traits can grow either uniformly or phasically (Cattell, 1973). Fluctuation or uniform growth will give trait-change factors closely mimicking the trait pattern. The differentiation of traits, states, and of uniform and phasic trait-change patterns rests on (1) comparison of *P*-, *dR*-, and *R*-technique patterns and variances, and (2) the *T-S* (trait-state) index (a ratio of inter- to intraperson variance). Although it seems likely that both traits and states have significant differences among

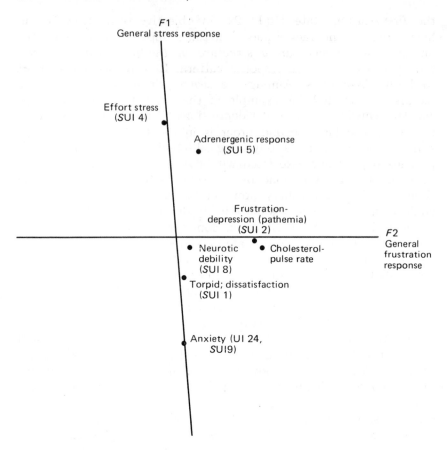

Figure 5-5. Second-order factors among primary states in *T*-data. Evidence for third-stratum state structure for *T*-data measures of states (third stratum in *Q*-data, second stratum in *T*-data).

individuals in the means of the internal fluctuation ranges, it is nevertheless very possible that their *T-S* indices will have a bimodal distribution, cleanly separating traits and states.

9. Modulation theory introduces a model that explains the level of a state in a given individual at a given moment as the product of his natural susceptibility or liability (L_x) to that particular state, x, and the provocative or modulating power s_{kx} of the given ambient situation, k, for all people on that emotion, x. In the introduction to this model we also take a first step toward precisely defining ambient psychological situations. The *global* situation of an act is divided into a *focal* stimulus, h, and an *ambient* stimulus, k. This brings behavioral

prediction, using states as well as traits, again into the practicable domain of applied psychology, because the L_x's can be scored, like traits, once and for all, for a given individual and the s_k's, expressing the average person's reactivity to a given situation, can also be experimentally determined and filed.

10. Experimental research on modulation requires careful attention to scaling and so far supports the model only if attention is given to providing higher test ceilings and with recognition that experiments are operating far above the level of minimum stimulation. It can be shown, algebraically and geometrically, that with a minimum of six measures we can check the modulation principle and that with a minimum of four we can establish first a true zero on the S state scale and then a true zero on the ambient situation modulation intensity, s_k, for situations. This, as an avenue to ratio scales, is of importance to psychometry as such.

11. Although some 12 general source states have been located, there are also state axes corresponding to every known dynamic (E and M) structure. Thus we can speak of ergic-tension levels and sentiment-excitation levels as important patterns in the domain of states along with general states. There are also higher- and lower-strata states, as there are traits. Finally, there is some evidence that abilities show trait-change factors.

12. A process was initially present here in simplest form geometrically (or in matrix terms) as a thread weaving along a time axis across k state response dimensions. It is now pointed out that the data that go as variables into the P-technique analysis of a process must include intensity measures on stimuli as well as responses, and may yield separate factors for environment and responses. There are likely to be departures from typical factorings because (1) many variables will have zero scores for long tracts (many occasion entries) in the process. This would yield in the last resort an unfactorable "chain-reflex" model of single variables in succession. (2) In life the co-ordination of the appearance of requisite stimuli with requisite response potentials often breaks down so that analysis can produce clear results only with successful runs. In the matrix representation of a process with p (stimuli and response) variables, n occasions, and k factors, the representation requires (1) a $p \times k$ factor-pattern matrix showing the structure of the variables in factors, and (2) an $n \times k$ matrix showing the involvement of each factor on each occasion over the time sequence.

13. The above is a system of analysis for describing a single process economically and precisely in a factor matrix, such as might occur once in one person (through a P-technique factoring). A Q-matrix can be built up, however, of pattern-similarity coefficients between

such single process matrices for different people, or for the same person at different times. (Or, indeed, to matrices with both person and time differences.) r_p is applied then to the complete matrices in Table 5-1, A and B above. This permits, by essentially the same Taxonome program as is used for locating types of personalities (Cattell & Coulter, 1966), the discovering of instances of recurrent "types" among singly observed processes. Thus processes, like traits and states, permit and require a taxonomy of common and unique patterns, and of surface and source patterns, and so on. Such a taxonomic approach leads to concepts of source processes, process components, and protoprocesses, which we will discuss where they are most relevant, in Volume 2.

NOTES

[1] In Chapter 1 we have pointed to events of great significance in history when a decision "out of keeping" with a leader's character traits resulted from a mood. The reference of Osler (p. 29) reminds us that a sister science, medicine, has also sought a balance here, though approaching from the opposite pole, by realizing that the *state* of a given disease is not everything, and that the constitutional *traits* of a given man have a role in the outcome, too.

[2] States are naturally thought of as good and bad, healthy and pathological, just as are traits. It is useful to think of healthy states, which oscillate in level about a mean, and are "pathological" only when extreme, and states of another class, such as fatigue, regression, and anxiety, which deviate only in a downward direction from a maximally adaptive healthy "zero" condition. The term *malergies* has been suggested for the latter, which coincide with those with which the clinician is largely preoccupied. Malergies are thus a subdivision of states.

[3] Confactor rotation is a basic principle independent of simple structure for unique rotation. It requires that the same variables be measured on a sample from each of two different populations, and then locates the position in which the loadings in one are proportional to those in the other. The postulate is that such a relation would arise only when the same functional unities are operative in both. Though simple structure and confactor are independent techniques, they should reach the same unique resolution.

[4] In that case the v, which we shall later define as the *involvement index*, will remain constant across ambient occasions while the term sL will vary in its sigma. But, as fitted to the standard-score variable and standard-score factor model, of the ordinary specification equation, v will vary inversely with s in order to keep all in standard scores. This may seem to intrude only as a technical statistical point, but it will be shown later to have psychological implications.

CHAPTER **6**

QUANTIFYING THE CONTRIBUTIONS OF STIMULUS, SITUATION, OBSERVER, PERSONALITY, AND ROLE: THE ECONETIC MODEL

6-1. Attaining a Taxonomy of Environment for both Person and Process Psychology

Recently, criticisms of personality theory, and indeed of all individual difference models, have arisen on the ground that they neglect the environment. The criticism is thoroughly justified in regard to much of the psychometry of individual differences. And the more statistically refined the latter has become the more it has tended, unfortunately, to ignore that wholeness of person and environment known to common sense.

It is not our purpose here to make a study of the history of academic rigidities. Whoever eventually does so, hoping to show new generations how to avoid them, will in this field have to recognize a reciprocity of rigidities. Many personality theorists handled trait behaviors without stimuli, but quite as many reflexological learning theorists handled stimulus responses without traits. One recognizes that the personality theorist's neglect of the situation is, nevertheless, no more disabling of good prediction that many reflexological learning theorists' attempt to formulate everything in terms of environmental stimuli, ignoring the characters of the organism.[1] What we shall call the *econetic model* offers an integration, and an end to this isolation in psychometrics of personality theory and learning theory.

Although it is vital that we do not proceed further without developing traits in an econetic framework we should note that much remains to be done in refining trait, state and process as such and that the present enterprise in econetic developments can only proceed to completion together with those developments in Chapters 7 and 8. Let it be recognized at the outset that it is only through the concept of the *data box*, with its five coordinates of people, focal stimuli, responses, ambient situations, and observers, that the hope of a thorough integration (as raised, for example, in enquiries by Spence, 1956; Cronbach, 1957; and others, as mentioned below) can be brought to a systematic fulfillment.

Our treatment so far, focussed on personality constructs, has been both cross-sectional (as in CORAN designs such as *R*-technique) and longitudinal, in the study of processes (in extended CORAN methods such as *P*-technique). If we ask at what points and in what ways the environment has already entered into these models, three developments can be recognized:

1. In the behavior specification equation the environment enters most obviously in the *behavioral indices*, which are peculiar to each stimulus-situation and the response that has to be made in it, and therefore in some sense quantify the former.

2. The environment is implicit, however, in a different sense in the T (trait factor) patterns themselves, which complete the specification. For these are abstractions from behavioral measures made upon a given sample of people *in a given physico-cultural environment*. They would change their loading patterns with changes in that cultural population and the surrounding stimuli in relation to which the responses are measured. The trait itself thus takes its definition in part from the environment and the population factored.

3. We need not, however, leave the main environmental representation, in (1) above, grossly in the form of the vector of *b* values. For in Chapters 4 and 5 on modulation of motivation and other states we have since broken the *b*'s down into *v*'s and *s*'s. The former reflects whatever is due to the focal stimulus *h* and to whatever the environment demands through the form of the response behavior *j*. The latter expresses whatever the modulations produced by the environment, *k* (as ambient situation) in the trait or state liability themselves do, by changing the factor size, to the latter's contribution to the response.

The novelty of conception in the present chapter is that the representation of the environment (both as it implicitly enters into structural trait measures, as in (2) above, and also as it enters through (1) and (3) above and into learning change measures as in (4) below) appears *through the terms* v, s, *and* T *developed in an adequate behavior specification equation.*

Hitherto personality psychologists have been accustomed to leave the complexity of the everyday environment to description in physico-cultural terms—largely qualitative—such as are used by the cultural anthropologist and sociologist. Other psychologists, for example, brass instrument psychologists in the laboratory, have cut such pattern complexity out by holding all constant except, say, the pitch of a note, as in the psycho-physical experimentation, from Wundt to Stevens and Helson. This relating of a single variable in environment to a single response has achieved one or two laws, but not of a kind useful to the personality theorist. Our ambition here is to face the problem with which personality theory is really confronted, as shown by certain systematic qualitative treatments (Craik, 1973, is a good example) and to solve it by a theoretical model capable of handling what is already known and of provoking crucial research advances. An important first step is to develop a method for representing the *physico-cultural* environment in *psychological, psychometric* terms. This in turn will lead to an objective taxonomic classification of environmental situations. Secondly, we propose a quantitative development which analyzes situational and organismic contribution not merely in a statistical variance breakdown relative to traits as in Endler and Hunt's (1966, 1969) approach and the dozen articles which have followed in their footsteps, but in terms of structural factors in the environment interacting with structure in the organism. This more comprehensive conception is possible only through the data box.

4. Continuing, however, with the ways in which the situation has

already entered into our model, we note in (1), (2), and (3) that we asked how environment enters into the standing structure of traits, states and processes. Our answer was that it is involved in all elements of the specification equation, in implicit form in the definition of T's, and overtly in the v's and s's. The latter tell what the h and k terms mean in terms of determining behavior and in deciding which traits will get involved in it. To complete our look at environment, however, we have to turn, in this fourth and last aspect, from behavior in static, reliably-repeating situations viewed in (1), (2), and (3) to what environment and environmental change mean in the phenomena of behavior *change* which includes learning. Later, in Volume 2, we shall systematically analyze the varieties of behavior change, but for the present purpose it suffices to consider two main forms; (a) learning as a definite trend in scores through environmental experience, and (b) fluctuant, reversible change through temporary effects of environment.

It is not possible, however, to penetrate effectively into the fourth domain, as (a), until the general paradigms of learning itself have been classified in Volume 2 (Chapters 3 and 4), and the finer points in (b) must escape us until the phenomena of temporary roles have been studied below. Accordingly, and fortunately without any major restriction on the general principles, the learning aspects of situations must receive deferred study while we handle the prior question of the representation of effects of environment in immediate general behavior. As indicated above, the main change in thinking required is a turning from analyzing the mere gross measurement of behavior in a_{hijk}, for example, by an ANOVA breakdown into inter-situation and inter-person variance contributions, to a structural analysis of the contributions of v's, s's and T's in the specification equation. In the past it was generally considered enough simply to relate changes in the magnitude of behavior, a_{hijk}, to different environments—for example, one compared judgments of distance perception with different intensities of light, or changes in attitude with different atmospheres in a social group. From now on we propose to go further and relate the changes in the conceptual terms on the *right* of the specification equation—principally in v's and s's since the changes in T's are familiar—to the changing environments. These behavioral indices, it will be found, provide an hitherto unavailable basis for measuring environments *psychologically* and obtaining therefrom a classifying taxonomy. Since most actual research has so far been done with such indices in the L- and Q-media of measurement, it is to that area—the in situ life area—that we shall first give most systematic attention.

6-2. Ecometric and Psychometric Bases for Dimensionalized Taxonomies of Environment in Econetics

Principle (1) above—that the meaning of the situation is expressed primarily in the b's—is obvious enough to need no immediate expansion. It has been interestingly illustrated in factoring of single individuals in a recent pioneer study by Pervin (1975a, 1975b) and is shown in R-technique in specification in the *16 P.F. Handbook* (Cattell, Eber, & Tatsuoka, 1970). But (2), concerning the extent to which environment enters into the definition of a trait as such, needs a little development. For it seems not to be widely realized that although a trait *score* is assigned to an individual and not explicitly referred to an environment, its *definition*, and therefore its mode of measurement, *is statistically rooted in a given population and a given culture*. The score on the trait is something the individual carries around with him: it is entirely his. But the definition of the dimension along which he is scored involves the whole population and the environment, for the factor gets its meaning from the variables used and its shape—as a loading pattern—from the sample of people factored.

In using the concept of a totality of human traits we have resorted to the necessary foundation of a totality of behavior variables which has been provided by the *personality sphere* concept (in turn based on sampling across a typical day's environmental situations in that culture). From a taxonomy of traits we thus find our thinking naturally moving on to a more recent concern of psychologists, namely to the associated need for a more comprehensive and firm taxonomy of the total environment. The notion of a total human interactive environment, from which sampling can be made, is in fact implicit in various ways in such diverse approaches as Allport and Odbert (1936); Baker's studies (1950) of social environment; Baldwin's studies of family dimensions (1948); Brunswik's "representative experiment" (1956); Burt's (1940) emphasis on variable sampling in multivariate analysis; Pervin's (1975a, 1975b) approach to a taxonomy; Craik's review (1973); the extensive naturalistic view of the physical environment by Proshansky, Ittelson, and Rivlin (1970); in the present writer's *personality sphere* concept (and in his points (1951) regarding the disabling inadequacies in Q-technique as practiced by Stephenson (1936)); Rogers (1940); and more recently in Magnusson's (1976) approach to the statistics of situations.

Like any other taxonomy, that of the human environment depends logically first on (a) some objective reduction of innumerable objects and situations into *species types* (including genera and families) and then (b) upon the discovering of those dimensions whereby a unique combination of scores defines any given particular psychological situation *within* any such species or type of situations, just as personality dimensions do within say, a special cultural or age group.

Ultimately, we may need to consider this mapping problem *separately* for the two aspects of environment (the two data box coordinates) into which we have already divided the global situation—namely, the focal stimulus and the ambient situation. But the general principles can for a while be developed and illustrated on either. The production of a good "map" of environment has rightly been seen by perceptive researchers as not just a theoretical "academic" need but as something highly relevant to the diverse problems with which several fields of personality study are now wrestling.

Before looking in any more detail at proposed maps of environment let us remind the reader that our interest is not simply this mapping in itself but in the development of a model that will enable us to bring properties of environment and types of environment into equations predicting behavior, through person-situation laws.[2] However, the statement that the econetic model is represented in the specification equation by indexing a focal stimulus, h, and an ambient situation, k, in connection with the response j, on the one hand, and by v and s terms affecting the action of traits, on the other, is a bit bare. The psychological naturalist, as well represented by Barker, Craik, Proshansky, Ittelson, and Rivlin, requires that we begin with concrete physical and social realities of environment. Unfortunately, for lack of a reducive taxonomy and a model he commonly gets lost in endless anecdotage. A taxonomy is the first need and a model to integrate it with personality the second. Although there is at present scarcely the beginning of a taxonomy, let us at least take a brief look at some actual attempts to map the diverse physical, social and cultural environment. In Table 6-1(a) we give an excerpt to illustrate the approach of Sherif and Sherif (1956) and the very different approach of the present writer from sampling every tenth page of a well-known encyclopedia; in Table 6-1(b) Sells (1963) set out a good methodological example of the more adequate naturalistic, ecological approach of *behavior time sampling* advocated by the present writer and others as more ideal. He restricted the approach only insofar as he centered his enquiry on a practically important piece of behavior; "the hours of study and recreation a student puts in per week," looking however at the rest of the student's time too. Using Murray's language (1937) of "environmental presses" (which was a useful early emphasis on environment and consistent with more refined quantitative developments in this book) Sells enumerated the environmental elements (1963, p. 5): "distance of residence from school, mode of transportation, hours of required chores, . . . extracurricular activities, frequency of dating, amount of spending money received, number of age mates nearby, attitudes of parents, religious affiliation, nature and frequency of illness, illumination of home, air conditioning, availability of private room, . . . characteristics of teachers, class size . . . etcetera."

Sherif and Sherif, asking how to cover an "environmental sphere" as we may term it, in relation to the personality sphere, set out more subjectively, but with systematic intent, a useful index running from 100,000 to 530,000 which we have sampled in Table 6-1. Other investigators, notably Asch (1963), and Mausner and Block (1963), have concentrated on what they deem to be theoretically outstanding features of the social environment, and numerous investigators have studied intensively some particular "bits," for example, the effect of a sib, the role of athletics. If properly conceived the global lists all illustrate that it is necessary to conceive both type groupings and vector dimensions in describing environment. For example, Table 6-1 has a dimension of the atmosphere—humidity—(to which temperature and pressure would be added if we first systematically recognized atmosphere as a type entity); a geographical vector—altitude; but it also runs to types— types of religious affiliation, hazards, social institutions.

These maps suffice at least to remind us that personalities operate in very different profiles of environment. Rarely do people "know how the other half lives" and one may wonder how far even the average professional psychotherapist at the couch realizes how differently people of different classes and occupations spend their 24 hours. It was an eye-opener for the busy executive and keen professional to see, for example, in E. L. Thorndike's results (1935a, 1935b) what a fair slice of the day the average person spends in chat and gossip (before the advent of TV however!).

Necessarily, a scheme for life situations must cover both the physical-organic *and* the social environment. The psychologist has disdained too much the purely physical environment, yet, as Huntington (1960) has adequately shown, the creativity of whole cultures can be related to temperature and humidity. Nevertheless it is in general admitted to be decidedly more important to cover the social and ideational worlds. The latter is needed because the social world is no longer adequately described by a social environment, of people alone, but also represents people long dead, in the vast

TABLE 6—1. Illustrative Sampling from a Proposed Environmental Sphere or "Total Stimulus Situation"

(a) Sample of index proposed by Sherif

Index	
100,000	Natural aspects of the environment
122,000	Humidity
136,000	Altitude
141,000	Sources of food
220,000	Social institutions
221,000	Family
222,000	Religion
312,000	Hazards and risks
342,000	Traveling conditions
422,000	Factors defined by marital status
427,000	Socioeconomic status
428,220	Family role
521,212	Group membership requirements

(b) Divisions of environmental interests proposed from children's essays

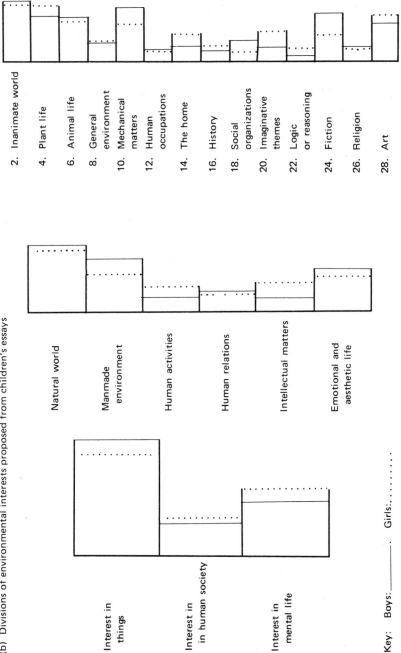

2. Inanimate world

4. Plant life

6. Animal life

8. General environment

10. Mechanical matters

12. Human occupations

14. The home

16. History

18. Social organizations

20. Imaginative themes

22. Logic or reasoning

24. Fiction

26. Religion

28. Art

Natural world

Manmade environment

Human activities

Human relations

Intellectual matters

Emotional and aesthetic life

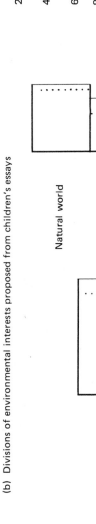

Interest in things

Interest in in human society

Interest in mental life

Key: Boys:————. Girls:..........

217

symbol batteries of books and words. In the modern world of advanced education and mass media for rapidly communicating ideas it is obviously of major importance to include concepts and symbols in description of the environment. Consequently the environment is best handled as a trinity: the *physical world*, the *social world* of groups and institutions, and the *world of ideas* and cognitive systems.

As a first systematic practical step within this triadic framework, and seeking to achieve the concept of a stratified sampling of a vast environmental sphere, the present writer (1935), as mentioned in the introduction, began a new methodological approach toward sampling and representing the environment for any given culture, namely, by taking every tenth page from a first-class encyclopedia for that culture. It did what Allport and Odbert (1936) were doing for words descriptive of personality traits by using a dictionary. This approach yielded some encouraging consistency of percentages in different categories when different encyclopedic sources were used, and presented no great difficulty in getting a consensus on categories, but has so far not been followed up (see Table 6-1(b)). The failure to follow these pioneer trials seems to be partly due to the psychometrist's lack of appreciation of the importance of environment in the model, partly to the exacting demands of such a task, and partly to confusion in not recognizing the distinction between a phase of searching for *types* (species) and one of locating *dimensions*, which two distinct steps are actually the warp and weft of *all* taxonomies.

The wavering of research effort from a systematic type search of environment by objective (taxonome) technique is partly due to the fact that in the physical world the job has long since been done for us by common sense. Common sense recognizes houses, schools, guns, and automobiles by sight, and, even without factor analyses, we proceed further, pretty reliably, to name their dimensions: cost, number of rooms, caliber, horsepower, etcetera. It is frequently overlooked that nothing of comparable dependability has been done in the other two domains—social group institutions and ideas—which will undoubtedly need factor analysis and reliable objective discovery of types and classes by the taxonome principle or others like it. Neglect of the real problem may actually have been aided and abetted by the psychologist's pride—or complacency—over the scientific status of his first incursion into environment-response relations in *psychophysics*, which gave psychology its first law—the Weber-Fechner. As illustrated by, for example, the relation of loudness to discriminating responses among tones, as covered by experiments from Fechner to Stevens, there arose no difficulty in proceeding immediately to describing the sound environment in "tones," and to meaningful psychological dimensions thereof, such as pitch or loudness (though one may ask if the loudness of complex tones from a nightingale and a pneumatic drill would yield the same laws).

By contrast, the necessary reduction procedures now required over the enormous range of human cultural environments call for more creative thought than the problem has yet demanded and commanded in psychophysics. Sells (1963) is almost certainly right in calling, in connection with social entities, for an objective factor analytic approach, following searching for type clusters by such methods as the Taxonome program. But the strategies, the judgment, and the research resources demanded in this work are going to be great. Meanwhile, also, we must recognize the right (and duty!) of the psychologist's neighbors—the sociologist and the cultural anthropologist—to propose taxonomies of environment based on *their* interests, hopefully to be pursued by equally objective means. And we must finally recognize that, regardless of academic origin, these type entities—men, cars, families, bank accounts, political parties, illnesses, births, games, roles—will be sometimes patterns in *time* as well as *space*, that is, they will be environmental *processes*.

At this point in research, the development of a "reduced," representative taxonomy of the environment may therefore seem so overwhelming a task as to cause dismay. Nevertheless, *econetics*, the title we may appropriately give to this broader concept of study of the ecology, is likely to become a major study in the domains particularly of social psychology and cultural anthropology—which hopefully will concur and cooperate in methods and concepts. At times, the baffled researcher may look enviously on that branch of econetics which we call psychophysics, since it can reduce its environmental terms to the centimer-gram-second-degree units of the physical sciences. However, the "intangibles" of the social features of the environment will not long be beyond our grasp. One can surely, as of this decade, take heart from the fact that two prominent parts of the social environment of a person, namely, other people as "stimuli" and group as groups, have already been brought quite substantially into reliably and validly measurable sets of dimensions. Inter-personal interaction has become an area of systematic research and the increased completeness of precision of measures of personality and motivation described in the preceding chapters, as well as the analysis of the interaction process by clear process models, promises real advance in this aspect of the environment. (The specific analysis of friends and enemies (Cattell, 1939) and of married couples' relations by Nesselroade and by Krug constitute some developed points in this interpersonal action field.)

The beginnings of firm measures of the environmental dimensions with which to relate the individual are also seen in determination of the dimensions of small face-to-face groups in which the individual operates (Hemphill & West 1954; Roby 1957; Cattell & Stice, 1960), of national culture patterns by Rummel (1972) and of dimensions of business organizations by Fredericksen (1970), Bass (1963) and others. These important cultural intangibles of the environment are studied more systematically in Volume 2, but they need to be mentioned in getting a true perspective of the environment in the present connection.

As soon as the psychologist gets to taxonomizing, he must firmly distinguish, if he is to progress in clear-minded fashion, between what we have called the objective, *physico-social-ideational description* of environment and the *psychological meaning* of these objects or dimensions, as seen by a perceiving individual or a group of individuals. It is easy for anyone preoccupied with the importance of perception and psychological meaning to slip into the assumption that all that matters in any perception is the subjective *psychological meaning* of the perception and that in seeking laws this need not be related to any external cues. The much used classroom illustration of the man who thought he was on firm ground and suddenly realized he was standing on a thinly frozen lake, and thereupon had a heart attack, should not obscure for a moment the fact that, except among the insane, perceptions *are* normally positively, and consistently related to the properties of the physical world. Consequently some fairly close relation can in principle be worked out between real properties and psychological subjective meanings just as the psychophysicist does in the simpler sensory domain—though the connections now are more arbitrarily tied to personal or group experiences. However, it is obviously true that the relation of physico-socio-ideational measures to response measures is not going to be simple, as Magnusson and Ekehammar's work (1975) shows. Socio-physical objects as different as a wild bull, a dentist's waiting room, and a red line in a bank statement may all provoke much the same kind of anxiety, and conversely the same physical object, a plane overhead, can evoke very diverse emotional meanings.

What the objective stimulus means, psychologically, will depend on the person, his mood, and the total situation, as recognized by our specification equation. In order to examine this we need a clear terminology and so we shall refer to the properties of the physico-socio-ideational-historical of the external environment as *ecometric* properties, and contrast with this the *perceptometric* (or *psycho-*

metric if a familiar word is preferred) properties of the psychological meaning of the environment. Econetics is the branch of psychology concerned with laws *relating ecometric to psychometric* properties, and psychophysics is an early and simple branch of it. Ecometrics is nothing more than classifying and measuring the social, physical and ideational world around us efficiently. Perceptometrics deals with affective and cognitive perceptions of that world and its taxonomic categories may turn out to be somewhat different from those of ecometrics. (The term eco for environment comes from the Greek word for house, as in economics, and is thus a very suitable symbol for the house of the world in which man lives.) Econetics has to broaden from the methods of its existing subdivision, psychophysics, in the new direction of handling *patterns* as such, over and above single *dimensions* (loudness, brightness) alone. In this direction one can already see a few promising developments in the work of Arnoult (1960), Atneave (1957), and Hake (1966) in achieving psychometric relations to ecometrically measurable aspects of *patterns* and objects in the visual field.

Though the development of a science of econetics may be a long task, the psychologist would have only half a science, and indeed, a "private world" if he were content to continue simply to describe and measure situations solely in psychological terms, unattached to an outer taxonomy. He would be confined to a world of circular definitions. For example, he could state that a situation is perceived as fearful because people are afraid of it, but he would be unable to state what features make it fearful or to predict how fear would increase as the situation develops. In a hundred years of perception and learning experiments, a few links, beyond the Weber-Fechner law, have been expressed in at least contingent and approximate laws. For example, fearful objects tend to be large, fast moving, loud, or associated with previous experience of pain.

As the study of personality progresses there will be a demand, especially in the applied field, that we reach quantitative predictions as to how a measured change of the objective situation will produce a measured change of behavior, personality remaining constant.

In a categorical, typological way we have already made some progress in this direction, in that we can describe the change in b's and modulations (s's) in moving from situation and performance X to situation-performance Y, but this is not as good as a relation of score on an ecometric dimension of environment to the value of psychometric b's, v's, or s's. The ideal econetics we have just described would find lawful relations of the b's to ecometric features of the environment, permitting extrapolation from one particular situation to another for which no *b*'s have previously been experimentally ascertained, as discussed in Sections 6-5 and 6-6 below.

6-3. The Five Sets of the Data Box—*P, E, R, S,* and *O*—as the Bases of Behavior Variance Breakdown

Virtually all research developing in this decade on evaluating the environmental situation has approached the problem in the restricted form imposed by Endler and Hunt's early (1966) questions. "How much of the variance in a response is due to differences in situations and how much to differences in people?" The question is a good beginning, but although it recognizes individual differences it still does so without the vital reference to *personality structures*. Quite apart from the error which critics soon noted in the first statistical method proposed, Endler and Hunt, by using an anxiety questionnaire ignoring the evidence on the structure of anxiety (one factor or many?) compared "anxiety" responses in different situations that were not unitractic and of known loading, and in many items were in fact measuring depression, stress and other responses.

In principle, such a person-situation breakdown is nevertheless a beginning. One can take some quite *specific* response, unreferred to any unitary trait, such as GSR magnitude, and measure it over a number of people and a number of situations. To avoid the above statistical defect one would take care to have, say, half a dozen responses in each person-situation cell to provide a basis of error variance, and then, by ANOVA methods, compare the relative variances of person and situation "effects." One would also look to the possibility of interaction, for example, of persons with stronger mean response being more responsive to differences of situation. In the next section we shall follow this up, particularly with regard to the strange interpretation that has been made by some writers, namely, that significant variation over situations (relative to persons) means that the unitary trait concept is upset! In this section, however, we propose to remain with the question as stated and with the objective of examining relative variances in personality behavior emanating from different stimulus-situation sources. However, in addressing ourselves to this "structureless" breakdown approach we propose to conceive it in the more comprehensive terms in which it needs to be tackled. That is to say we shall remember that human behavior is comprehended by a data box (Cattell, 1946, p. 96; 1966, p. 67) in which not only person and stimulus bound the score matrix, but also occasion (situation), mode of response and observing experimenter.[3]

In taking this comprehensive view we do not overlook that there are limits to the interchangeability of sets in the data box, notably in that it is relatively meaningless to score different kinds of responses all in the same raw units, for example, to compare degrees of liking an object, and speed of copying a square. Consequently, in that setting an analysis of how much variance is associated with, say, differences in kind of stimulus and how much with differences in kinds of response is not to be made operational and is meaningless. It happens that some of the Endler and Hunt work has nevertheless been of this kind, measures of the frequency and intensity with which an individual reports that he makes this and that response being analyzed. One may wonder how far such results for, say, intensity, are spurious. For example, "Does your heart beat fast when you go to the dentist?" and "Do you walk faster on the street on a dark night?" are respectively pulse and walking speed measures not to be compared (because in different units) across people, occasions, observers or anything else. The particular developments in the Endler and Hunt framework will be discussed later. But here, in connection with the comprehensive overview, it suffices to note that one co-ordinate of the data box—that of different kinds of responses—cannot be used in such analyses of variance except under the condition when the units happen to be the same, as in seconds to complete a task, frequency, rise of temperature in performing, etcetera. Otherwise, however, sets can be experimented on in all possible pairs among four (responses being ruled out) which are six: people-situation, people-stimuli, people-observers, situations-stimuli, stituations-observers, and stimuli-observers.

One can readily see substantive issues, especially in applied psychology, to which variance analysis (ANOVA, but used for more than significance testing) would be relevant. For example, in social evaluations of individuals, how much of the variance is due to observers and how much to the people observed? In responses to questionnaires (stimuli) how much is due to the stimulus constituted by the question and how much to the social or other situation in which it is asked (stimulus defined here as usual as h and ambient situation as k). In clinical psychology an interesting application would be to find out how much depressive responses are situational and how much endogenous (in an ordinary personality sample). And in personality how much of behavior resides in steady personality factors and how much is in role factors brought into action (modulated) by ambient situations?

The quantitative answers one gets will, of course, depend on whether the people, occasions, observers, etcetera, are taken (selected) to stand at some special, arbitrarily-fixed intervals or as random samples. And, as discussed elsewhere (Cattell, 1977b), the random or stratified sampling of situations, stimuli, etcetera, cannot be considered yet worked out as well as for populations and samples of people. An attempt at a rationale for sampling stimuli and, more specifically, "tests," along some half dozen descriptive dimensions has been given, however, by Cattell and Warburton (1967).

Because the implicit assumption above that the reader has been familiarized in psychometrics with the data box may be only partly correct this page will digress into a somewhat more complete statement of its nature. For the data box or basic data relation matrix is central to many issues touched upon in the broader psychometric perspectives of this book. The data box recognizes that *all psychological events concern a stimulus, a response, an ambient situation (or occasion), a person and an observer.* The historical development of this "box" of fundamental relations began with only three of these (persons, tests, occasions) in what was initially called the *covariation chart.* It was later expanded (Cattell 1966) to *five* Cartesian coordinates, each a set of "ids," in what was named the *basic data relation matrix* (BDRM) or complete data box (Figure 6-1).

The data box, whether 3 or 5 dimensional is nothing but a score matrix, with response measures as dependent variables in the cells, as shown in Figure 6-2. It is nothing but an extension of the common classroom or *R*-technique, "individual difference" score sheet, with performances (responses to stimuli) across the top and people down the side. An example of how the data box can be spread out in a flat *grid* is shown in Figure 5-3. The person coordinate—the vertical in Figure 6-1 and labelled by *i*'s in Figure 6-2—consists in general terms of a set of organisms in some indexed sequence. (They could be people, countries, rats, etc.) The ordinary classroom score sheet, with the coordinate of people arranged in merely alphabetical order down the side and with tests or dates of presence in class along the top, is called a *facet* because it is a "slice" cut from this box. Along the stimulus coordinate, there would be a variety of stimuli, each of a different pattern, but usually in practice belonging to some fairly definite class, for example, a series of pictures of automobiles, a number of animal sounds. The response patterns and the ambient situations would similarly be a series of *ids* (individual patterns) in a known recorded sequence but normally not placed in order on any continuum, though all belonging to the same id *set* or species.

The *sets* in the five coordinate Basic Data Relation Matrix (BDRM) are thus organisms, stimuli, responses, ambient situations, and observers, along each of which sets there is a variance contributed

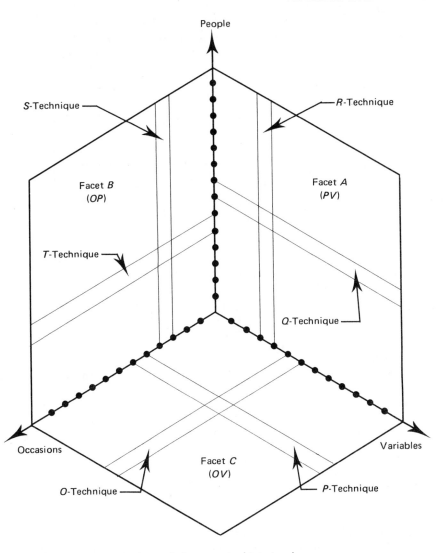

Figure 6-1. The basic data relation matrix (data box).

Only three of the five dimensions can be shown pictorially here. The missing coordinates are "observers" and "stimuli" (When variables are split into responses and stimuli).

to the response measures, which are the dependent variables placed in the cells of the score grid. (A useful mnemonic for these sets of ids is *PERSO*, since we normally name the five sets *p*ersons, *e*nvironmental backgrounds (ambient situations), *r*esponse types, *s*timuli, and *o*bservers.) In the usual case where we hold to one type of response, or at least one kind of score unit for the responses through-

People

		i_1	i_2	i_3	i_4	i_5	i_6
j_1 Stimulus situations	h_1k_1	5	4	5	4 ,	3	1
	h_2k	4	4	6	3	1	0
	h_3k_3	7	3	8	2	5	1
j_2 Stimulus situations	h_1k_1	6	5	7	3	2	1
	h_2k_2	9	4	8	0	4	3
	h_3k_3	3	0	4	7	2	0
j_3 Stimulus situations	h_1k_1	2	1	3	2	2	0
	h_2k_2	8	9	9	5	6	3
	h_3k_3	3	1	0	3	8	4

Responses { (bracketing j_1, j_2, j_3 Stimulus situations)

Figure 6-2.   Illustration of variance breakdown across people, responses, and stimulus situations.

In data box technical terminology, this is a grid, that is, a three-dimensional box unfolded by facets (see Figure 5-3). Note that for "error variance" we would want at least two measures in each cell. The table is left as is in this respect because it is clearer for the later CORAN discussion.

out the data box, any score will be identifiable by its being opposite a particular person on the person coordinate, a particular stimulus on the coordinate occupied by stimuli and so on. In other words a given response score in the full hyperspace data box is related to (placed in regard to) an id on each of four other coordinates. The actual measurement of the response, act, or performance we have consistently symbolized in all specification equations (here and elsewhere) as "a". The BDRM shows that it actually needs five signatures (not two or three as hitherto) to fix its uniqueness as a psychological event. Henceforth, wherever we wish to be completely adequate in a statement of a behavioral event we should write five *referents* as subscripts, as follows:

$$a_{hijko} \tag{6-1}$$

where i indicates the given individual; h, the particular stimulus; j, the form of the response which the person agrees to make; k, the ambient situation; and o, the observer (and his measuring instrument). Note a is the *size* of the response according to some agreed measuring operation, of which several might be possible, while j is the *kind* of response being made.

It should be noted incidentally, that the series of ids in any one set can be either a freely chosen and randomly ordered sample, or restricted and allowed to vary in a sequential way along just some one dimension (or special combination of dimensions). The stimuli, for example, could be repetitions of the same particular stimulus at different positions along a continuum, for example, a light bulb at various powers of illumination, and in that case the conclusion from the subsequent analysis will be different in nature from that with a class of ids, for example, a great variety of light sources, randomly ordered and differing in all directions. For in the former case the coordinate is a single dimension (and if carefully controlled will yield only one factor dimension) rather than a set of ids varying along all dimensions on which their natural patterns can possibly differ. Some confusions have resulted from lack of explicitness about which of these id designs—a difference of (a) patterns or of a (b) single dimensional score—is being used, but the former is the usual design.

Table 6-2 is an attempt to summarize for the reader this difference in the use of the data box between inserts of ids (people, tests, situations) in the coordinates and inserts of values on some parameter of the ids. It does so in connection with the earlier discussion on econetics. Under design (a) any breakdown of the relative variance from people, situations, etcetera, will have meaning in regard to the sample (and therefore population) of people and situations used. In (b), on the other hand, the coordinates will represent dimensions of people and a defined, pre-set range, for example, a defined range on verbal ability, and dimensions of stimuli and occasions, for example, the range of uncommonness of words on Thorndike's semantic count. Almost all factor analysis is on design (a) in which we set out to *discover* the dimensions of subjects, situations, modes of response or observers, permitted by the wide choice of ids in any set.

More relevant to our present discussion is that virtually all these factor analyses have so far dealt with dimensions of people, rather than of situations and stimuli, with which we are concerned in this chapter. At this point we are concerned with their psychological rather than their physical dimensions. However, let us note that the

TABLE 6–2. The Chief Econetic Relation Matrices

(a)   *By types of situations and stimuli (Discontinuous values)*

(i) Ambient situations				(ii) Focal stimuli for specific response j			
Liability trait				Trait			
Situation (k)	T_1	T_2 $\cdots$	T_x	Stimulus (h)	T_1	T_2 $\cdots$	T_x
Type (Id) 1	s_{11}	s_{21} $\cdots$	s_{x1}	Type (Id) 1	b_{11}	b_{21} $\cdots$	b_{x1}
Type (Id) 2	s_{12}	s_{22} $\cdots$	s_{x2}	Type (Id) 2			
.				.			
.				.			
.				.			
Type (Id) u	s_{1u}	s_{2u} $\cdots$	s_{xu}	Type (Id) u			

(b)   *By dimensions of one situation and stimulus (Continuous values, manipulable)*

(i) Ambient situations				(ii) Focal stimuli			
Type x Dimension p_k	T_1	T_2 $\cdots$	T_x	Type x Dimension p_h	T_1	T_2 $\cdots$	T_x
p_1				p_1	b_{11}	b_{21} $\cdots$	b_{x1}
p_2				p_2			
.				.			
.				.			
.				.			
p_u				p_u			

In the dimensions case $p_1, p_2, \ldots p_u$ are different numerical scores on some ecometric dimension p of the situation x.

data box remains a *psychological* data box only so long as it enters *behavioral responses* on the the score cells of this multiple coordinate matrix. It is *possible*, however, to enter measures of other kinds that still relate to these id sets. For example, a facet of stimuli by ambient situations, taken from our cultural environment, could have as entries the *frequencies* with which certain stimuli are encountered in certain situations. The resulting *ANOVA*, (*an*alysis of *va*riance), *CORAN* (*cor*relation *an*alysis) or factor analysis would tell us about the structure of environment as such, not about human behavior patterns in relation to it. It will belong to the ecometric not the psychometric aspect of econetics. In the former we can enter the stature of people, the weight of apples, the cost of automobiles, etcetera. The concepts emerging are then no longer psychological, but geographic, economic, chemical, etcetera.

A second tricky point, already briefly mentioned, is that the hitherto habitual use of the data box and factoring mainly with tests as variables in the score matrix has obscured the *separability* of the stimulus and response sets. It was the initial simpler convention which permitted, however, the original easier introduction of the data box concept as the three-dimensional "covariation chart"— people, tests and occasions. It may be true that in practice there are certain limits to the linkages of stimuli and responses that are experimentally possible. (This suggests that we should use topological boundaries like those of the phase rule in physical chemistry.) For example, to measure the individual's laughter response to a series of geometrical figures, or to ask whether a steak and kidney pie is more pitiable than a rasher of bacon gets us to nonsense measurements (though ones not much more unreal than those asked for in, say, judging "distance" in the "semantic differential" and some multidimensional scaling procedures!). In general, within limits, however, stimulus and response ids can be independently chosen with the expectation that a meaningful psychological measurement can be made from every possible combination. Thus in general we retain the use of the ten pairings presenting the basic possible relations among the five sets of ids, and, if analysis of variance contributions is our aim, the relative contribution of referees (rows) and relatives (columns) to the dependent behavioral score can be obtained for each of these ten relational matrices (provided we have more than one entry on each cell, to get error variance). Properly conceived, therefore, the econetic problem is not one of "the relative contribution of people and situations" to behavior, but of people, situations, stimuli, modes of response, and observers (when behavior has to be humanly recorded).

A third issue over which one might stumble in the use of data box measures concerns the difficulty already mentioned of getting the same type of measurement from many types of response. In CORAN approaches we do not usually notice this problem since all variables are brought to standard scores in their own sort of unit and we can correlate a response measured in seconds with one measured in inches, but ANOVA cannot usually do this without losing part of what it is looking for. The response scored as number of synonyms produced to a word stimulus and that scored as reaction time to a buzzer can be correlated because implicitly the calculation of a correlation uses only standard scores. But ANOVA requires that the dependent variable be in the same units for comparison of variance associated with the several effects. Incidentally, a useful overview of this *ANOVA-CORAN* contrast and comparison is available in Burt (1966). Often the above difficulty can be overcome by a sufficiently ingenious choice of a type of score that will be applicable to all. For example, such diverse responses as answering a multiple choice intelligence test item, answering a questionnaire item, avoiding an electric shock, shooting at suddenly exposed objects, etcetera, can all be scored with some meaning as response time in seconds. Others can be scored on number of errors, acceleration of pulse in responding in different j forms etcetera. Or one might measure the response on the same particular 40 item anxiety scale score to a diversity of focal stimuli over a diversity of ambient situations. An alternative, when search for common units ceases to make sense, is discussed in note 4 below.

Finally, let us take a retrospective appraisal of this data box or *BDRM* (Basic Data Relation Matrix) that claims to contain all the possible raw material (the id relations) within its walls. A doubt is sometimes raised whether the five signatures of the data box are enough completely to fix the uniqueness of an act. The question is sometimes raised whether the fact that a type of response, j, and the mode of measuring it, a, are two different things does not create a sixth coordinate. Also one asks whether notice should not be taken of the fact that an id changes from time to time, that is, it suffers "states" and is not fixed, so that coordinates might need to be introduced for the states of the ids at the experimental moment. As to the first, in describing objective personality tests in Chapter 3, we already recognized the difference between the nature (pattern) of a response as such, j, and the mode of measuring it, a, in that we indexed the stimulus-response patterns (tests) by $T.1$ through $T.500$, but the more numerous ways of measuring (applying a scale to) the responses by Master Index numbers, $MI.1$ to $MI.2000$ odd. As many as four or five different aspects of a response can be measured, commonly on different scale units, for example, time, curves, etcetera. The scale units are taken care of in the a term in a_{hijko} and it is thus appropriate that a is different in class of symbol from h, i, j, k, and o, for the latter are ids around the data box and a is the numerical entry in the cells. [4]

The terms *relatives* and *referees* have consistently been used for some years (Cattell, 1966) to refer to the two vitally different sets of ids which bound any two-coordinate score matrix, that is, a facet. A parting word on their definition is appropriate here. The relatives are the ids *to be related* by correlation, and are most typically tests or responses. The referees are the ids *over which the correlation is made*, such as people or occasions. It should be noted (a) that transposing the matrix will reverse these labels, and (b) that either can also be entered as a *composite* of ids making two coordinates into one. Ten tests over 10 occasions would give 100 test-occasion relatives, which could be correlated, for example, over, say 500 people as referees. Alternatively, one could correlate, say, 30 responses as relatives over 100 referees, the latter formed by 10 people each scored on 10 occasions. Such a score matrix with composite sets has been called a *grid*, to contrast with a simple *facet* or *face* of the data box. Figures 5-3 and 6-2 illustrate this creation of a grid matrix. It can be thought of as making a three dimensional score matrix two dimensional by laying out measure facets (slices from the data box) end to end. Most commonly, however, neither relatives nor referees are composite.

This digression into the nature of the data box (more fully analyzed in the *Handbook of Multivariate Experimental Psychology*, 1966) has been necessary to enlarge and bring into perspective the questions of personality and environment that have hitherto been treated more narrowly under such queries as "Is it individual differences or differences of situation that predict more of behavior?" Variance over "environment" indeed, is seen to be too global and crude an expression for good theory, since it can mean over stimuli, over ambient situations, and even over observers. One could, for instance, take as scores the grades of 100 students over, say, 20 school subjects as stimuli, over 200 ambient situations constituting different availabilities of reference books, and over 20 different examiners, constituting the observer coordinate—and all of these last three are "environment." In any case the data box reminds us that there are five sources of variance in the behavior response measures themselves—not just the two approached in the Endler and Hunt stimulated line of studies—and that these add up their effects to the total observed variance from the grand mean of the data box.

In any two-effect analysis we collapse the other dimensions and thus get several entries in each cell, as needed for ANOVA, the "error" variance within the cell being the contribution from the collapsed dimensions (literally error of measurement in the case of the observer set contribution). In this field of investigation the alternative is possible of either artificially fixing sub-groups of ids uniformly at different levels or allowing the natural distribution to hold. Most social and personality generalizations probably demand the latter, using representative, stratified samples of the four kinds of population. Except for the pioneer work of Endler and Hunt and its repetitions, *psychology at present lacks concrete evidence on the relative contributions of the data box sets* even to such central measures as intelligence and the personality factors, and it is uncertain on the equally important question of how significant various *interactions* of the sets may be.

6-4. Breaking down the Variance of Particular Behaviors into Person, Stimulus, Observer, etcetera, Sources of Variance

Recent discussions (well surveyed by Magnusson 1976, Golding, 1975 and others) of approaches to analyzing personal and environmental sources of variance in behavior show (a) certain misapprehensions of what the breakdown means, notably, as stated above, in regard to trait concepts, (b) a restriction of interest to what may not be the most important, and is certainly not all, of the non-personality sources, such as we have surveyed under the symbols P, E, R, S, and O above.

Despite having shown through the five coordinate sets of the data box how many and diverse the possible comparisons of variance sources are, we shall find it convenient for exposition initially to proceed to the next step by illustration within the more common people-stimulus relation matrix. (To be exact, the person-test matrix, with stimulus and response combined in test.) The next step sharpens the issue by emphasizing that the person-test comparison needs to be conceived in trait-vs-situation terms, and it aims to show incidentally that wrong conclusions about trait structure have been rather widely disseminated from the first experiments on situational effects. The present trait question issue applies mainly to people and stimuli. Except for the more numerous interaction terms to be coped with in more than two sets, this much illustration should suffice.

Figure 6-2 sets out raw scores for six people in three responses over three stimulus situations. For the sake of some simplification, focal stimuli and ambient situations are locked in pairs, so that the grid represents the unfolding of a three-dimensional box only. We shall assume, in general, as in this example, that the three responses are measurable in the same units.[5]

Granted more than one entry in each cell—say entries by different observers—this table could be used to obtain the variance contributions and interactions among situations, forms of response, and people. The significance of mean score differences for different groups of individual's (i's) and ambient situations (k's) could be tested by the usual F ratios:

$$F_i = \frac{\sum x^2{}_i/dfi}{\sum d^2/dfe} \tag{6-2a}$$

$$F_k = \frac{\sum x^2{}_h/dfi}{\sum d^2/dfe} \tag{6-2b}$$

(The degrees of freedom, df, are to be entered appropriately for i and e error.) Here $\sum d^2$ is the residual variance (when divided by dfe) after the person mean and stimulus mean variances have been taken out. (This residual "error" variance, if we use a score matrix in which each person is a row and each column is a stimulus and in which, consequently, there is only one entry in each cell, would be the sum of both interactions and error, which cannot directly be separated.)

However, in the general evaluation of the magnitude of different contributions, such as form of response, j, person, i, difference of stimulus h, and the remaining two sets in the data box, a ratio of any particular two, for example, persons, i's, and stimuli, h's, is a less important object of inquiry than a partitioning of the whole system. Getting this latter information simply requires us to collapse the data box down each dimension (in turn), producing what have been defined as *face* scores matrices, of which there are ten. For example, we can virtually eliminate the person variance by reaching the face score matrix in what was, say, a three dimensional box—people, situation, and stimuli—by adding and averaging for each situation-stimulus across all the scores of a large sample of people in the third set of the box. In more limited contexts, the application of the intra-class correlation (or one of the indices suggested by Golding, 1975; Glass and Hakstian, 1969; or Cronbach, Gleser, and Rajaratnam, 1972) to the score matrix will provide it. A glance at Figure 6-2 will show how this collapse of facets in relation to situations could be made.

The possible usefulness of knowledge about the above relative variance contributions and interactions, concerning some particular response measure, to psychological theories is becoming increasingly recognized. Aspects of learning theory hinge on the relative contribution from differences of stimuli; perspective on modulation theory requires appreciation of the amount of variance from situations relative to persons, and concepts in social psychology are assembled in importance by knowing the ratio of variances of behavioral measures respectively from situations and observers. However, as indicated above we need now to move in from this general, unstructured analysis to the relevance of those sources of variance to the trait concept and the use of traits in prediction. Ambiguous conclusions have been drawn in this matter—particularly the strange conclusion that much situation variance is incompatible with unitary traits—from the researches on situation or stimulus effects by Endler and Hunt, Moos, Argyle, and Little, etcetera. Part of the confusion arises from the fact that the usual set of items as used in such studies as met in our earlier comment, has begged the question of personality structure. These studies assumed that if one puts together items to measure say anxiety or depression by "face validity" the results are those for a unitary trait. Actually these scales have not been demonstrably unifactorial, but have contained several factors, as commonly happens with subjectively composed questionnaires.

Several writers who need not be mentioned have fallen into the error of supposing that if the variance of, say, items in an anxiety response scale, is decidedly greater over situations than it is over people, a trait cannot be said to exist. The ordinary factor analytic demonstration of a source trait holds the stimuli and situations at a constant level for all people, but not the same level for each h or k, that is, it recognizes that as between one particular h or k and another there may be substantial differences of potency. It is understood that the *mean* raw score on response to a strong and a weak anxiety situation for N people will differ considerably, but that the rank order of the N people will be very similar on the two when a unitary source trait exists. As Golding has well said (1972) "the classic [trait theory] psychometric position has been that situations 'constrain' individual differences [affecting] both the mean and variance of these differences, though the rank order of individuals on the 'trait' should remain relatively invariant across . . . situations [which the trait loads]." (Bracket inserts by this writer.)

Without going into factor analysis, and by accepting for a moment a simple correlation cluster concept of a surface traits, we see at once that substantial differences between the response score sizes in different situations in Figure 6-2 are entirely compatible with substantial correlations among the variables across people. For example, rows $h_1 k_1$ and $h_2 k_2$, in response j_3, are at entirely different levels (means 1.7 and 6.7 respectively) yet the response variables correlate substantially. Situations, k's; response forms, j's; and stimuli, h's; may each have characteristic effects on the mean and sigma of the response measure; but so long as their rows (rows here, columns in most score matrices, with people down the side) intercorrelate to yield a cluster or factor, the gross differences of mean, etcetera, present have no relevance to nor offer criticism of, the theory of unitary traits.[6]

Indeed, when a trait is rightly conceived in the perspective of the environment, as we have attempted here, one *expects* (a) that the actual magnitude of expression will vary, as a mean for people, across different situations, *according to the modulation model* we set out in Chapter 5 and discussed in the next section, and, (b) that if we take any specific bit of behavior only moderately loaded in the unitary trait, and not some pure factor measure, the correlation of the manifestations over people, that is, of different situations and stimuli, will fall well short of unity. (The failure of Endler & Hunt to use an available relatively pure factor scale for anxiety, rather than items only face valid, would account for some noticeable reduction of correlations in their data.) Clinical-type observation alone tells one that in a person high on an ergic level of fearfulness, one does not expect him to show equal fear response (on, say, the GSR) to a barking lapdog and to a revolver pointed at his head.

6-5. **The Additive Attribute Model for Assessing Structurally the Relative Roles of Personality and Other Influences in Behavior**

The reader will probably find the above arguments in ANOVA and CORAN terms concerning single behaviors reasonably familiar. They lead to an acceptable form of solution to the main question or questions commonly raised about evaluating the relative importance of personality and environmental determiners (situations, stimuli, observers) but so far only concerning *some specific piece of behavior.* Just as the more sophisticated personality theorist has been more interested in understanding specific behaviors through broader structures in personality, however, so also here he will want to reach structural concepts of environment and to bring them into meaningful relation to personality structures.

Two theoretical models are here proposed which shift the treatment of environmental variance into the main framework of the behavioral specification equation. The first will be described here as an "additive" model and the second in the next section as a "product" model. Both give a possible fourfold extension of the environmental contribution as treated above, in that they analyze for stimulus variance, observer variance, ambient situation variance, and variance due to the form of the response, that is, they include all dimensions of the data box.

The concept here carries us into the domain of *three-way* factor analysis, and the first thing we must do is to avoid confusion with Tucker's brilliant and recondite *three-mode* analysis. Potentially we are actually speaking of n-way factoring (n up to five) but for ease of illustration let us keep to three way. Three-way analysis differs (see Cattell, 1978) from three mode in not conducting a single analysis of the three way score matrix, but in unrolling the data box in three different directions and doing three analyses. One is over people as relatives, one over tests, and one over situations. Each score matrix is a *face*, not a *facet*. That is to say, when we correlate tests over people, the scores are averaged over all situations, and when we correlate situations over people the score for a person i in situation k is averaged over all his tests, and so on.

As there are three id sets to be considered we have three possible score matrix combinations (each of which could give also an inverse factoring). They are the familiar persons by tests (but averaged over all situations), the tests by situations (score averaged over all people) and the situations by people (scores averaged over all tests). Since correlating brings to the same mean and sigma we have, in the first, deviations from the grand mean due only to people's factors on tests, in the second those due only to test's factors on situations, and so on. The mean scores across these three score matrices will estimate the total score for a given person, on a given test in a given situation due to the three separate deviations.

The factoring of these three matrices will yield in the first the v's (loadings) for particular tests, and people's personality trait scores (from test scores) that derive from them. This will be like an ordinary R-technique except that the test score is averaged across many situations of administration. In the second it will yield weights, which we will label w's, for dimension of tests, P's, as they affect all people's performances on situations. That is to say, any particular situation will have weights on the general factors in tests, which will be scored in terms of situations most affected. In the third the factors will be marked by loadings on people, which we will call x's, and each situation will get a score in terms of people's factor scores from situations (Q's) weighted by the weights of the situation factors on people.

It should be observed that we are paralleling the ordinary analysis of variance (deviation) of any particular measurement by factor analysis of that deviation. As to deviation of a particular a_{ijk} score we could write it as a deviation of the facet mean, for example, for test j, from the grand mean, plus the deviation of the mean scores on situation k in that facet from the facet mean, plus the deviation of person i in that situation vector from the vector k mean. Actually here, if we consider the factoring described in the last paragraph, the corresponding deviation breakdown is collapsed. The factored matrix is the face formed by adding scores over all situations, and its mean is the same as the grand mean. Since correlating tests eliminates differences of test means the deviation we are actually explaining in factored terms is that deviation of a_{ijk} from the grand mean that is due to the person alone. And we are explaining it in the familiar psychometric form of factor scores in people defined as functions of standard scores on tests as in Figure 6-3(a).

We thus reach three specification equations, which we necessarily represent as estimates because of omitted specifics:

$$a_{ij} = v_1 T_{1i} + \cdots + v_n T_{ni} \qquad (6\text{-}3a)$$

$$a_{jk} = w_1 P_{1j} + \cdots + w_m P_{mj} \qquad (6\text{-}3b)$$

$$a_{ik} = x_1 Q_{1k} + \cdots + x_z Q_{zk} \qquad (6\text{-}3c)$$

where T's are person traits, P's are test attributes, and Q's are situation traits (respectively n, m, and z in number), and a_{ij}, a_{jk}, and a_{ik} are respectively i's performance on a situation-averaged performance, j's contribution in a people-averaged performance and k's contribution in a test-averaged performance (The second subscript in each case describes the set in which the factor patterns are calculated, and the first that to which scores are given.)

Just as in single deviations the estimation of the deviation of a given a_{ijk} from the grand mean can be broken into three parts:

$$\hat{a}_{ijk} = (\hat{a}_{ij} + \hat{a}_{jk} + \hat{a}_{ik})/3 \qquad (6\text{-}4)$$

so the factorings of these parts above, in equation (6-3) can be put together to represent (with specifics as shown in the end parentheses in 6-5) factorially the total a_{ijk} deviation (standard) score thus:

$$\hat{a}_{ijk} = [(v_1 T_{1i} + \cdots + v_n T_{ni}) + (w_1 P_{1j} + \cdots + w_m P_{mj}) \\ + (x_1 Q_{1k} + \cdots + x_z Q_{zk})]/3 \qquad (6\text{-}5)$$

(As noted before, j here is a test and thus actually covers a combination, hj, of stimulus and response as we would usually write it in the full five set data box.)

A query that naturally arises here is whether it is sufficient to describe the person i in factors in *tests* alone (as we commonly do) since we now have situations also and could from a *persons* $\times$ *situations* score matrix (averaged over tests), get a description also in factors describing how people react as regards situations. Cattell, Blaine, and Kameoka (in preparation) have examined this and concluded that since the transpose of that score matrix— *situations* $\times$ *persons*—already contributes dimensions in equation (6-5), it is unnecessary, if Burt's position (1936) is correct, to involve six matrices in reproducing a_{ijk}.

The aim of equation (6-5) is to permit us to grasp not only the magnitude but also the nature of the contributions to the final act from person traits, *T*'s, test (stimulus-response) traits, *P*'s and situation traits, *Q*'s. We are thus permitted to *understand* and predict final behavior from a meaningful integration of attributes of people, tests and situations. At the moment research has given concrete meanings only to source traits of persons, but psychologists who write on the environment will hopefully open up discoveries regarding situational and stimulus traits. Incidentally if this illustration in 3-way analysis is extended to the full 5-set data box there will be five bracketted terms in (6-5). One could indeed open up two sources of meaning for traits of each of the h, i, j, k and o ids. Those of observers, o's, and situations, k's, will be of particular interest to econetics.

Among further technical problems that can be glanced at but not pursued here is the possibility that the above treatment would be more apt in real base than in traditional (unit factor variance) factor analysis. Also one may ask whether there are any special problems in connection with particular BDRM sets. Observers can obviously be easily handled. Different forms of response, however, among the j's, present some problems through non-comparable score units, and if we bring them to standard scores we lose something. A possibility is to let the *populations* be standard scores, so that the given sample need not have the same mean and sigma on all performances.

Finally, it should be realized that the "additive attribute" model is still essentially a psychometric not an ecometric one, that is, the dimensions found for situations, observers, etcetera, are in psychological not physico-social terms.

6-6. The Person-centered Product Model for the Assessment of the Influence of Environment and Other Data Box Sets

The second model for defining understanding and calculating the other influences than personality itself which determine recorded behavior retains personality traits as central and expresses the rest by *coefficients affecting the trait expressions*. The basic model was stated 15 years ago in Sells' *Stimulus determinants of behavior* (1963) and has been carried a step further in modulation theory here (Chapter 5) and elsewhere.

The most elementary form of this model recognizes that the environment (actually the stimulus, response and situation, hjk, together) is represented as a vector of behavioral indices in the specification equation for that response situation. The theorem follows that two stimulus response events are similar in meaning to the extent that the vectors of behavioral indices in their specification equation are similar. Actually the relation of two such vectors, as for behavior in stimulus responses j_1 and j_2 in the following

$$b_{j1a}, b_{j1b}, \ldots, b_{j1k}$$

and $\quad b_{j2a}, b_{j2b}, \ldots, b_{j2k}$ \hfill (6-6)

(where j_1 and j_2 are two behaviors determined by factors a through k) would be better determined by the *pattern similarity coefficient* r_p than the correlation, r, of these series of b's. An objective taxonomy of perceived situations, that is, a psychometric taxonomy, can thus be reached as suggested in more detail elsewhere (Cattell 1963), by setting up a matrix of situations with r_p's in the cells and either applying Taxonome to find types of environment as suggested (Cattell 1963) or factoring for dimensions as Bolz (1972) suggests.

In the last paragraph we moved immediately to illustrate the essential use of this mode of environmental representation in achieving an objective taxonomy of situations. But more development of the model itself is desirable both to reach a more refined meaning of taxonomy and to understand the variance contribution analysis offered by the model.

The main development is an extension of analysis of *behavioral indices* in the specification equation initially developed in Section 6-3 above and in modulation theory. Six special developments are involved, as follows: (1) a refinement of the concept of the modulation mechanism developed in the preceding chapter, (2) an ultimate breakdown of the behavioral index, b, into four rather than three components, (3) a second way, derived from this model, of reaching the relative variances due to persons, situations, response forms, and so on, beyond that set out in Section 6-5 above, (4) a more analytical treatment of the taxonomic classifications of environment, (5) the definition of a *perception* of environment psychometrically in vector terms, (6) a model for roles and role adoption in relation to personality.

To approach the remainder of these questions let us begin by some expansion of the modulation model in (1).

From the preceding chapter the reader will recall that the modulation model supposes that an ambient situation, k, modulates a state proneness or liability, L_{xi}, to state x to produce a state magnitude at the moment (occasion) k, of S_{xki}. Now evidence over the last decade or so (Cattell & Scheier, 1961; Cattell, Schmidt, & Bjersted, 1972) is forcing us to recognize that practically *every* trait also modulates (though with much smaller s's than for k's) so that there is no need to complicate the specification with two kinds of structural terms, T and L, and we may simply write:

$$a_{hijk} = v_{hj}s_{k1}L_{1i} + \cdots + v_{hjy}s_{ky}L_{y1} \qquad (6\text{-}7)$$

where L is *any* kind of trait or state liability, and there are y such structures. Parenthetically the consistency of the modulation model with the ANOVA breakdowns above should be noted. It supposes that there is personality variance in the L terms and that everyone changes significantly in behavior level from one situation to another, that is, that both sources of variation are significant. Furthermore since a product term, $s_{ky}L_{yi}$ is used it supposes that the change from k_1 to k_2 is not the same for all people, since individuals of higher L will change more in going to the second situation. It thus agrees with present findings (Moos, 1970; Endler, 1973; Argyle & Little, 1972) in requiring significant interaction, though the detailed form of that interaction may well differ from case to case.

Regarding equation (6-7) it is well to point out before proceeding (1) that here and in later equations unless there is particular relevance of the specific error factors, we shall, for printing simplicity, omit them, (2) that the split of the b term into v and s terms will now be more fully explained, statistically and theoretically, and (3) that the subscripts of k and j for the v's and k for the s's may both prove to require additions. The s's may be affected by h's, and v's by k's, as only experiment can decide. However, what we are saying psychologically is as in Chapter 5, namely that the modulator s_k states how much of a state is produced by the situation from the individual's state liability, L_{yi}, and that v_{hj} then describes how much that state— or equally a trait—is able to contribute to the response behavior.

The experimental obtaining of the v (v for trait or state *involvement* in a behavior) value is through dividing an experimentally obtained b (a loading) by an experimentally obtained s, thus:

$$v = \frac{b}{s} \qquad (6\text{-}8)$$

The technicalities of obtaining the s values involve *real base factor analysis* and use of what has been called the multi-situation-multi-demo (*MSMD*) design (as shown in Figure 6-3) and which may be read at length elsewhere (Cattell, 1973). However, the essential step in procedure is to compare the standard deviation of a factor in an unstimulated condition (k_o) with its standard deviation in a stimulated condition, k_1. The *law of constancy of factor effect* (Cattell, 1972) supposes that for each unit increase in a factor score there will be a v_j increase in a given variable j. Hence if the factor actually increases in range, by a ratio s_{k1} (actually a ratio of s_{k1} to s_{ko}) its change effect on the variable will be $s_k v_j$ compared to the effect when the factor stands at unit variance at k_o.

To find the s_{kx} value for a given situation k_x, therefore, we need to compare the variance of the factor in situation k_x with that at k_o, which is either some assumed point of zero stimulation, or, more practically, a central mean value of many situations. This can be done either by (a) having a good factor battery and literally measuring the variances, over some standard sample of people, in the different situations, or (b) if no valid battery is available, factoring the variables over a variety of separate situations. The above reference to real base factoring means that in the latter case we must use real base rather than ordinary factoring, with unit length factors, because we want to be aware of changing factor sizes. In either case the calculation is that

$$s_{k1} = \frac{\sigma_{k1}}{\sigma_{ko}} \qquad (6\text{-}9)$$

where these are the sigmas of the factor at k_1 and k_o, the central core value.

Actually in real base factoring the factor variance size will depend on both the variance modulation due to the situation and that due to population or sample difference. Accordingly, to separate these, the fuller treatment of this matter elsewhere (Cattell, 1972c) calls for an MSMD design sampling both populations ("demos") and situations. Many such factorings yield a central standard core reference matrix fixing the unit length factor. The size of any factor at any other situation and demo is then given (with unity as "equal") by the calculation in equation (6-9) and Figure 6-3. To get a measure of s_k which describes only the modulation effect and not that part of the effect due to selection of the group for greater or lesser demographic variance, an additional calculation is necessary (see Cattell, 1972c). The experimental assessment is concluded when knowing the b loading value (in covariance terms) it is broken into the s_k by equation (6-9). We then get v by equation (6-8).

However, the further analysis of the specifications equation coefficients, as above, into s's and v's is not the end of what needs to be done to represent the environment. The s_k represents the emotional state or drive-exciting character of the ambient situation k. This leaves in v the description both of the stimulus properties and of the vigor and executive skill with which the response course of action, j, is pursued. In fact v must involve (a) cognitive perceptual skills, beginning with the recognition of the stimulus object,

	Situations				Mean Demo
	k_1	k_2	k_c	k_y	V_{fp}'s
$p1$	a_{j1}	a_{j1}		a_{j1}	
	a_{j2}	a_{j2}		a_{j2}	
	.	.		.	
	.	.		.	
	.	.		.	
	a_{jn}	a_{jn}		a_{jn}	
p_2	a_{j1}	a_{j1}		a_{j1}	
	a_{j2}	a_{j2}		a_{j2}	
	.	.		.	
	.	.		.	
	.	.		.	
	a_{jn}	a_{jn}		a_{jn}	
p_c					
p_o	a_{j1}	a_{j1}		a_{j1}	
	a_{j2}	a_{j2}		a_{j2}	
	.	.		.	
	.	.		.	
	.	.		.	
	a_{jn}	a_{jn}		a_{jn}	

Demos (N subjects in each)

Mean Situation V_{fp}'s

Figure 6-3.   Sources of modulator value change in the multisituation multidemographic group design.

Elsewhere (Cattell, 1971b) the writer began by designating this an MRMS design. In broader perspective this proved a misnomer and the present designation—MSMD, for multisituation-multidemographic group—is distinctly preferable.

(b) a dynamic value showing the intensity of motivational investment in j, from the aroused dynamic source trait $s_k D$, and (3) a
level in whatever executive (including motor) skills are involved in
j. Can these be equated in some way with the description of the
environment, that is, its psychometric meaning, and with the sets
of the data box?

The difficulty of fitting an operational to a conceptual distinction here lies in the often inextricable binding of goodness of
cognitive action with goodness of executive action in the stimulus
response process represented in our symbols by hj. The organic
whole of cognitive perceptions and execution that we recognize
when a tennis player returns a fast ball is typical of most human
behavior.[7] Nevertheless, an experimental separation of contributions from the cognitive recognition on the one hand and the
executive strength on the other would seem possible in principle by
linking k's and j's in different combinations, or holding k fixed and
attaching various j's to it, and vice versa. For example, one could
have a series of tests in which the appearance of a word for the
female of a species—doe, hen, cow—called for drawing a woman and
the male term—cock, buck, etc.—for drawing a man. In every case
part of the speed of performance would be due to the cognitive
perception of the stimulus, k, and part to the capacity to execute
the response, j. The aim would be factor analytically to determine
v's for various combinations, $k_1 j_1$, $k_1 j_2$, $k_2 j_1$, $k_2 j_2$, etcetera, and
work out, by simultaneous equations, the fractions of the experimentally obtained v associated respectively with h's and k's.

Parenthetically, the rather long persisting myth or prejudice
preventing recognition that multivariate (factor analytic) experiment
can and should use manipulation as freely as bivariate designs, has
resulted in our having no results to cite here. But one can conceive
several kinds of experiment here that could produce variance contribution separation. For example subjects could be instructed in
experiment 1 to press a button as soon as they recognized the
stimulus and, in experiment 2, to respond to it by some defined
motor action appropriate to the stimulus. We could obtain factor
loadings, b's, on the one hand for the *recognition* process alone and
on the other for *recognition plus action*. In principle by subtracting
the former from the latter we could get that part of the loading
value which is the effect of contribution by each trait upon the
executive action part of the score.

There are statistical and experimental technicalities in putting
these principles into action, of course. The measurement units
would have to be the same in both, for example, seconds, to re-

cognize the object, and to complete the task, and the factor analysis would have to be real base, and to ensure that the factors are the same in the two analyses and capable of assuming larger loadings over all in the second case. Alternatively, if one already had concrete batteries for the factors, the experimental comparison would be one of raw regression (B) coefficients. It is also an alternative possibility that sufficiently ingenious experiment could wipe out perceptual skills and obtain the v loadings for effectiveness of response alone, directly, that is, without having to subtract cognitive perception from perception-plus-response performance. Lastly, an experimental design to use the varieties of combinations as discussed above, and which might be called a *re-coupling design* could be tried. This is illustrated briefly in Table 6-3 and alluded to further in note 7 above. The breakdown into p and e terms shown in Table 6-3 as a derivative from experimentally coupling stimuli (h's) and responses (j's) in all possible combinations supposes that the s values have already been taken out (or held constant).

What is illustrated (for 48 test variables) in Table 6-3, could be carried out in a global way for the whole data box with sufficiently large samples of subjects. With w stimuli, x responses, y situations and z observers, combined in all ways (as for h and j in Table 6-3) we should have $w \times x \times y \times z$ experimental measures, which, for factoring would require 3 to 5 times as many people as $wxyz$. The correlations of the $wxyz$ variables would yield loading patterns

TABLE 6–3. Constitution of Variables in the Coupling Experimental Design to Separate Perceptual from Executive Action of Traits

	j_1	j_2	j_3	j_4	j_5	j_6	Row sums:
h_1	$p_1 + e_1$	$p_1 + e_2$	$p_1 + e_3$				$8p_1 + \Sigma e$
h_2	$p_2 + e_1$	$p_2 + e_2$	$p_2 + e_3$				$8p_2 + \Sigma e$
h_3	$p_3 + e_1$	$p_3 + e_2$					
h_4	$p_4 + e_1$						
h_5	p_5						
h_6	p_6						
h_7	p_7						
h_8	p_8						

Column sums:

$8e_1 + \Sigma p$ $8e_2 + \Sigma p$

from which, by the treatment indicated by summing all h_a's, all j_b's, all s_c's etc. (Table 6-3) estimates could be obtained, for every factor, of the size of p, e, l, and s in equation (6-11) below.

The concept we have now reached is that any trait or state liability (which we will represent generically as T) enters into determining the total response j, to a stimulus h, in an ambient situation k, in a way that requires *three* indices. They are s_k to represent its modulation, and what we will symbolize as p, to represent its aid to *perception*, and e its contribution to *execution*. We shall thus have in the specification equation a vector series of p's, constituting the *perceptual vector* for the given behavior, a series of e's representing the *executive skill vector*, and a series of s's, the *shift* or *arousal modulating vector*.

The model could treat the p and e indices either as additive—as would be required by the above initial experimental derivation from their additive contributions to the variance of the response, a_{hjk}—or in a product relation, which could be reached by a different derivation from the same experimental data. The modulator action is already committed to being a product, through the derivation from the core matrix being fitted to the postulated law that the sigma of a state will be simply proportional to its mean measured from an absolute zero. There exist ways in which an s could be defined with additive properties, but without digressing on that we have the alternatives for any term in the specification equation of

$$p \cdot e \cdot s \cdot T \qquad\qquad (6\text{-}10a)$$
or
$$(p + e) \cdot s \cdot T \qquad\qquad (6\text{-}10b)$$

There would be corresponding expression in the *matrix* representation, covering the relation of the matrix *vectors* **P**, **E**, **S**, and **T**, which we shall encounter in due course. The terms of the enriched specification equation, their definitions and relations to this point, are summarized in Table 6-4.

What we have reached in this section is a breakdown of magnitudes of effects from the five sets of the data box paralleling that in the previous section but utilizing a different mathematical model. Like the additive attribute model it can lead to a breakdown of behavioral variance into personality, stimulus, observer, and situation variance components, and also to means of describing the environment psychometrically in precise vectors of attribute measures. The observer component in the b term, incidentally, presents no problem inasmuch as it can be derived from the changes in b values when a range of observers instead of a single or mean observer is used. The terms then become:

$$p \cdot e \cdot l \cdot s \cdot T \tag{6-11a}$$

or

$$(p + e + l) \cdot s \cdot T \tag{6-11b}$$

where l is the observer (mnemonic: looker on) source, and p, e, l, and s are fragmentations of the loading b.

The terms just given will have subscripts p_h, e_j, l_o, s_k, and T_i, which reminds us of their operational alignment with the data box coordinates. It reminds us also of some lack of alignment with existing psychological conceptions of trait modality which we initially hoped to incorporate. For although perceptual processes are largely involved in reacting to the stimulus, they are not there alone, for they enter, as we have seen, also into action execution. And although dynamic modality is *largely* involved in the modulation term acting upon a drive, the tie up of motivation-interest with a particular course of action also affects the value of e. (In some representations we have therefore weakened on the exactness of alignment of p, e, l, and s with the nature, respectively, of h, j, o, and k, and permitted s to be fixed by both h and k, and e by both h and j; though strict application of the model requires a testing of the assumption of exclusive alignment.)

Even with strict adherence to the alignment with data box sets we shall still propose later a further conceptual step in which e is broken down into a motor executive effect of a trait, and an interest intensity effect, which we will represent by r for motor and n for interest-motivation. A person who habitually plays 9 holes of golf in 40 has a 40 score which partly represents the role of any given trait, say exvia, through some contribution to *skill* (let us assume, for example, that extroverts are more athletic) and partly through some contribution to interest in the game (an exviant person enjoying the company in a foursome). Additional experimental operations could split e into these r and n components.

The mathematical and conceptual relations of the additive attribute model in equation (6-5), to the personality centered product model here (in 6-11) can certainly be worked out, but we shall not stop to do the translation here. Conceptually the *attribute* model allows the stimulus, the observer, the ambient situation, etcetera, to express their influence in the subject's behavior by additions specifically from their own attributes, with no more than additive interaction with the attributes of the person. The *person-centered* model, on the other hand, expresses all the influences of environment, etcetera, *through* the person's traits. The former appeals by a simpler and cleaner separation of the sources of variance. The latter, one suspects, takes care of interactions that really exist psychologically. As to the mathematico-statistical translation from one to the other, it suffices perhaps to note that the variance of, say, the effect of attributes (dimensions) of ambient situation, k's, is paralleled in the latter by the variance in size of s's across the various behaviors, and similarly for the other terms.

The above two developments of specification equations for combining the effects of personality, stimulus, observer, situation and mode of response in estimating the magnitude of response have their primary importance in and of themselves. However, they lead also to several by-products, two of which—the development of a taxonomy of environment and the analysis of perception—we shall follow up here.

On the former only a brief comment is needed, since—at the level of depending on the total b values—it has been handled elsewhere (Sells, 1963), and will be met again under perception. In the initial statement each response situation was represented by the vector of b's in the given specification equation. From a collection of vectors from many situations it is then possible objectively to classify in species types by taxonome principles (Bolz, 1972; Cattell, 1970; Cattell & Coulter, 1966) and the taxonome program. Using the additive model for environmental effects, on the other hand, one would not enter with vectors of p's and s's but with vectors of the scores of situations, stimuli, etcetera, on the dimensions peculiar to each, as used in the later bracketted terms of equation (6-5). By either the additive or the personality centered approach the similarities and the species of environments can be expressed, of course, either for ambient situations alone or for stimuli, etcetera, too. This non-subjective approach to a psychometrically meaningful taxonomy and categorization of environments could lead to powerful developments in clinical, and social psychology, particularly concerning emotional meaning. It could conceivably give aid even in the narrower field of cognitive abilities and perceptions, for example, in relation to brain damage.

6-7. The Behavioristic Definition of Perception and a New Model for the Concepts Involved

A fashionable excursion occurred at the middle of this century from studying perception in traditional Wundtian and Titchenerian cognitive frameworks to what was called "the new look." This rightly attempted an assault on the emotional aspects of perception, but unfortunately it left nothing but a few model-less experiments and some psychoanalytic conjectures. Personality was brought in notably through projection and other Freudian mechanisms but, except for the work of Wenig (1952), there were only fragmentary attempts to verify the defense mechanisms as such as functional unities in experimental operations, which would have supplied the necessary quantitative basis for that kind of approach.

A sufficiently broad theoretical model, capable of expressing the personality as a whole, and in meaningful measurements was then lacking, but today, armed with objective evidence of personality and motivation structure and a systematic psychometric model of the environment, a broader theory of perception is at last possible. If one is a behaviorist—and virtually all psychologists are, since abandoning the introspectionism of Kulpe, Meinong, Stout, Titchener, and others in the late nineteenth century— a perception is something the existence and nature of which must be inferred from behavior. But if what the person *does* (or would do if not inhibited) in response to a stimulus is the true and only behavioral evidence from which to infer the nature of his perception, one might argue, as Cattell and Scheier (1961) did, that "a perception" might be a superfluous term and concept. What a person is perceiving they argued, is probably sufficiently defined and described by what he does, and therefore already resides in the specification equation, as a pattern of loadings on the personality and ability traits. This is a consistent behavioristic position, but it still leaves open the question of whether the vector of b's (or v's or s's) is solely concerned with the existing traits and state liability terms, or whether still others are needed. We must never forget that—at least with the list of broad personality, ability and dynamic source traits presently known—we scarcely account for two thirds of the variance of a typical sample of human behaviors.

Many psychometrists still use a traditional specification equation, that is, one with only fixed features, namely, fixed traits and total, unanalyzed loadings (b's). This kind of restriction would almost certainly make the proposed formulation of perception inadequate. Any perception would be simply a function of the unchanging personality (and the physico-social, ecometric situation) and would ignore, among other things, the undoubted fact that the same person sees things differently at different times. Perception seems to need also something more narrow than traits and states, as appears in the nature of cognitive "apperception masses" (to use Herbart's still valuable term), that belong to the person but can come and go. The recent work of Magnusson and Ekehammar (1975b) well illustrates, for example, the importance in perception of passing stresses, etcetera, as here envisaged.

The present model maintains the position that the nature of the perception is defined by the behavior, but in extracting a formula from the specification equation it recognizes (a) the full role of the state terms and (b) that the large unitary factors, whether cognitive or dynamic, are not the whole story and must be supplemented by much smaller and also more transient factor contributors. Pursuit of (b) will lead us into some developments about sentiments that are important and integrative in other areas of behavior, too. Meanwhile, however, let us look at the central statement, regardless of these newer "transient factor" notions.

The central statement is that the meaning of a total situation to which a person is reacting is, for the population to which he belongs, precisely described by the set of behavioral indices for that situation. This will be represented by a set of loading-derived indices which, omitting only the observer error, l, from 6-11 will be written:

$$(p_{h1}e_{j1}s_{k1})\,(p_{h2}e_{j2}s_{k2}) \cdots (p_{hw}e_{jw}s_{kw}) \tag{6-12}$$

assuming w to be the total number of ability, temperament and dynamic traits in people, and, of course, that some of them are state liability traits. Note we have kept specifically to subscript h for p's, j for e's, and so on, though doubt was expressed above that associations will be conceptually quite that neat.

By contrast to equation (6-12) which gives the meaning of a perception a_{hjk} to the general population the meaning of a_{hijk} will vary somewhat for individuals, since their traits will interpret the situation differently. The vector is now that of the full terms in the specification itself, namely:

$$(p_{h1}e_{j1}s_{k1}T_{1i})\,(p_{h2}e_{j2}s_{k2}T_{2i}),\ \text{etcetera} \tag{6-13}$$

Thus if T_2 happened to be the fear erg and k an air raid, the average person would react (a_{hjk}) to a fearful situation as shown by the $p_{h2}e_{j2}s_{k2}$ magnitudes, but a person high in T_2 would perceive it as a *particularly* fearful situation.

Finally, let us ask how the less fixed, more maneuverable cognitive "apperception masses" come into this model. The discussion in Volume 2 on the manner in which sentiments are acquired, as well as the analysis of sentiment structure in children by Sweney (1961) suggest that we have a hierarchical form in sentiments, with a broad factor over the whole domain concerned, and with narrower, lower order factors detectable at lower levels of factorization within it.

These latter ultimately splinter into what we would recognize as *mental sets*, and presumably further into single "ideas" and images—cognitive-dynamic *apperception masses*. It is customary to think of these purely as entities of the moment, quite different from traits. But we must remember that even large sentiments are subject to considerable modulation of strength with occasions (Cattell & Cross, 1952; Birkett & Cattell, 1978), and we deal in mental sets and cognitive apperception masses only with an extreme on the continuum of such modulation. The specification equation in complete form should therefore splinter at the right hand end into a number of increasingly minor factors, which, like the typical liability, L, structure will characteristically fluctuate appreciably in salience due to their high susceptibility to modulation. Our ultimate model indicates that their arousal is determined partly by the arousal of the broad unitary sentiment to which they belong and partly by the impact of specific external stimuli (see Volume 2).

A contingent summary of personality in relation to perception of the environment therefore requires us to recognize (1) That the perceptual meaning of a situation of action can be psychometrically precisely defined by the **P**, **E**, and **S** vectors of p, e, and s indices, for *common* meaning, and for any *individual* by the full specification equation entered with his trait scores. (2) This provides an objective basis, via pattern similarity indexes applied to these vectors, for different response situations, to provide a psychometric, typal taxonomy of situations. Such typing could be set out separately, if desired, in cognitive, emotional-dynamic, etcetera, domains. The psychometric meaning typology thus reached can then be related to the ecometric features of environment by whatever laws may appear. (3) That over and above the applied psychological utility of such handling of perception, interesting theoretical possibilities are opened up of predicting the meaning of new situations to individuals who have never experienced them from indices already known and traits already scored. The above is summarized in Table 6-4.

6-8.   The Definition, Experimental Discovery, and Measurement of Role Traits

Since by general consent of writers in the social area of role behavior such behavior is more tied up with environmental situations than are the general run of personality factors, the present systematic treatment of situational influences is the appropriate place to turn to a proper precision of definition of the role concept in personality.

TABLE 6—4. Distinctions and Relations of Environment Vectors
in the Specification Equation

Matrix Term	Single Index Term
Factor Pattern Matrix, V_{fp}	b, factor loading or *behavioral index*
Covariance Factor Pattern	c, covariance factor loading or
Matrix, V_{fpc}	*investment index*
Perception Vector, **P**	p, perception index
Execution Vector, **E**	e, execution index
Shift Vector, **S**	s, modulation index

$$b = vs$$
$$v = pe \text{ or } p + e$$
$$bS = b \, s \, L$$
Note conceptual difference of $b(sL) = bs(L)$

The last three rows are **P**, **E**, and **S**, presented as vectors, but could also, by conjugating
several such rows, be presented as matrices like V_{fp} and V_{fpc} above.

Role is actually one of several concepts that are likely to be
experimentally advanced in the next decade by application of the
modulation model. As we shall see, modulation lies at the heart
of role action as it did of psychophysiological state change, and
when we come to personality learning (Volume 2) we shall find
it pulling into its orbit Hull's (1952) and Tolman's (1938) notions
of "expectation" and "anticipation." In social psychology it handles
Fischbein's "behavioral intention" as an attitude parameter and
permits calculations on Stogdill's (1950) and Frederiksen's (1970)
"group atmospheres" (in administrative groups), while in the field
of perception it permits a restatement of Blake and Helson's (1960)
findings of "adaptation levels." These offshoots for application of
the modulation model must be left to the reader while we turn to
its detailed application to the important personality concept of *role*.

At the outset one should recognize that role is not only the
property of the personality theorist but also of the anthropologist
and the sociologist, and our treatment must integrate these views
which are at present as diverse as the descriptions by touch of the
elephant by the several blind men in the Sufi story. For example,
the anthropologist is struck by the enormous difference of pattern
or mean level of what the psychologist would think of as a "personality expression" for example, gregariousness or sex, due to the
mores and roles of different cultures. The sociologist, indeed, is
inclined to believe he can explain most of people's differences in
behavior *without* personality (certainly without inherited tempera-

ment!), simply by recognizing the roles in which they are placed. For these academic specialties there is almost an agreement that personality can be virtually squeezed out of any conceptual predictive importance.

The personality psychologist, who is often also a social psychologist, is not as unaware, however, as the sociologist sometimes thinks, that everyone may shout lustily at a football match, less lustily at dinner, and not at all in church, and he does recognize the cultural anthropologist's "customs and mores." He sees these as evidences of substantial modifiers of ordinary personality traits residing in a new class of traits which can generically be called roles. Roles can range from relatively permanent to transient ones, but even as transient sets they must possess a permanent underlying trait structure. The more permanent role reactions tend to be those recognized by being definitely present in some people and absent in others, for example, a mother contrasted with a non-mother otherwise similar in personality, and the transient ones are recognized by one and the same person stepping relatively completely in and out of a role, as say an officer does in relation to the parade ground. But the difference is only one of degree. What can be perceived to characterize them in all cases is a certain independence of the rest of the personality and a modulation of action to quite specific environments, contrasting with the more universal appearance of a personality trait. Thus they represent a break from ordinary personality behaviors, as estimated from personality traits measured across the majority of ordinary situations.

The environment thus assumes a degree of importance previously not so apparent, for these new role behaviors occur under the sanction and stimulus of some quite special situation, in which the more deviant pattern of behavior is approved and required. Because of these marked behavior changes it has not infrequently been explicitly argued, especially by sociologists, that as we mentioned above, role concepts should be sufficient to explain all behavior. However, if the reader has recognized the implications of Section 6-7 on perception, he will see that this is incorrect. In this section we shall describe what seems the best model to bring personality and role together.

Under the notion that roles are a strictly social phenomenon a considerable amount of experiment has focused on the change of individual behavior that often occurs between a nongroup and a group situation, notably in the work of Asch (1950); Hemphill and Weste (1950, 1952); Cattell and Stice (1960) and others in group dynamics; Blake and Helson on adaptation levels (1960); and Stogdill on group norms and expectations (1952). But change in and out of groups is not *the whole* of role behavior, a fair fraction of which, in fact, is not restricted to group situations. Robinson Crusoe's scanning of the horizon as a daily ritual, the self mortification of anchorites in the desert, or a farmer's attention to his fields have some role characteristics. Nevertheless much of the above work on group determination of behavior—as well as some research not specifically set in a group—can well be brought together under the single topic of *role behavior*.

The difference of role perception by sociologist and psychologist is essentially that between the outside and the inside of the same structure. To the sociologist, a role is a socially recognized and individually accepted status, with duties and privileges attached, defined by the group culture and important to the group. Further, especially to the cultural anthropologist, it has historically traceable roots and considerable resistance to change. Nevertheless, the social psychologist does not neglect these group status and group function aspects and has indeed moved further than the non-quantitative anthropologist in defining them by precise patterns and scales. This he has done through (1) finding and measuring the dimensions of group function, for example, measuring social status (Cattell, 1942; Cattell and Stice, 1976; Rummel, 1960; Sawyer, 1967) in relation to which role functions can be articulated, and by (2) tracing communication networks and cooperative role relations, for example, in leadership hierarchies, sub-cultures, etcetera. (Cattell and Stice, 1953, 1970; Asch, 1952; Bales and Strodbeck, 1951; Gorer, 1955; Kelley and Thibaut, 1969; Rummel, 1975; and Stricker, 1977.)

From the standpoint of personality and individual dynamics, however, a role has a very different appearance. It is constituted by an interrelated set of learned habits which are highly dependent on triggering by certain ambient situations and which are, through learning, connected with some institution, and possessed more by some people than others. As to the last—differences of degree—a role may appear to be an all or nothing matter in terms of psychometric distribution of scores, as when a man is married or unmarried, or when a person is equipped to step at a moment's call into a policeman's role, or not. Yet everyday observation shows that even in such categorical instances there are degrees to which a person is in the role, for example, the extent to which he takes on, say, the husband's or policeman's role. However, in virtually all discussions of the role model here, we shall not find it necessary to digress much into this somewhat secondary issue of whether the behaviors are continuous and normally distributed or bimodal. For correlational, structure-analytic purposes, for instance, we can handle any bimodal cases along with the general pattern of continuity of score distribution by using both biserial and ordinary correlations.

In regard to the more basic question of placing role structures among other personality structures, we have empirically recognized in Chapter 4 that they emerge from experimental data which show that they belong to the class of acquired dynamic structures which we call *sentiments*, that is, acquired aggregates of attitude actions, though some may be limited *parts* of sentiments.

The peculiarity of the role among sentiments probably will be found to reside in two features (a) a far higher sensitivity to modulation by situations, and (b) a special kind of pattern, not necessarily broader or narrower than other sentiments, but more tied to social involvements. Indeed the line between a role sentiment and other sentiments cannot be sharply drawn by any one feature, and the question could be raised, for example, whether a sentiment to one's career is not also a role sentiment. However, in the transient type of role sentiment it is clear that a distinguishing feature is that the *same* focal stimuli are often met by any individual both inside and outside the role but are reacted to *quite* differently in the two cases. Further we note that the difference in the ensuing response is due specifically to the different ambient situation. In short, the ambient situation and its modulating action are the key to role action. For example, a teacher may witness two children fighting in the classroom or on the way home from school and is likely to feel that interference is called for, as part of the teacher role, only in the ambient situation of the classroom. Very often the crucial ambient situation is well marked, as when a policeman steps into and out of his role with the donning and removing of his uniform, or a tennis pro with stepping on the court. In the case of a permanent role, say, that of a mother, the ambient situations are equally clear by activating the given person quite differently from another. Thus only in temporal respects is it necessary to think of any difference of the essentially similar models of permanent and transient roles.

Although quite different in secondary respects, *states* (with state liability traits) and *roles* are *formally* in the same class. They are similar in showing an unusually large change of level of action through the modulating action of an ambient situation. However, in the case of the state, the situation arouses an innate erg or an inborn pattern of, say, physiological anxiety response, whereas a role is a learned sentiment and consequently is more activated and expressed through a cognitive network.

Here we have to ask a question, since a role is a species of sentiment, that will be more fully pursued in the dynamics of sentiments in Volume 2, namely: "Is there evidence that the parts of the cognitive system of a sentiment not only grow together, but are activated from time to time, as just assumed, as a functional unity?" Experimentally, the best test of this is whether its pattern appears not only in R-technique factorings, but also shows rise and fall as a single functional unity in dR- and P-technique, that is, is it excited as a unitary whole? The early work of Cross (1951) (see also Cattell and Cross, 1952) indicated strongly that a sentiment does modulate simultaneously in all the attitude strengths which define it. The more recent work of Birkett (1977), Kline and Grindley (1974), and, indirectly, Cattell, Kawash, and DeYoung (1972) and others now brings sufficient experimental evidence to show that, like any other sentiment, a role sentiment does undergo a change of cognitive excitation and shows a *general* readiness to respond. This activation tends to extend simultaneously through all its attitude parts when the right ambient stimulus situation impinges.

By analogy with state liability, therefore, the simplest model for role action is obtained by adding a role action liability factor to the usual trait and state specification equation. This could be written M, since it is a sentiment, but to indicate its special character among sentiments, we shall designate a role as R and add it to the general specification equation thus:

$$a_{hijk_r} = \sum^{y=q} p_{hy}e_{jy}s_{k_ry}T_{yi} + \sum^{z=w} p_{hz}e_{jz}s_{k_rz}R_{zi} \qquad (6\text{-}14)$$

where there are q personality and state liability traits and w role patterns, and (kr) is the role-stimulating situation. (The p and e subscripts are here in their simplest form.)

This will meet the demands of the sociologist for prominence of the situation because the weights on R, when a_j is largely a role action, will be much greater than those of the T's, the personality traits. For it is the weight of s_{k_r} terms that particularly causes the level of action to be dependent on whether the person is in a role situation or not. It will also satisfy the psychologist in that within the range of role behavior it still allows for effects of differences of personality by the first term. "Level of action" refers to deviation from the person mean. The mean itself, that is, that from the score for *all* people, will, however, be brought to a higher level when the role is operating, if real-base factoring is used.

If equation (6-14) is accepted as our main role model, then we have to proceed to define in research the conditions whereby a role factor, R, can be recognized and distinguished from a personality factor, T. Elsewhere (Cattell, 1960), this has been discussed in detail with the conclusion that, *if the personality sphere has been followed* in choosing the variables: (1) the R's will distinguish from the T's (though not from the L's) first by much larger modulator values; (2) secondly by the fact that the loadings, b's, of any personality trait will extend over a large *variety* of ambient situations, k's, whereas those of an R will typically be restricted to a few definite, related, social situation variables; (3) when examined qualitatively, these situations will be perceived to be largely those of social demand and to coincide with what are recognized sociologically and anthropologically to be role expectation situations, whereas the T loadings, by contrast, will extend equally over social and nonsocial situations; and (4) when scores on factors are calculated, we may expect personality traits almost invariably to be essentially normal in distribution, whereas R's may be bimodal (or skewed) through individuals being either "in" or "out" of role positions, and often by only a minority of the population ever being in the role.

It will be seen that the theoretical framework here calls for an objective basis of separation of personality and role traits (for a role liability is a sentiment trait) from evidence on the *pattern of loadings* in a factor matrix, and the distribution of factor scores, etcetera, as above. To work well this design will need to have variables strategically chosen to bring in diverse situations, some believed to be role-evoking and others believed not to be, and to bring in the *same* stimuli (h's) in both of these kinds of situations. It is, however, only on initial circumscribing, to be enriched by further developments.

To illustrate more fully the principles of separation, Table 6-5 sets out 16 variables representing the possible combinations of four focal stimuli and four ambient situations. The factor analytic experiment has been carried far enough to yield the v's (not p's and e's) and the s's, set out in separate matrices for the four factors extracted. (There is no point here in breaking down the b's, the behavioral indices, as far as into p's and e's, since stimuli and responses are considered inherently tied.) The design for identifying roles calls, however, for a further experiment, re-shuffling the combinations of stimuli and ambient situations in different pairings, to test that the factor patterns found "move" with the h and k elements in the variables as they should. Thus, if the first two factors are personality factors and the last two (3 and 4) are role factors, we would in general expect, as illustrated here (to the limit of possible combinations in a small, simple example) that:

TABLE 6–5. The Expected Contrasting Loading Patterns on Involvement, v, and Modulator, s, Indices for Personality Traits and Role Traits

Variable	Elements combined in the variable		Loading pattern of factors in involvement indices, v's				Loading pattern of same factors in modulator indices, s's			
	Focal Stimulus	Ambient Situation	T_1	T_2	R_1	R_2	T_1	T_2	R_1	R_2
1	h_a	k_a	L		L		S		L	
2	h_b	k_a	L	L					L	
3	h_c	k_a	S	S	L		S		L	
4	h_d	k_a		L	L	S			L	
5	h_a	k_b	L			S	S		S	L
6	h_b	k_b	L	L	S	S			S	L
7	h_c	k_b	S	S		S			S	L
8	h_d	k_b		L	S	S		S	S	L
9	h_a	k_c	L		L				L	
10	h_b	k_c	L	L					L	
11	h_c	k_c	S	S					L	
12	h_d	k_c		L	L	S			L	
13	h_a	k_d	L							L
14	h_b	k_d	L	L						L
15	h_c	k_d	S	S		S				L
16	h_d	k_d		L		S				L

L means a large loading; S, a small; and a blank, a zero loading. There are two personality and two role structures. Ambient situations k_a and k_c invoke R_1 strongly, and k_b does so weakly. Situations k_b and k_d evoke role R_2 strongly.

1. The pattern of modulator indices, s_k's will follow the ambient situations, so that the role factors, R's, will be more largely and systematically loaded on them than will the personality traits (T's).

2. Personality factor loadings will attach themselves to, and repeat themselves most consistently in relation to, particular stimulus-response variables, that is, the same set of h's such as h_a, h_b, and h_c for T_1.

3. Mutually among personality traits there will be the usual randomly overlapping loading pattern on the variables. Between personality and role factors, however, a still more distinct difference of patterns will be expected. For the variables well loaded on a personality factor will distribute rather evenly over roles, as those of T_2 in Table 6-5 do over R_1 and R_2, and reciprocally the variables well loaded on some role will have loadings rather evenly scattered over several personality factors.

Point (1) above does not deny that there will be *some* large loadings on variables that are role traits (R_1 and R_2 in Table 6-5) and *some* large s loadings on personality traits (T_1 and T_2 in Table 6-5), but refers only to a preponderant incidence. Parenthetically, there will almost always be some tendency for variables with high s modulations on a role trait also to have some *significant* v loadings, for learning theory suggests there would be no point, dynamically, in a role trait being brought into action by modulation unless it also produced, by involvement, v, appreciable action on the variable concerned.

One notes from this that the same stimulus-response may come into action as part of the action of two or more roles and, conversely, that appreciable modulation of variables for one role factor can arise from two or more ambient stimulus situations.

The conceptual and operational separation and scoring of personality and role traits by the above model should not lead us to the illusion that (a) a person has to act in one role at a time, or (b) that a person can act at times *purely* in terms of his personality, without role intrusion. The first is obvious from common observation. For example, when entertaining guests with his family at dinner, a man may be in the social roles of a host, of a husband, of a father, and, if he happens to be professionally a specialist in the topic discussed at dinner, also of an authority.

The second principle—that a person is *always* in some degree acting in some role—is perhaps not so self evident, unless we recognize that roles as operationally defined here are occasionally not social in nature and setting, as occurs when, say, a forester switches from an esthetic enjoyment of the view to the care of his trees, or a cook is recalled from TV by the smell of burning in the kitchen. In any case the conclusion for psychometry is clear: to get the least biassed measure and conception of a personality trait we need to choose the variables by which it is scored by sampling behaviors *across a wide array of roles*, to produce attenuation of any specific role effects. To do this insightfully it is necessary to know what the role factors are, and to adjust weights according to their degree of intrusion. Conversely the scoring of a role trait requires sampling across all the different personality factors that express themselves in the role behaviors. Thus ideally one would not simply go to the nearest random factor pattern matrix (V_{fp}) and correct it (by R_v = correlation of variables and R_f = correlation of factors) to a factor estimation matrix of ($V_{fe} = R_v^{-1} V_{fp} R_f$), but would first select from a larger V_{fp} a smaller one with balance across the personality factors. The question of whether some necessary and systematic relation of certain personality factors with a particular role factor exists and should be heeded will be discussed as a secondary principle below.

As far as a first definition of a role is concerned the upshot of this section is that in internal, strictly individual psychological terms each role is definable by a two-column matrix, one giving the v's and the other the s's—as if we put the two R_1 columns together from Table 6-5. As just mentioned, the question of whether the definition of a particular role by a map in the form of a matrix of stimulus-situation-response loadings has a need to be extended to take account also of relations to particularly involved personality and dynamic factors remains now to be discussed.

6-9. The Dynamics of Role Traits and Other Sentiments
and the Formulation of Perception Changes
by People in Roles

Many questions are asked in textbooks about roles and their relations to personality, some of which admit more precise answers in terms of the above, and others of which stimulate a need for further conceptual development before they can be answered. Among those questions one encounters: "When a person steps into a role does his personality change?" "If the change in behavior in a person entering a role is not due to his personality changing, is it instead, due to his *perceiving* the same things differently?" and "Do certain roles give especial expression to certain general personality and dynamic traits, so that one may be forced to conclude that a certain personality will favor assumption of certain roles and certain roles develop particular personality traits?" This last would imply either that personality and role are not so distinct as so far said or that we must look further for special correlations and interactions among them. In tackling these issues the present section will become involved in basic issues of (a) the dynamics of sentiments, which apply to roles, and (b) some further development of the psychology of perception beyond that in the last section.

Before considering these rather complex new questions, let us recognize that some alternative models of a role itself *might* better fit certain analytical results. The principal alternative is to suppose that a role expresses itself—not just by a modulation on a role factor itself (over the situations which provoke it) but also by the role exercising a *pattern of modulations on a set of personality and dynamic factors*. This would require that the role be represented not just by *a role factor* and its *v*'s and *s*'s but by a pattern of weights, like modulating *s* indices, applied to primary personality factors. Psychologically that would express a capacity and need of the role regularly to invoke these factors in its expression.

The difference of this from the initial model is that therein the role is viewed as contributing an addition to what various personality factors do to *particular variables*, whereas in the alternative model the role is assumed to modify whole personality factors, affecting variables only at one remove. It is perhaps unlikely that an ability or temperament trait would be so modified, because the evidence suggests that they modulate little. But dynamic factors such as ergs and sentiments get modulated as a whole by situations and might easily participate in this way. The model is analogous to, and might even be identical with, the role as a second stratum factor. The alternatives are to take our first model—a single role factor—and evaluate the ergic content of all the particular behaviors the role factor loads strongly; or to take the second model and consider the ergic expressions of the role marked by its second stratum loadings on ergs. One could argue that this second stratum effect should be evaluated strictly by the modulation part of the loadings on primaries. Like any other sentiment learning, role learning occurs in the interests of ergic satisfactions (means-end learning) but the somewhat more popular view that certain roles are adopted *mainly* because they give more expression to certain dynamic needs also deserves investigation, which can be done in this model.

With this much approach toward sketching the more complex dynamics of roles let us return briefly to tidy the simpler issues such as that of role and perception—which may now be shown to be largely a question of semantic choice. The question of whether entering a role produces a change *of personality or of perception* seems to have been philosophically or semantically intriguing to psychologists. The issue is most evident in a temporary role, as when we ask whether a policeman in plain clothes is able to ignore a traffic violation to which he reacts brusquely when in uniform because his personality changes or merely because his perception is different. Of course, as far as an individual is concerned (equation 6-12) the perception is invariably defined in part by the personality. So the question becomes essentially "Are we to define the word personality only by the vector of permanent trait scores, or is it to be applied to the person with his states alongside his traits, at the given moment?"

The perception of a stimulus has certainly changed when a person steps into a role; for we have agreed that perception is a simple function of behavior, and the behavior potential has changed because the role factor is now modulated into action. Similarly, for that matter, the individual with a state liability modulated to some high state score certainly has a different perception, and if we choose to let semantics admit personality as temporary, his personality has changed at the same time.

The simplest way to verbal clarity here is to differentiate two terms, one for the "permanent," abstracted or latent personality, defined by the trait and state liability scores which, by their nature, are considered averaged across all situations, and one for the current, active or extant personality which is defined by its traits and states at the moment. Probably *latent* and *extant* are best, because active suggests only external stimulation, whereas the extant deviates at any moment from the latent by internal, for example, hormonal, effects too.

Even with the elimination of "deep questions" that are merely semantic we still have a quaint problem here of a conceptual and mathematical "reversible perspective" figure. In the ordinary R-technique model the change in behavior ($a_2 - a_1$) between situations k_1 and k_2, which we have accepted as a change in perception on entering a role, is representable in two ways according to where we put the bracket

$$a_{hijk_2} - a_{hijk_1} = [v(s_{k_2} - s_{k_1})]L_r = v[(s_{k_2} - s_{k_1})L_r] \qquad (6\text{-}15)$$

Here situation k_1 is out of the role and k_2 is in it, and L_r is a role liability trait (R in some other formulae). The first of the two analytic expressions keeps the personality, *per se*, intact and at its abstracted level as L_r, the latent personality, whereas the second says v operates on a changed personality—the new extant personality from modulation, shown within the brackets.

The conceptual equivalence in equation (6-15) may seem to have only theoretical or even semantic interest, but in forensic psychology it can become real—at least for the accused—in that if his courtroom personality is not that of the formerly extant personality which committed the crime he may escape punishment.

Even if we admit a probability of easier adoption of certain roles by certain personalities, the role and the personality can still be well separated by the above model. To speak in everyday terms, the model is saying that the same role can be found in persons of very different personalities and the same personality—in terms of general personality factor scores—can be found in individuals whose roles are strikingly different.[8]

6-10. Expressing the Environment Ecometrically in a Cultural Matrix, a Personality Expression Matrix and an Individual Impact Matrix

Our analysis of environment in relation to personality has so far covered the chief angles psychologists have commonly considered, namely, the ratios of variances from person, situation, stimulus, observers, etcetera, in any behavior; the effect of cultures and populations on trait structures; the understanding of perception of the environment in exact formulae; and the nature of role behavior—as well as some noval relations through the p, e, and s breakdown of behavioral indices, leading to an objective environmental taxonomy in psychometric terms.

At this point we devote two sections to a more ambitious but more complex calculus. The general reader is advised either to skip it at first reading or to be prepared to devote especially concentrated study to it, according to his degree of psychometric preparation and his desire for immediate completeness of treatment. The principal new concepts here are those of *scales of modulation intensity*, of *cultural presses* expressed in a matrix for a given culture, of *dynamic relevance* of cultural elements and of a matrix for each individual defining his *accessibility* or *vulnerability* to the standard features of the environment. The treatment, it should be said, is one for the general population and only in final aspects brought down to evaluations for the individual personality.

It will be remembered that as conditions of successful application of the trait modulation model, and of experimental solution of terms therein, it was required that (1) the state scale have equal interval properties (which might be sought by pan-normalization) or relational simplex (Cattell 1962, 1973, 1978) properties, and (2) that all members of the experimental group stand exactly at the same ambient stimulus modulation strength level. The latter is only a condition for the simple solution. However, in daily life, and perhaps even under laboratory control it is not sufficiently achieved. Due to different life backgrounds subjects are affected at the time of testing not only by the experimenter's controlled situation level but by many other ambient situations. The s_k acting on L_x at any given moment is actually a combination of several situations simultaneously producing the emotional state S_x. Thus among those people measured in the laboratory on response to the controlled anxiety stimulus k, Mary is to be married tomorrow, John needs to go to the dentist, and so on. As stated this may complicate but does not present a solution for modulation values, for De Young has shown (see Cattell, 1972) that if the law of proportionality of mean to sigma holds when all subjects are at the same s_k it will hold also when they are normally distributed around that value.

Consideration of this point introduces us, however, to a new domain of treatment of the environment which has to do with the relation of ecometric distributions to psychometric distributions and might be called *environmental impact theory*. It brings together the distribution of environmental elements and population trait elements, as might be seen in simplest form in the statement that the actual sigma of emotional states in the population will be the product of the sigma of L's and the sigma of k's. In these further developments we need the following concepts:

1. *The Cultural Press Matrix.* The notion of a totality of *entities* (types, patterns, for example, houses, banks, fraternities, families) in the real environment is involved here, plus a concept of their prominence in the given culture relative to one another and to that in other cultures. The entities will thus be given ecometric values in certain units that represent their sociological *importance* to the *average member* of the culture. The entries in the cultural press matrix will be both parametric and categorical, covering such things as cost of living, presence of religious institutions, city or country life, marriage features, wage distribution, etcetera. These real "cultural presses" as we shall call them could be either psychometrically or ecometrically expressed, but we will suppose in Figure 6-4 that we are dealing with the socio-physical entities initially in the terms of the sociologists and economists and therefore ecometric. Matrix C (for cultural press) in Figure 6-4 is a diagonal matrix, of one value for each press, and the values c_1 throught c_u, could perhaps for uniformity be represented as to their importance in ecometric units by the money the culture invests in them. It will be noted these are for the *average* person. The reason for arrangement as a diagonal instead of as a single vector will become evident in the ensuing calculation.

2. *The Individual Personal Position Matrix.* The second concept introduces the notion of the contact, relevance, or accessibility to each particular individual of each of these environmental entities as the result of the individual's special position in the culture. It is his

Possible examples

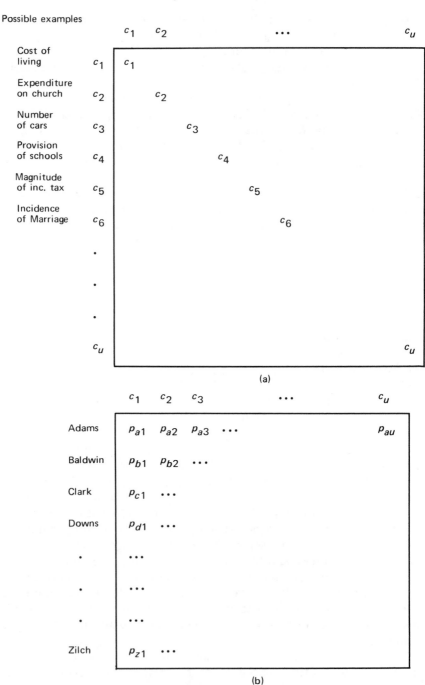

(a)

(b)

Figure 6-4. Illustration of the cultural pressure and personal position matrices, C and P. (a) Cultural pressure matrix: C; (b) personal position or relevance matrix: P.

personal statement of how cultural presses impinge upon him. Thus, if the individual has no car, he will have a zero entry for relevance of that element; if his house is quite inexpensive or rented, he may have less than average concern with what happens to cost of houses; or if he does not go to church, he may not be interested in what happens regarding the church. Note that relevance, exposure, or interaction score for a person in *P* does not here mean emotional relevance in the sense of how he reacts emotionally to it. It is a statement about the external stimulus—of how much the given cultural press in fact impinges on his life. He may very much *need* a car, but if one is not accessible to him the concerns of a car will not affect his behavior. This relevance, or accessibility of the environmental element in relation to the person's position in society, we may call a *p* value, and there will be *N* (×) *u* such entries—*N* being the number of people in the sample and *u*, as indicated, the number of cultural elements, the same as in *c*. The entries will be *p*'s for his relative position deciding his "vulnerabilities" or "accessibilities" to each element, that is, the relative relevances of the *u* elements to him. (See Figure 6-4b.)

From the interaction of the cultural press matrix, *C*, values and the personal exposure or interaction matrix, *P*, we can calculate (if we accept *products* as evaluating the effect) an *actual, personal impact* matrix (Figure 6-5), showing what influence is actually brought to bear on each given individual, through his *position* in the culture, in matrix *P*, being taken into consideration. *I*, the impact matrix, is, as it were, the pattern of any given individual's personal fate (but perhaps by unconscious or undesired choice) of involvements in the cultural environment, and, as the *P* × *C* multiplication in Figure 6-5 shows (recorded here in equation 6-16), it arises from considering the importance of a feature in a given culture

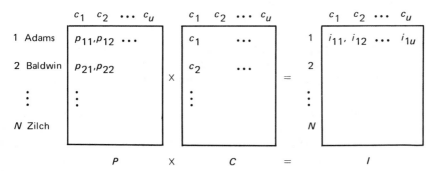

Figure 6-5.   The matrix multiplication to obtain the impact matrix, *I*.

and the degree of an individual's exposure to the elements of the culture, thus:

$$P \times C = I \qquad (6\text{-}16)$$
$$(N \times u) \; (u \times u) \quad (N \times u)$$

The impact matrix we have reached is still essentially in situational terms and in ecometric units, of whatever kind would derive from the terms in C, for example, economic, and those in P, for example, number of contacts the person makes per month with the object. For example, person x, living in a culture assigning small support to universities (C matrix), and himself having no contact with them, will have a decidedly smaller product value in the impact matrix, I, than will person y in a culture with prominent universities and at one of which the individual attends classes regularly. Our next step in the following section is to move from this ecometric description of the individual's situation to a psychometric calculation of his motivational involvement.

6-11. Expressing the Ecometric Environmental Impact Psychometrically, in Individual Matrices of Stimulation, Satisfaction, etcetera

The resolution of the environment so far reached remains, in the I matrix—the impact or contact matrix at the ecometric level. It says nothing about psychological reactions but attempts to state how the environmental presses impinge on the given individual. It states what amount of contact, dealings and involvements he has with the cultural elements first stated in the C matrix, that is, with wife, with car or public transport, with the supermarket, the library, local government, etcetera.

In transforming this impact to effects on personality and dynamics at least two intermediate transformation concepts have to be expressed in matrix form if calculations and checks on theory are to be made. Let us consider each and every individual represented by a profile (vector) of z scores on z dynamic structures such as the ergs and sentiments to home, school, hobby, career, etcetera. Since sentiments tend to arise around institutional elements of the culture some of these z items will bear the same name as some of the u cultural elements in the C and I matrices but we cannot assume anything approaching a one to one relation. The ergs, at least, among the dynamic structures, will have no one-to-one cultural element counterpart, and a sentiment, say, to photography will have dealings with decidely more than one cultural element, for example, with chemical industries, the imposition of tariffs on lenses from abroad, photographic clubs, etcetera.

The absolute level of the elements in the impact matrix, as well as changes in them, will have effects upon the individual's dynamic traits. These effects will be varied in emotional direction, and, as will soon be seen, we shall need a separate matrix for each kind of dynamic-emotional effect. What we are saying at this point is that for a given real world impact, as expressed purely in the ecometric $(N \times u)$ impact matrix, I, for a given individual (row i) the effect will depend (a) on the relation to his interests and purposes, to the degree and mode of impact, and (b) on the strength of his interests and purposes. The first requires attention to each of many kinds of effect, each of which will need to be expressed by a separate matrix. For example, one could consider (1) How far contact with each of the u elements leads to learning growth in each of the y dynamic traits, (2) How far it leads to stimulation, as by s_k terms, of those traits, (3) How much satisfaction it gives, or, (4) alternatively, how much frustration a given u pressure brings to bear on each of the y dynamic traits with the ensuing generation of pugnacity, anxiety, depression and other products to be studied systematically in the *adjustment process analysis chart.*

Before considering these latter diverse subsequent effects one has to make the transformation from the ecometric to the psychometric perception of environment in terms of sheer magnitude of involvement of the individual's dynamic systems. This comes about through introducing a matrix expressing the strength of the individual's various dynamic traits in an $N \times z$ matrix, which we will call D, the *dynamic patterns* of the individuals in the group. It is possible—even probable—that there will be *some* correlation between amount of an individual's contact with an environmental element and the strength of his or her interest in it, but we must proceed by permitting them initial independence. For, though there may be *some* relations of I and D terms of the kind just discussed, there can be appreciable differences between an individual's amount of contact (I matrix) with a cultural element and the strength of his interests and dynamic relation to it. A man may commute by the X railway line every day and yet be quite uninterested in it so long as it works; the same degree of daily contact of two husbands with their wives may be accompanied by very different emotional involvement; and an adolescent who is allowed the family car only once a week may yet be intensely interested in it.

Accordingly, if we accept both amount of contact (I) and intensity of interests (D) as finally determining, by a product, the effect on a given dynamic structure, product terms in the $I \times D$ product matrix would express this. However, we cannot take this simple immediate product, in the first place, because the I ($N \times u$) and D ($N \times z$) matrices are not conforming, and secondly, because there is, in any case, a need in *psychological* terms for an intermediate term to relate dynamic endowments to effects.

Thus it is necessary, in this ecometric-psychometric bridge or transformation to introduce an intermediate matrix which, as indicated above, will be specific to a particular kind of psychometric generation, for example, of anxiety, of learning, of satisfaction to the self-sentiment, and so on. An element (cell) in this matrix will describe what a unit of a given c value in the I matrix (of which there are u such values for each person) will in general generate from a unit endowment in a particular dynamic trait, d (of which there are z for each person). This whole new intermediate matrix will be written with respect to one particular psychological feature or expression, of course, for example, anxiety generation. We will call it E, an effect matrix, with the understanding that at this point in the series the calculation would branch into many psychological directions, marked by many different subscripts for the E's, for example, anxiety, depression, learning. Any one e entry in E will multiply many different d's for a given individual. For example, one e might be a rise in inflation, which will increase anxiety through the dynamic term concerned with interest in feeding his family, but reduce it through his interest in certain property, and so on. E will be a *common to all* people $u \times z$ matrix, therefore, relating each of the z dynamic traits to each of the u cultural elements which have *unique personal* values in the I matrix. This *eco-psychometric transformation matrix*, as we may call it (represented by E) must have empirically discovered values that are the average for all people.

The criticism may be raised that this *should* have individual rather than general properties, since the way in which some ecometric change will affect an individual's dynamic, psychometric satisfactions will depend on his position in society. Our reply is that (a) this individuality is already taken care of in the statement of his individual contacts in the I matrix and his individual interests in the D matrix, and (b) that there must exist dependable general laws about the *average* effect of a cultural element change upon the satisfaction (or frustrations, etcetera) of any prominent sentiment. For example, the advent of a safe and easy method of birth control produced effects in the sentiments and behaviors relating the sexes, and a steeper income tax might tend to reduce the average young man's interest in business as a career relative to say, a civil service position. The E matrix, indeed, promises to be no empty abstraction but the repository of some important social-psychological and economic empirical laws, even though reduced to linear expressions.

Granted such a matrix is conceivable and obtainable the eco-psychometric bridge is crossed in the following equation:

$$I \quad \times \quad E \quad = \quad G \qquad (6\text{-}17)$$
$$(N \times u) \qquad (u \times z) \qquad (N \times z)$$

Here G is a matrix of generated psychological effects for each person in a position defined by a row in I, if possessed of *average* endowments in dynamic traits. (For it to be other than average we would have had to introduce the individual D matrix of unique dynamic endowments, and the matrix multiplication sequence is more easily handled if we withhold the introduction of D to the next step.) Thus, here, we go so far as to generate matrix, G, as above, which says how far each given individual's z dynamic traits get involved in the culture, as the summed results of its u cultural features (c's). G is thus a mixture of individual-specific and common properties and though it has inherent meaning, as just stated, we use it only as an intermediate operator. To get where we really want to—namely, to a statement of the psychological effect on the given individual— we can proceed in one of two ways according to whether we want a *single* score for him, measuring, say the total anxiety created summing across all his dynamic systems, or some effect on *single* dynamic traits. The former is most neatly handled by two diagonal super-matrices. The first will be G, re-written as a super matrix $|G|$, each row in G entered as a diagonal entry, and the second D above, similarly re-written as $|D|$ thus

$$|G| \quad \times \quad |D| \quad = \quad S \qquad (6\text{-}18)$$
$$(N \times N) \qquad (N \times N) \qquad (N \times N)$$

S is used as the symbol here because it would be most commonly a general *state*, for example, anxiety, satisfaction, that is in question.

If a value specific to a particular dynamic trait is in question, such as the amount of stimulation or growth given by the cultural position of the individual to his endowment in this or that erg or sentiment, then the calculation becomes

$$G \quad \cdot \quad D \quad = \quad Q \qquad (6\text{-}19)$$
$$(N \times z) \qquad (N \times z) \qquad (N \times z)$$

where the dot between G and D indicates a multiplication different from the common matrix rule, becoming a multiplication of each cell in G by the corresponding cell in D. For example, the first cell in the first row of G might be the expected generation of stimulation on the trait of "need security" (an erg) per unit of strength of that erg in a person in that individual's cultural position. It is multiplied by the value in D which gives that person's actual endowment in that erg, thus issuing in the stimulation level of the security erg that he will actually show.

Whether equation (6-18) or (6-19) will be used depends, as will be realized, on whether the result can be reduced to some single characteristic of the organism, such as anxiety level, general integration, etcetera, or whether we are interested in the individual effects of all z dynamic structures. It should also be clearly kept in view that the key matrix is E, the eco-psychometric transformation, which will be changed among the series of E's according to the type of psychological effect it is ultimately desired to estimate. One may anticipate that both individual and social psychology will be interested in such dependent variables as anxiety, depression, average gratification, etcetera, in using equation (6-18), and in the major ergs and sentiments in using equation (6-19).

The problem of reaching the various concrete matrix values from experiments and surveys will naturally be next in the reader's mind; but in this condensed treatment we must, without evasiveness, point to the similarity of the problem to that handled in Volume 2 with learning matrices. If we put the steps above together, from beginning to end of the above model, we have a single matrix multiplication chain, in equation (6-20), which could be variously cut for experimental purposes:

$$(P \times C \times E) \cdot D = Q \tag{6-20}$$

and which may be called the *general cultural environmental equation* or general econetic model for defining cultural effects on the individual personality.

From this general equation one can obtain results that are psychologically important not only for individual adjustment problems but also for understanding social distributions. The question of sources of variance contributions to behavior with which we started can be answered in a more sophisticated and meaningful way here, recognizing that the final distribution of something like an anxiety scale score must depend on distributions occurring at any one of the intermediate matrices such as P, C, E, and D. An initial attack on this complex question has been offered elsewhere (Cattell, 1972b). Finally, as to changes over time let us note that the general importance of elements in the given culture, as represented by C, might be expected to change more slowly than the values in P, an individual person's position (accessibility, exposure or vulnerability to cultural elements), and perhaps the general laws of relation, in E, would change least of all. Parenthetically, in getting at distributions it is of primary importance that the P matrix contain a sample of N people that is well stratified.

Probably, as suggested in our initial attack on person-situation variance analyses, the relations of behavior variances to the cultural matrix noted in this section will be more important to social psychology, sociology, and economics than to personality theory per se. Changes in the level and distribution of educational achievement, the vagaries of values on the stock exchange, the relation of war interest to journalistic writings, the relation of crime to diminished ergic investment in the family sentiment, and so on are issues, however, needing the above model.

6-12. Summary

1. A psychology of personality which has no models or methods of research for incorporating the environment is justly criticizable, and predictively inadequate. However, the necessary model is complex and many faceted, unavoidably making this chapter one of the most difficult in the present book. There are two stages in studying environment: (a) As it relates to traits and repeatable processes in the personality *in being*, at equilibrium, and (b) As it relates to learning. The latter belongs to Volume 2, on learning.

2. An elementary and merely statistically-oriented attack on the question has been in vogue, which roughly gives the answer that variance due to different stimulus situations is about as important as variance to interpersonal differences, and that some interaction of the two sources is often significant. Oddly, this demonstration of the expected environmental variance has been misinterpreted by some theorists as unfavorable to the theory of unitary trait structures. Actually it is consistent both with trait structure and with the theory of situational modulators (s_k's) of traits. It also fits our theory of instrument factors (page 371) but is quite beside the point in relation to the reality of trait correlation of behaviors across persons in trait factors.

3. More broadly conceived in the framework of the box (BDRM), psychological interest and theory calls for analysis of variance contributions with respect not only to stimuli and people, but also

to kinds of response form, observer differences, and differences of ambient stimuli. The breakdowns in design (2) above have been made only where the *same* type of response measure could be applied to all stimulus responses; but with certain assumptions differences in the kind of responses can also be included. But in any case a comprehensive treatment of the system of personality and environment requires a data box, five-way (not a two-way) breakdown of sources of variance.

4. To develop the full meaning of the five sources of variance a further installment concerning the previously briefly mentioned BDRM or Data Box is entered upon, as a brief digression. The central concept is that every unique psychological event has five signatures, which are the bases for all psychological analyses of behavior. Actually the data box can be entered with other than behavioral response scores, but if so its extracted concepts are likely to cease to be psychological. The five sets of ids bounding the data box can themselves be either series of discrete patterns, or single continua of variation using a single particular dimension score for each id. The former is the common usage and is necessary if dimensions of ids are to be found.

5. Two major models which have some systematic mutual relations—not yet explored—are available for bringing environment into personality-environment interactions. The first simply proceeds further with the breakdowns of variance on *ANOVA* lines already begun in (2), but instead of stopping with a bare statement of the contributions to deviation sources from the grand mean, it structures these contributions. That is to say this *additive attribute* model as we may call it, takes each response behavior measure, and breaks it down (as a deviation from the grand data box mean) into additive components from, say, a four-part specification equation, one part being the weights of the particular behavior on the factors of the person, another the weights of the stimulus on the factors among stimuli, another the weights of the particular situation on the factors which fix situations, and so on. The fact that a given response can be assessed by a combination of these separate specification equations for person, stimulation, situation, and observer, etcetera, is called the first law of econetics.

6. The second major model arises from manipulative factor analytic experiment by which the single initially obtained loading, b, on a trait, in the specification equation, can ultimately be broken down into four behavioral indices. It is called the person-centered product model because the terms for the environment, etcetera, all express themselves in product form through the personality factors. The breakdown of the behavioral index term is into p_h a perceptual

ability weight for the personality factor, e_j, an execution weight connected with performance in j and a modulator index, s_k, associated with differences in the situations, k's. By calculating the variances of p_h's, e_j's, and s_k's across a suitable sample of events one obtains the relative importance of stimuli modes of response, and situations, in relation to a particular personality factor (unit variance) or as an average over a desired set of personality factors. There are variants on the p, e, s analysis such as $(p + e)s$, or alternatively breaking down e into r (motor skill) and i (interest strength in action).

7.   A prime need of psychology today is a mapping of environment leading to an objective taxonomy and a basis for sampling stimuli and situations. Such a taxonomy can be in physico-social terms external to the person, which we call ecometric, or in terms of meaning to human or other subjects, which we call a psychometric taxonomy. The latter can be objectively reached by either the additive or the product representation of environment. In either, the r_p coefficient of pattern similarity and the Taxonome program for finding species types are used. (In the former on dimensional scores; in the latter on the vectors of b's—or p's, e's, and s's.) The classifications will have different meaning and natures for the different sets of behavior indices. For example, if on s's the classification will be on the emotional, dynamic meanings of situations.

8.   In behavioristic psychology, that is, not depending on introspection, the meaning of a perception is given by the response to the object concerned. In regard to what is common to all people its meaning and identity are fixed by the behavioral indices—p's, e's, and s's. The s vector, for example, defines the emotion-arousing meaning of the object for people generally. However, for a given individual, on the other hand, the trait scores must also enter. Thus, for example, a timid man (low H factor) sees a threatening situation as more terrifying than does a man less so.

However, the perception is by no means fully accounted for by the indices and scores for the major personality traits alone. It is recognized that the dynamic traits we call sentiments are hierarchical, splintering into mental sets and apperception masses (memories, images) which also have index weights in determining the nature of a perception, and the action, external and internal, which follows from and defines the perception. The appearance of these is partly caused by specific stimuli and partly by the broader sentiments the arousal of which make higher order contributions to them.

9.   Environment, especially social, is commonly thought of as playing a larger part in role behavior than in general personality behavior and the large s_k's found with roles would support this. Roles are definable both by inner structure features in personality and by outer

cultural functions and expectations. The outward, social-function and status-position aspects of a role are here largely left to sociology and cultural anthropology.

The internal, dynamic structure belongs to psychology and is recognized in personality research as a special type of an acquired sentiment. A particular role sentiment can be defined as a matrix of v's—$(p + e)$'s—and s's, which show the particular situations in which it operates and with what force. A role matrix of v's and s's has particular general pattern properties which permit its distinction (in a general, experimentally-obtained, factor matrix) from a personality trait. Since a person's behavior is *always* in one or more roles, obtaining the best score on a pure personality factor requires taking personality-loaded behavior variables across a judicious sample of many roles. Conversely, the cleanest, least-confounded role score requires even sampling of role response scores across behaviors also involving a diversity of ergs and other personality factors.

10. An alternative somewhat more complex model for a role which current experiment should be comparing for fit, supposes that a role is not simply one among the total series of dynamic personality traits but a second order factor which simultaneously modifies (contributes to) several *factors* (not acting directly to the variables also affected by them, as in the first model). Such a mode of operation would be demonstrated if a role were shown to be a second-stratum factor, the modulation of which would produce a characteristic constant pattern of modulators, as weights, across all members of a particular set of factors. Although a preponderance of needs or temperament traits in certain personalities may favor the seeking of roles characteristically giving more scope to those traits and needs, personality and role can be clearly separated, and any endowment in role can go virtually with any personality.

11. The question "Does behavior change when a person steps into a role because his perceptions change or because his personality changes?" is purely semantic and to be settled by a convention deciding whether personality shall be defined as covering only the occasion-averaged traits as such (as the *latent* personality) or be semantically permitted to refer to the *activated* personality level in moments of modulation. A change in perception *always* occurs in the role, but only through the modulated part. The extent of general and physiological changes in modulation might incline one to accept the definition of personality as including modulations, and law courts have to some extent and in a confused manner accepted this when a man is sometimes not held guilty in "crimes passionel."

12. Since the ultimate aim of econetics is to develop systematic relations between ecometric and psychometric parameters, that can be used to understand not only individuals but also the mass social phenomena of economics, politics, etcetera, a general econetic model is developed here which respects multiple causation by using matrix concepts. Beginning on the ecometric ("objective") side it represents a given culture by a C matrix quantifying the prominence of each of a total of u cultural features. It follows, still ecometrically, with a P matrix of degree of individual personal contact with those features, yielding a resultant individual impact matrix I. At that point by an E matrix—an eco-psychometric bridge—showing the typical psychometric effect on each of z dynamic traits of u cultural impacts (with respect to one specific psychometric entity, for example, anxiety) it moves to psychological effects. To express these for given individuals a matrix of individuals' endowments in the dynamic traits, D is introduced.

The end result, which might be called the general cultural environmental equation, states the effect upon the given psychological state or need of the impact of all this individual's dynamic traits of all cultural elements. This is expressed as the product of two super matrices

$$|G| \times |D| = S$$

as shown in equation (6-18) where S will be an ordinary diagonal matrix of N state scores representing the final effect on each individual. One such S will, of course, be available for each psychological state or trait. It is suggested that practical technical development of concrete solutions for this model will help both in individual predictions from environment and in understanding the distributions and the variance breakdowns of behavior in regard to various aspects of the culture.

NOTES

[1] It would be hard to find, in any mature science, such a studied aloofness as has characterized the areas of learning theory and personality research from the days of Watson and Freud down to 1970. Perhaps this is part of a still wider defensive habit more prominent in psychology than in well established sciences of moving behind a fence of jargon into academic ghettos. Actually, there has been no lack of appeals, by writers as diverse as Borgatta and Cottrell (1956, 1958), Brunswick (1956), Burt (1940), Barker (1962), Fiske and Maddi (1961), Pervin (1975a, b), the Sherifs (1956, 1965), Sells (1963), McDougall (1932),

and the present writer, calling for a rapprochement. They fell in the main on deaf ears of learning theorists interested only in what could be done with "peripheralistic" S-R paradigms, on the one hand, and on the indifference of traditional psychometrists, on the other, unconcerned to define and attend to the stimulus situations *implicit* in their trait measurements. Such leaders in their fields as Spence (1950), who saw the antithesis in terms of SR vs. RR approaches and Cronbach (1957), among psychometrists, who spoke of two psychologies, recognized a problem; but unfortunately they did not focus it in the full perspective of the Basic Data Relation Matrix. Only in that clear context can one see the way to structural formulae that will encompass meaningful dimensions of both person and environment, as proposed in this chapter.

Equally slow to be recognized as requiring a systematic synthesis were a number of enterprising special forays across borders, made from different angles by half a dozen or more researchers over the last forty years. One thinks of Murray's (1936) concept of "environmental presses," of Helson's (1963) "adaptation level" approach; of writings by Barker (1950), Borgatta, et al. (1958), Pervin (1975a, b), Sargent (1961), Sells (1963) calling for taxonomies of social and environmental stimulus situations; Cattell's (1935) proposal for defining a total interest sphere; the Sherifs' (1956, 1965) and Hemphill and West's (1954) models of group environments, and Stogdill's (1950) and Frediksen et al.'s (1970) studies of the administrative frameworks in which decisions are made. It seems fair and correct to point out that these concerns with the role of environment and experience came largely from the personality theory side, and that learning theory (reflexology to be precise) had little to say (except in the first work of Pavlov) about temperament or ability traits in rat or man. This glance at a history of segregation and narrow approaches may be unpleasant; but it should be salutary in encouraging the reader to face here the difficulties and complexities of a multivariate and many faceted formulation.

[2] Since the two introductory statements above about expression of environment in the specification equation are novel it may be desirable to reiterate their implications before proceeding. They are (1) that the nature of the stimulus response setting of the behavior is "read" through the *behavioral indices*, and (2) that the cultural environment and the group nature are also entangled in the trait structures themselves. The latter says the loadings in the pattern of a trait are *not* something fixed only in the structure of an individual. They rest on relationships in a group of individuals to a given shared environment. Thus we are used to thinking of traits, as patterns, as belonging to people but they are indeed in no sense independent of environment in definition. Further we should keep in mind that the behavioral indices in the specifications equation for any behaviors and the trait pattern used in obtaining trait scores are closely related—in fact as rows and columns in a matrix. True, the actual trait score is a level of expression in the individual, independent of the provocations and facilitations presented by immediate environmental situations, and carried around independently thereof in the individual. But its form is rooted in the population and its permanent environment.

[3] In psychology both the issues of sampling and the issues of dividing up behavioral variance have persisted in very partial, not to say parochial, frames of reference for a rather surprisingly long time. The desirability of applying population-sampling principles to response variables as well as to people was apparently first given explicit consideration by Burt (1940) in connection with Q-technique; Brunswick (1956) in relation to representative experimental design; and Cattell (1946) in relation to developing a personality sphere concept of

human response behavior. It was reiterated in relation to factor analytic variables by Cattell (1952) in relation to due proportions of hyperplane stuff and by Kaiser (1965) in regard to image analysis. This has born fruit in systematic statistical treatments in the generalized reliability concept of Cronbach, Gleser, and Rajaratnam (1972) and the expressions proposed by Lord (1963).

Up to the present, however, most psychometric thinking and practice has considered this sampling and breaking down of variance only in regard to two coordinates—people and certain variables rather nondescriptly called "situations." The data box, now to be discussed in this connection, and which defined *five* sets of ids (entities—persons, stimuli—each a specific pattern on the dimensions of its species type) or *ten*, if one chooses to double each by giving both the individual and his position on some most relevant dimensions, opens up, however, an altogether wider treatment. Any one of the five coordinates then has on it an unordered sample of individual ids from the given set—ideally a random or stratified sample. A breakdown of response measure variance is then possible with respect ultimately to five sources of variance.

[4] If one wishes to pursue the logical possibilities in the data box and its arrangement much more could be said, but for the reader who wishes to go beyond the traditional psychometric realm of interest this footnote must suffice. A distinction has been drawn between the usual use of the data box, where the coordinates are sets of ids, that is, each is a pattern of measures, and the "dimensional use" in which the coordinates represent a series of score values on some chosen variable, either for the same person or the same average groups of persons, such as stature, level of excitement, age. The coordinates for stimulus and ambient situations could similarly be set up as scores on agreed features of the stimuli or situations. Actually, the data box could have an infinite number of coordinates in this case, since any one type of id has an infinite number of measurable aspects.

Except for the special case of splitting each coordinate into two—an *"organism" or pattern and the "state" of an organism at a given moment of testing*—there is little point in pursuing these extra models. This special dimension-scoring case the present writer has pursued in the *Handbook of Multivariate Experimental Psychology* (1966), as a *ten-coordinate* data box. Whenever an *entity* and a *state* that can characterize all the entities can be identified, so that the entities can be measured on the dependent variable at all states, this can be used. Thus one could have 50 animals with their characteristic individual properties and ten states of hunger on another coordinate for every animal; or 50 stimuli at 12 different intensity levels. Probably, the ten states of hunger in the first example would normally be handled adequately by placing them along the ambient situation axis—unless that were already occupied by, additionally, changes in the external situation. The need for a ten-coordinate system is thus problematical; but if adopted it would require an event definition as follows:

$$a_{hh',ii',jj',kk',oo'} \qquad (6\text{-}2)$$

the splitting of subscripts into two indicating the average condition of the id and its state at the time of experiment.

[5] In researches so far, for example, those of Endler and Hunt, Moos, Argyle, and Little, the question of how to handle responses in different units has not arisen, as it does in our broader, more generalized treatment here. If using the same type of measurement units when responses are actually very different, for example, taking reaction time across questionnaire items, GSR, fluency,

etcetera, as described above, loses the essential behavior meaning, an alternative is as follows. Take for each variable a population distribution, and express the given sample in standard scores from that population. The scores will now differ in mean and sigma from response to response, situation to situation, and of course, person to person, permitting an analysis of variance with respect to the various sets, in terms of magnitudes of differences of samples from populations.

[6] For reasons of space we have been compelled to set out the important concepts here without undue digression into statistical groundwork, and also without participating further in the debates which have stirred up—not to say muddied—the waters around the Endler and Hunt type of approach. That the latter missed some necessary statistical principles has been fully conceded by them, and Golding (1974) has pointed to other flaws. (See also Hakstian's comment (1972) on use of omega squared.) The necessary statistical caveats are well set out by Cornfield and Tukey (1956). Actually, other researches (see Magnusson, 1975) by Rausch et al. (1959, 1960), Moos (1968, 1969, 1970), Nelson, Grinder, and Mutterer (1969) and Argyle and Little (1972) reach situation-person variance ratios, little different from the roughly 50/50 ratio of Endler and Hunt. The conceptual problems in this field, as stated in the text above, arise rather from the misinterpretations than the findings themselves.

To say that sets of situations are all substantially and about equally loaded on intelligence, for example, is not to say that the mean scores or sigmas of each are alike. Speed of completion of a certain synonyms test and an arithmetic problem test may both have a +0.5 loading on the intelligence source trait but the first may have a mean time of 3 minutes and a sigma of 1 minute and the second a mean of 7 minutes and a sigma of ½ minute.

If speed of solution of a problem is what one is interested in, then the above change in mean and sigma in shifting from one situation to another is, however, a statement of the importance of environmental difference relative to trait difference. That relative importance can be worked out, as far as means are concerned, just as in equation (6-3) above, except that one will now want to use subjects varying in intelligence but controlled to equality on other traits. If that is not possible, then the correlation of intelligence with the performance variance should be used to define that fraction of the variance which is due to intelligence, and it is this fraction the variance of which, across situations, provides the basis for trait intelligence-vs.-situation comparisons. In connection with this point, it is evident that for a population of a given variance on intelligence, the variance of certain particular subtest performances would be expected to be partly a function of intelligence variance, partly of variance on other traits which enter the performance, and partly of situational variance inherently associated with the particular subtest stimuli and response measures. In correlational and factor treatments, we eliminate the last—the test differences which are h and j scale peculiarities—by using standard scores. Here we convert the particular variable scores into a single composite factor score. But we can still retain it, if we eliminate the "other factors" variance by fractioning the variance according to the loading. We are thus gaining a measure of the relative contribution of the trait of intelligence and of the situation to the changing variances of performance across situations and people.

[7] An extreme in entanglement is presented by, say, performance in a track-tracer experiment, where perception and execution are so intimately related that this division may be artificial and break down. But in others, as when a

person realizes his bank account is low and sets out to do something about it, the difference in the traits affected by the *p* and *e* loadings is obviously considerable. As here suggested, results from the proposed operational separation of these indices *may* lead psychologists to the view that the traditional terms "perceptual" and "motor" may not precisely define the dichotomy; but we have to *start* with familiar terms.

One must recognize that statistical and experimental difficulties will be encountered by pioneers in this field. Experimentally, there will be many stimulus-response units that will neither split clearly into stimulus and response parts, as required by the first research design, nor make sense in recoupling, as required in the second. The difficulties lie in finding the same units of measurement applicable to the perception and the response behavior, and, in the case of the experimental design we have called *re-coupling*, of finding lists of stimuli and responses that can be combined in all mathematically possible combinations and still constitute psychologically realistic responses to presented stimuli. One cannot easily respond to a presented difference of tones by saying which is brighter in color, as required by recoupling, and the separation of a kiss from the response to a kiss might defy the demand for isolation.

[8] Eysenck has argued at some length from questionnaire evidence that in our society individuals with extreme left (communist) attitudes and those at the extreme right (fascist) in beliefs are very similar in personality, and many such instance of interests and roles being independent of personality could be found.

7

THE MORE REFINED DEFINITION
OF THE MODELS OF TRAITS, STATE, AND TYPE RELATIONS

7-1.   *Higher- and lower-strata source-state organization*
7-2.   *The scientific conceptual status of factors at all stratum levels*
7-3.   *Reticular and strata models and factor emergents: The Cattell-White and Schmid-Leiman equations relating strata*
7-4.   *The universal model, stub factors, and depth psychometry*
7-5.   *Variance sources in the specification equation using trait, trait-change, and state factors, with enlarged meanings of the latter*
7-6.   *Proceeding beyond the linear and additive form of the specification equation*
7-7.   *The discovery and use of types in relation to traits*
7-8.   *Summary*

7-1.   Higher- and Lower-Strata Source-State Organization

The central behavioral specification equation expressing personality structure and environmental structure that we have used to this point may be oversimplified. We have kept it so partly for didactic purposes, skating lightly over complications that would distract the entering student, and partly because the directions of modification require more investigation than could be given until this point.

Our core model is plain enough, being that linear, additive equation, with oblique factors as the main terms, which was favored by Thurstone and followed by the present writer and others. The student should be aware that until recently the bulk of multivariate analysts did not follow this model, Burt treating factors only as classificatory principles (1941), Guilford (1959, 1975) fitting all data to an orthogonal model, Eysenck (1960) ignoring the verdict of tests for factor number and the difference of first and second order factors, and most analysts paying only lip service to establishing uniqueness and replicability by simple structure, confactor and congruence procedures. These are nevertheless workers developing psychological theory from real data: what the pure mathematician, by contrast, presents as the factor—usually the component—model is something still more remote from the model here. Our model here is governed by several extra principles and checked empirically at several points with which the pure mathematical use of factor analysis is not concerned. The reader wishing to brush up on the main framework of the present approach need not lack for excellent texts, in Gorsuch (1974), Harman (1977), Mulaik (1972), Uberla (1970) and others; more slender and easy in Child (1970), Fruchter (1954), Lawlis and Chatfield (1974), and Guertin and Bailey (1970), and closer to practical use in the present writer's *Scientific Use of Factor Analysis* (1978).

An indication of these readily available sources is desirable because hopefully the present chapter can concentrate on the more refined developments of our behavioral model without undue digression on the statement of the mathematical under-pinnings as such.

One direction in which the reader may have felt the pavement ended rather abruptly was in our discussion of the statistical and psychological meaning of higher strata states and traits.[1] Another concerns the general relative magnitudes of variance contributions to behavior from states and traits. Another has to do with the perennial debates on the extent of approximation involved when our behavior predictions stay with linear rather than non-linear curves. And finally there are subtle issues about the proper combined use of species type and dimension descriptions that we have skated over rather quickly.

Let us begin with the as yet scarcely touched problem of higher-strata states. Rotation to unique meaning, by simple structure (or, in a few cases, by confactor) (Cattell & Brennan, 1978), proceeds as well with *dR*- and *P*-technique states as with traits. The conclusion from present data (Curran, 1970; Cattell & Brennan, 1979; Wedding 1977) would probably be, however, that, at the unique resolution position, states tend to be decidedly more highly intercorrelated than do most traits. One must distinguish between state levels at a given moment being correlated, as is commonly shown in the Curran and Cattell batteries (1976) and which could be due to presently unavoidable trait contamination, for example, of high *O* factor (guilt proneness) underlying both anxiety and depression state scales, and correlation of *changes* of state level between one day and another. Both correlations are substantial, for example, 0.6 to 0.7 of depression with fatigue. Time is so powerful a determiner of states that it is not surprising that changes in any two states should become strongly correlated, but if the correlation is repeated and systematic some common real cause must be hypothesized.

The distinction of *primary state* is as appropriate here as the use of *primary trait*. The primary states, like primary traits, break down into certain classes, notably, *general states*, like anxiety, fatigue, elation, stress; *dynamic-emotional states*, like fear, parental pity, anger, and lust; and *trait-change* dimensions, which, conceptually are not really states but as we have seen, often cannot yet be more than arbitrarily separated from ordinary states.

The same initial uncertainty about the proper stratum level of a given factor, and the same unevenness of levels across media occur with states as with traits. Fortunately, the translation from, say, Q- to L-data, seems very similar to that for traits. Thus it can be shown that in Q-data there are *primary* states or trait-change factors corresponding to the twenty or so Q-data primary traits A, B, C, D, etcetera. The initial research of Cattell and Scheier (1961) showed that the familiar states of anxiety, exvia, depression, arousal, etcetera, are *second* stratum to these and later research shows that in provable instances these second order Q states align with primary states or trait-change factors in T-data. There is tentative evidence that these Q-data states which we have called general states (fatigue, elation, anxiety, and so on) appear to be second order not only to the above primaries but probably also to the specific ergic tension states (fear, hunger, sex, etcetera). Thus anxiety is clearly a state measure $Q(S)II$ in questionnaires at the second order, loading primaries $C-$, $H-$, L, O, Q_3-, and Q_4, and probably at second order to the MAT ergic factors. But as Scheier, Hundleby, Bolz, Nesselroade, and others have shown, in behavior and physiology (T-data) anxiety comes out as a first-order state, aligning with UI (S) 24. Thus second order Q aligns with first order T in states as in traits.

In factor analysis the term "factor order" is used, as initially here, where "stratum" would be more correct. The nature of the difference has been only mentioned briefly, but should now be explained. The *order* of a factor is named from a factor-analytic operation, and typically refers to one experiment only. Factoring a set of variables yields primaries; factoring correlated primaries by this mode of definition necessarily yields secondaries, and so on. Occasionally, however, it happens in an experiment that a scale for a pure primary factor is included among scales otherwise merely for variables. The situation is revealed, though it needs an alert eye, in that the factoring—provided a bit of communality is provided for the factor scale—results in the pseudo variable marking a factor practically on its own; that is, it has virtually only one loading: on itself. It is thus saying that though factored among variables, it is not a variable but a primary factor, and was, so to speak, factored in lower company when it actually belongs to a stratum above. A fuller discussion of the technicality of the process of identifying *strata* positions from combining operational evidence on a number of *order* experiments is given in technical factor-analytic discussions (Cattell, 1978). Suffice it that the aim in a stable scientific model is to assign permanent *strata* levels to factors rather than doubtful order levels in single experiments. With this note we shall henceforth use the term strata rather than order when there is evidence, from several order experiments, to support a stable stratum identification.

What we have called *general* states, as instanced in Curran's *Q*-data 8 State Scale (1976), or, in *T*-data, Nesselroade's 8 State Battery, are typically at the second stratum (relative to 16 PF, HSPQ, CAQ, etcetera, *Q*-data primaries) though there is evidence that the stress-reaction state, and the curious pattern of high pulse rate and high serum cholesterol (Cattell & Scheier, 1961), are probably primaries. The ergic-tension and sentiment-excitation state dimensions in the MAT (Sweney, 1969) are also probably properly considered as primaries. They have always merited this primary designation because they arise directly from variables. The statement already tentatively made here that the general states of anxiety, depression, arousal, regression, and so on, are at the secondary-stratum level relative to the ergic-tension primaries will be found later to provide a basis for an intriguing argument in the dynamic calculus concerning the derivation of the general states from environmental effects on particular ergs (see Volume 2).

It will be psychologically illuminating first to consider the general principles in this area in relation to the general states of anxiety, depression, arousal, and so on. There are two explanations of second order factor findings we shall finally need to consider—the *higher influence* and the *spiral feedback*—but both fall essentially within the *multi-strata* model, which may be but is not always hierarchical also. In attempts to fit factor results to more extended models one must recognize that the generally accepted strata model is not the only one, and that the very different *reticular* model must ultimately be given a chance.

Meanwhile, the strata model is tried because it is simpler, and science, after all, bids us espouse simpler models unless they become untenable. The facts presently available indicate that so far the stratum model has given reliably replicable results through the third and fourth strata in traits and the second and third in states. Pawlik (1967), for example, has broken into the third order in objective personality trait measures and argued for the appearance of three major factors in *T*-data traits at the third order; and Cattell and Schuerger (1976) have confirmed their patterns. They would actually be at the fourth order if we started with primaries in the *L-Q* medium, but good replication in the *Q*-medium has so far extended only to locating five or six factors at the *third* order.

Because at each step there are fewer common factors than variables factored, any ordinary empirical pursuit of higher-strata traits or states ends by giving us a pyramid. Several writers in the field have been so entranced by their hierarchy, often with a single supreme factor at the top, that they have espoused this "monarchic" model as the essential structure of the human personality, assigning supreme importance to the top factor. But to assign such uniqueness and importance to the top of the pyramid is to be fooled by an artifact. For if we started with a broader base of variables, we would have several factors at the top where we previously had but one and so would be able to go a stratum higher still (see Cattell, 1971, p. 106; 1977).

At the moment, we know relatively little experimentally about what happens in the third and fourth strata, except that patterns seem less stable than lower down. Whether this is a real changeability of form or the result of accumulating measurement and method error as one moves further from the actual measured variables is uncertain, but one may suspect the latter, because rotation is rarely so thoroughly done at the primary and secondary level as to fix cosines firmly, and error then increases with stratum level. Because of this uncertainty, it is not appropriate at present to delve into psychological theories of third and fourth strata state factors in detail. However, in Section 7-5 some discussion is given to the fact that anxiety and stress seem to fall on opposite sides of a certain higher stratum factor, which suggests, along with other loadings thereon, that this higher dimension represents a situationally-determined pattern. The dimension, indeed, seems to be one of tackling a problem (becoming stressed) versus retreating from a problem (becoming anxious and guilty). If other such instances arise, a higher-stratum factor in states may need to be considered typically not as one more physiological state, but as a pattern in the joint appearance and disappearance of states due to a repeating environmental situation and to one's reaction to that situation. We similarly have concluded that high-stratum personality trait factors may reach back to psychology into physiological or sociological origins. Encountering these problems in higher orders requires for perspective that the next section revert momentarily to discussing more fully the scientific status of *all* factors.

7-2.   The Scientific Conceptual Status of Factors at All Stratum Levels

As explained at the outset, a purely mathematical factor, such as an unrotated factor or principal component, can be related to calculation operations, but is, from a substantive scientific standpoint a dimension without meaning in the real world. As any one of an infinite number of possible combinations of the variables, it will give various kinds of mathematical prediction (by multiple regression), but need have no identity with any scientific concept or model. By contrast, a factor rotated to a unique position by simple structure or confactor rotation (Cattell, 1944, 1966; Cattell & Cattell, 1955; Cattell & Brennan, 1977)—these independent procedures being mutually consistent—is a dimension that can claim to correspond to the conceptual status of a *determiner*, an *emergent*, or a *causal influence*, by some operational definition of these latter.

Using a common-sense meaning of these related but distinguishable terms, it would seem that for the moment we must retain all three, in the light of present empirical results from factor analysis. For example, in the Thurstone (1937) factoring of several measures on many boxes, the factors come out as length, breadth, and height. And in the Cattell and Dickman (1960) factoring of 32 "behaviors" of balls on strings, the factors came out as volume, weight, length of cord, and elasticity of the ball. Conventional language might justify our saying that the length of the cord is the causal determiner of the rate of swing of the pendulum, or that a ball's elasticity is one cause of its bouncing higher than another. But in the Thurstone case (which, in many ways, is an unhappy illustration, all its factors being of one nature—spatial), we would scarcely say that height, length, and breadth are the "causes" of the box's volume. "Determiners" would here be more acceptable.

As to "cause" philosophers have gone in circles over various limits to its definition and some have said it is a false concept created by an anthropocentric projection of the human will. However, most philosophers are ready to accept that in the definition of cause and effect there must be *invariable temporal sequence*, so that time sequence observation, in an experiment, *but not necessarily experimental manipulation*, must be involved. "Invariable sequence," however, is not so easy to define for any effect may have several possible causes (not requiring that any particular one be always present) and conversely any one cause may have several effects. But the generalization that a factor, when accepted only at a unique rotational position, meeting simple-structure or confactor conditions, can correspond to what is commonly accepted as a cause or influence is now supported by numerous experimental studies. In the factoring of cups of coffee by Cattell and Sullivan (1962), the cause of a particular cup being hot or cold was the temperature reached by the pot at time of pouring (a factor affecting some other things, too); in the ball problem, the weight of the ball was the cause of its rolling further, against carpet friction; while for differences in number of arithmetic problems solved by schoolboys, differences in intelligence were the cause, and so on.

Some sort of continuum can be supposed across the terms "determiner," "influence," and "cause," from Thurstone's length of box factor, as a determiner, to such concepts as engine power, in a factoring of airplanes, or barometric pressure in a meteorological factoring, which become true causes or influences. However, adequate proof of such causal action, in the case of factor-analytic experiment, usually comes from evidence outside factor analysis, as when factors and effects are observed for succession effects over time, with or without manipulation. For example, we observe that as intelligence score increases with time (over age) the rate of learning becomes faster, or that an increase in anxiety is *followed* by an increased ketosteroid excretion.

Although it can well be argued that factors uniquely placed by simple structure or confactor rotation are, by the implication of those methods, causes, added observations of the constancy of sequences of their effects over time is the most common way of confirming causality. As to the implications of the initial methods we note that simple structure rests on the assumption that it is unlikely in any large number of diverse variables *that any one influence will affect all*. This is why we seek, in simple structure, to rotate to where each factor loads *only* a subset and leaves all others alone. At that position we can argue that we have a factor that is most likely to correspond to a natural influence. It can rightly be objected that in a comprehensive and random array of variables, though a cause would generally be expected to affect only a minority of variables, the argument is not necessarily reversible, that a factor affecting only a small subset *is* a cause. Thus it is not an infallible argument, but a probability. However, it is a probability that gets larger if we are unable to think of any other reasons for such restriction of action to a subset.

The second available rotational procedure for discovering a unique rotational position is confactor rotation. This requires two experiments with the same variables, from which we find the position where the loadings in one study on each factor can be shown to be *proportional* to those of some corresponding factor in the other. It has been shown (Cattell, 1944) that if such a position exists in the data, it is unique. The obtained parallelism of loading patterns connotes that the same influences are at work in both, though to different degrees, as would be expected. If such a confactor position cannot be found—and let us note that neither simple structure nor confactor positions can be found in random correlations or correlations of random normal deviates—then there are no distinct separable influences at work in the observations. Cattell and Gorsuch (1963) have shown empirically that simple-structure cannot be found, nor confactor relationships reached with random scores or random correlations. Therefore these patterns are a special sign, found in most real data, of causal structuring. Cattell and Cattell (1955) and Cattell and Brennan (1977) have shown how to locate the position respectively for orthogonal and oblique cases.

Granted that a factor with these special conditions is a determiner or cause, we still must consider whether it is a present or a past cause. In other sciences researchers are often aware of an orderliness in data that arises not from present but from preserved results of earlier influences, as in the inferences that can be made from the rings of a cut tree about past years or rainfall and sunshine. As a geologist travelling from Africa to Northern Europe compares valleys, he finds a correlation in the U-shapes of the valleys, the long scratches in the rock bed, the numbers of geologically misplaced boulders, and the presence of moraine lakes, which points to a single factor behind all—a great glacier having moved through each valley. Similarly, when a factor is found in psychological data, it may represent an active, existing single influence, like a present anxiety-state response pattern, or it may point to a pattern of habits and skills in crystallized intelligence formed through a particular pattern of learning experienced long ago.

The assignment of a given discovered factor either to the class of acting influences, or that of patterns from past influences, is a secondary task. It is not usually a difficult step. For example, hyperthyroid temperament trait or an anxiety state is generally clearly traceable to a presently acting influence. Such states or traits, as individual-difference factors, represent a correlation of behaviors through some presently existing single power, that is, for example, power of inhibition, or power of relation-eduction. On the other hand, in developmental studies we may better search for an explanation in some past common growth. A cardinal instance of debate on this issue concerns intelligence; the present writer hypothesized (1971) that g_f, fluid intelligence, is a presently existing power of mass neurological action, whereas g_c, crystallized intelligence, shows a correlation between verbal and numerical skills because they have been learned together in the past. The most direct test of past or present is to reduce, modify, or remove one of the loaded variables. In the extreme case, the loss or suppression of one can occur without any loss occurring to the other (as in brain damage producing specific aphasias), if the connection is only historical.

Though a uniquely resolved factor, having thus claim to be in the class of influences, must apparently be one or the other of these types, a taxonomist could probably proceed to many subdivisions. A pattern belonging to the class of past developments, for example, can still be either an inherited, genetic pattern, which appeared by maturation, or a learned pattern, as discussed in Volume 2. And according to the variables we put in, that is, to the zone of the personality sphere covered, it can have ability, or temperament, or dynamic modality. In short, the psychologist *must not think of the several factors emerging together directly in any given factor analysis, in the personality and state domain, as necessarily being all of a kind, i.e., in one class.* Once they are indexed and replicated, then further examination is needed to see what kind of structure or state they represent; and an open mind and psychologically alert experimentation will commonly lead to differentiation.

Accepting the proposition that the uniquely determined factors known to us are largely determiners or causal influences, and returning now to the question of second-order structures, we are bound consistently to recognize that a (simple-structure) second-stratum factor is essentially some additional influence contributing to the variance of several primary factors as factors. It contributes to them directly just as they do to the variables, but it does not act directly on the variables themselves. For example, the second order Q-data factor we call *control* or *good upbringing* suggests that good home upbringing, that is, concern for good values and readiness of parents to spend time and effort in inculcating those values, should help simultaneously to produce increased superego growth (G, on page 64), self-sentiment development (Q_3), and some restraint on native surgency ($F-$). Consequently we might expect such a second-stratum factor to load G, Q_3, and $F(-)$. Precisely such a factor is found in the form of QVIII (p. 81). Or again, if we consider social status a molding influence on personality, so that it would augment such T-data primaries as independence (QIV), intelligence (QVII), and good upbringing (QVIII), we might expect a third-order factor to be found loading these secondaries. There the secondaries will have been brought into positive correlation by the selection, promotion, education, and so on, associated with social status. Such a factor pattern, indeed, we find in the third-order pattern labelled Q δ (though the intelligence loading is rather small in student groups, as would be expected from selection on intelligence; Cattell, 1973, p. 135).

From such examples it is evident that higher-strata factors may be very different in their scientific domain from the lower-strata factors they organize. Thus that just instanced in $Q \delta$ at the third-order trait level is a factor more in the realm of sociology than psychology. It is brought about by the tendency in a mobile society for upward mobility to be favored by certain gifts and for social status, in turn, to confer certain extra education in manners and morals. The structure of such a factor is originally in society and only secondarily in the produced individual personality makeup.

Similarly, though it is at present not so easy to produce a good example for scrutiny, a higher-stratum factor may step across the other main frontier of psychology, namely into physiological structure. There is some evidence that in children fluid intelligence and anxiety are positively correlated, possibly because of a single third-stratum factor. This, if true, is surprising, and perhaps points to a physiological root in that a larger cortex could be a "playground" in early life both for greater relation perception and greater stimulation of anxiety. Conceivably, in other words, a large and efficient cerebral cortex not only correlates substantially with intelligence but, in early childhood at least, renders its possessor more liable to imaginatively produced anxieties (see Cattell, 1971). Two or more primary traits might thus be augmented in common by some underlying single physiological factor that would emerge in research as a second-stratum factor. This possibility that high-strata factors may not be psychological at all, but go into and come from other domains, is an argument additional to the statistical one (of more *efficient* prediction from primaries—see Section 7-3) for considering primaries more psychologically important, and for treating secondaries and tertiaries as, sometimes, more extraneous modifiers of primary psychological structures.

In the realm of traits there are enough well replicated second and third stratum factors to provide the psychologists with rich food for thought about these concepts; but the recency of true state study by P- and dR-techniques gives only relatively tentative guidance. However, we have in Figure 5-5 (p. 206) results at the second stratum for T states and third for Q-data which point to the interesting possibility that a general factor exists which shows a general tendency to grapple with problems rather than retreat—a state of courage versus cowardice. Descriptively we are saying that the person who confronts difficulties experiences stress and other physiological responses of a psychosomatic kind, whereas he who retreats experiences guilt, anxiety, and regression. And we explain the relatively substantial correlation among such states by saying that if, for example anxiety and depression are involved in the same impact of an external problem, they will tend to mount together as the problem impinges, and recede together as it withdraws.

Not only should we expect higher-strata patterns to emerge from this common responsiveness, but we might also expect them to be tied to regularly repeating external situations, such as are analyzed in the Adjustment Process Analysis Chart in Volume 2, Chapter 4. Thus, in states as in traits, the primary and secondary strata—in Q-data the 16 PF primaries, in T-data the UI factors—are likely to be most psychologically meaningful, whereas the third and fourth strata may take their form from physiological, situational, or socioeconomic background influences.

A last glance is appropriate in their methodologically "polishing section" at the general relation of unique to common factors, as defined in Chapter 1. Both deal with identical data—an array of raw-score personality variables—but analyzed in two distinct systems. As shown earlier, to detect and record structure in terms of unique trait patterns, it is essential to study fluctuations of performance *in the given individual*, over occasions and stimulus situation, essentially by P-technique. This contrasts with what is done in individual-difference, common-trait analysis, as in R-technique. From this difference of the statistical framework of the two kinds of experiment we run into problems, in establishing the psychological identity of unique traits, in scoring them comparably from individual to individual, and in making score comparisons from unique to common trait domains. The logical basis for recognizing several similar unique trait patterns as essentially the same, but in different individuals, is the same as in showing replication in R-technique, namely applying the pattern similarity coefficient to demonstrate, for example, by the Taxonome program, their belonging to a segregated type. The significance limits for congruences in P-technique, however, remain to be worked out.

Once this identification of the central tendency in unique trait or state patterns across many individuals is established, and the matching with a common R-technique completed, the problem of comparing scores on some basis of standard scores is not insuperable. Initially, in any given case, the standardization framework for unique traits is necessarily encapsulated in the series of occasions for the given individual. For example, "a university education" factor, which may exist, has a uniqueness of pattern for every university and country and, ultimately, for every individual. But a reasonable equivalence of *raw* scores for factors can be reached by working from the *mean* V_{fe} (factor estimate weights) matrix among them.

A more accurate comparison can be based on the *equipotent* or *isopodic* principles, the technicalities of which we leave to other articles and books (Cattell, 1969, 1970, 1977). Standardized scores across different *P*-technique, unique-trait, or state scores can be reached either relative to the population of occasions of each individual or occasions across all individuals.

This section has been built entirely on the hypothesis that a factor is a determiner of (1) the variables, or (2) the lower-order factors that a second stratum factor loads. In the next section we must turn to the alternative models we briefly introduced of reticular and spiral emergent forms.

7-3. Reticular and Strata Models and Factor Emergents: The Cattell-White and Schmid-Leiman Equations Relating Strata

Before examining the statistical models for a non-strata interaction of factors, it may offer some perspective to look at one or two examples suggesting a need to go further. Two of the most important and statistically largest second-order factors, anxiety (QII) and exvia (QI), have psychological associations suggesting that the model of the second order as an extra influence affecting first orders may actually have to be, in a special sense, inverted. That is to say, there is an argument for making the second order a product of actions of the primaries.

In the case of the second-stratum factor that has been recognized as general anxiety, one school of psychology at least—psychoanalysis—has very definitely adopted a theory that requires this inversion of the model. There it is argued that ego weakness, $C-$, guilt proneness (or affronted superego), O, and libido, or undischarged ergic tension, Q_4, operate as the *causes* of anxiety. We do not necessarily have to accept this, for some modern experimental work (for example, Rickels et al., 1966), although bearing out that these primaries come together with substantial correlations in the second-order anxiety factor, has been compatible with interpreting anxiety conversely as the cause of weakened ego ($C-$), and so on, that is, in the pattern of second orders as influences of primaries. However, we must note that what we shall call the spiral emergent view of QII would fit the psychoanalytic summary in that it recognizes $H-$, natural timidity (or tendency to overreact to threat) to be important in the pattern, which could also be seen more easily as cause rather than consequence of the second order, anxiety.

There is sufficient reason, therefore, for considering an alternative explanation of a second-stratum factor, which we have called the *emergent* or *spiral emergent*, or *spiral-interaction* hypothesis, in that it supposes that certain primary factors have inevitably mutual interactions, beyond the additive action model, producing a new emergent dimension. For example, psychologically we can see that higher ergic tension, Q_4, may weaken control by the ego, C, and the resulting impulsive action could in turn provoke guilt, O. The term "spiral" is retained in the designation not because it may be *precisely* a spiral sequence of action among the primaries, but because interaction is likely to have some sort of sequential or chain action, leading, by feedback, to the first term, into some rise in level of *all* of the interacting primaries relative to other primaries that do not interact. As to the exact form of the productive interaction, several theories are possible of which we consider two representatively diverse. The first is that actual behavior variables are not appearing by linear and additive action of the primaries, but that in some cases, at least (in this case anxiety manifestations) they depend on, say, the product of the primaries. Another possible instance of this is that acquisition of intellectual skills may not depend on an *additive* action of fluid intelligence, g_f, and years of schooling, but analogously to energy, in physics, on a product of force and distance (time in this case), that is, on intelligence-hours. The crystallized intelligence factor, g_c, thus appears as a demand for something to account for the variance beyond the additive contribution.

The second model for this extra variance among interacting primaries, appearing as an emergent second order, is what might be called *situation-mediated interaction*. Here the behavior stemming from one factor propels the individual into a situation favorable to the development of another. (This could also operate in the above emergence of g_c insofar as scholarship selection places higher g_f individuals in positions to receive longer schooling.) Thus in the extraversion second order an individual with innately low tendency to inhibition, that is, an $H(+)$, parmic person, would appear more readily in social groups and get more change to acquire the quick social thinking and wit of surgency, $F(+)$. The popularity which surgency brings would in turn incline the individual to take a warm rather than a cold and withdrawing attitude to his fellow men, and hence score higher on A, affectia. (The misanthropy of such geniuses as Michaelangelo, Cavendish, and Schopenhauer seems to have begun with an unusual sensitivity.) The self-sufficient, group-rejecting style of trait Q_2 can also be seen as a derivative.

To this theory of interaction of primaries, in either of its forms, as alternative to the single-influence theory of the origin of secondary patterns it may be objected—in general, not just for anxiety and exvia—that some formal properties of uniquely simple structure rotated secondary factors may not fit the idea that they are emergents from interaction effects. Chiefly a critic might ask, "How should interaction explain the existence of simple structure since its origin has hitherto been ascribed to the influence model?" "If interaction does produce such new variance, why does it not simply produce a surface-trait cluster rather than a new dimension?" "If we grant that interaction occurs among the primaries is it inherent in their natures, in any situation, or is it dependent upon and mediated by a particular environmental situation?"

As to the first question, if an increase in a certain primary tended to result in an increase in another, with mutual feedback, the extra variance (especially in dR-analyses) would appear as if a second order factor affected both. That such mutual interaction should be relatively restricted, to a limited set of primaries, with special causes for interaction, is no more surprising than that a higher order factor should operate only on a few primaries. In short this limitation would produce the same kind of simple-structure pattern in second-order factoring as does an ordinary second-stratum factor.

As to the second question, concerning surface trait possibilities, the answer simply requires a clear recognition of the difference in the model between a set of what have been called *cooperative factors* (Cattell, 1977), that is, a set all of which act with linear additiveness on a *common* set of variables to produce a surface-trait correlation cluster, and the very distinct model considered here. There have been confusions in this area before in the literature from time to time between a cluster as a *product* of cooperation, as here defined, and, on the other hand, a higher-order factor as a *determiner* of the same cooperative factors.[2] Let it be clear that what we have here is something different; a mutual augmenting effect of a set of factors in what for lack of a better term we will call *spiral interaction* (though it may be feedback in all possible directions). At its simplest, in a set of three factors which we may designate A, B, and C, the following relations would be expected:

$$B_0 = B + xA, \quad C_0 = C + yB, \quad \text{and} \quad A_o = A + zC \qquad (7\text{-}1a)$$

where A_0 is the final A score, and A the original A, and so on. Or there could be a general network of interaction, such that:

$$B_0 = B + xA + zC; \quad C_0 = C + pA + qB; \quad \text{etcetera.} \qquad (7\text{-}1b)$$

and so on. This interfactor effect has not been represented before in the factor-analytic model and would complicate the specification equation if it had to be represented in any behavioral action. But actually it does not, for it is hypothesized to occur as a purely developmental process such as would appear in dR-analyses, not in the effect of primaries at a given moment of behavior, though it would produce correlations among the A_O's, B_O's, and C_O's.

By either spiral or general interaction, indeed strong inter-correlations will be generated among A_O, B_O, and C_O that did not exist in the original A, B, and C primaries, and these will appear as a factor at the second order, which we may call an interactional emergent to contrast it with the higher-order factor the appearance of which is due to an external influence.

As to the third question, both possibilities need to be experimented on. Conceivably, as in the chemical elements, there are inherent properties in some subgroups of primaries that cause them to interact. More probably, however, they have some interaction caused by a very specific recurrent situation, social or internal and physiological, that causes an increase or decrease in one to be accompanied by produced correlated changes in the other. Such a mechanism has been briefly suggested above for exvia and we will now expand on it a little. Let us suppose a student to be in a situation where he can either studiously keep to himself or encounter an increasing number of lively, small-group circles. Higher endowment in primary A, affectia (an unsuspicious enjoyment of other persons) and H (parmia, a thick-skinned absence of shyness) would lead to more frequent group encounters; and if the skills and attitudes of F (surgency), E (social dominance), and $Q_2(-)$ (group dependence) are learned through group participation, they would become higher in individuals already initially high on A and H. The existence of a situation presenting a range of possible group participation in the environment—a "life situation"—would thus be responsible for the rise of interaction effects. It has to be noted that this emergent model comes fairly close to the simple second-order *influence* model for exvia, group learning there being the influence. However, there are important sequential differences, although we recognize that both the *emergent* and the *influence* model would fit the fact that simple structure appears, making possible the definition of second-order factor.

To complete this survey of possible types of higher-strata models, we must recognize a third type representing *joint selection* occurring on several primaries at once. This could occur first as a phenomenon in some separated subgroup in which there is selection for level on all the involved factors relative to the general population. This "type" will exaggerate any correlations that already exist among the factors.

For example, the second-order factor of intelligence stands out with much larger variance in a population ranging from defectives to geniuses than in a middling-range group. Secondly, it could occur through educational or genetic influences operating to increase the frequency of certain combination as such in individuals. For example, as R. A. Fisher (1930) argued, social promotion selects for intelligence, ego strength (freedom from mental disorder), and physique. It does not increase the number of persons deviating positively on all of these, but it does cause them to correlate over people. This follows because social status, as a dependent variable, will correlate positively with each. In Fisher's argument the correlation becomes genetically cemented and a more permanent feature of the population. For social-status differences mean segregations on interaction and mating, and a person who rose by intelligence might produce offspring with a person who rose by greater emotional stability. Parallel educational mechanisms can be imagined, the final effect of which would be to generate more than chance associations of, say, high intelligence and introversion (love of reading) producing a second-order factor (in this case "scholarliness") among the primaries.

Regardless of origin the operational detection of second-order patterns proceeds on the assumption of a model of successive strata. This has already been explored in personality and ability structure up to a third- and even a fourth-order stratum. Virtually all factor-analytic work has so far proceeded within this simple strata model, yet we now have to introduce a broader model, which has been called the reticular, or network, model. The reticular model, as shown in Figure 7-1(a) (Model V), is free of all conventions restricting interaction. It deserves consideration because although we have readily agreed that hierarchies are artifacts we have not recognized enough that even strata may sometimes result from modes of experiment, and that results may not in fact point to the existence of precise successive strata themselves. In a world of numerous influences, the manners in which they may interact are in principle unrestricted, and in practice are manifold. Psychologists have discussed taxonomies for models of interaction among factors and variables, and sometimes among factors themselves. Numerous and varied though they are (see Figure 7-1(a)) it is most desirable that the psychologist keep them in mind as experiment penetrates into various new regions, for any one of them might suddenly prove more apt than the common strata model. Figure 7-1(a) (discussed further in Cattell, 1977) shows the main possible varieties of alternative structure, using terms for them that in some cases have already become established, notably in the discussions of ability by Thurstone, Holzinger, Spearman, Burt, and others.

In this survey of possible models we have retained the labels of variable, primary factor, and higher-order factor (recognizing, however, that the last, in the emergent-trait form, has a possible alternative form to the strict earlier influence definition). In the last resort the various designs in the second and third rows of Figure 7-1(*a*), which are not strata models, can be brought under the general heading of *reticular models*, that is, models admitting *a general network* of influences interacting in all directions. Among other relations, the reticular model admits those known in systems analysis as positive and negative feedback. Thus trait *A* might load trait *B* positively, so that every increase in *A* would tend to bring about an increase in *B*; but, by negative feedback, every increase in *B* might tend to reduce *A*. Such relations will not be immediately evident or provable in correlations. We are dealing here in fact with path coefficient analysis (Morton & Yee, 1977) in which a given set of correlation coefficients might fit several causal path coefficient analysis models (Cattell, 1978). The effects will be visible in loadings, but again with some ambiguities. For, at a simple-structure or con-factor position, where a factor is likely to be identical with an influence, the loading (but not the correlation) will be a statement of the magnitude of that influence, and, of course, of whether it is positive or negative. (For the distinction of loading and correlation see Gorsuch, 1974 or Cattell, 1978.) This proposition will become evident only as the student works with oblique factors and recognizes that causal sequences, at least in the strata model, are defined by sequences of simple structures.

If we suspect that the door must be opened wide in some substantive regions to the reticular model, then such tools as factor analysis, manipulative research, and path coefficient analysis (Wright, 1927; Morton & Yee, 1974; Cattell, 1976) will need to be jointly and ingeniously brought to bear. Factor analysis alone will no longer provide the relatively straight and royal avenue to structure as it does when the relations in nature readily fit the strata model. Because this is not a book on method, the reader must be referred elsewhere (Li, 1970; Cattell, 1978), for use of the valuable tool of path analysis. As stated below in connection with the nonlinearity problem, so here in the "nonstrata" problem, the general methodological solution seems to be to use factor analysis for a first—if distorted—picture of the particular factors that are at work. Then, measuring these as the basic entities to a first approximation, we can sharpen their definition, meaning, measurement, and inter-

(a) *The basic strata model, III, among more complex models*

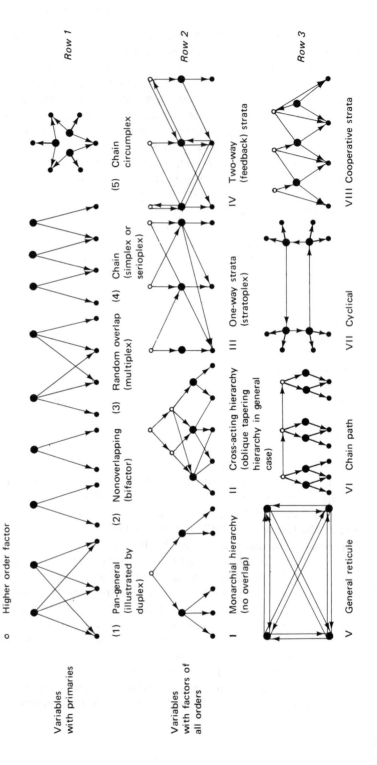

• Variable

● Primary factor

○ Higher order factor

Variables
with primaries

Row 1

(1) Pan-general
(illustrated by
duplex)

(2) Nonoverlapping
(bifactor)

(3) Random overlap
(multiplex)

(4) Chain
(simplex or
serioplex)

(5) Chain
circumplex

Variables
with factors of
all orders

Row 2

I Monarchial hierarchy
(no overlap)

II Cross-acting hierarchy
(oblique tapering
hierarchy in general
case)

III One-way strata
(stratoplex)

IV Two-way
(feedback) strata

Row 3

V General reticule

VI Chain path

VII Cyclical

VIII Cooperative strata

(b) *A typical problem in deriving true strata levels from order levels*

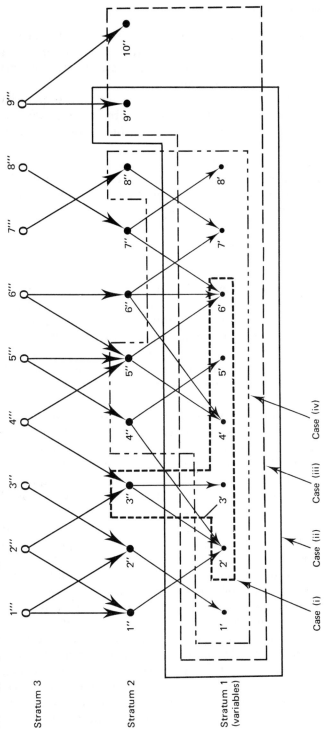

Possibilities of mistaking the stratum level of a factor. Case (i): One primary factor from stratum 1, and it has psychological representation in the other first-stratum variables. Case (ii): One primary factor from 2 is included in 1, and it has no psychological representation in stratum 1 variables. Case (iii): Two or more primaries from 1 are accidentally included in 2, with no psychological representation in first-stratum variables. Case (iv): Two or more primaries from 1 are included in 2, and they have psychological representation in first-stratum variables.

Figure 7-1. A taxonomy of the chief possible relational models among factors and variables

relations by piecing together the evidence on more complex relations of interaction from manipulative or sequential experiment, using these factor scores, notably with path coefficients and with bivariate studies, as in scientific research generally.

Since the strata model seems to hold, however, in the majority of areas investigated, we shall now turn to a more explicit examination of the model and the calculations among the strata, as summarized in Table 7-1(a) and (b).

A specification equation for estimating primary factors from secondary factors is precisely analogous to equation (2-1), used for predicting variables from primaries. Keeping to our convention of Roman numerals for secondaries, it becomes:

$$F_{gi} = b_{gI} F_{Ii} + b_{gII} F_{IIi} + \cdots + b_{gP} F_{Pi} + b_g F_{Gi} \qquad (7\text{-}2)$$

where F_{gi} is a measure of individual i on primary g and the F's with Roman subscripts are second order factors. The estimation of secondaries from tertiaries, for which we use Greek alphabet subscripts, is precisely analogous. Incidentally, the lower, (b) part of Figure 7-1 is a diagram to illustrate the problem of passing from factor *order* findings to factor *strata* conclusions when entering a relatively new field, with initial uncertainties about the variables chosen really all being on the same level. The reader not presently in actual research need not study it in detail.

Two interesting possibilities present themselves as sequels to equation (7-2). First, although we consider the actual action is one of secondary traits on primary traits, it is possible and useful to calculate the *loadings of a second-order factor directly on variables*. Secondly, it is possible to set up a behavioral specification equation that uses both primaries and secondaries together—or, indeed tertiaries and higher-strata factors too—in company. If these higher-strata factors have psychological meaning—as indeed they must have—then it would be advantageous to present a specification equation for a certain piece of behavior that allots effects to the separate primary and secondary strata of traits. It would be advantageous because it would permit us to use what knowledge we have of the different properties and natural history of the primaries, secondaries and other strata. For example, the second-stratum factor might be known to increase rapidly with age and the first-stratum not, so that a prediction two years hence, that recognized the secondary and made an allowance for age change, would be better than an ignorant use of the simple statistical prediction from the primaries.

There are two ways in which the effects of secondaries directly upon variables can be expressed, namely, through the Cattell-White (or CW) formula and the Schmid-Leiman (or SL). However, let us bear in mind from the beginning that our most favored model considers that secondaries act on primaries and primaries act on variables. Hence the CW and SL calculations are only "as if" statements describing a final *statistical* magnitude of effect of secondaries directly on variables. Similarly part of Mr. Smith's income may go via IRS to an HEW ministry, which then pays it to Mr. Jones' family, but Mr. Smith has no part in the action of paying it to Mr. Jones.[3]

Knowing the projection of higher orders directly on variables has three notable uses: (1) It leads conversely to weights of variables in estimating the scores of secondaries directly from variables. This is less clumsy than estimating the scores of primaries from variables and then of secondaries from primaries. (2) Knowing the actual behaviors ultimately affected helps in interpretation of the higher order. (3) It permits secondaries to be used jointly with primaries in the specification, as we are now setting out.

The two different ways (CW and SL) referred to for calculating the ultimate effects of higher strata factors on behavioral variables actually involve two different models. The first (CW) simply assumes that factors are oblique as they appear to be. The second (SL) handles the matter as if there are what we may call *stub primaries*, cut down in variance relative to the observed primaries, by taking the second order common factor variance out of them, leaving them uncorrelated. The understanding of these two forms of calculation may require the student to seek some statistical help at this point. We shall simply state the form of the calculation and then go on to the new models which are the psychological important part, and which can be understood in purely logical concepts.

The calculation of the weights of a secondary directly on variables by the C-W is as follows, using the notation $V_{fp\,IIv}$ for the projection of a second order directly on the variables:

$$V_{fp\,IIv} = V_{fp\,I}, V_{fp\,II} \tag{7-3}$$

where $V_{fp\,I}$ is the first-stratum factor-pattern matrix and $V_{fp\,II}$ that of the secondaries on the primaries. Similarly, for the projections of third orders on variables, we have:

$$V_{fp\,IIIv} = V_{fp\,I}\, V_{fp\,II}, V_{fp\,III} \tag{7-4}$$

On the other hand the S-L equivalent of equations (7-3) and (7-4) that is of projection of second and third on the variables is:

$$V_{fp\,IIv} = V_{fp\,I} U_{II} V_{fp\,II} U_{III} \tag{7-5a}$$

and $\quad V_{fp\,IIIv} = V_{fp\,I} U_{II} V_{fp\,II} U_{III} V_{fp\,III} U_{IV} \tag{7-5b}$

where U is the diagonal matrix of unique factor loadings.

TABLE 7-1. The Four Ways of Conceiving Higher-Order Structures

The convention of representation here is to write oblique matrices in italics, V_{fp}, and orthogonals in roman, V_{fp}. Projections of higher on lower are written V_{fpI-II} (II on variables at the first order).

(a) Oblique Factors at Each Stratum

(1) Primary stratum; oblique V_{fpI}

			Primary factors				
Variables	1	2	3	4	5	6	h^2
1	0.00	−0.80	0.20	0.00	0.40	0.00	.89
2	0.00	−0.60	0.00	0.20	0.20	0.00	.47
3	0.00	0.20	0.00	0.80	0.00	0.40	.86
4	0.00	0.00	0.00	0.20	0.00	0.60	.42
5	0.50	0.00	−0.70	0.20	0.40	0.00	.73
6	0.30	0.00	0.80	0.00	0.40	0.00	.78
7	0.00	−0.40	0.300	0.50	0.00	0.20	.70
8	0.30	0.00	0.40	0.60	0.00	0.50	.96
9	−0.30	0.20	0.00	0.00	0.60	0.00	.55
10	0.00	0.00	0.40	0.30	−0.60	0.20	.67
11	0.00	0.20	0.30	0.40	0.00	0.30	.39
12	0.70	0.30	0.00	0.00	0.60	0.00	.79
13	0.00	0.00	−0.60	0.00	0.00	0.50	.63
14	0.00	0.70	0.00	0.00	−0.30	0.00	.57
15	0.20	0.00	0.00	0.60	0.00	0.00	.40
16	−0.20	0.20	0.00	0.00	0.20	0.40	.36

(2) Correlations among primary factors, R_{fI}

	1	2	3	4	5	6
1	1.00	−0.16	0.20	−0.01	−0.11	0.22
2	0.16	1.00	−0.20	0.14	0.01	0.03
3	0.20	−0.20	1.00	0.17	0.02	0.04
4	−0.01	0.14	0.17	1.00	0.05	0.09
5	−0.11	0.01	−0.02	0.05	1.00	0.08
6	0.22	0.03	−0.04	0.09	0.08	1.00

(3) Second stratum V_{fpII}

		1	2	h^2
Primaries	1	0.30	0.50	.39
	2	0.40	0.00	.16
	3	0.50	0.00	.25
	4	0.40	−0.30	.21
	5	0.00	−0.20	.04
	6	0.00	0.40	.16

(4) Correlations of second-stratum factors, R_{fII}

	1	2
1	1.00	0.18
2	0.18	1.00

(5) Third stratum, V_{fpIII}

		1	h^2
Secondaries	1	0.60	.36
	2	0.30	.09

(b) Stratified Uncorrelated Determiners (SUD)

(1) Primary "stub" stratum factors (This matrix V_{fpI} is identical with Schmid-Leiman first stratum in (d)(1) below, left.)

(2) Second-stratum stub factors, V_{fpII}

		1	2	h^2
Primaries	1	0.24	0.48	.29
	2	−0.32	0.00	.10
	3	0.40	0.0000	.16
	4	0.32	−0.29	.19
	5	0.00	−0.19	.04
	6	0.00	0.38	.14

(3) Third-stratum factors, V_{fpIII}

		1	h^2
Secondaries	1	0.60	.36
	2	0.30	.09

TABLE 7-1 (continued)

(c) Higher Strata Projected on Variables, C-W Model

(1) Primary stratum is identical with V_{fpI} in (a)(1) above

(2) Second stratum on variables, V_{fpIIv}

	1	2	h^2
1	0.42	−0.08	0.17
2	0.32	−0.10	0.10
3	0.24	−0.40	0.18
4	−0.08	0.30	0.09
5	−0.12	0.11	0.02
6	0.31	0.07	0.09
7	0.51	−0.23	0.27
8	−0.53	−0.23	0.29
9	−0.17	−0.27	0.12
10	0.32	−0.05	0.10
11	0.23	0.24	0.09
12	0.09	0.23	0.07
13	−0.30	0.20	0.15
14	0.28	0.06	0.08
15	0.30	−0.08	0.09
16	−0.14	0.30	0.12

(3) Third stratum on variables, V_{fpIIIv}

	1	h^2
1	0.23	0.05
2	0.16	0.03
3	0.02	0.00
4	−0.04	0.00
5	−0.04	0.00
6	0.17	0.03
7	0.24	0.06
8	0.25	0.06
9	0.18	0.03
10	0.18	0.03
11	0.07	0.00
12	0.12	0.02
13	−0.24	0.06
14	0.15	0.02
15	−0.16	0.02
16	0.17	0.03

(d) Higher Strata Projected on Variables, S-L Model Transformation

(1) Primary stratum, V_{fpl}

	1	2	3	4	5	6	h^2
1	0.00	0.73	0.17	0.00	0.39	0.00	0.72
2	0.00	0.55	0.00	0.17	0.20	0.00	0.37
3	0.00	0.18	0.00	0.69	0.00	0.37	0.65
4	0.00	0.00	0.00	0.17	0.00	0.55	0.33
5	0.41	0.00	0.61	0.17	0.39	0.00	0.72
6	0.24	0.00	0.69	0.00	0.39	0.00	0.69
7	0.00	0.37	0.26	0.43	0.00	0.18	0.42
8	0.24	0.00	0.35	0.52	0.00	0.46	0.66
9	0.24	0.18	0.00	0.00	0.59	0.00	0.44
10	0.00	0.00	0.35	0.26	0.59	0.18	0.57
11	0.00	0.18	0.26	0.35	0.00	0.27	0.30
12	0.57	0.27	0.00	0.00	0.59	0.00	0.74
13	0.00	0.00	0.52	0.00	0.00	0.46	0.48
14	0.00	0.64	0.00	0.00	0.29	0.00	0.50
15	0.16	0.00	0.00	0.52	0.00	0.00	0.30
16	0.16	0.18	0.00	0.00	0.20	0.37	0.23

(2) Secondary stratum, V_{fpllv}

	1	2	h^2
1	0.34	0.08	0.12
2	0.26	0.10	0.17
3	0.19	0.38	0.18
4	0.06	0.29	0.09
5	0.10	0.10	0.02
6	0.25	0.07	0.07
7	0.41	0.22	0.21
8	0.42	0.22	0.23
9	0.14 0	0.26	0.08
10	0.26	0.05	0.07
11	0.18	0.23	0.09
12	0.07	0.22	0.05
13	0.24	0.19	0.09
14	0.22	0.06	0.05
15	0.24	0.08	0.06
16	0.11	0.29	0.09

(3) Tertiary stratum, V_{fplllv}

	1	h^2	Σh^2
1	0.23	0.05	.89
2	0.16	0.03	.47
3	0.02	0.00	.86
4	0.04	0.00	.42
5	0.04	0.00	.73
6	0.17	0.03	.78
7	0.24	0.06	.70
8	0.25	0.06	.96
9	0.18	0.03	.55
10	0.18	0.03	.67
11	0.07	0.00	.39
12	0.12	0.02	.79
13	0.24	0.06	.63
14	0.15	0.02	.57
15	0.16	0.02	.40
16	0.17	0.03	.36

TABLE 7–1. (Continued)

(e) Correlation Matrix of Variables from which Above Four Solutions Were Derived, R_{VI}

	1	22	3	4	5	6	7	8	9	10	11	12	13	14	15	16
1	0.89	0.61	−0.04	0.03	0.00	−0.09	0.52	0.28	0.03	−0.04	0.00	0.06	−0.21	0.70	0.12	−0.11
2	−0.61	0.47	0.12	0.07	0.07	−0.02	0.44	0.26	0.03	0.03	0.04	−0.02	0.08	0.50	0.19	0.09
3	−0.04	0.12	0.86	0.45	−0.07	0.08	0.49	0.72	0.10	0.33	0.51	−0.02	0.19	0.05	0.46	0.25
4	0.03	0.07	0.45	0.42	−0.00	0.03	0.26	0.43	0.07	0.17	0.29	0.06	0.30	0.02	0.13	0.28
5	0.00	0.07	0.07	0.00	0.73	0.70	−0.15	−0.10	0.13	0.43	−0.14	0.45	0.33	0.08	0.12	0.00
6	−0.09	−0.02	0.08	0.03	0.70	0.78	0.33	0.35	0.22	0.57	0.25	0.33	0.45	−0.03	0.05	0.08
7	0.52	0.44	0.49	0.26	−0.15	0.33	0.70	0.69	−0.11	0.40	0.35	−0.09	0.16	0.37	0.39	0.02
8	0.28	0.26	0.72	0.43	−0.10	0.35	0.69	0.96	0.10	0.51	0.55	0.14	0.09	−0.14	0.48	0.10
9	0.03	−0.03	0.10	0.07	0.13	0.22	−0.11	0.10	0.55	0.40	0.06	0.18	0.13	−0.01	0.08	0.31
10	−0.04	0.03	0.33	0.17	0.43	0.57	0.40	0.51	0.40	0.67	0.31	0.32	0.19	0.09	0.24	0.09
11	0.00	0.04	0.51	0.29	−0.14	0.25	0.35	0.55	0.06	0.31	0.39	0.02	−0.03	0.05	0.26	0.17
12	0.06	−0.02	−0.02	0.06	0.45	0.33	−0.09	0.14	0.18	0.32	0.02	0.79	−0.09	0.02	0.10	−0.01
13	−0.21	0.08	0.19	0.30	0.33	0.45	0.16	0.09	0.13	0.19	−0.03	0.09	0.63	−0.08	0.08	0.29
14	0.70	0.50	0.05	0.02	0.08	−0.03	0.37	0.14	−0.01	0.09	0.05	0.02	0.08	0.57	0.08	0.09
15	−0.12	0.19	0.46	0.13	0.12	0.05	0.39	0.48	0.08	0.24	0.26	0.10	0.08	0.08	0.40	0.06
16	−0.11	0.09	0.25	0.28	0.00	0.08	0.02	0.10	0.31	0.09	0.17	−0.01	0.29	0.09	0.06	0.36

These matrices can be looked at concretely in Table 7-1. In (a) we have the actual strata matrices as obtained in the usual way: a primary $V_{fp}I$ of 16 variables by 6 primaries; a secondary $V_{fp}II$ of 6 primaries by 2 secondaries, and finally a third stratum $V_{fp}III$ of 2 secondaries by one tertiary.

In (c) the secondaries and the tertiary are projected on variables by the C-W calculation. Therein the primaries are left at their full variance. Consequently in (a) (1) when we put alongside that matrix the projections of the secondaries by the C-W, as in (c) (2), the common variances of the variables (sum of the h^2 columns) is seen to be excessive; for the second order variance has gone in twice, once in the original obliqueness of the primaries and once in the secondaries that derive from that obliqueness.

By contrast the three matrices in the Schmid-Leiman (S-L) are made by that calculation (7-5) not to overlap in this way. One can add the h^2 variances across the three matrices in (d) (1) and reach a $\Sigma\ h^2$ that is the same as for the original primary (oblique) matrix at (a) (1). This is due to the projected factors in the S-L all being mutually orthogonal. The process of bringing them to orthogonality cuts down their size to what we shall call "stub" factors. This is done by multiplying the loading in the original column (say factor 2 in (a) (1)) by its uniqueness in the second order matrix, that is, the fraction of it that is not accounted for by the common second order factors above. For this fraction is the stub part that is left orthogonal to the other first orders. It is analogous to the specific factor left in a variable when primaries are taken out, but in this case it is the "specific" left in a primary factor when secondaries are taken out. If the reader will compare the loadings for, say, factor 2, in (a) (1), the original, with those in (d)1, the S-L matrix he will see they are all proportionately reduced and by the fraction .91 which (a) (3) shows to be the uniqueness for factor 2, namely $\sqrt{1-h^2} = \sqrt{1-.16} = u$.

These two systems—the CW in which the next higher orders show what they do regardless of the still high orders implicit in them and the S-L which, analogously to a partial R, removes from each the effects of correlated influences—have their various practical uses. But as psychologists we are more concerned, in the next section, with what the implications are for psychological structure and development.

7-4.   The Universal Model, Stub Factors, and Depth Psychometry

At this point in the trait and state strata structure we approach issues concerning joint action and also emergent development that are intriguing and subtle, but not too subtle for our mathematical model to catch and test.

The empirical evidence in personality has been overwhelmingly that the source traits are oblique, and that they retain their characteristic obliqueness in most ordinary populations.[4] Physical examples (Cattell, 1978) and general considerations suggest that such obliquity should prevail. For example, if we took 100 positions on the way up to the summit of Mount Everest and measured, at each, some 10 variables of size and greenness in plants, signs in rocks of ice action, speed of chemical actions, and so on, dependent on oxygen pressure and on temperature (some, of course, on both), we might expect two major primaries; one expressing effects of oxygen tension and one of temperature. But scores on these two primaries would *tend* to change together, perhaps with a correlation around 0.7, as we climb to higher locations. (Though accidents of sun and wind exposure would prevent any perfect correlation.) In short, at simple structure they would be oblique and the obliqueness would be due to common variance from a second-order factor of altitude.

Elsewhere, with more extensive reasoning than can be given here, the present writer (1978) has concluded that the most likely model for psychological data (so long as we remain in a system recognizing strata) is what has been designated the *stratified uncorrelated determiner*, or SUD, model. This supposes that influences, as isolated by factor analysis for example, are in their original existence to be considered independent and uncorrelated. There is no reason why things should become correlated unless some further influence acts jointly upon them. They become correlated only when two such factors are both acted upon, for example, augmented, by a third. On analysis the two first will appear as primaries, and the third will emerge from calculation as a second-order factor. At the next stratum, however, some further common influence will act on two or more secondaries, and this will emerge from calculations as a third-stratum factor. The SUD model thus supposes that secondaries are orthogonal to each other and to all primaries—as well as to tertiaries. This model—which in itself says nothing about the projection of the higher strata on variables—is shown in Table 7-1(b) and is to be compared with the full length oblique factor model in 7-1(a) (2). However, as will be most readily seen from a comparison of the C-W and the S-L formulae for factor loadings of primaries projected on variables (Table 7-1(c) and (d)), the true orthogonal primaries have only a fraction of the variance of the original oblique primaries and can best be called the *stubs*. The original primaries and the stubs have the same factor patterns except that all loadings are reduced on the latter, as will be seen from comparisons of the Schmid-Leiman (Table 7-1(d) with (c) and (a)). Incidentally, Table

7-1 finally gives, in (e) the original correlation matrix from which solutions according to these different models are derived, so that the reader may check as he wishes.

There are unfortunately three rather prevalent misunderstandings of the SUD model. First, the acceptance of orthogonality here is confused with the sense in which orthogonality is accepted by, say, Burt, Guilford, Horst, and many others. The latter usage prevents any appearance of second and higher strata, and recognizes no obliquity at any stage, because the primaries themselves cannot go oblique, whereas the former has to *start* with recognizing obliquities as a basis for finding the higher-order factors. This means that the SUD model has to give careful attention to determining the obliquities at each stratum, beginning with the R matrix in Table 7-1(e), though it proceeds *ultimately* to locating the psychological entities as orthogonal (stub) influences.

Second, the SUD model can be wrongly thought of as identical with the Schmid-Leiman mode of calculating a matrix, because the latter deals with the same stub factor matrix. The difference is that the S-L calculates the loadings of the higher-order factors as projections directly on the variables, whereas in the SUD model there is no false assumption that higher strata act directly on variables. Each operates only on that immediately below it. Causally, there is no "vaulting" of strata as in the S-L formulation.

Third, it is sometimes forgotten, since factors *end* orthogonal that, as a consequence of the first point above, one must still go through the experimental determination of *successive oblique strata*. Thus the SSS, successive simple-structure model, Cattell (1978), reached by the usual methods (simple structure and confactor rotation) is still the only approach to the SUD solution.

Although there is no intention to make this a text on multivariate models and statistics a proper understanding of the nature of psychological concepts and interactions in themselves requires that we be precise for the reader with statistical background, by expressing in formulae what is being said. Table 7-2 sets out in general terms what has been illustrated concretely in Table 7-1. It directs us essentially to (a) two models of factor resolutions—the familiar SSS and SUD, and (b) two modes of calculation of relations to variables, the CW and the SL. The necessary equations for all but the stub SUD have been set out, and the last may now be seen as:

$$V_{\mathrm{fpI(SUD)}} = V_{fpI} \, U_{\mathrm{II}} \tag{7-6a}$$

and $$V_{\mathrm{fpII(SUD)}} = V_{fpII} \, U_{\mathrm{III}} \tag{7-6b}$$

where V_{fpI} and V_{fpII} are the matrices as initially reached in rotation,

TABLE 7–2.   The Four Main Designs for Representing Factor Action

	Oblique	Orthogonal
Loadings given by each stratum only on next-lower stratum	Successive simple-structure oblique model (SSS or common oblique model)	Stratified uncorrelated determiners (SUD) model
Loadings projected ("vaulted") from higher-strata factors directly on variables as measured	Cattell-White matrix of oblique factor loadings on variables	Schmid-Leiman matrix of ortho-gonal, stub factor (SUD) loadings on variables

and U_{II} and U_{III} are the uniqueness of those matrices. These $V_{fpI(SUD)}$ and $V_{fpII(SUD)}$ are shown in Table 7-1(b).

As for estimating a particular factor from a higher to a lower order instance, and ultimately estimating a variable, the computation is only a matter of keeping the strata in order. Let us adopt the convention of Greek subscript for third order, Roman for a second and Arabic for a first. Then a specification can be set up for a second order factor, a first order, and a variable as follows, in the ordinary oblique (successive simple structure) system with b values from the V_{fp}'s.

$$F_{Ii} = b_{I\alpha} F_{\alpha i} + b_{I\beta} F_{\beta i} + \cdots + \text{other third orders and a} \qquad \text{specific} \qquad (7\text{-}7a)$$

$$F_{1i} = b_{1I} F_{Ii} + b_{1III} F_{IIIi} + \cdots + \text{other second orders and a} \qquad \text{specific} \qquad (7\text{-}7b)$$

$$a_{ji} = b_{ji} F_{1i} + b_{j2} F_{2i} + \cdots + \text{other first orders and a} \qquad \text{specific} \qquad (7\text{-}7c)$$

It will be realized that the ordinary (SSS; sequential simple structures) model in these 7-7 equations is a prediction of oblique factors from oblique factors—at the next higher order. The matrices in Table 7-1 are also concerned with predicting oblique factor scores, but in that case the writing out of equations equivalent to equation (7-7) would be from orthogonal stub factors, which we could distinguish by a bar on top, thus: $\bar{F}_I$, $\bar{F}_x$, etcetera. In this SUD form the b's would be only relevant to that immediate upper stratum and not imply the influence of still higher strata.

Indeed, in the SUD model we encounter two pecularities. First, equations like those in (7-7a) and (7-7b) cannot be written, because a lower order trait factor is an independent entity, not to be reconstructed from higher order factor with which, in fact, our un-correlated determiner model says it is uncorrelated! Only the corresponding oblique factor for, say $\bar{F}_I$, namely F_I, as in equation (7-7b), can be so estimated. ($\bar{F}_I$ can of course be estimated as a factor score from the *variables* it loads.) The second peculiarity of the SUD is that the different strata of factors can, in the case of trait factors, be brought into the same variable specification equation. (It has already been pointed out that in the SL matrix—Table 7-1 (d)—the 9 factor columns can be put side by side, the squared loadings in the whole row for each variable adding up to h^2, whereas 7-1(a) and 7-1(c) cannot be put together in that way, since the oblique factor columns overlap in their variance.)

Without falling into the assumption that the Schmid-Leiman equation describes what is *functionally* happening we can yet get valuable perspective on what the various strata levels of factors (stub factors) are contributing to any variable by writing the following all-strata-embracing specification equation.[5]

$$a_{ij} = b_{j1}\bar{F}_{1i} + \cdots + b_{j6}\bar{F}_{6i} + b_{jI}\bar{F}_{Ii}$$
$$+ b_{jII}\bar{F}_{IIi} + b_{jIII}\bar{F}_{IIIi} + \text{specifics} \tag{7-8}$$

where the stub factors, $\bar{F}_{Ii}$, $\bar{F}_{Ii}$, $\bar{F}_{xi}$, and so on, are estimated from the V_{fe}'s implied by the V_{fp}'s in (d) in Table 7-1. The properties of this SUD-derived S-L model equation have been developed particularly by Bentler (1976).

Some psychologists may yet wish to debate whether equation (7-8) may not be *more* than a convenience, actually representing some functional action; but we have given our arguments for treating it largely as a convenience in predicting a specific action, a_{ij} and for giving the statistical relative importance of primary, secondary and tertiary traits.

Where different strata undoubtedly exist we would argue for putting personality structure in all three or four matrix forms, as in Table 7-1, after the SSS solutions have been reached. This not only helps interpretation of higher-strata source traits but also puts issues of the applied psychometric use of factors of different strata into due perspective. For example, in this decade some practising psychologists, less at home in multivariate analysis, have been prone "for simplicity" to use questionnaire scales for secondaries but not for primaries. They seem ready to sacrifice accuracy and under-standing for convenience and brevity by using, say, just three or four personality scales—secondaries—instead of the 16 to 29 primar-ies that research indicates to be present. The argument is put forward, notably by Eysenck and Eysenck (1960, 1969) regarding the use of their trinity of scales—neuroticism, extraversion, and psychoticism—that secondaries, being broader, are more important. Quite apart from the general scientific argument that anything as complex as human nature is unlikely to be well described by three scores, there is statistical evidence against the safety of this casual practice of operating with two or three measurements when important diagnostic decisions are being made that greatly affect a patient's life. The statistical fact is that if we take almost any criterion behavior prediction—job success, clinical prognosis, scholastic performance—the percentage of the variance predicted is higher and sometimes decidedly higher, from the primary scores than from the secondaries. Investigation remains to be done to see how widely this is supported for the "stubs" in equation (7-8), but it is undoubtedly true of the usual psychometric predictions from oblique primaries, as measured in the ability field by Hakstian and Cattell (1976), and in personality in the 16 PF, HSPQ, CPQ, O-A Battery, and so on, as instanced by Cattell, Eber, and Tsujioka (1970), Porter and Cattell (1974), Cattell and Schuerger (1978), and others.

Actually, the argument for using just a few gross secondaries is awry in two senses: in trying to give psychological priority to them, and in setting up a rivalry and antithesis of primary and secondary use that misrepresents the real problem. The correct perspective is to use both. In what the present writer has proposed to clinicians and industrial and educational psychologists as *depth psychometry*, it is argued that insightful use must include and employ intelligently the facts about *all strata simultaneously*. However, this statement, in a precise sense, refers to measures of the orthogonal source traits in the SUD system, which recognizes that the upper-strata factors are real trait influences, with very different characteristics and natural histories from those in the lower strata. They are not just *statistically* different pieces of variance, but psychologically different source traits with different natural histories and properties. Furthermore, we can achieve this joint use of primaries and secondaries without using additional scales for secondaries. For when we are using the usual primary batteries, the standardization and scoring tables permit the test results, for example, of the 16 PF primaries, *to yield at once both the scores on primaries* (which are, in fact, estimates of the stub primaries) *and the scores on the secondaries*, also as stub factors.

What depth psychometry adds to the ordinary psychometric examination is simultaneously information about the possible diverse action of the different strata of source traits. For example, one and the same score on the secondary we call anxiety (QII) may, in two different patients, be very differently constituted in terms of relative scores on the primaries of ego weakness $(C-)$, ergic tension (Q_4), guilt proneness (O), and so on. This difference in mode of expression, or, in the balance of the set of primary factors adding up in a given individual to some surface trait or symptom score, could be very important for the design of therapy. At the moment, the possibilities of depth psychometry cannot be case-illustrated because its use has yet been little realized by clinicians. Accordingly the topic must be set aside here while we proceed to basic science propositions as such.

In summary, we have accepted as the most likely universal model of structure a set of essentially independent orthogonal fundamental factors that can ultimately be recovered by analysis, but only by proceeding through SSS—oblique factors at different levels. What will thus normally emerge initially from any careful analysis of primaries is a set of obliquely well-defined, correlated source traits. This model permits the higher-stratum influences to be recognized as of various types, such as direct influences or interaction products. Any statistical problem or properties associated with this model, the reader is reminded, can be well handled in existing statistical methods, though it has not seemed appropriate to pursue pure statistics to ultimate detail here.

7-5. Variance Sources in the Specification Equation Using Trait, Trait-Change, and State Factors, with Enlarged Meanings of the Latter

Two important concepts developed as we advance toward increasing precision in this chapter are, first, the ultimate relation of factors in the stratum (SUD) (and, implicitly, the reticular) model, already pursued sufficiently above, and second, a shift from the older psychometric fixed-trait model. That shift is toward a psychological and statistical integration of trait and state action, to which the present section is addressed.

The propositions that need now to be stated more clearly about relations of trait-difference and state-change contributions to behavior may seem at first to be purely psychometric in nature. Further, they may seem to resolve into statistical technicalities we have promised we would, as far as possible, avoid. Yet in the next decade progress in discovery of the main structures of states and traits and their interrelationships is unlikely to move clearly and rapidly unless more refined models are made explicit and brought to application in student research.

First, we need to focus on the simple fact that the distinction of trait, trait-change, and state factors will depend partly on establishment of their relative variance magnitudes as factors in cross-comparisons of R-, dR-, and P-technique results. To begin with, let us proceed on the probability that, in the ultimate formal psychometric sense, *both traits and states will modulate*, that is, change in level and variance, with ambient situations, though to perhaps decidedly different degrees, as suggested by our hypothesis of a bimodality of TS (trait-state ratio) distributions. An additional differentiator will be that traits may show steady long-term maturation and learning trends. We are familiar with the idea that even a trait *not* undergoing development will need (on account of temporary modulator fluctuation) to have measures taken on several occasions and averaged if a reasonably correct score is required. Recent evidence from the proper comparison of dependability-reliability and stability coefficients indicates, as expected, that the departure of stability coefficients from unity is not due merely to error of measurement.

As to the state model, we have already noted that it is conceivable that state variance occurs for all people either about the *same central* mean value, or from the *same extreme, zero* level. Tentative evidence suggests it is more likely that each individual will have his or her own characteristic mean level on each state, about which he or she oscillates. Our bimodality hypothesis suggests that calculation of the intra-interindividual variance ratio index, TS, will show an altogether higher ratio of intra-individual to interindividual variation in states than in traits, and the bimodality of distribution of this index will aid us in recognizing two distinct classes: traits and states.

Nevertheless, we have recognized that states will appear as factors in ordinary single-occasion R-technique as "frozen waves," and we may add that even if we averaged measures over several occasions to get relatively pure trait R-technique structures, state patterns would still appear, though as very small variance factors—if our assumption is correct that individuals oscillate around characteristic state levels. In seeking a statement of the relative sizes of trait and state factors in R-, dR-, and P-techniques, we must remember that ordinary factor analysis, beginning with unit-length (standard-score) variables, "artificially" makes all factors of unit length too. Only if we use *real base* factor analysis shall we be able to make statements about relative factor sizes.[6] This is essentially the same as saying that if we keep to raw scores (but take a wide array of variables sufficient for specific test sigmas to cancel out when tests are added to give factor scores), and then estimate factor-score variances therefrom, we shall find state factors larger in dR-technique. The fact that *difference* scores of uncorrelated repeat measures each of variance σ^2 will have a variance of $2\sigma^2$ shows that state factors will have half the variance in R- and (person-averaged) P-techniques that they have in dR, whereas trait factors will be completely missing from dR and P. A summary of the essential relations is given in Table 7-3. Such a comparison of sigmas alone should go far to enable research to identify trait and state factors. Table 7-3 says nothing about the relative variance of states as such in relation to trait factors as such, about which matter, important for behavior prediction, little is yet known empirically. The table above thus only sets out variances of state in relation to state, and trait in relation to trait, in different experimental systems. To this general statement we should add the additional observation that as the modulation diagram (p. 193) shows, the state variance will climb relative to that of traits as we move into more "high-powered" stimulating ambient situations.

A question we have raised in connection with state-factor definition is whether the patterns of change in rise and in decline respectively, are identical, or whether, as seems more likely, more exact research will show a process of sequential substates in the rise and fall each with a somewhat different pattern. Similar to that is the question whether in the rise and fall of ergic tensions and sentiment excitations, some genetically prescribed sequence in the former, or some learned association paths in the latter, will cause each cross sectional increment or change to be somewhat different in pattern from the summed pattern across all stages of elevation or decline. The latter hypothesis—that the pattern of covariation of variables will change with level—is surely more probable, and the methods exist (factoring over short ranges) to permit the answer to be researched. If we say that $\mathbf{C}_{s1}$, $\mathbf{C}_{s2}$, and $\mathbf{C}_{s3}$ are three column vectors showing the effect of state S on the score changes on variables a through n, through the first, second, and third fraction of the score range of the state, then we are saying that the expression for the full range of the state on these variables is:

$$\mathbf{C}_{st} = \mathbf{C}_{s1} + \mathbf{C}_{s2} + \mathbf{C}_{s3} \qquad (7\text{-}13)$$

In the case of trait-change factors, the question of what they will look like in R-technique (granted their appearance in dR and P) can be answered only if we carry the above concept of changing state

TABLE 7–3. Relations of Sizes of Trait and State Factors in R-, dR-, and P-Technique Domains of Data Analysis[a]

(a) Assumption: All People Have the Same State Mean and Sigma. There is only one trait and one state involved so that the variance of the variable is wholly accounted for by them. State factor sigma equals trait sigma equals unity in the R-technique case. With both assumptions (a, and b below), the basic treatment is by covariance factor analysis. Thus in (a) dR, we have the alternative of saying the loading is $2b_{js}$ or of keeping it at b_{js}, as in R, allowing the factor to be twice as big. The variance of the variable is the same for R and dR, if $b_{jt} = b_{js}$, but the state change variable is twice as big as the state variable in R. With these conditions, the variance of the variable should be half as big in P as in R and dR.

R-technique:

$$\sigma_{ij(k)^2} = b_{jt^2}\,\sigma_{ti^2} + b_{js^2}\,\sigma_{sk^2} = b_{jt^2} + b_{js^2}$$

dR-technique:

$$\sigma_{ij(k2-k1)^2} = b_{js^2}\,\sigma_{sk^2} + b_{js^2}\,\sigma_{sk^2} = 2b_{js^2}$$

P-technique:

$$\sigma_{ijk(i)} = b_{js(i)}\,\sigma_{sk^2} = b_{js^2}$$

Note: Subscripts in parentheses indicate what is constant for all measures: i in P, k in R. j is the specific variable, k the occasion. By contrast a roman letter shows over what the variance is measured. b_j is the loading for variable j. k is roman in R and dR because, although it is the same occasion in time, the condition is different for each person in regard to his state provocation.

(b) Assumption: People Have Different Means and Sigmas for Their States, Which Are Positively Correlated Over People.

R-technique:

$$\sigma_{ij(k)^2} = b_{jt^2}\,\sigma_{t^2} + b_{js^2}\,\sigma_{smi^2} + \sigma_{ski^2} + 2r_{mki}\,\sigma_{smi}\,\sigma_{ski}$$

Note: σ_{smi} is the variance of state means across people; σ_{ski} is the variance of individuals from their means where both occasions (k's) and the sigma of individuals (i's) vary. This sigma across two sources is considered approximately the mean of the sigmas of all individuals.

dR-technique:

$$\sigma_{ij(k_2-k_1)^2} = 2bjs^2\,\sigma_{ski^2}$$

P-technique:

$$\sigma_{jk(i)^2} = b_{js(i)^2}\,\sigma_{sk(i)^2} = b_{jis}$$

Note: This P-technique differs from that in (a) only because σ_{sk^2} is peculiar to the individual, whereas in (a) it was assumed the same for all individuals. Otherwise, the variance of factors and variables is the same for dR and P in (b) as in (a). But in R, the variance of the variable will be greater and the variance of the state factor will be considerably greater (using raw scores and covariance factors). Such experimental comparisons are the means of deciding between models (a) and (b).

---

[a]From Cattell, R. B., *Personality and Mood by Questionnaire*, 1973, p. 227. Reproduced by kind permission of Jossey Bass Publishers.

patterns to more extreme form. This we do in the concepts of *phased* and *uniform* growth (or decline) processes. Uniform (unphased) growth is approximated by the growth of a pine tree or a shape painted on a balloon expanded by successive breaths. A variable initially larger (in raw scores) like the height of the tree trunk, will show a proportionately larger growth increment, whereas a smaller one, like the diameter of a branch, will show a smaller dR change (in absolute measures) in covariance dR-factoring. (This difference would not appear if trunk and twig changes are standardized.) If measures are taken at yearly intervals, the dR-factor loadings for successive years will be much the same (even if each year the trunk grows relatively twice as fast as a branch). In other words, in a situation of uniform growth, the dR-loading patterns will tend to be the same from year to year and the same as the individual-difference R-technique loading pattern in any given year.

In the growth of a house or of an automobile, on the other hand, there are phases of growth of one part unaccompanied by growth in some other. Thus dR-factors for houses would show, first, high loadings on features of the foundations and zero values for walls, but later, loadings on walls and zero on foundation. This we call *phased growth*, and although it occurs more with inanimate objects, most organic growth has some phased effect and some (a butterfly) is wholly phasic. Human psychological growth (an excellent general methodological treatment of which can be found in Nesselroade & Reese, 1973) has features of both uniform and phasic growth. In bodily growth head size develops fast in infancy and limb growth in early adolescence, scholastic skills develop over the school age, and human skills probably later.

Nevertheless, whether we deal with factors of phased or uniform growth, the relation of those trait-change factors to trait (individual difference) factors at various absolute levels can be worked out. Without full elaboration here of the derivations, it can be seen that the specification equations (and the associated factor-estimation equations) for individual-difference factors (R-technique) will, as a mathematical necessity, bear a relation—in the first case when all growth starts from zero—to those from dR-technique. If, for precision, we step into real base (covariance) factor analysis, the factors and weights for the R-technique statement at full growth will be a summation of the dR-values for the successive years of growth, as in equations (7-10a) to (7-10c):

$$a_{ij(1-2)} = b_{j1(1-2)}T_{1i} + \cdots + b_{jp(1-2)}T_{pi} \qquad (7\text{-}10a)$$

$$a_{ij(2-3)} = b_{i(2-3)}T_{1i} + \cdots + b_{jp(2-3)}T_{pi} \qquad (7\text{-}10b)$$

$$a_{ij(3-4)} = b_{(3-4)}T_{1i} + \cdots + b_{jp(3-4)}T_{pi} \qquad (7\text{-}10c)$$

assuming the periods taken add to the total years of growth. If not, and we do a single dR over the three periods, we would similarly expect (if the factor is measured in weights transcending any one phase) that the loadings b_{j1}, etcetera, in (7-10a), (7-10b), and (7-10c) will be added (and averaged if T's are restandardized), to give loadings appropriate for the total change dR-analyses. We can readily see on a logical basis that if the type of growth is absolutely uniform, the R-technique interindividual weights will be a simple multiple and averaging of any one-year dR-pattern, for the differences among persons become nothing but differences in rate of growth over the same time.

Consideration of these similarities of R and dR in the case of uniform growth—which must often be approximated in human maturation and learning—suggest that what we have called trait-change factors, which theoretically should appear alongside state factors in R-technique, will often not do so. They will—unlike states—be too similar in pattern to the trait factor itself to be separable from it. On the other hand, when phasic growth prevails, the increment pattern should, not only in theory but in practical factoring, split off more readily from the individual-difference pattern factor that existed before the anomalous phasic growth pattern augmented it. It may well call for extremely good factor-analytic technique to do this, but if research can rise to the challenge, some intriguing possibilities of more insightful understanding of personality structure arise. It has been said already that the concept of a factor as an influence includes the "archaeological" deposit of a past influence. We now add that if a trait went through two or three distinct forms of phasic growth, it should not be beyond the capacity of sensitive factor methods to uncover these superimposed patterns instead of delivering, as is now probably the usual outcome, a somewhat blurred compromise pattern across the phases, impeding both interpretation and scoring.

The above concepts of uniform and phasic change, along with the distinction between the state and trait-change models to which both apply, have vital relevance to the growing practice of measuring states as well as traits in, for example, clinical and experimental areas. They have relevance both to factor score estimation and to that use of standardized scores that psychologists wish to follow in states as they have in traits.

Returning to states, let us now recognize some further refinements and some practical problems in applied personality practice. We have recognized that probably the best fitting model is one in which different individuals have different means on state scores.

But we must also recognize that they probably have different sigmas. When we assign George a standard score on anxiety, do we need to measure him on a large sample of occasions in order to be able to say that, *for him*, he stands today at, say, the ninetieth percentile on anxiety, fatigue, or whatever? Or should we be content with the more practicable but gross alternative of measuring everyone (a large sample) on one occasion, and recognizing that the variance on this distribution adds (and, therefore, confounds) the usual psychometric variance of individuals on their state means, about the grand mean, and the variance within individuals (which without measurement occasion would be a mean of within variances)? If each of all the individuals were measured several times and the result contrasted with that just mentioned it should be possible to estimate these variances separately. The practitioner has no alternative but to recognize that assigning a standard score to any individual in a population, in terms of his *own* state variance (both his mean and his variance by hypothesis being different from those of anyone else), can approach accuracy only through a large number of measures on each individual. In short, state-level standardization is more complex and a far greater practical problem than the more familiar trait-standardization task.

Furthermore, we must recognize that in states we can standardize for tables both of *levels*, as above, and of *amount of change* between one occasion and another. Precisely parallel meanings of standard score arise, incidentally, for trait-change factors. As an additional consideration in the psychometric aspects, we must point out in this connection that in assigning standard scores to *dR*-data we deal with *changes* in state (or trait change) level, not absolute level, as in *R*-technique data, and it is *change score* standardizations that are the basis of comparisons. So far as the writer knows, no tables for state-change score standardization have been published, although they would be useful in clinical practice and drug research.

However, we are not quite at the end of the conceptual refinements needed for state concepts. First, in scoring, a really refined treatment will eventually have to bring in the changing standardization related to change of weights of variables in factor scoring in states with phases, taken, for example, "on the way up and on the way down."

Such changes of the pattern of weights interact with and bring us to consideration of "ceiling" and "floor" effects in scaling the individual variables. As a practical instance, if an individual's blood pressure is already high for some organic reason, then a change in it due to an anxiety state is unlikely to be properly represented in the usual loading of blood pressure on the anxiety state. There are actually two sources of complication here: (1) ordinary problems of getting equal interval scores on constituent variables in the face of ceiling and floor effects, and (2) the problem that the score on any variable used in state measurement also may appreciably involve some trait factor. The former problem, which is probably serious in state scales, needs to be tackled by the pan-normalization and relational simplex methods (Cattell, 1973, p. 383), and there is also every hope that in the near future data will present a true zero to be estimated by the method described under modulation.

As to the second—the practical measurement—problem there is much evidence that it is very difficult indeed to find items for state measurement that do not also appreciably involve traits. At the moment no "state sphere" of variables has ever been set out comparable to our *personality sphere* of trait variables. Moreover, in order to "place" states relative to traits our first step was to use this same sphere for both, though later we developed a vocabulary of a rough nature for states. Until some years of "progressive rectification" (Cattell 1973) have taken place, therefore, it is likely that all state scales will contain noticeable trait variance—and, of course, vice versa.

This question of trait contamination has been raised as a possible explanation of the embarrassingly high correlations found between state scales, even in a well groomed instance like the Curran (1968) 8 state battery. Typically there are large positive correlations of anxiety, depression, fatigue, and regression, which correlate regularly negatively with arousal and exvia. The inclination of practical workers making rough judgments is to say that there is really only one large second order—positive on anxiety, depression, guilt, etcetera, negative on exvia and arousal—but this is too simple. The fact is that statistical tests show eight primary factors, and that even though they correlate highly they have readily determined, distinct hyperplanes and cannot be reduced to one factor.

The possible explanation just considered—that there is contaminating trait variance from a trait which pre-disposes people to mark themselves high on anxiety and depression and low on exvia state and arousal—has essentially been disposed of by the recent work of Brennan and the present writer in *dR*-technique and of Birkett and Cattell (1978) in *P*-technique. These studies show that when change scores only are used the big second order factor (indeed more than one) still persists. One theory must be that there are physiological changes common to anxiety, depression and stress which, as a second order, produce common movement in change. The chief alternative theory, that it is in the nature of life situations to produce one of these when they produce the other is strongly indicated by the adjustment process analysis chart (Volume 2) but not so clearly by initial empirical results.

Throughout this book we have given attention to the psychometric recognition and matrix representation of *processes*, particularly as a development from state measurement. A necessary methodological step in illuminating the interweaving of a succession of states in a process is the introduction of *lead and lag correlation* procedures, and specifically of factor lead and lag analysis. In a rising state of stress, for example, the pulse rate may rise mostly in the first minute and the release of ketosteroids or cholesterol more in the second minute or later. Consequently, the observed correlation of these two variables, permitting easy recognition of the unified nature of the functional process of responses in the stress state will reach a maximum only if we lag all pulse-rate measures, in the *P*-technique score sheet, by one minute on those of ketosteroid measures. The same kind of "lead and lag," by trial and error, to maximize *r* between two variables, is often done in research on business cycles in economics. It will be seen readily that in a matrix of many variables internal inconsistency could arise rapidly when variables are assigned, in pairs, particular mutual lags. What we have proposed as *factor lead and lag* (Cattell, 1973, 1977) proceeds first to a *P*-technique factor analysis in the ordinary way, and then, with estimates of factor scores on each occasion, proceeds to lag variables on *factors* to discover the delays maximizing the loadings. This should give the best view of the unitary action of the factor in a process. Factor lead and lag, of course, is a trial-and-error procedure for which there is no royal road by analytical methods, but computers now make such comprehensive exploration easier.

From what has been surveyed in this section, it will be evident that two further types of specification equation need to be recorded. The combination of present traits with present states has been expressed in equation (5-2) (p. 187 et seq.) for a performance at a given moment. The need may arise, however, for expressing a performance at a given moment with regard to specific growth on a trait-change factor since some earlier event, for example, entry into psychotherapy. Granted phasic growth, permitting separation of the form of the trait and trait-growth change factor, for the group concerned, we would then have:

$$a_{hijk} = \overset{x=m}{\underset{}{\Sigma}} v_{hjkx}\, T_{xi} + \overset{y=n}{\underset{}{\Sigma}} v_{hjky}\, T_{yi} + \overset{z=o}{\underset{}{\Sigma}} v_{hjkz}\, s_{kz}\, L_z$$

$$+ \text{ specific and error} \qquad (7\text{-}11)$$

where there are m trait scores (T_x's), n trait-change scores (T_y's), and o state-liability scores.

The second formulation is in the realm of analyzing scores purely of changes in performance, in connection with dR-analyses and the standardization of state change scores per se. Here traits will not enter, but only trait-change and state-change measures. The latter, for uniformity, can be put in the form of a modulator difference between two occasions, or left as a simple state-score difference, but we choose the former:

$$a_{hij(k_2-k_1)} = y_{hjx}T_{xi(k_2-k_1)} + y_{hjy}s_{y(k_2-k_1)}L_{yi} \quad (7\text{-}12)$$

It is unnecessary to write this separately for dR- and P-situations, but the T and the L will be common traits in the former and unique in the latter.

7-6.   Proceeding beyond the Linear and Additive Form of the Specification Equation

The refinements of the model to fit emerging research findings have so far been concerned largely with recognizing diverse varieties of factors. We have looked at the nature of higher- and lower-strata source traits and at the conditions of factor-analytic designs and formulae required to handle concepts of trait, trait-change, and state-dimension patterns.

A more fundamental question, frequently posed by those who proceed to multivariate models, concerns the possibility that curvilinear rather than linear relations are demanded by psychological causality and other conditions. There must have been several points at which we could speculate whether the *multiplication* of two influences, or even some exponential relation, might perhaps be more likely to predict the behavior accurately than the most simple additive and linear model we have uniformly pursued to this point. Let us consider this model and its possible modifications more closely.

1. *The linear relations in the model.* In these it is assumed that each equal successive increment in a factor brings a successive increment in a variable, which is also regular, though different for each variable. Thus, if we plotted the essential relation $a_{ij} = b_j F_{xi}$, we should have a straight line, and the loading b_j would simply be the

tangent, showing how the behavior, a_j, on the ordinate increases for each unit increase along the abscissa, F_x. The relations among variables are also expressed linearly, consistently with those of variables to factors. This assumption is made to fit the correlation coefficient, which reports only the linear part of a relationship.

2. *Additiveness among factor effects.* This assumption supposes the effect of each trait on any variable is simply added to that of others. (Incidentally, the converse is also consistently true, that a factor score estimate is treated as a weighted addition of scores on variables.) As Tucker points out, the factor model does not assume that the total intervariable relations must be entirely linear (it handles only the linear part) nor does it assume linear relations among factors.

It needs no great imagination to think of many situations in psychology where relations might be nonadditive and curvilinear. But we should not let boldness of imagination in this respect lead to any supercilious disparagement of the simpler model, so long as it actually works. It is historically noticeable in the literature that during the 1930s and 1940s the impact of factor-analytic and related methods on certain writers unused to and untrained in mathematical psychology was, in some cases, to engender what must charitably be regarded as defensive rationalizations. Probably the most common defense against experimenting with the factor model was that the additive restriction made it altogether too crude for the subtleties that certain clinicians believed they saw in operation. The next most common was that factors were arbitrary abstractions which could not be reliably scored from one sample to another, as representative of a real entity, because the weighting pattern on variables altered grossly from one sample or population to another. A glance at the same literature will show that these psychologists proposed constructively no more subtle but precise models to rectify their discontent, nor did they contribute to the production of tables of different weights which are undoubtedly needed to estimate the same factor in different social, age and sex groups. Thus those who, mathematically, could not walk, upbraided those in the new field who did not run fast enough. But the historical fact is that for the first 50 years the linear additive model has shown itself capable of fitting most psychological data so well that it has opened up vast fields of trait, state, process and type structure knowledge previously left to speculation and myth.

Just how frequently have non-linear relations been encountered? In 1955 the present writer examined scatter plots of some 2,000 correlations among personality measures and found roughly 5 percent with a significant departure from linearity at the 5 percent level! Just possibly the 200 variables did not constitute a stratified sample of personality behavior, but evidently the need to abandon a linear assumption is not urgent. And, when apparent instances exist, they can sometimes, but not always, be shown to be due to unsuitable scaling on one variable.

However, consistently with taking the above wider perspective, we *can* point to a handful of reliably replicated curvilinear relations that apparently cannot be cured by rescaling. One is the parabolic relation, $C = K - R^2$, reported by the present writer (1935a) and Pinaar between C, ego strength, and R, motor-perceptual rigidity. Another is the relation reported Sarason (1966), Taylor (1951), and others between achievement in certain performances and anxiety, in which maximum achievement is found at moderate (central) values of anxiety. There must be many others, even though they seem likely to remain a minority among known psychological relations—at least until altogether better scaling properties are achieved.

Incidentally, it will be evident, as implied above, that by rescaling variables that are initially very arbitrary in their raw-score scaling, it is generally possible—as between *any pair*—to eliminate a monotonic curvilinearity in favor of a more convenient linearity. But this convenience may not represent any underlying truth, as we can be reminded sometimes by the same rescaling making some *other* relations (than that pair) of these same variables worse! However, strictly it is only when a genuine basis for equal-interval scaling has been introduced that we can ask, without waste of effort, whether real curvilinearity exists.

In investigating possibilities of true curvilinearity of factor-variable relations, one possibility is to shift to a non-linear form of factor analysis. At present McDonald's (1962) is the only practicable form, but it is very difficult to apply especially beyond two or three factors. An entirely practicable alternative is what might be called the *successive ranges* approach. Therein, by choice of population or situation, the investigator takes, say, initially, a lower score range on the variables, and, therefore, by probability on the factors, and finds the weights and loadings by factoring that range. This is repeated, as shown in Figure 7-2 at other ranges. The different loadings, which are tangents, can then be joined up into a non-linear form, if that is what emerges, as shown in Figure 7-2. For precise comparability this calls for real base factor analysis.

A second procedure for finding just what is happening regarding curvilinear relations of factors and variables is one of successive approximation on factor score estimation. One estimates the factor score to a first approximation as a linear combination of one subset

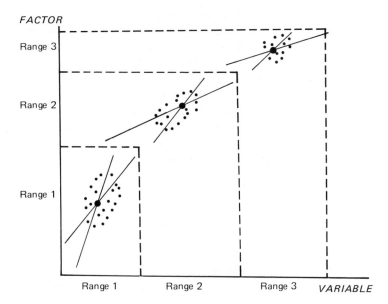

Figure 7-2. Discovering curvilinear relations by factoring over successive limited ranges.

Here a factor analysis is carried out at each of 3 selected levels of the variables (and of other variables known to be well-loaded on the factor). The regressions of factor on variable and variable on factor (the loading) change at each level. From putting these together, in covariance analysis terms and with factor sizes adjusted to comparability, a curvilinear plot can be reached transcending the usual linear restriction relating factor to variable.

of variables and then plots that score against each of, say, a dozen other significantly loaded variables. It is likely that among these some will be found to be significantly nonlinear relations. A more complete estimate of the factor can then be made, based on curves (generally quadratics) for the nonlinear contributions. When this is again plotted against each variable, we will iteratively approach an estimate more correctly based on some variables being treated as linear in relation and others on the best equation fitting the nonlinear relation. At that point we achieve a specification equation expressible in a polynomial of first, second, third, degree relations, according to the particular variable as illustrated by some speculative terms in equation (7-13).

$$a_{ij} = b_{j1} \left(c_1 F_{1i} + c_2 F^2{}_{1i} + \cdots + c_y F^y{}_{1i} \right) + \cdots + b_{j2} F_{1i} F_{2c}$$

$$+ \cdots + b_{jn} \left(d_1 F_{ni} + d_2 F^2{}_{ni} + \cdots + d_z F^z{}_{ni} \right) \qquad (7\text{-}13)$$

where c's and d's are various numerical weights.

Without further elaboration, we are, in effect, saying that, granted the existence of factors as influences and behaviors as dependent variables, the relations can be of any nature and are by no means restricted to what we think of as the ordinary specification equation. However, statistical methods at present provide us with no royal road from the matrix of linear and non-linear relations among variables, in the square matrix we get from experiments, to any equation like the above. Factor analysis, provided relations are linear, is perhaps the *nearest* among scientific methods to such a royal road to systematic and comprehensive discovery of relations. Indeed, when aided by ingenious computer programs, it carries the experimenter much of the way in approximately linear systems toward complete concept formation. But in the last resort it still falls far short of "a mechanical discoverer," for nowhere in science can one be sure beforehand that the data fits precisely a particular model. All is trial and error, hunch, shrewd logical inference, intuition, and inspired probing. So both in the search for equations more precise than linear ones, as above, and in the next step to be discussed, which is the search for relations other than additive ones, we must step outside factor analysis into that two-handed use of multivariate and bivariate methods advocated in our general introduction.

Nevertheless, it is plainly written in the history of psychology, that factor analysis has worked excellently as a first model and has produced not just "taxonomic factors" but entirely new concepts of causes and structures, rich in implications for quite new research trails. What we have to recognize is that its initial restriction to linear and additive action requires often to be surpassed by applying to the concepts it initially delivers appropriate bivariate and manipulative experimental methods. Statistically, this means in most cases analysis of variance designs in which factors are introduced as independent or dependent variables. Some fine technical treatments of interaction and nonlinearity in multivariate experiment can be pursued in a chapter by Digman (1966), in MacDonald (1962), in Horst (1966), and in Saunders (1956).

In regard to the introduction of nonlinear *product* relations among *factors* in determining behaviors, which we are now discussing, it is obvious that analysis of variance, by its capacity to reveal interaction—that is, something more than additive action, among uncorrelated "effects" (factors)—can first put us on the track of recognizing and formulating such product action. The problem in factor-analytic investigation is whether the existence of product action might throw the factor-analytic discovery of the distinct factors out of gear in the very first approach. In various plasmodes (arithmetical examples made to fit a particular model—in this case, one of factor multiplication) by Bargmann (unpublished), Cattell and Dickman (1962), Gorsuch (1963), Saunders (1956), and others not formally published, it has been shown that factor analysis *does* in general succeed in finding the factors even when there is really product rather than additive action among them. It does so by representing the product relation in the approximate terms of a summation, that is, an actual $b_{xy} F_x F_y^2$ in the true specification equation becomes $b_x F_x + b_y F_y$ in the additive representation. This fits the recognition throughout mathematics that a product relation can be approximated, over small ranges, by a sum. And as such approximation is better when the range is small, this points us to the practical strategy of doing our refined later factor analyses successively over rather restricted ranges of variables (and therefore of factors) as described above.

Although our concern here is a condensed statement of the main new possible developments in the model as such, we will not confine ourselves to the bare mathematical model, but add some psychological flesh to the skeletal bones by taking behavioral examples. It is in fact not difficult to indicate some psychological findings fitting these mathematical forms. One such repeated finding is found in reports on *moderator variables*, as investigated by Digman (1966), Saunders (1956), and others. The notion is that the relation of variable x to y differs according to the level of the subjects on a third variable z. If we switch to factors instead of variables, the same concept has been dealt with by the present writer under the label "permissive factors" (1972), and by Coombs and Kao (1955) under the label "disjunctive relations."

An obvious example of permissive action among factors occurs in educational testing. In a polyglot group doing an examination in arithmetic written in English, a candidate's numerical ability (Thurstone's N) will not get him very far unless his reading of English (V) is at a respectable level. If a_j is the examination performance, the true relation of a_j to the primary N cannot emerge until the permissive factor V reaches a certain level. The psychologist will have no difficulty in thinking of several interesting examples of this kind. For example, because dominance, E, and freedom from shyness, $H-$, are distinct factors (whatever the popular stereotype may be!), a dominant person may not be able to express himself in a group situation unless his H (parmia) is above a certain level. The psychologically permissive mode of action requires that we resort in the mathematical model to a product term, with perhaps a threshold constant introduced. Thus the variable "expression of dominance in a strange group" just mentioned would contain in the specification equation $a = E(H - k)$, where k defines a threshold on H below which E cannot function. A special case of permissive action is what the present writer has called catalytic action (1972), a term and a mode of action self-explanatory from chemistry.

Early in the history of personality factoring (Cattell, 1952), the appearance of what were called *cooperative factors* was noted. These are distinct factors (vouched for by a test for number of factors and hyperplanes) that nevertheless load markedly the same variables in common. Cooperative action may occur when two distinct uncorrelated influences, despite their independent origin, have a common tendency to impinge on the same organs or targets. A striking example is the common organ targets (but in opposite directions of action) of the sympathetic and parasympathetic nervous systems. Another example is seen in the parallel effects on various aspects of human health of cold and damp, themselves little correlated. Alternatively, it is possible that what looks in an ordinary factor pattern matrix like such a parallelism of column loadings could arise from the factor model seeking to express as an additive relation what is really a product relation of the two factors. Use of the factor-product formula (with a subtracted constant) would probably fit, and explain many clinical phenomena, such as, the tendency to diagnose some schizophrenics also as mental defectives when actually the emotional block is something preventing use of a good intelligence; or the failure to recognize high ergic tension (Q_4) in a very desurgent $(F-)$ individual, because of the degree of general inhibition.

Although the instances of nonfit that may require modifications of the linear-additive specification equation may crop up at bewildering moments, and although definitely *establishing* the need for a change of model may involve massive research trial and error, it is heartening to reflect that no matter how complex the plotted curve of a factor score to variable score may turn out to be, a definite polynomial specification equation for predicting criterion from factors can always be fitted to it. The development of personality theory as refined to exact forms in the next two decades is going to require attention to these further models of the specification equation, using concepts of permissive and cooperative factor action, product and exponential terms.

7-7. The Discovery and Use of Types in Relation to Traits

The introduction to the type concept in Chapter 1 averred that, of some 45 uses of the term type (Cattell, 1946), the most useful and operationally definable is that of a "species type." This statement rests on the observation that when individuals are placed as points in multidimensional factor space, they may cluster and segregate, as shown in Figure 1-8, whereupon any type is defined as the *modal* value (or centroid) calculated for such a definite, recognizable cluster.

Biological observations at present give us the most likely and the most sophisticated concepts of natural types and subtypes, in *order*, *genus*, and *species*. In biological species-types and also in many psychological profiles that cluster and point to the existence of such regions of dense representation, we can see that there is a special functional success for individuals with the given combination of traits, which causes it to flourish and multiply. Conversely, there are regions in the multidimensional space that are relatively uninhabited because the given combination would be functionally relatively useless. For example, an architect usually has, simultaneously, good knowledge about the engineering quality of materials and good geometricial and esthetic ability to draw an attractive structure. There is less demand in society for people possessing one without the other than for people possessing both together. It is beyond our scope here to go into the causes of segregation in the biological world, but obviously nature has produced only a few out of all mathematically possible combinations of traits. Sometimes this may be due to the evolutionary difficulty of moving by small increments across unrewarding interspaces but more likely there is simply no value or practicality in the combination. Men with one eye in the back of the head might have greater survival in modern traffic, but it is a long way for the organ to migrate!

Elsewhere (Cattell, Coulter, & Tsujioka, 1966), two major causes for types have been more systematically considered—one is *functional advantage* (social or genetic) for particular combinations, as just discussed, and the other has been called origin by *inherent development pathways*. The latter is best illustrated in nature by the type of rivers, or the characteristic form of ocean cliffs, but in living beings more often by the syndrome of a disease process (Cattell, 1966, p. 292). These could account for the origin of species types in general, that is, for uneven densities of possible combinations, and they have considerable relevance to psychology, where researchers and writers constantly refer to species types in occupational skills, political attitudes, the sexes, clinical syndrome groups, racial temperaments, and cultural patterns. It will be recognized that assignment to types has practical usefulness because all members of a type are likely to have many other predictable properties in common than those by which they are initially classified. They also tend to experience a common life course and a shared general fate.

Thus, if we say that under the table there is either a cat or a rattle-snake, we usefully "predict" that among other things one may meow and the other may bite. Less important, when an employer sees that a job candidate is a man and not a woman, the employer can predict (*pace* women's lib) that the male employee will *not* take maternity leave. Similar "extra packaged information" through "typing" occurs often in clinical psychology, for a clinician who diagnoses one patient as neurotic and another as schizophrenic is adding to the immediate information the implicit prediction that the first may respond well to therapy whereas the other will present a less promising case.

Much factor-analytic research is compelled, through lack of resources for preliminary reconnaissance, and through initial ignorance of the distribution of types in the population, to get its first major source-trait dimensions from factoring a population that is actually a conglomeration of types. Incidentally, as Figure 7-3 shows, it is possible to have a continuous and normal distribution on the variables, even when there are many such distinct, discontinuous, modal groups in the data. The source-trait patterns found when we factor across many subtypes will, however, tend to be less clear than those found within one species type alone. For example, if we factor boys and girls separately on physical variables, we get relatively clear-cut loadings of the body-depth factor on various variables, loadings that are reduced and blurred if the two subpopulations are factored together.

Description and prediction by types and by traits have long histories. The former has been called the Aristotelian and the latter the Galilean method, usually with the implication that Galileo's approach of analyzing and describing by measures on continuous variables is superior. But actually the two approaches have a logically inescapable reciprocity and both are necessary for the best prediction. Indeed, description by *sorts* and by *sizes* runs through all human attempts at defining and predicting with respect to the environment. It is rooted in language in nouns on the one hand and adjectives (and adverbs) on the other.

Consequently, most refined taxonomic procedure requires (as briefly pointed out in Chapter 1) that we *first assign the individual to a type and then define his position within that type along the source traits found by factoring people in that type.* The analogue in analysis of variance consists in fixing the individual by the deviation of his group mean from the grand mean and then by his personal deviation from his group mean. But in the multivariate, correlational treatment, there is more to it in that the statistical and structural natures of the "subgroups" themselves are different.

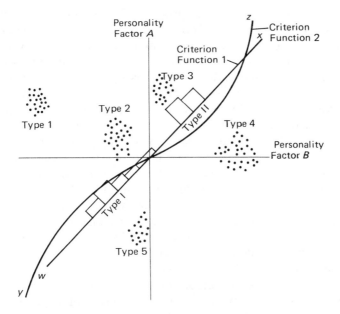

Figure 7-3. The use of a single value from weighted elements, according to a criterion performance function, in locating types, showing reduction of types and loss of information when projected on one dimension.

Histogram drawn of Criterion Function 1 shows two modes (types) replacing the five modes (types) on the profile elements themselves. The projections on Criterion Function 2 are too complex to be readily drawn. Criterion 1 is a simple linear additive function and 2 a curvilinear function. (From Cattell, *Handbook of Multivariate Experimental Psychology,* 1966, p. 306.)

When the population falls into many true species, only a restricted fraction of the variables on which the members of this and that particular type can be measured *within* their type can also be measured *over all* types. In a population of mammals, for example, only some can be measured on length of horns, and in a human prison population only some criminal types on number of murders committed, and so on. Consequently we must *first* locate the types themselves by measures on *population-common factor dimensions,* and, having so placed the types in a framework of broad dimensions, we can take up additional variables for getting *dimensions within each type.* Any individual can be assigned scores on both the dimensions stretching across types and the dimensions within his own type; but frequently the former, pin-pointing the central type, can be taken for granted when he has already been assigned to a named, indexed type.

This brings out the reciprocity of type and trait concepts and measures, for to discover trait dimensions (over types or individuals), there must be in existence individuals or types who show them—there is no dimension of redness to be brought out among types of flowers that include no red varieties. Conversely, to "place" types originally, we must have a framework of broader dimensions. The reciprocity is brought out with even more dramatic simplicity when a score matrix with information about traits (a matrix of peoples × variables, as used in R-technique factoring) is simply turned over and on its side (variables × people, as used in correlating people in Q-technique) in order to get types. In short, the *same* information, identical in the two transposes of the matrix, can supply both type and dimension concepts. Parenthetically, however, we must avert the misunderstanding that *ordinary* Q-technique as just mentioned, can yield types immediately: the coefficients of similarity of individuals must cease to be correlations and take on the special properties of profile-similarity concepts for that purpose.

With this recognition of the type-dimension reciprocity, let us turn to types, noting that the psychology of types requires principles concerning (1) how to define any given type; (2) how to discover existing types by objective procedures; (3) how to find the origins of types; and (4) how to use knowledge of types in predictive laws.

To make precise (1), the *definition* of the type as a mode in multidimensional space, it is now necessary to go further to the concepts of (a) the *homostat* and (b) the *segregate* already briefly introduced in our earlier, rougher account of types (Chapter 1). Both take into account *density of person points in one zone relative to other zones*, but with different restrictions. Distance between points can be expressed either as Mahalanobis's d or as the present writer's profile similarity coefficient, r_p.

$$r_{p \cdot ab} = \frac{2k - \Sigma d^2_{ab}}{2k + \Sigma d^2_{ab}} \tag{7-14}$$

where k is the number of elements and $2k$ yields the expected chance value of Σd^2, d being the difference on any one element of the profile between person a and b. Certain advantages can be claimed for the latter (see Cattell, Coulter, & Tsujioka, 1966, p. 293), but for the moment we can use *either* generalized distance or r_p, recognizing that a *high* r_p value means two people are close together ($r_p = 1.0$ when identical; 0.0 when unrelated). A homostat (or stat; "a set of people standing in the same place") is defined as a collection of

Segregates ("Aits") and Homostats Illustrated in Two Dimensions

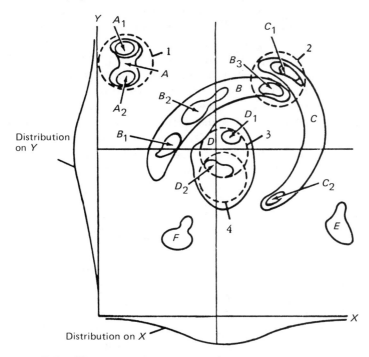

Figure 7-4.   The nature of homostat and segregate types.

people all mutually similar, above some agreed high r_p value—perhaps
0.7. Such a group would stand within one of the dashed line circles
(of radius fixed by r_p) in Figure 7-4, and if we agree further on a
density requirement—say, at least 10 people to give a "mode"—then
it is clear that whole regions in Figure 7-4 will be devoid of homostats (henceforth "stats" for short). Thus the high-density stats stand
at A_1, A_2, B_1, B_2, B_3, C_1, C_2, D_1, D_2, F, and E.

However, a second type of grouping is recognizable, as in the
long shapes shown at B and C (outer boundary). Here an individual
at one end has no great resemblance (in fact, a near-zero r_p) to an
individual at the other, but they are joined by a continuity of closely
mutually resembling individuals. This is called a segregate (*ait* for
short). One might encounter such a set of people in, say, some
religious denominations, where the measured attitudes of the "progressive" end are very different from those of the "conservative," yet
there is an unbroken spread from one to the other, and they do in
fact segregate, by lack of any connecting intermediate individuals,
from some other religious denomination. Darwin recognized such a

segregate type biologically in what is now called a "ring species." Briefly, lesser black-backed gulls in England do not mate with herring gulls in England, but they do with a somewhat different variety to the east in Scandinavia, which in turn mates with and differs little from a variety still further to the east. By the end of this polar circle of interbreeding varieties one comes to the herring gull which no longer breeds with the original black-backed gull. Many instances of such "long" segregates, with continuity throughout but with marked differences developing between the ends, can be found. However, the objective statistical location of such a ring species, or segregate of wide range, like B and C in Figure 7-4, presents some special statistical problems. Nevertheless, a process and a computer program for locating *aits* has been presented by Cattell, Coulter, and Tsujioka (1966).

Numerous taxonomists in other fields have been particularly interested in the phenomenon of *dendritic* types. This is a typical phenomenon in the biological world—as yet not well documented by psychological examples. It presents the form of a "tree" branching from classes into orders, families, genuses, and species, and finally into varieties. Special programs have been proposed for locating the "trees" in psychology, (Sokal & Sneath, 1964) but actually successive application of the Taxonome program (see Bolz, 1972; Coulter & Cattell, 1966) to individuals, then to the centroid of each of all segregate patterns, and so on should be sufficient to reveal a dendritic structure. An excellent survey of this and other taxonomic methodologies is given by Sokal and Sneath (1964).

Psychologists at present need only particular aspects of this total methodology, which we can only briefly indicate here. At present most psychologists have concepts that resolve methodologically into locating stats, aits and dendritic heirarchies. The concepts and calculations can be pursued in detail in Bolz (1972), Cattell, Coulter, and Tsjioka (1966), McQuitty (1963), Guertin and Bailey (1970), Sokal and Sneath (1964), and elsewhere. The computer program called Taxonome has been constructed to handle both stats and aits (and, ultimately, dendritic structure) by Coulter and Cattell (1966) and has been successfully used in classifying naval vessels, separating breeds of dogs (Cattell, Korth, & Bolz, 1973), grouping musical instruments (May, 1971), and other problems. A very thorough review has been given by Bolz (1972). It must be stressed that Taxonome and similar programs can be objective only so far as any device can be that seeks to say where one mountain or cloud ends and another begins. The fact is that the natural data on which we work is intrinsically not absolutely discrete and therefore not capable of being resolved purely objectively without injection of standards and limits. We are dealing with the statistics of topography, not the mathematics of topology. The Taxonome procedure is objective, in the sense that different experimenters will get the same results, only when certain constants—either the r_p or the distance cutting-point, the number of cases accepted for a significant homostat, and so on—are chosen at the same values.

Thus any sound decision on cutting point must be achieved by a proper preliminary appreciation of the particular *texture* of the data. In short, what constitutes a separate crowd is inevitably differently defined in the Sahara and in Times Square. And the shapes that emerge will necessarily and unavoidably be different with different cutting points, as the map of sand bars in an estuary changes with a falling tide. By the nature of nature, there is no single, elegant mathematical solution. But the reader who gets clear ideas of the concepts of stats and aits, of nuclear and phenomenal clusters, as defined in the reading above, can learn the necessary scientific and artistic skills and can hope to play Taxonome like a musical instrument, with different stops and keys, to get consistent results.

As to points (3) and (4) above—the laws explaining the origins of types and the principles of their use in prediction—the use of Taxonome and similar methods on measures that are factor pure and valid is still too recent to have opened these doors to understanding in an empirical sense. We can surmise that some types will be the results of what we call above, for lack of any better expression, "inherent development properties," as the type of topography we call "a river" is, or the pattern of schizophrenia, whereas others will reflect the functional advantage concept, as when people learn by social reinforcement to shape themselves to a social institution impress, in discrete attitude and skill patterns corresponding to and giving success in occupations and political affiliations. It is a fact of research that at the moment very few studies indeed have been sensitive enough in measurement and correct enough in procedure to have given us a type taxonomy in either clinical or social areas that is truly objective and specifiable in a vector pattern of personality and dynamic-trait measures.

Finally, we should note the connection between type analysis in this section and nonadditive and nonlinear relations in the previous section. As to linearity, if the distribution of individuals caused by the incidence of types is as in Figure 7-3 or 7-4 the ordinary correlation will not do credit to a "curved space." The requirements of linearity and homoscedasticity will not be met in this space of uneven densities. Only correlation ratios accepting curvilinearity will, in the last resort, express most of the relationships. As to nonadditiveness, we have suggested that one of the reasons for the multiplication of individuals at a mode is that some peculiar advantage in adaptation arises at certain combinations. The long forelegs of the giraffe, which enable him to reach the higher leaves, must be accompanied by an equally long neck if he is to drink from a brook. Granted this combination, such a variant proliferates and becomes a type.

In integrating concepts it will be noted that what we called above the permissive relation among factors is also operative here. Permissive action appears in the positive sense that a particular criterion variable suddenly receives a great increase in contribution from an increment in a particular factor when some other factor simultaneously reaches a certain range. We have used the term emergents (Cattell, Coulter, & Tsujioka, 1966) for such sudden crescendos in existing functions or the creation of entirely new effects from particular combinations of existing factors. Zeeman (1976) interestingly applies topology to such "fits and starts" prediction but much of it can be handled in equations simply by the polynomial forms indicated above (equation 7-13). We have spoken above of *two* distinct factor or dimensional frameworks in which types need to be handled, and which may be called the *cross-type* dimensionality and the *within-type* source-trait dimensions. The emergents belong to interaction in the cross-type framework of source traits; the within-type dimensions are less likely to produce emergents and are sometimes themselves emergents from cross-type dimension interactions.

Although psychologists seem eager to investigate the conditions that make types appear—in the functional advantage sense—such research is better tackled after we have mastered the basic research task of finding and defining types themselves. This includes, besides discovering types, the polishing of the applied-science procedures of deciding how much a given individual belongs to certain types. A few developments in the latter deserve our present comment. One is the possibility in *finding* types of using r_p, but with the new feature of giving *unequal weights to the profile elements*, on the assumption that some dimensions are more important in testing resemblance than others. (Similarity of engines in two cars may be considered more important than similarity of paint.) A solution for such *weighted* r_p Taxonome use has been worked out by Cattell, Coulter, and Tsujioka (1966), and perspective on such problems is given in the excellent chapter by Bolz (1972). Related to this "uneven emphasis" procedure is the use of the *discriminant function* to give special importance to those variables that most effectively separate the types.

The fact that we might weight the scores differently on different elements in a type, and combine them in nonadditive ways, raises two questions. First, would it in many cases be an improvement to use the profile similarity coefficient with *weighted* elements as just mooted? The answer to this by many taxonomists has been that it would. As Cattell and Coulter (1966) show, Taxonome can legitimately be used with r_p's so calculated. However, they point out that r_p is intended for uncorrelated elements, and that when factors are oblique an undetermined weighting is already taking place. An intention to weight therefore requires that an ideal weighting be converted to a nominal weighting with regard to the weighting from existing correlations of elements. The second question is, would it be an advantage to convert each profile, by a weighted combination, to a single *functional effectiveness* score, and to use the distribution along this single continuum for final decisions on type belonging? The problem is that there could be quite a diversity of functional-effectiveness scores and weightings and a choice has to be made, just as with a specification equation. There is no reason why we should not re-group people in types according to particular combinations of elements and particular kinds of effectiveness, but we should remember that a type does not survive by any *one* type of performance and that nature has given equal weights for good reasons.

A practical answer to the last point could be that some single score might reasonably be reached as a combination of functions representing what the type is most frequently required to perform. For example, a car has to move swiftly, to carry enough people, and to use little gas, and some mean of the specification equations for these applied to the main factors of cars could be reached. Cars could then be grouped by their values on this single composite function. It is interesting to note what this means geometrically in terms of Figure 7-3 where the line xw represents a function (nearly equally weighted, as it happens) of two elements, factors A and B. Any such function could include many factor elements and obviously there *could* be many such lines. Figure 7-3 served the purpose of showing that a population divided into many discrete species can still give normal distributions on the factor scores as such. It further shows here that the five existing types projected on (resolved by weighted scores into) the criterion function score would yield only two types (modal groupings) on the xw function. It reminds us also that the number of types we are able to recognize will change with the nature of the weighting of profile elements.

If weights were very different and other than additive functions were used—as would be appropriate for certain types and functions—the appearance of particularly "successful" *emergents* (as we call points at which individuals proliferate by their success) could be very sudden and extreme. As mentioned, Zeeman (1976) has suggested that we even abandon ordinary mathematical treatment for such "catastrophic" happenings. However, in psychology at least, we need to meet these demands only when they arise, and no demand has yet required abandoning ordinary polynomials.

Related to this concept of weighting elements in profiles, either to aid proper separation of types or better to express their essence, is the application of discriminant functions (Tatsuoka, 1970). Apparently some users need to be reminded that the multiple discriminant function (Tatsuoka, 1970) is *not* an independent, additional means, over and above the Taxonome procedure, for *finding* types. It is only a useful means of weighting r_p to *accentuate* separation when an *initial* recognition of types has been achieved by taxonomic procedures. The values of the discriminant function will in any case alter with the particular company of types, as initially found by Taxonome. Nevertheless discriminants could usefully help in clearer final separation in an agreed population of types, for example, among a dozen psychiatric syndrome types.

After types have been found, the degree of belonging by any particular individual to any type can be estimated if we calculate his r_p to the mean profile that defines the given type, allowing the standard deviation of the r_p of existing members within each type also to enter into the evaluation of degree of belonging. Here we meet the notion that a person can be "placed" by values on a series of continuous functions each yielding a set of graduated measurements in terms of his resemblance to one of several types. It is a complete analogue to placing him by graduated measurements on a set of trait dimensions. To do this we simply list the r_p's of each person to the centroid profiles of each and all of a standard reference set of types. In refined form this must recognize also the dispersion within each type. Actually, we are merely conceptually and statistically making more precise the usual typing performed by the man in the street, the novelist, and the poet, as in Wordsworth's "I saw her upon nearer view / A Spirit yet a Woman too!" (Indeed, we are lucky if our grasp is not strained by such reference to half a dozen types: "He had all the characteristics of genius. Like Napoleon he was short; like Alexander he was an alcoholic; like Carlyle he could not be contradicted. . . .") But for most calculations, first placing an individual in one type, and then using source-trait measures to define him in detail, offer a probably more precise and certainly more negotiable framework than giving distances from various types. A bridge for calculating from type information to factor specification use has been presented by Tatsuoka and Cattell (1970).

7-8. Summary

1. Higher-order factoring of primary states and primary traits leads in both cases to firmly replicable higher *strata* factors. These secondaries and tertiaries have recognizable meaning, which may be psychological, sociological, or physiological. The existence of a series of factor strata does not necessarily or usually connote the existence of a hierarchy (as anything but an accident of calculation and a particular choice of variables in the strata system). In any case we ultimately have to see nature as a reticular system of factor interaction, with the strata model as a special case.

2. The basic meaning of a factor (uniquely determined by simple-structure or confactor rotation) is: (a) most commonly a broad *influence* or determiner. However, the observed pattern may result from either a *presently acting* influence (power, capacity) or one that *has operated in the past*, leaving a set of habits, and so on, no longer functionally connected. Three other possible general interpretations are however, possible: (b) as an *emergent* from interaction (typically "spiral interaction") of primaries; (c) as the result of selection in the population, notably one increasing the relative frequency of individuals with certain factor combinations, as sometimes in types; and (d) as the result of an external situation, especially in the case of higher-order *states*, which naturally and repeatedly evokes two or more particular states together.

3. Correlations among factors and the rise of higher-order factor patterns must ultimately be considered in regard to a general reticular model, in which factors act on factors and variables in all directions and sequences. Reticular patterns can be explored with their complex positive and negative feedbacks, only by piecing together different factorings, by trial and error with path coefficients, and by manipulative experiments with relevant sections of the structure. But the strata model, which holds well up to a point, can be comprehensively investigated by ordinary factor analysis, systematically carried from level to level.

4. Within the strata model, the expression of the action of factors on lower-order factors and variables can be set out in either the ordinary SSS formulation, which preserved the obliquities natural among factors at simple structure or the SUD (stratified uncorrelated determiners) formulation, which takes the oblique positions and resolves them into orthogonal higher-order factors explaining the initial obliqueness. We conclude the latter better represents the actual action in the most likely natural events, in which correlations among lower orders only result from their sharing the contributions of higher-strata influences.

With either of these two models (SSS or SUD) one can develop matrices in which the higher-order factors become represented by their projections as loadings directly on variables. The oblique form uses the Cattell-White formula and the orthogonal the Schmid-Leiman equation. It is more correct, however, to regard the CW and SL as calculating conveniences, for example, when higher-order factor scores need to be estimated or interpreted from the foundation of variable scores, rather than as representations of actual factor action. For in both the SSS and SUD we assume factors act only on the next lower stratum. This conclusion that "vaulted" factor patterns are artificial is supported by absence of clear simple structure of higher orders when examined on variables and by the results of manipulative experiment.

5. The models that on general consideration—factor analytic and general experimental—best fit evidence on structure are the SUD, within stratified material and the general reticular model when stratification does not hold. To fit data to the latter there is no single simple procedure like straightforward factor analysis, but only careful tactical combinations of manipulative, sequential and factor analytic experiments.

6. From the SUD model it is evident that applied psychology should not be trying to "get by" by use of just a few second or third orders, since first orders have greater predictive power. But in any case evidence on *all* strata scores needs to be considered in *depth psychometry*. The score of an individual in any stratum can only be insightfully interpreted with knowledge of scores at other strata.

7. The specification equation typically contains contributions, in the *R*-technique situation, from traits, trait-change factors, and states, whereas *P*- and *dR*-techniques reveal and predict only from trait-change and state factors. Separation and identification of the different kinds of contributor are aided by the fact that in the *P*- and *dR*-techniques the resulting state and trait-change factors have different absolute variances from those that they have in *R*-technique. These variances are related however, in a simple way, which aids in separating the three kinds of structure.

8. Trait-change factors can be either of *uniform* growth or *phasic* growth in type. The former cannot be expected to be easily factor analytically separated from the corresponding traits in *R*-technique, but in *dR*- and *P*-technique will stand out as the only factors present, along with state patterns. With more refined research, state factors will probably be found to have somewhat different patterns going up and going down. A more complete definition of a state as a process is obtainable from staggered *P*-technique (lead and lag of factors on

variables) directed to maximizing loadings. Assigning standard scores to states involves a problem created by the probability that people stand at different mean state-score levels when averaged over time. It is hypothesized that the trait-change and state-fluctuation measures nevertheless, in the last resort, follow the same model of having both within- and between-person variance, but that the fluctuation ratio index (TS) values (intra- to interpersonal variance) for trait-change and state fluctuation will be bimodally distributed, thus giving us a categorical basis for separating traits and states. The summation of *dR*- loading matrices obtained on developmentally successive phasic state-change factors at intervals from birth to maturity should, with appropriate statistical allowances, average to the trait-loading matrix from individual-difference *R*-technique factor analysis at maturity.

9. Although research is now being conducted to explore possibilities beyond the linear and additive specification equation, proof of significant lack of fit of the simpler model is quite uncommon. Rescaling for "ceiling and floor distortion" in scales sometimes resolves such uncommon cases, but true cases of curvilinearity are known. Factor analysis can adapt to non-linear relations. In discovering factors despite existence of non-linear relations, the linear, additive model usually approximates sufficiently to non-additive (product) relations in data to permit the inherent factors to be severally recognized. On this basis specification equations set up on obtained plots of experiments at restricted successive ranges can be used as a step toward obtaining the true curvilinear relations. Psychologically interesting examples of the phenomena defined as *moderator variable* action, *cooperative factors*, and *permissive relations* between factors are discussed. When approaches sensitive to evidence of this kind are combined we are likely finally to depart from the linear additive specification equation—for many variables—toward higher degree polynomials fitted to various curves.

10. Most natural populations, even when seemingly multivariately normally distributed, show some heterogeneity of person density and therefore some partial or complete "coagulation" into emergent species types. Species types are defined by distinct modal densities in multi-dimensional distribution. Psychometrically, it is an improvement on a gross factoring across the whole population first to locate types by factoring with a few strategic variables relevant to *all* types across that whole population. The experimenter thus reaches inter-species dimensions permitting recognition and location of species. From this he can proceed in each species to more precise within-type factor analysis, to get the within-type source traits by which the individual can be uniquely placed. Stopping at a gross Aristotelian assignment to types does give predictive information, but such

assignment followed by Galilean use of within-type graded scores on dimensions, in a Cartesian plot, is decidedly more precise and informative. Type and trait descriptions are mutually bound by Q- and R- use of the same matrix of observations, though ordinary Q-technique actually only places people in space as a *preliminary* to typing.

11. Recognition of species types begins with a Q-matrix and proceeds, through the r_p coefficient, or some inverted distance function, in such programs as Taxonome, to find homostats (stats) and segregates (aits) as in the biologists' ring species. Repetition of the process, entering with one central profile for each type found, can then lead to recognition of dendritic, heirarchical structures among types.

12. Types arise either through *functional advantage* of certain score combinations on the dimensions, leading to proliferation of individuals at certain places in the former multivariate normal distribution, or through *inherent development pathways*, which, by the nature of things, cause a certain entity with characteristic associated elements (a "glacier," a "river," a "cliff") to appear with high modal frequency. In psychology, species types often result from a functional advantage conferred by society, and later educationally shaped by social institutional learning in the interests of society. Such types are seen in roles, occupations, and team types, but psychology, notably clinical psychology, also recognizes disease syndrome types arising from an inherent development pathway kind of origin.

13. Refinements of type methodology and conception include (a) the use of discriminant functions to give cleaner separation of types already located by Taxonome methods; (b) the introduction in r_p calculations of differing weights for profile elements, and recognizing also the effect of correlation among the factor elements; (c) the examination of distributions of single "type-function" values obtained by inserting element weights into a specification equation showing what a type *does* in terms of some criterion. The groupings of individuals from this last process will differ appreciably according to the function chosen for special emphasis and will be a projection of the types in k-space on a single line, which projection will cause a simplified re-sorting of the full multi-dimensional roll-call of types.

14. The mathematical functions that best describe the expression of different type patterns with respect to their action on some criterion are likely to be more complex than ordinary specification equations in presenting quite sudden changes in the curve ("catastrophic" effects in Zeeman's terms, but often highly beneficial "catastrophes").

For it is in the nature of many types that they lead to combinations of elements producing sudden maxima and minima.

15. A radically different method of describing individuals from that of scores on dimensional continua is to describe each by degree of resemblance to several important type referents or landmarks. Such expressions of degree of belonging to each type must include reference also to the sigma within each type. A means of translating information about relations to types into dimensional specification equations has been proposed by Tatsuoka and Cattell (1970). As far as can be seen presently, the type distance (belonging) approach is less generally negotiable in various predictions than the dimensional approach.

Because the models developed here are both more elaborate and more flexible than those in common forms of factor analysis, the reader may find it useful to consult at this point some background mathematical statistical works. (For example, those of Gorsuch (1974), Harman (1971), Horst (1965), Mulaik (1972), and the present writer (1978).) In terms of progress through the main areas of this book the reader with insufficient background to absorb these concepts can with reasonable maintenace of continuity defer closer methodological re-reading to a later occasion.

NOTES

[1] There are two ways of factoring factors: (1) by *scale factoring*, resting on estimated factor *scores*, for example, by a good primary scale, and then correlating and factoring these; (2) by *pure primary factor factoring:* recording the cosines of the angles among primaries *on the plots* at the point where unique maximum simple structure is reached. In most work with the 16 PF, HSPQ, etcetera, the results of the two approaches are very similar, the scale factoring giving slightly attenuated second-order loadings because the intercorrelations are attenuated by the imperfect validity (error) of the scales. However, the results of factoring the pure primaries has the reciprocal defect of angular error in rotation, if great care has not been taken by persistent hand rotation (Rotoplot) to reach an absolutely maximum simple structure, fixing the cosines close to true values.

Parenthetically, there is a clash between the use of the term "primary factor" or "primary" in the psychological sense, in reference to first-stratum levels, and a usage common among mathematical statisticians in which "primary factor" is contrasted with "reference vector" (Harman, 1976; Horst, 1965). In the latter setting, the traditional use of primary is a redundancy, and, in more recent factor-analytic textbooks (Gorsuch, 1974; Cattell, 1978), "factor" is simply contrasted with "reference vector" whereas primary factor or primary refers, as here, to the *first stratum* or order of analysis.

[2] Additive, cooperative action of factors will produce only a variable *cluster*, not a new factor. However, if the factor interaction is more than additive—if it is some product effect such as produces significant *statistical* interaction effects—then a new variance will appear not simply accounted for by the added factors, and a new factor may appear. What may become the classical instance is that of a schooling factor and a fluid-intelligence factor generating a new dimension of crystallized intelligence (Cattell, 1971; Horn, 1972).

[3] Against the argument occasionally met that secondaries *do* act directly on behavioral variables—an argument implicit in Eysenck's direct factoring of variables to second order factors—the objections arise (1) that if this were so secondaries would have simple structure directly on the variables, and (2) that the tests for number of factors in the variables should show the number of primaries plus number of secondaries (and tertiaries) though in fact they converge only on the first.

[4] This statement does not overlook that some leaders in the field remain in disagreement with this position. Among these we may take Burt (1940), Horst (1965), Guilford (1975), and, until recently, Eysenck (1960).

[5] One thought that will, for example, occur to the alert statistician is that in the Schmid-Leiman model we could run into the indeterminacy of having more factors than variables. This is true, but the situation is unlikely. It is rare to have primary factors more numerous than half the number of variables. If, at each step in the strata, this limit is reached, the number of factors is $(n/2) + (n/4) + (n/8) + \cdots$, which has n as its limit. Incidentally, the number of factors given by the scree and other proved tests for number of factors turns out to be the number of *primary* factors only.

[6] This is not the entire story. In ordinary factoring the factor itself may be of unit length and variance but the mean squared loadings of a given set of variables on it and other factors may vary considerably from factor to factor and this latter value is in a sense a statement about relative factor size.

CHAPTER **8**

RELATIONS OF THE OBSERVER AND THE OBSERVED: ERROR, PERTURBATION, AND TRAIT-VIEW THEORIES

8-1. Classification of the Main Error Categories in Observation and Inference

Every mature science has had to come to terms with the demon of error. Even astronomy, with its glittering precision, recognizes a "personal equation" of the observer, and goes a little red-faced over such items as Schiaparelli's fine maps of the canals on Mars. In psychology, as in the social sciences generally, discovering the real sources and limits of error, and dealing with them, is a major problem, and we shall devote this whole chapter to it in concluding our theories of personality structure.

Our alleged knowledge of human nature, which has descended to us from novelists, historians, biographers, and eventually clinicians, is a sorry tangle of sound observation and inference combined with myths, stereotypes, and personal biases. Experimental psychologists, on the other hand, always have had a sharp perception of the demon "error," and have tried to contain it, as tightly as the djinn in the Arabian Nights was contained in a bottle. Strictly speaking experimentalists have two bottles, one labeled "experimental error of

345

measurement" and the other "sampling error," and these do indeed neatly cover and contain the error sources in psychological research. The first concerns any sort of error by instrument or observer whereby the recorded value differs from the true value. The second concerns any fallacy in drawing conclusions about the main population from any mere sample of it.

Intensive and sophisticated treatment of error characterizes psychometric work of the last half century. Cronbach, Gleser, Nanda, and Rajaratnam wrote a whole book (1972) on the reliability coefficient, and the pages of *Psychometrika* are rich with refined handling of sampling error for almost every kind of statistic. With these sources for reference we can fortunately here leave routine technicalities and turn to a broader approach to error and distortion. The intrusion of error affects both raw *measurements* and the *relations* of measurements. Most statistical texts are properly concerned with the range of uncertainty of individual measurements, means, and variances but in the domain of theory we are most concerned with errors in *relationships*—in correlations, multiple regression and factor matrices. Ultimately we are here concerned to know what error of observation and sampling inference can do to our *concepts* of factor structures, types, states, and processes, that is, with *patterns*.

It would be hard to say whether psychology has suffered more, especially in the pre-experimental period, from error by observation or of sampling. Both have at times been large and systematic. When Freud based general theories of personality on fin-de-siècle middle class Viennese neurotics, or the faculty member bases all his experiments on undergraduates, a *systematic* and considerable sampling error is likely to be involved. And when much personality research is based on ratings, by minds beset by stereotypes and cliches, we have systematic "experimental" error in the observations themselves. It has taken a good novelist, Somerset Maugham, to remind theorists of the consulting room that (Maugham, 1940): "We can only know the world through our own personality. Because the behavior of others is similar to our own we surmise that they are like us: it is a shock to discover that they are not." What we call "naive projection" (Cattell & Wenig, 1952), distinguished from "true projection," could scarcely be better described. Indeed, the intrusion of the observer's position is so great in psychology that we shall here develop general principles of "psychological relativity," analogous to the latest frameworks of the physicist, to handle these problems.

Somewhere along the line error of inference about relations due to sampling shades off into epistemological and other philosophical questions. These we shall leave to many good available texts such as Cohen and Nagel (1934), Feigl and Brodbeck (1953), Royce and Buss (1976) and less tried recent texts. However, the first chapters of the *Handbook of Multivariate Experimental Psychology* also handle related methodological aspects of inference, and we shall certainly not ignore such problems when they are touched here.

In the personality area the effects of sampling error as regard single parameters are in general well worked out. Error of measurement in the T-data domain is no greater than in experimental work generally, but in Q- and $L(R)$-data (self-rating and observer rating) it obviously can be considerable and systematic. Both kinds of error are most comprehensively dealt with by returning to the five dimensional *basic data relation matrix* (BDRM). As far as sampling error is concerned we are then saved from any narrow habit of considering sampling only on people, being thereby reminded that biased inferences may be entertained also by sampling oddities on situations, stimuli, observers, etcetera. It enables us also to handle error of measurement as deriving from a single coordinate set: that presented by the observers and their instruments. This helps us also to see that we have to deal with a *psychological relativity* of observer and observed. For like physics, psychology has its Newtonian world, operating, in its case, in four dimensions of errorless entities, and the equivalent of an Einsteinian world of relativity, in psychology, added by the fifth dimension: that of the recording observer. In this world of relativity, we fully recognize that any statement of A about the attitudes and personality of B is in part determined by the personality of A and in part also by the relative movement of A and B in the social field. Parenthetically, the measurement error will probably not lie just in the observer qualities but in their interaction, also, with other dimensions, notably with the ambient situation coordinate.

Curiously, psychology has been slower than the physical sciences to develop precise models about this relativity of an observation to the observer. It is more than 100 years since astronomy talked about the "personal equation" of the observer, and it is 70 years since physics introduced the special and general theories of relativity. Psychology has still to work out general principles of relativity in regard to measurement. Of the three sources of observation for personality theory, T-data is of the same order of precision as general experimental data, but regard for effects of error is urgently needed in L- and Q-media, where the natures of observer and observed interact in peculiar ways. The present chapter is largely a first limited draft of principles of psychological relativity in that area. In ratings of others, it has long been recognized that the observer may project features of himself, either by *true* projection (Freud, 1920) or *naive* projection (Cattell & Wenig, 1952). In questionnaires, the observer may introduce gross effects when he attempts to fit his own image to a job he is keen to get, patterning his distortion on one of several social desirability images; or he may err simply through ignorance, for example, rating himself unduly high on fear of heights because he has never realized how much other people are afraid. The distortions in *Q*- and *L*-media are thus both greater and more complex than those in *T*-data. For this reason, following the educational maxim to "go from the simple to the complex," we shall tackle first the problem of ordinary "instrument factors," primarily in *T*-data, and proceed thence to the more complex issues of observers, in *trait view theory*. Our concern, as stated above, will be almost entirely with the effect of error upon relations, and not so much in simple correlations as in the form of factors and loadings in the behavior specification equation. Here we need first of all a general taxonomic overview of what the forms of error in pattern investigation are likely to be.

8-2. A Systematic Analysis of the Varieties of Perturbation Factors

Error, as defined generally, can affect (as experimental or sampling error) individual scores, means, variances, correlations, and factors. As stated above the general treatment of such error by statistical texts is too well known to call for repetition here, nor are we most interested, in the applied psychology problems of errors in individual measures, means, and so on, as such.

Our concern is with those errors, whether of the experimental or the sampling class, which produce distortions in the number and forms of those factors on which trait and state theory rest. Several of these effects are analogous to the perturbations which initially permitted wrong concepts about the motions of the planets, in astronomy, so we have, in the writings developing understanding of such effects in psychology, called it *Perturbation Theory*.

As far as factor structures are concerned we have labelled as perturbation factors those that appear over and above what we should expect from the nature of personality and the form of the model we have reason to believe, from other evidence, best fits personality structure. Note it is not being said that the perturbation factors are causeless and unreal. Indeed, as in the astronomical case, their investigation can be very profitable in throwing light on unsuspected sources of variance which, though "outside the system," are real. What we are saying is that if their existence and intrusion is ignored, the main behavior patterns considered to be personality factors will be distorted and yield false concepts.

The main discussions and derivations of perturbation concepts must here, for condensation, "be taken as read," permitting us simply to state the considered conclusion. The foundations in earlier trains of thought leading to Figure 8-1, as the most comprehensive taxonomy of structures purely due to perturbations from modes of observation, can be consulted elsewhere (Cattell, 1961, 1968, 1973; Cattell & Digman, 1964). The hierarchical "tree" of subdivisions is probably sufficiently self-explanatory; and the brief descriptions of each type, if carefully read, should give sufficient definition.

The first division of factors occurring in Figure 8-1 is that between those that appear only in one factor matrix (one experiment) and those that replicate reliably across several experiments analyzing the same data. (Correct factoring and simple structure rotation are assumed.) All the "only one experiment pattern" appearances are "false," in the sense of being unreplicable, accidental products of bad sampling, poor measurement, or erroneous calculation that can distort any *single* experimental conclusion. The particular influences in observing and calculating that produce them are listed. But, on the other hand, not all of the factors that are faithful across experiments are "true." The perturbation factors that consistently reappear in several studies are not in the ordinary sense *substantive* traits and states, of importance to psychological theory. We shall see that they arise from particular methods and instruments or biased samples and can be separated as real but "irrelevant" factors.

The persistent perturbation factors—those that produce disturbance in our attempt to find true factors even when method is good—spring from four main sources, two of which subdivide further, one into two and the other into three subforms. The four main sources begin with the case of artifacts from *data treatment*, including scaling peculiarities. The question of whether scaling properties are truly part of the data or not is sometimes not easy to answer, but certainly the form of test answers often introduces artefactual factors, and modes of calculation, for example, undue dependence on the "group method" of factoring, can do the same. By and large, however, false factors from the first of the four sources appear in studies conducted with poor training and lack of alertness at a common sense level to combatting disturbing influences. De Young (1972), Gorsuch (1974), Cattell (1972, 1973, 1974, 1978), and Vaughan (1973) among others have pointed out how editors often permit publications of factor

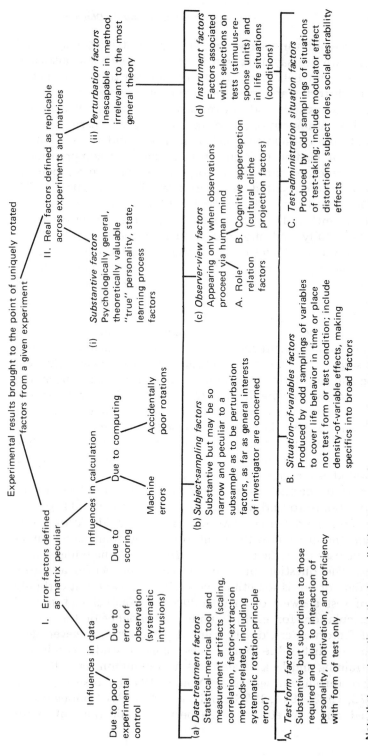

Experimental results brought to the point of uniquely rotated factors from a given experiment

I. Error factors defined as matrix peculiar

Influences in data

Due to poor experimental control

Due to error of observation (systematic intrusions)

Influences in calculation

Due to scoring

Due to computing

Machine errors

Accidentally poor rotations

II. Real factors defined as replicable across experiments and matrices

(i) *Substantive factors* Psychologically general, theoretically valuable "true" personality, state, learning process factors

(ii) *Perturbation factors* Inescapable in method, irrelevant to the most general theory

(a) *Data-treatment factors* Statistical-metrical tool and measurement artifacts (scaling, correlation, factor-extraction methods-related, including systematic rotation-principle error)

(b) *Subject-sampling factors* Substantive but may be so narrow and peculiar to a subsample as to be perturbation factors, as far as general interests of investigator are concerned

(c) *Observer-view factors* Appearing only when observations proceed via human mind

A. Role relation factors

B. Cognitive apperception (cultural cliche projection factors)

(d) *Instrument factors* Factors associated with selections on tests (stimulus-response units) and in life situations (conditions)

A. *Test-form factors* Substantive but subordinate to those required and due to interaction of personality, motivation, and proficiency with form of test only

B. *Situation-of-variables factors* Produced by odd samplings of variables to cover life behavior in time or place not test form or test condition; include density-of-variable effects, making specifics into broad factors

C. *Test-administration situation factors* Produced by odd samplings of situations of test-taking; include modulator effect distortions, subject roles, social desirability effects

Note that a systematic relation is possible between certain categories here and those of the five dimensions in the data box. Thus, II(ii)(b) deals with sampling on the subject coordinate; II(ii)(c) with the observer coordinate; II(ii)(d)A and B with the stimulus-response coordinates; and II(ii)(d)B and C with selections on the occasions coordinate.

Figure 8-1. Sources of structural misinterpretation focused on perturbation theory

analytic researches that fail to report the vital procedural steps that could inform us whether the contribution is valuable or useless and misleading.

Briefly, regarding such error, it may be said that the absence of any one of some eight basic requirement (Vaughan, 1973; Cattell, 1973, p. 283), including (1) a reliable test for number of factors, (2) iteration of communalities, (3) evidence of having adequately reached a true maximum hyperplane count in oblique simple structure, (4) use of a test of significance of simple structure, and, finally, (5) a test, by salient variable or congruence coefficient of goodness of replication, can produce gross artifacts and errors of conclusion regarding factor patterns. False factor patterns in this area II(ii) (a) in Figure 8-1 will, in general, have no more particular or general meaning than will a false mean or variance resulting from a slip in calculation.

The second form of disturbance II(ii) (b) in Figure 8-1 brings us back to subject sampling error, which is not usually important in reasonably designed experiments surpassing a minimum of, say, 200 subjects, provided we are using the right population. Maximum-likelihood factor analysis (Rao, 1965; Lawley, 1943; Joreskog, 1967; Cattell, 1978), a "deluxe" method not always available *will* yield reliable decisions as to how many factors can be taken out with a given number of subjects, but the scree test (Cattell & Vogelmann, 1977; Hakstian, Rogers, & Cattell, in press) which is psychometric in principle is adequate for most occasions. Moreover, against the statistical principle in maximum likelihood it may be urged that as sample sizes become large and begin to include rather peculiar subsets of people, new factors not found in most (smaller) samples will rise into statistical significance. Thus it is useful in such situations to check the maximum-likelihood decision on number of factors against that by a psychometric decision based on the scree test. The final decision may then be reached that the large-sample, maximum-likelihood number includes trivial factors that can be set aside as not constituting patterns of wide occurrence. In any case a factor analysis without a thorough test of number of factors is going to be wrong in all subsequent steps and to generate false perturbation factors, or false patterns in real factors.

The third and fourth types of perturbation source have greatest relevance to observer and instrument effects as here considered. The *observer view* factors appear only when a human observer is organically involved, *perceptually*, as an instrument in getting the scores, for example, in ratings. By "perceptually involved" we mean involved in making subjective mental estimations of the abstractions from behavior we call traits, as in *L*- and *Q*-media, not merely involvement in reading answer sheets and writing down the objective-test performance scores from a test, as in the *T*-medium, or in such objective sciences as physics or astronomy. The observer view class of perturbation factors, as we shall see, comes broadly from two sources: (1) the relation of the observer to the observed, in the sense of their role situation relationship, and (2) the properties of the observer himself, in his personality and cognitive equipment, operating by projection and stereotyped perception as well in other ways we shall detail. To these important third and fourth types of distortion we shall return.

Finally, in Figure 8-1 we meet those perturbation factors that are called instrument factors. First, as the classification there indicates, these are factors other than the true substantive ones, and they intrude through *the particular form of the tests themselves*, and have their distinct traceable origins. An early gross example, pointing to the reality of this sort of effect, was that found by Cattell and Gruen (1955) in using the same physical instrument, the GSR, over a number of diverse response measurement variables. If correction for individual differences of initial skin resistance is not complete, an individual with higher skin resistance will have a lesser score to various stimuli, over all these diverse response variables, and a factor will be created having nothing to do with the psychological substance but running across all tests that chance to use this measuring device.

In other instances of tests yielding an instrument factor, the intrusive factor is seen to be in an undeniable sense psychologically meaningful (as the above GSR instrument factor was physiologically meaningful), but of a trivial, irrelevant nature and having nothing to do with the broad personality factors under examination. Just as dirt is matter out of place, so this covariance in our tests is not unreal, but it is irrelevant and unwanted. For example, in the Music Preference Test of Personality, which hinges on liking or not liking certain kinds of excerpts played on the piano (Cattell & Saunders, 1954; Cattell & Eber, 1966), some pieces were recorded on a better recording instrument than others. All items with "a scratchy noise" (slight though it was) tended to be less liked by those who noticed it, so a single factor runs across this subset of response variables that has nothing to do with the domain of emotional response to musical forms as such.

Another instance is that of using a relatively demanding vocabulary in fashioning certain groups of items, for example, for a test of the arithmetic skill factor, *N*, and the spatial factor, *S*. An instrument factor, which is a kind of verbal ability, will then spread across subsets in the distinct *N*- and *S*-factor loaded variables using a large instructional vocabulary. Instrument factors from the test-form source, incidentally, are usually quite shallow (small loadings) but can be extensive in area. It has been argued, for instance that an instrument factor might be expected running across all questionnaire scales that use a certain device, for example, forced choice, multiple choice, or self-rating on a graphic scale. Such could spread each across several substantive factors, but not, of course, into a different medium, such as rating. This would be what is labelled in Figure 8-1 as A, a "test-form" instrument factor. The B and C instrument factors are discussed in the next section.

8-3. Instrument Factors from Test Form, Behavioral Area, and Situations of Testing

Before examining evidence for the second and third forms of instrument factors, it will help if we ask more explicitly what the relation of any and all instrument factors to personality factors is *expected* to be, as manifested in factor matrix patterns. In other words, what are the signs and conditions for their adequate recognition? Table 8-1 shows a typical real-data example, simplified a little by some exclusion of irrelevant parts, and rounded as to its loading values. It concerns seven attitudes, known from previous work to mark three particular dynamic-structure factors, so that all seven together suffice to reveal and mark the given dynamic traits: escape erg (two attitudes), parental erg (two attitudes), and the self-sentiment (three attitudes). These attitudes were measured by the objective motivation-strength measurement devices of Chapter 4, the first seven using information and the same seven content attitudes re-appearing as 8 through 14 in Table 8-1, then being measured again with the autism device. The simple-structure resolution with five broad factors taken out (according to the scree) came out as in factor matrix (a), Table 8-1.

Here the first three factors clearly reveal the substantive, psychological traits and the next two equally clearly point to some kind of instrument factor associated (a) with the information device and (b) with the autism measures. These latter *could* just be due to some mode of scoring, which happens to be shared by all instances of one device. But fortunately for the breadth of our illustration, they are not that trivial and bring out a fact we must never overlook, that the instrument factor itself can sometimes have real psychological meaning and substance as an individual-difference factor. In this case information may tap an ability trait, probably general intelligence

TABLE 8–1.   The Separation of Personality and Instrument Factors: An Experimental Illustration*

(a)	Psychological Factors			Instrument Factors	
	Escape Erg	Parental Senti- ment	Self- Senti- ment	Infor- mation Device	Autism Device
Information Measures					
1. Desire for good self-control	00	-02	26	54	03
2. Wish to know oneself	03	-05	31	27	19
3. Wish never to become insane	-06	12	22	43	04
4. Readiness to turn to parents for help	-02	35	09	28	-01
5. Feeling proud of one's parents	-06	28	-01	24	01
6. Desire to avoid fatal disease and accidents	16	04	13	65	-05
7. ·Wish to get protection from A-bomb	14	-08	03	14	-05
Autism Measures					
8. Desire for good self-control	01	-04	30	02	22
9. Wish to know oneself	-08	07	37	-01	31
10. Wish never to become insane	00	-01	16	00	25
11. Readiness to turn to parents for help	-08	18	09	-08	42
12. Feeling proud of one's parents	-03	14	01	06	14
13. Desire to avoid fatal disease and accidents	26	20	01	04	17
14. Wish to get protection from A-bomb	23	13	09	15	10

Note: The theoretically required salients to define the factors are boxed. Except for two values at the bottom of the parental sentiment column, the salients are high (above 0.09) where and only where they are theoretically required to be. Attitudes 13 and 14 are the same as 6 and 7 but in a different medium, and similarly for the other cross-media personality factors. Decimal points omitted as in other factor matrices.

*Example from Dynamic Structure Trait Experiment (Cattell and Digman, 1964). All 14 attitudes are factored together.

(first seven variables), and autism, in the second seven, a temperament trait. This illustrates that the character of an instrument factor arises from the fact that it is "out of place." In this case the instrument is the ability or personality-response *vehicle*, as we shall call it, which has "carried," in the actual measures, the expression of the dynamic interest area factor we want to measure. As a practical scoring matter we want to get rid of it, and that is achieved, as far as it can be achieved by reduction of particular specifics, by measuring the required dynamic trait through *several* different instruments and adding scores. With only two specifics available in Table 8-1 we would add scores on 1 and 8, 2 and 9, 3 and 10, and so on. With four to six vehicles we see that too much confounding with any one instrument tends to get "washed out."

TABLE 8-1   *(continued)*

(b) (i) Plasmode with *L*-Data Variables Cut from Multi-instrument Matrix (Cattell, 1964)

	1	2	3′	L
1	53	13	17	-03
2	-37	-01	01	57
3	38	-28	01	39
4	-02	65	01	13
5	-13	34	72	-08
6	14	05	-57	56
7	-06	04	67	08

	1	2	3′	L
1	100			
2	32	100		
3′	08	-22	100	
L	-09	11	-06	100

Mean correlation among factors = 0.02.

Note: Factor analysis with allowance for fourth (instrument) factor. Clear, correct outcome except for some unevenness of instrument factor.

(ii) Plasmode with Variables from Table (b)(i) Factor Analyzed One Factor Short (no *L*-instrument factor)

	1	2	3′
1	53	18	-12
2	-45	36	-23
3	27	-01	-57
4	00	57	18
5	-03	82	50
6	-01	-11	-63
7	00	64	22

	1	2	3′
1	100		
2	38	100	
3′	11	-18	100

Mean correlation among factors = 0.10.

In this "applied" problem it may seem that we are concerned simply with error of measurement on some single individual score, but actually our preoccupation is still with error of pattern conception, and we have just shown how necessary concern with pattern effects is, even to handle insightfully error on a single score. In regard to structure, the important principle is that if the analysis does not locate and set aside instrument factors, but confounds them with the true factors, distortions will ensue, not merely of score, as here, but also of interpretation of patterns and of approach to concepts and meaning, regarding the personality structure itself. For example, in another real data illustration, in ratings, in Table 8-1(b) where the true number of factors is three substantive and one instrument, as in 8-1(b)(i), we show what happens (Table 8-1(b)(ii)) when the experimenter takes out the wrong number of factors—three, instead of four—ignoring the fact that these data would be expected to have one instrument factor beyond the substantives. Thereupon, in the attempts at rotation it is shown that we *can* still lock into a simple-structure resolution of a sort, but it will be more approximate, as shown in b(ii). Moreover, the correlations among the factors will be unduly large, as indicated by a moderate increase of the mean *r* from on (i) to (ii) at the right of the example.

A rough practical way of handling what we here define as the instrument factor problem, but only with the applied aim of reducing bias in scoring (not of illuminating the form of instrument and substantive structures), became popular in the 1960s under the name of multitrait-multimethod scoring. (Actually multi-instrument would have been a better name than multimethod, for it is not a question of a whole scientific method but only of a test instrument form). The MTMI (multitrait-multi-instrument) method—as we may best call it, was suggested by Campbell and Fiske (1959) and contained the proposal to choose variables so that each assumed trait would be represented by several different kinds of instrument, and each kind of instrument would be used across several traits. As a practical reminder in test construction of the need to attenuate instrument effects, MTMI has been valuable. But, like cruder concepts elsewhere popular in practice, it has tended, among those unfamiliar with factor methods and the instrument concept, to encourage them to dispense with the prior need to discover the exact relation of instrument and trait structure that is important to theory and in practice a necessary prelude to insightful, precise use of instrument attenuation corrections. For in MTMI practice not only have the boundaries of the *substantive* trait itself been assumed to be those set by the psychologist's subjective choice of variables, but the boundaries of the instrument factors have also been set by fiat. Thus in the choice of instruments there has been uncritical acceptance from superficial examination that when an *apparently uniform* form of instrument has been used ("all these variables have been measured by only *one* kind of instrument"), only one single instrument factor must run through them. Actually (and sometimes at odds with such models as our own simplified example in Table 8-1), what is apparently the same measurement device may involve two or three instrument factors, when factorially examined.

In Table 8-1(b)(i) we showed simply that if an instrument factor (there labelled L for L-data instrumentality) is not given room to appear (because of underfactoring) and thus does not get set aside, it will disturb the patterns and intercorrelations of the true, substantive factors. But it has been shown, theoretically and empirically, that unfortunately the confounding *can* at times produce a seductively spurious order such as does not happen to appear in the small example in Table 8-1. When there are actually one substantive factor and two instrument factors, the accidental extraction of one less factor than is required—that is, of just two—will tend to produce two factors that have *almost* tolerable simple structure (provided there is additional "hyperplane stuff" in the form of other variables). It then turns out that one of the simple structure factors reached is a blend of the substantive with instrument number one, and the other a blend of the substantive with instrument factor number two. These are being called, for lack of a better term, *refraction factors*, because, like a single object seen double through a prism, they present essentially the same pattern with different "coloring" from the instrumentality. Real examples of these are given in Cattell (1961) and a clearer, schematically simplified, example, from use of the MAT (Motivation Analysis Test, Sweney, 1969) is shown in Table 8-2.

Here the two instrument factors, information and autism, clearly appearing in (a) are absorbed in (b) into an alternative simple structure which appears as the most feasible solution in rotating a matrix in which there has been a mistake on the number of factors, through taking out one fewer in (b) than in (a). That is, there has been an underfactoring mistake by taking only one factor short of the number *properly* taken in (a). The instrument factors in Table 8-2(a) are recognized by each running across *six* different attitudes, and by each corresponding with attitudes covering one particular method of measurement.

As soon as some preliminary factorial exploration has occurred in a domain, a design with suitable choices of variables to test alternative resolutions (a) and (b) can be made. It calls for a similar strategy of choice of marker variables as we met in separating personality and role factors. Granted attention to due proportions of markers, such design in choice of markers should suffice for recognizing instrument factors in the most general sense.

Recognizing the existence of instrument factors is one thing and getting rid of undue instrument factor contamination from a substantive factor score estimate is quite another. In getting rid of instrument factor contamination from a particular trait measurement, it has often been suggested, as an alternative to attenuating instrument contributions by averaging across several instruments, that every individual be measured "on the side" on the "pure" instrument factor itself. His score thereon would then be partialled out from his substantive measure. This alternative is psychometrically

TABLE 8–2.   Relation of Instrument to Substantive Factors in a Well-developed Research Design; Handling of Instrument Factors in Dynamic Domain: Alternative of (a) Separation and (b) Hybrid Refraction Factors

(a) Clean separation with five factors

| | Factors | | | | | |
| | Dynamic Traits | | | Instruments | | |
Variable	Esc.	Par.	S.S.	Inf.	Aut.	Specific
Attitude 1	.4			.7		.6
Attitude 2		.4		.7		.6
Attitude 3			.4	.7		.6
Attitude 4	.4			.7		.6
Attitude 5		.4		.7		.6
Attitude 6			.4	.7		.6
Attitude 7	.4				.7	.6
Attitude 8		.4			.7	.6
Attitude 9			.4		.7	.6
Attitude 10	.4				.7	.6
Attitude 11		.4			.7	.6
Attitude 12			.4		.7	.6

(b) Refraction factors appearing with six factors

Variable	Esc. Inf.	Esc. Aut.	Par. Inf.	Par. Aut.	S.S. Inf.	S.S. Aut.	Specific
Attitude 1	.8						.6
Attitude 2			.8				.6
Attitude 3					.8		.6
Attitude 4	.8						.6
Attitude 5			.8				.6
Attitude 6					.8		.6
Attitude 7		.8					.6
Attitude 8				.8			.6
Attitude 9						.8	.6
Attitude 10		.8					.6
Attitude 11				.8			.6
Attitude 12						.8	.6

Note: Among the best worked-out examples of instrument factors are those in dynamic traits measured by objective motivation tests. The above is a simplified rounded and smooth "ideal" from the original values.

clear, but in practice we meet difficulties in getting a pure instrument factor measure. It is as hard to find a single variable free of substantive factors as one free of instruments. For example, if memory is the vehicle for interest measurement in several areas we would want to find the individual's general goodness of memory. But to be sound the latter must in turn be averaged across many fields of interest.

With this grasp of the instrument factor concept, let us consider the next and last two chief influences, B and C, listed in Figure 8-1 as causing instrument factors. B has to do with special peculiarities of time and place in the content of the variables, not in the mode of measurement. For example, if we were to take 30 measures of forms of conscientiousness at home and another 30 of conscientiousness in the office (on the same persons, of course) or 30 variables dealing with persistence in class and 30 with persistence on the playing field, it is likely that beyond the main conscientiousness and persistence traits we should find in the total 120 × 120 correlation matrix two instrument factors, corresponding to the two areas of expression, sharing each of these trait measures. (This problem was considered from another angle in Chapter 6 in connection with environmental sources of variance.) The instrument factors in this case might be nothing more than other dynamic traits—say, sentiments to home, to class, to business, and to sport—or they might be a pattern of *s* indices associated with patterns of past reinforcement peculiar to but uniform across each of these areas. Nevertheless, the choice of variables and the carefulness of rotation could be technically good enough to separate them, and the scoring should aim to balance (attenuate) or partial them out. In this case we primarily would want to eliminate contamination from these areas in the estimation of a *general* personality trait (conscientiousness) or perhaps an ability factor. However, the instrument factors here might also be interesting in themselves as "area of expression factors."

If a sufficiently broad range of measures can be chosen for a factor (covering, say, as many instruments as there are, usually, subtests), correction by attenuation is a reasonable solution. Then the instrument factor variance will appear only as a balanced, attenuating, "specific factor" variance, which is ideal. But the mistaken aim—traditional among some psychometrists—of getting high homogeneity among all subtests or items in some intended measure of a broad personality factor will generally ensure the opposite effect! It will pile up instrument variance into what has been called a "bloated specific" (Cattell, 1973). That is to say, getting items of high homogeneity will tend to introduce an instrument factor conterminous with the trait-factor itself, and completely confound instrument and trait variance in the resulting score.

Test administration condition instrument factors—C in Figure 8-1—are neither in the test form itself, as in A, nor in the area of the behavior itself, as in B. They are related to some condition prevailing over the administration situation—anything from poor lighting to a powerful pressure toward socially desirable responses. Obviously, any factor that appears tied to the administration situation *could* also come from modulator effects and represent the genuine creation of a state or role factor of too small variance to be noted in some other situation. In that case, the intruders illustrate again that some instrument factors can be true individual-difference factors, which are intrusive and "perturbing" only in terms of the aim of measuring certain other personality factors. The danger here is no longer that of mistaking an instrument for a substantive factor, but failing to set aside separate factors on intrusive variance distorting the patterns of the main substantives.

Instrument factors Type II(ii)(d) in Figure 8-1, unlike error factors of Type I, but like all perturbation factors under Type II(ii), will replicate themselves recognizably as long as the test forms, measurement situations, and so on, are maintained. Yet in terms of basic personality theory they are essentially error. However, it is desirable expressly to recognize that an error term has not generally been introduced into specification equations as hitherto set out here. Therein, so far, the "tail end" of the equation—error and specifics—has appropriately been neglected as irrelevant to our main propositions. However, it becomes necessary now to recognize and add two types of common error factor—those from random error of measurement, E_r, and those from instrument effects, E_n. In passing, let us note that, as Horn, Humphreys, and others have shown, random error, especially in small samples, *will* give a few appreciable loadings on *common* factors arising purely from error. This simply means that correlations among random numbers, which in an infinite population would be zero, will rise in a small sample—say, of 50—to some appreciable positive values beyond zero. (Actually, on $N = 50$, one in twenty will reach above plus or minus .28 justifying loadings on two error factors of over 0.5 on each.) Thus, in the usual moderate-sized sample we really have the following structure (throwing all substantive factors together for the moment as T's, and the p's and e's as v's):

$$a_{hijk} = \overset{x=q}{\Sigma} v_{hjkx} s_{kx} T_{xi} + \overset{y=m}{\Sigma} v_{hjky} s_{ky} I_{yi} + \overset{z=u}{\Sigma} b_{hjkz} E_{zi}$$

$$+ \overset{j=t}{\Sigma} v_{hjk} s_{kj} T_{ji} + b_{hjk} E_{hji} \tag{8-1}$$

where the first term is the substantive trait and state factor effect from q structures; the second is the effect of m instrument factors; the third is from u random error, broad common factors (in practice, often only one or two); the fourth, T_j, is a set of t true, substantive specific factors (commonly considered for simplicity as one, but conceivably more and the last is error. This E_j, the measurement error specific to measuring j, is often written just as an error term but, for consistency, is here presented as a specific error *factor*, the loading of which brings the variance of a_{hijk} up to unity. The opportunity has been taken here to remind the reader that although statistically we are forced to calculate the specific T_j as a single value, it is conceptually more correct to consider that there may be several different skills or interest contributions peculiar to the behavior j, just as several specific errors could contribute to E_{hj}. Although equation (8-1) is a statement of what must be added to the specification equation when the observer set of the data box is brought in, it will be realized that the error is in the interaction of observer and situation. Influences that cause error of measurement exist outside the observer but register through him.

8-4.   The Basic Data Relation Matrix and Its Encompassing of Observer Traits

Of the three types of perturbation factor that remain in Figure 8-1 after instrument factors are dealt with, two—data treatment and subject sampling—are sufficiently obvious in nature for the brief descriptions in the Figure and earlier (Cattell & Digman, 1964) to suffice. Before handling the remaining source of perturbation factors—observer-view factors—which covers a fascinating variety of distortions and often constitutes the greatest—we shall get the observer effects in perspective in this section by referring again to the framework of the data box.

The BDRM, or data box, has been glimpsed in efforts to clarify earlier issues. It was involved most systematically in the description of the environment in Chapter 6. In handling observer effects we come to the fifth, the last and as-yet little studied coordinate therein; that of the observer set.

Let us remind the reader that there are just five types of entity involved in the description of any psychological event, as follows:

1. A *person* or organism. Class symbol P, from 1 through N, with i as specific instance.

2. A *focal stimulus*. Class symbol S, from 1 through q, with h as a specific instance.

3. A particular kind of *response*. Class symbol R, from 1 through n, with j as an instance.

4. A particular *ambient situation*, which is variously called background occasion of measurement or treatment. Symbol E (for environment), running from 1 through u, with k as an instance.

5. An *observer* (using either human powers or mechanical recording). Class O, from 1 through f, with o as an instance.

From these, as set out in equation (8-2) (but without development of the error term), we have a five-signatured statement of any psychological event. To this could be added, in equation (8-1), E_z and E_{hj} error terms to describe the difference between what actually is and what gets recorded.

In equation (8-1) we have kept to what is conventional in most textbook treatments of error. The error is the difference between the observed score, a_{hijko}, and the true score contribution from the real substantive broad and specific traits. For general consistency with the specification equation the error is added as a broad (common) and a specific factor score which belong to the subject—the erroneous part of his score.

Here we break away from this and represent the experimental error as a function of the observer and his instruments, though we present three somewhat different models for doing so—the two already described in Chapter 6 and the new *trait view* model. The gain from this change—apart from the elegance of the symmetry of the data box—is considerable, since it leads to bringing "random error" within the scope of prediction from observer and instrument properties.

Our existing two models (Chapter 6) are the *additive attribute* and the *person-centered product* model. The latter is nearer to current modes of thinking in that it retains a specification equation in which the T's are all traits of a person. The amount of variance from stimulus, situation and observer is handled by the product of T respectively with p_h, e_j, s_k, and q_o, the breakdown elements of the factor loading, the last being the observer effect. The form for one trait is as in (8-2):

$$a_{hijko} = p_{hx}e_{jx}s_{kx}q_{ox}T_{xi} \tag{8-2}$$

The breakdown of the initially obtained loading, either as

$$b_{hjko \cdot x} = p_{hx}e_{jx}s_{kx}q_{ox} \tag{8-3a}$$

or as

$$b_{hjko \cdot x} = (p_{hx} + e_{jk} + q_{ox})s_{kx} \tag{8-3b}$$

is obtained in one of the two or three ways mentioned in Chapter 6, namely (a) experimental control to constancy of all but one coordinate of the data box, (b) re-shuffling of h, j, and o combinations, or (c) factoring of a *grid*, involving correlation over people of response performances for all combinations of stimuli, situations and observers, with subsequent averaging of b values for each set, for example, of the set of loading of the variables constituted by the combination of stimulus h with all situations and observers or the observer q with all stimuli and situations. The end result, as far as the observer coordinate in which we are now interested is concerned is a q value peculiar to each observer describing the error he contributes to the estimate of a_{hijko} through a distorting weight, q_o, applied to each trait of the subject. (Wrong here simply means peculiar to the given observer.)

By contrast the *additive attribute* model has as many subequations in the specification equation as there are coordinates in the data box used, each adding the contribution to a_{hijko} that comes from the attributes of the given coordinates, particularized in factor scores and loadings for the given h, or i, or j, or k, or observer, o. As we saw (Chapter 6) these sub-equations are obtained from factoring face matrices in which the scores are averages across all coordinates except the two that bound the matrix. As far as the observer faces are concerned the factors will be dimensions of observers as they contribute to the mean scores across three coordinates. A given a_{hijko} score as a deviation from the grand mean is now predicted (if we throw h and j together as tests, in the most familiar way) by addition of four attribute subequations as follows:

$$\hat{a}_{hijko} = \overset{p=a}{\underset{}{\Sigma}} b_{yip} T_{pi} + \overset{s=x}{\underset{}{\Sigma}} b_{ks} T_{sk} + \overset{t=y}{\underset{}{\Sigma}} b T_{t \cdot hi} + \overset{e=z}{\underset{}{\Sigma}} b T_{e \cdot o} \qquad (8\text{-}4)$$

where there are w personality traits, x situational trait factors, y test type dimensions, and z dimensions of observers. Each individual person is an i, each situation a k, each test an hj, and each observer an o. The traits of people have subscript p, of situations, s, of tests, t, and of observers (experimenters) e. No interaction is assumed.

The ingenious psychometrist will see many interesting lemmas that can be developed from the person-centered product and the additive attribute modes (the first from a grid and the second from orthogonal faces in the data box) which, however, cannot be pursued here.

Here we propose to turn instead to a special possibility that arises from subjects and observers both being human and describable in the same attributes. Conceivably the attributes of observers in the above second model can be partly derived from personality attributes, but this we leave. The point is that by turning to observer effects in terms of their personalities we link with much existing psychological speculation about the misperception of person by person. Unfortunately much of that speculation has confined its experiments to projection rather than broader personality action and has been reduced to trivial conclusions by lack of a comprehensive model.

8-5.   Trait View Laws Regarding Distortion Error in Observer Ratings

The additive attribute model is at present rather remote from common psychological discussion, requiring as it does that we think econetically of five sources of measurement contributions in any psychological event. The person-centered product model, by contrast, is less remote from the familiar specification equation, but involves the unexplored concept that the observer misperceives behavior by weights on the real traits of the subject. The third model—trait view theory—that we shall now follow, is much nearer to everyday psychological thinking. It supposes that the distortion in an observer's measurement or rating is a function (a) of the personality of the rater, (b) of the personality of the subject, and (c) of the situation, both h and k, in which they stand. It will be noted in passing that no one of the three models ignores any element of the total data box data. Indeed, persons assessed, ambient situations, stimulus-response properties and observer characteristics are incorporated in different ways in all three models.

As indicated, conceptions of how observer traits affect perception of a subject began to crystallize prematurely in specific clinical convictions before operational general models were developed. Since psychoanalytic defenses implied misperceptions Freud's writings (1920) and Anna Freud's incisive analysis of defense mechanisms (1928) offered specific hypotheses, provided those defenses were accepted. However, it was not until the multivariate experimental study of Cattell and Wenig (1952) when the number and nature of the sources of defense misperception were correlationally checked and significant relations shown to personality traits, along with such new distinctions as that between true and naive projection, that quantitative experiment on stably defined mechanisms could begin. (Parenthetically that pioneer study still awaits the necessary consolidation and extension.) Meanwhile, outside the clinical domain, an unrelated set of hypotheses grew up in psychometric literature.

They included halo effect in observer ratings, social desirability in questionnaires, acquiescence and extremity of response sets in questionnaires. These earlier essays are exhaustively evaluated by Messick and Ross (1962) on "response styles"; by Edwards (1957) on "social desirability"; by Campbell and Fiske (1959) on "multitrait-multimethod" and "convergent and discriminant validity"; Dahlstrom (1962) on lie scales; and especially Wiggins (1973), taking a more modern look at acquiescence and desirability. The reader should also study a critical review by Rorer (1965) on response sets, and Cattell, Eber, and Tatsuoka (1970) on construction of simple distortion-correction scales in questionnaire practice.

Many of these lines of thought have led into blind alleys. For example, evidence has accumulated that there is no *single* social desirability, but two or three distinct factors, and that acquiescence and extremity response are expressions of *T*-data personality traits more profitably researched in the broad context of objective personality (behavioral) tests. As far as test practice is concerned, lie and distortion scales grossly oversimplify correction, and extremity of response and acquiescence can readily be reduced to unimportance by proper design of questionnaires. Trait-view theory, as now to be described, on the other hand, locks into general personality theory and general sources of misperception. Along with scale vulnerability concepts, it presents a more stimulating and fruitful approach to discovering the possible range of traits and associated mechanisms that influence misperception.

Trait-view theory belongs in the same class as the above two models, in giving a role to all attributes of the observer, and applying coefficients also to the traits of the subject. It has the attractive simplicity, and the consistency with the behavioral specification equation, of treating the perception of the subject (and therefore the distortion within that perception) as an act by the observer, *expressible like any other behavior as a function of his personality and the situation*.

Trait-view theory is best initially illustrated in the psychological setting of observers rating subjects, but in principle it covers any kind of assessment in which humans are involved. The only difference is that the dimensionality of instruments—in fact *instrument factors*—come more to the fore in situations where test devices rather than people predominate in determining the scores. Let us note, additionally, that it is part of the powerful comprehensiveness of trait view theory that it also covers the case of the person *rating himself*, that is, of the ordinary answering of questionnaires. Let us put the model together by first considering its parts, which are five, as follows:

1. *The Effects of the Observer's Traits: the Construing Effect.* We call this the construing effect, that is, how the observer's own traits cause him to construe the subject, rather than the "projection" effect because it is not at all to be assumed that projection is the only mechanism. This will be expressible by an ordinary specification equation, covering the ability, temperament and especially dynamic traits of the rater, and it does not matter whether we write this for the assessment act for the whole trait T_j in the subject, or for the erroneous, distorted part thereof, for we can later handle transformation by:

$$T_{ijo} = T_{ij} + T_{d \cdot ijo} \qquad (8\text{-}5)$$

where T_{ijo} is the observer's rating of i on trait T_j, and $T_{d \cdot ijo}$ is distortion.

The effect of the rater's personality on a given rating situation k can therefore be written:

$$T_{ijo} = b_{jk1} T_{1o} + \cdots + b_{jkn} T_{no} \qquad (8\text{-}6)$$

That is it involves all n traits of the observer. The question arises whether the subscript for b should include i or only jk, k being the observer's situation. If we are concerned with how the traits of the observer o will affect his rating *anyone* on T_j we can dispense with i, but if the subject has some special role relation to him then all the b's in (8-6) must carry i as an additional definition of the situation.

How will the values in (8-6) be obtained? In this case we must take a sufficient sample of observers rating a single subject on trait T_j. If we have sound measures of the spectrum of traits T_1 through T_n in the observers, say in the 16 PF or CAQ, we then correlate his trait scores with the T score or scores assigned to i. Otherwise the subject must be rated also on *other* traits, at least $2n$ in number, so that T_{1o} through T_{no} are located, by factoring, as traits in the observers, duly loaded and scorable from the scores they assigned the subject. (Parenthetically, if we want to keep i in the subscript all raters must at least stand in the *same* role relation to the observed, for example, parents, wives, teachers.)

From solutions to equation (8-6) general laws could be formulated about the relation of traits in observers to distortions of each kind of trait in the subject. This supposes that we are willing to accept the *average* rating by many raters as the true value so that the deviations therefrom (the standard scores of the estimate T_{ijo}

on the left of 8-6) are taken as rater distortion (as far as construing is concerned).

2. *The Effect of the Subject's Other Traits: the Contextual Effect.* Unless we think we are running the play without Hamlet, the feature of the subject that will most determine his rated score on trait T_j being rated is his true endowment in T_j. However, there is sufficient psychological evidence that there will be a *contextual* effect from the context of his other traits. For example, the estimate of a person's intelligence could be affected by his level on such traits as shrewdness (N factor) or surgency (F factor).

We must initially take the simplest model: that the contextual effect will be the same for all observers. Thereupon we can set out an equation expressing the effect of different subjects upon all observers, thus:

$$T_{ij\bar{o}} = c_{j1} T_{1i} + c_{jj} T_{ji} + \cdots + c_{jn} T_{ni} \tag{8-7}$$

We assume that subjects and observers, both being human, will have the same n traits. A k, for ambient situation, could be added as subscript all across $T_{ij\bar{o}}$ and the contextual loadings, c's, in (8-7).

3. *Restrictions on the Range of Situations in which the Subject is Observed.* A disastrous source of error in ratings and questionnaires and even (as discussed under homogeneity) in tests, is restriction of the area of behavioral observation. In ratings a comparison of the results of the studies by Cattell (1945a, 1946) and Cattell, Pierson, and Finkbeiner (1974), which had extended daily observation, over a long period, with others done just in classroom or on scant acquaintance, shows considerable difference. In particular, factors faint to the point of disappearance in the latter are firmly replicated in the former. Parenthetically this is a place where the questionnaire, with its round the clock and years' long observation is superior to observer rating.

No new equation is necessary to handle this restriction effect. If k_1 is a restricted and k_2 a less restricted observation we may expect the c's in equation (8-7) to predict less of the trait with k_1 than k_2 subscripts. The estimation of the trait in itself is from the weight on T_{ji}—the true score—and some idea of what restriction to various areas does to this value can be obtained by obtaining the multiple R for the prediction of T_j, and from correlations of T_j's from various areas of k's. This question has also been looked at (p. 359) in terms of area instrument factors.

4. *The Role Relation Effect.* This again is a possibly strong effect; one cannot entirely trust the ratings of, say, a foreman or a parent. It needs no other representation than the adding of a role factor,

R_o, to the construing equation and another, R_i, to represent the subject's role in the contextual equation.

5. *The Cognitive Cliches and Sterotypes about What May Be Desirable or Undesirable in Certain Roles.* This source is the lineal descendant of the "halo" effect (in rating others) or "social desirability" in rating the self; but with the difference that it conceives the possibility of several desirabilities rather than one desirability. In this connection we may pause to point out that the recent work of Cattell, Pierson, and Finkbeiner (1974), comparing comparatively unbiased ratings (10 observers) with personal questionnaire response has shown that the bulk of the desirability distortion falls in *two* major factors, one that might be called the "good fellow, peer-pleasing" pattern and the other the "respectability super-ego-satisfying" form of desirability. Each of these is guided by a cognitive stereotype of what is wanted.

The question of cognitive stereotypes and cliches is taken up in more detail in Section 8-7, but in order to place it in perspective in the totality of trait view theory, we shall here take a simplified position that a stereotype or cliche is a factor, largely cognitive, in the observer, which comes into action with certain situational weights, that is, a b value peculiar to a situation and the trait being rated. It might be represented by one or more Y terms added to the construing equation (8-6).

The main stereotype that has been under discussion for years (Edwards, 1957) is social desirability. As stated, a study (Cattell, Pierson, & Finkbeiner, 1974) which for the first time included questionnaire and observer rating data in the same factoring, to see what might be in the questionnaire that is not evident to the outside observer, found *two*, not one social desirability. Doubtless there are desirability faking patterns that are as numerous as examination situations and goals, but these two are most prominent. One loaded shifts on personality factors to make the person a popular "good fellow" in terms of peers; for example, a shift toward exvia. The other loaded "respectability" prestige, in the eyes of the establishment, affecting gains on super ego, self-sentiment, etcetera.

The forces making for distortion of rating or self-rating can be psychologically analyzed into the five above, but in the model they can all be expressed in the two-part trait equation, as follows, by addition of R and Y classes of factors (Y's being stereotypes, largely desirabilities).

$$T_{ijko} = c_{jk1}T_{1i} + c_{jkj}T_{ji} + \cdots + c_{jkn}T_{ni} + b_{jk1}T_{1o} + \cdots$$
$$+ b_{jkn}T_{no} + b_{kr}R_o + b_{ky}Y_o \tag{8-8}$$

which is simply equations (8-6) and (8-7) joined together to add *both* of the sources of perception and misperception—plus R and Y.

In the case of rating this equation can be obtained either by (a) having all raters rate one (or the average) subject to get the part on the right, and then all subjects rated by one (or the average) judge to get the part on the left (followed by adjustment of weights for a standard score on $T_{1jk\bar{o}}$), or (b) factoring a score matrix (of $T_{ijk\bar{o}}$'s and other traits) in which both sources of variance are present (a sample of $p \times q$ cases, with p subjects and q judges). The $2n$ factors will need to be sorted into n subject and n judge factors in the latter approach and it may be more practicable to correlate or factor all subjects for the average judge and all judges for the average subject, as above, separately.[1] The meaning of true value and distortion has been defined as far as the judges are concerned by making the average value *true*, so that each judge's deviation therefrom is the distortion the source of which we are tracing to weights on his traits. In the case of the contextual distortion since

$$T_{ijk\bar{o}} = T_{ij\bar{o}} + T_{d \cdot ij\bar{o}}$$

where $T_{d \cdot ij\bar{o}}$ is the contextual distortion. Substituting in (8-7);

$$T_{d \cdot ij\bar{o}} = c_{jk1} T_{1i} + (c_{jkj} - 1) T_{ji} + \cdots + c_{jkn} T_{n1} \tag{8-9}$$

That is to say the true value for T_{ij} (or T_{ji} in the usual convention) operates on the distortion with a value $(c_{jkj} - 1)$. However, in estimating the true score, T_{ij}, free of contextual effects, we would use equation (8-7) employing all the weights on T_j (in V_{fe} form) upon the various observed scores $T_{ijk\bar{o}}$ for scales largely concerned with T_j.

Naturally we have suggested starting with the simplest formulae, but one must keep an eye open to the possibility that there is some interaction of observer-rooted construing effects and subject-rooted contextual effects, in place of the linear additive model above. Perhaps the most likely form for this would be:

$$T_{xikk'o} = b_{xk'1} T_{1i} (b_{xk1} T_{11} + \cdots + b_{xkn} T_{n1})$$
$$+ b_{xk'2} T_{2i} (b_{xk1} T_{11} + \cdots + b_{xkn} T_{n1}) + \cdots \tag{8-10}$$

and so on, for each trait of the individual observed. (An alternative interactive formula is given in Cattell, 1968.) Here k and k' are the situations respectively for subject and observer.

8-6.   The Uniting of Observer and Observed in Q-data, and Some Comments on Instrument Factors

Trait view theory has been first set out here in terms of subjects observed by judges, but it is part of its elegance that it handles also self rating by questionnaires and indeed brings "social desirability," "projection" phenomena, etcetera, into a single system. As Block (1976) has brought out, L- and Q-data contrast with T-data in accepting perceptual values of the fallible human mind, and it is not surprising therefore that their errors yield to the same decontaminating approach.

In the rating situation the weights for the subject's factors in the contextual effect on the one hand and for the rater's factors in the construing effect on the other are different. But if we carry out the corresponding factoring for *self* ratings the values of equations (8-6) and (8-7) cannot be separated. For they combine, as weights on the same personality factors those of the person as subject and as rater. Regardless of whether we use $2n$ or $4n$ variables we shall now get only n factors, each with its "combined" loading, thus:

$$T_{ijk} = (b_{jk1} + c_{jk1})T_{1i} + \cdots + (b_{jk} + c_{jk} - 1)T_{ji} + \cdots$$
$$+ (b_{jp} + c_{jp})T_{pi} \tag{8-11}$$

Fortunately, as far as practical utility is concerned, we experience no loss, for we can see that this equation, given by experiment with a single value for any $(b + c)$ term, enables us to proceed to true factor estimates at least as readily as from the two-part equation (8-12), with its fuller information. The drawback remains a theoretical one, namely, that since we can no longer combine different subjects with different observers, or average over all observers for one subject, the patterns of construing and contextual effects as such cannot be separated. One can suggest an experimental approach, however, that might be evaluated by the internal consistency of its results. This is to have many acquainted observers fill in a questionnaire for one subject (to cancel observer construing by averaging over these observers). Then the same would be done for several different subjects and by factoring across these the contextual pattern obtained. By subtracting these common observer c's from the $(c + b)$ values obtained by factoring different self-rating questionnaire responds the separate b values could in principle be obtained.

One must not close discussion of the above trait view model procedures, at least as they affect questionnaires, without distinguishing them carefully from the recently developed technique of *variance reallocation* or *computer synthesis* in getting the most information from a set of scales in an omnibus trait questionnaire (Cattell, Eber, & Tatsuoka, 1970).

Computer synthesis is essentially a practical device for raising the validity of each individual factor scale when one has omnibus scales for a whole series of traits to draw upon. It aims to collect bits of score on factor x that are available, scattered by the inevitable factor complexity of items in other scales than x, in an omnibus test with scales for several factors. The principle assumed is that this weighting reflects contaminations in the test scales as such by items partly suitable for other factors, and that the reallocation weights hold over all situations, that is, are situation-free. Computer synthesis augments the x scale by weights on other scales that are simply functions of the composition of the scales. In trait view theory, on the other hand, the weights are recognized to be *peculiar to each situation* and to belong to the observation process. This difference means that the computer synthesis weights become in fact defined as *an average* of the many diverse *situational trait view* weights.

In retrospect on this and the previous section, it will be recognized that although obtaining behavior indices giving us a new domain of possible laws and generalizations about the perceptual effects of traits in the observer, upon traits as recorded about the observed, is the *main* aim of trait view theory, there are certain by-product conclusions and gains, too. In the simplest of formulations we are saying that what we call a true instrument- and observer-transcending trait is, both in pattern and score level, an average across many *observers*, many *ambient situations*, and many contextual *trait surroundings* in the individual rated. The philosopher may conceivably entertain some other concept of a true trait and trait score, somewhere beyond space and time, but the operational psychometrist can only mean by the *true* score one that is balanced by averaging, across a stratified sample of all sources of error and distortion, as were discussed under five headings above.

Elsewhere (1973) the present writer has argued for the usefulness of the concept and measurement of an instrument-transcending trait pattern. The concept was defended first in face of allegations (Becker, 1960, and others) that the same traits could not be found simultaneously in different media. This could be refuted in the sense that when markers for the same putative trait factor in L- and Q-data, for example, were factored together they turned out to mark the same factor. But, in general, instrument factors appeared, often as refraction factors (p. 358), bound to the factor in each medium, and this irrelevant variance at least resulted in much reduced correlations between measures of the same trait taken from different media, which reductions seemed to justify doubt about the trait as a unified entity.

The *theory of indifference of indicator* (Cattell, 1957, 1973), which said the same trait structures would appear in different observation media, was proved correct in the sense intended—that patterns would be matchable, that is, would factor out together and match by configurative methods (Cattell 1965c; Kaiser, Hunka, & Bianchini, 1971). But it had never connoted that correlations between the same personality factors evaluated in different media would be high. The concept of instrument-transcending factors carries the notion of indifference of indicator to greater precision. It says that when instrument factors, including the distortions from trait view effects, have been set aside by suitable factor-analytic procedural care, the pattern of loadings that emerges for a particular personality factor will load across all media with high values on expressions of similar meaning in the different media. Secondly, it says that the truest *measure* of a personality factor will be one in which the effect of instruments is attenuated and balanced by evenly sampling of variables across the instrument factors from all three media—Q, L, and T. This requires more careful delineation of what those instrument factors are than we yet have reached. It also warns again against high homogeneity as a basic psychometric aim in test instruction, and suggests that most current personality measurement scales are two narrowly based. Setting L-data aside and keeping to tests (Q and T), it suggests that the low homogeneities aimed at and reached in the 16 PF (Cattell, Eber, & Tatsuoka, 1970) and the O-A Battery (Cattell & Schuerger, 1978) will provide a better measure, especially together, of the instrument-transcending personality source traits. The better life-criteria correlations achieved with these latter tests support this conclusion.

8-7. The Effects of Observer Roles, Cognitive Stereotypes, and Cliches

We now turn to more intensive study of a source of perceptual distortion that is narrower, more specific and transient than the effects of the broad personality and ability structures in the perceiver. It concerns the fifth and last of the sources listed above (p. 350, (c)B), namely the effect of cognitive stereotypes and cliches, but involves also to some extent, the first, third, and fourth sources.

It may be objected to the bringing together of role action with the effects of cognitive furniture—as in stereotypes and cliches—that they are disparate. Indeed they are, for a role trait is just another personality trait, though of a dynamic and special kind, and is already included, therefore in trait view treatment. (Krug, 1971, made a special study of the comparative action of general and role traits in test distortion.) However, the invocation of stereotypes and cliches is seen more clearly in roles; so some consideration together is appropriate.

The calling up of an apperception mass such as a cognitive stereotype is part of the general action of what we have called (Chapter 4) a *sentiment* of which a role is only a special subspecies. There is contingent evidence that the dynamic structure of any sentiment is hierarchical, showing narrower sub-factors within it. The latter are subsidiated to the total goal of the sentiment and often acquired as necessary supports, by later learning. Our theoretical model has been perfectly clear here (a) that these contributory systems may also, at lower levels, be increasingly transferable to other sentiments, as when a man who learns to handle computers for his engineering sentiment may later use the skill in connection with a sentiment to his bank account, and (b) that as one goes backward down the subsidiation chain to smaller and smaller subsystems one comes eventually to fractionated elements, mental sets and cognitive apperception masses used in recognition of what to do in particular situations. Here we encounter the concept of *activation* of an acquired sentiment system by outside stimuli; which is supported by dR technique observations. Using the SUD model (p. 308) of higher- and lower-order factors operating together, we are supposing that activation of a main sentiment M also brings some excitation of a subsentiment m. The latter however draws part of its activation from a particular situation k' and stimulus h, for the response j, so that the response strength of an act or perception a is also determined by the second term expressing

$$a_{hijkk'} = v_{hjm}s_{km}M_i + v_{hjm}(s_{hk'm} + s_{km}M_k)m_k \qquad (8\text{-}12)$$

the joint activation of m by M and k' (k is the stimulus situation for the *whole* M).

This hypothesis, as shown, is thus that the excitation of m is a function both of the direct effect of k' on m in the specific subsituation k', and of the general activation of M in the global situation k. This is a fairly marked departure from the simple specification equation and will be discussed and developed further, in Volume 2, Chapter 2. Meanwhile we shall lean upon it in this perception context. The m's might well be called "apperception masses," and are brought into a state of greater excitation as the role as a whole becomes more excited by modulation. In what follows, it is desirable to remember that the M in equation (8-12) is generally a role factor, and we shall in appropriate contexts symbolize it as R_x, a role in action, or L_{rx}, a liability to a role action.

Among the apperception masses that come into action when R_x is large will be special cognitive perception capacities appropriate to the role action. In the special area of score distortion considered in this chapter, the role under consideration is that of an inventory test-taking examination, perhaps as a patient, or, alternatively, an observer role as rater, perhaps as a teacher or foreman. The apperception units that operate there will be those concerned with describing some individual—in Q-data oneself, in $L(R)$-data someone else. In describing the self, the role we shall consider is that of aiming to describe the self favorably. In describing others, the role may be one of several, some inviting favorable perceptions, some overcritical, and so on.

The coinage of cognitive ideas that the roles use in this transaction—that is, the cognitive apperception masses that they may call on—are cognitive maps about the way human traits work and express themselves, and how they are related. These maps have often been called sterotypes, for example, that "quick eaters make quick workers" or "shifty-eyed people are dishonest" and sociologists in particular have warned us against their use. However, it is necessary in fact to recognize two kinds of maps or apperception masses, those which, apart from a little random error really do correctly represent environmental relations, for example, "a thing that glows hot will burn me" and those which are badly biased, for example, "fair women are arrogant." We will call these respectively "stereotypes" and "cliches" and define them in personality perception as follows:

1. A *stereotype* consists of a belief not necessarily fully conscious, that certain traits go together, and is ultimately based in largely correct fashion on actual probabilities. Thus a person might have a stereotype about extraversion, the core of which is actually the second-stratum factor evidence that A, F, H, and $Q_2(-)$ tend to go together. A subclass of stereotypes concerns not what actually goes together in people, but what society typically *asks for* in certain positions, and these we might call "demand stereotypes," of which Edward's "social desirability" is alleged to be one.

2. A *cliche* we shall define as a stereotype that is false; that is, the elements of the assumed pattern in fact do not go together. If differs from a figment (below) only by being *common* property in some

population and established by fashion. Many "prejudices," for or against, are cliches. The line between stereotypes and cliches is not sharp, but the difference between a minimally distorted stereotype, reality-rooted and a completely fabricated or extraneously developed cliche is important enough to be handled by using two terms. Sociologists in general have done thinking and research a disservice here by making no distinction between stereotypes and cliches, and by insisting that all stereotypes are misleading and incorrect. A recent volume, for example, warns against accepting stereotypes that nations, classes, races, sexes have any psychological differences. It asks us not to believe Swedes on an average are taller than Japanese, that men average higher than women on spatial ability, or women higher than men on verbal ability, and so on.

3. A *figment* we define as a false stereotype or fiction *peculiar to the mind of one individual.*

As far as true stereotypes are concerned, there seems little doubt, as argued by Passini and Norman (1966), Mulaik (1964), and others, that they do enter into rating acts and help to determine the correlations found among rating variables. The problem of deciding whether stereotypes or cliches are involved could not be answered in psychological data because no one could trust (seemingly even in abilities!) values for the *true* correlations and configurations, against which observer ratings could be compared. The problem was solved by Dickman (condensed in Cattell & Dickman, 1962) by taking "physical" behavior, of objectively determinable structure (the behavior of balls, in bouncing, rolling, etcetera), and comparing the factors obtained from measurement with those from ratings of the behaviors. It was found that for adults, and even six-year-old children, the cognitive maps that might have guided the ratings were indistinguishable from the true relations. Thus by trial, and reward and punishment in daily life respectively for apt response and error, the stereotype or cognitive map becomes an apperception mass that on the whole is correctly modeled on reality. Its function is to aid quicker perception—even if occasionally it lays one open to a conjuring trick. Its effect is such that the beholder of one element of a common trait pattern in the subject will be inclined to see the other elements that belong, too.

Concerning the prevalence and magnitude of the effect of cliches and figments, little is know. However, when we shift from patterns of behavior that normally go together to conceptions of what society—this or that society—believes is *desirable* in personality, we may well prove to be moving in general from the domain of stereotypes into that of cliches, for bias is more concerned with desirabilities. The error may either be random or it may be systematic.

TABLE 8–3. Demand Stereotypes of What is Desirable in Various Test-taking Roles; Change in Mean Score from Anonymous to "Desirable Role" Situations[a]

		Job Seeking	Socially Ideal Self	Date Seeking
A	Affectia	1.2	1.6	1.0
B	Intelligence	-.1	-.3	0
C	Ego strength	1.9	2.9	1.7
E	Dominance	-.2	-.6	0
F	Surgency	-.7	-.1	0
G	Super ego	2.1	2.5	.6
H	Parmia	1.9	2.3	1.7
I	Premsia	.2	-.2	-.4
L	Protension	-1.6	-2.1	-1.5
M	Autia	-.5	-1.1	-.7
N	Shrewdness	1.1	1.4	.8
O	Guilt proneness	-2.3	-3.0	-1.9
Q$_1$	Radicalism	.9	1.0	.7
Q$_2$	Self-sufficiency	.8	-1.3	-.9
Q$_3$	Self-sentiment	2.5	2.9	1.4
Q$_4$	Ergic tension	-2.8	-3.6	-2.2

[a]From p. 401 of Cattell, R. B., *Personality and Mood by Questionnaire*.
Note intelligence is essentially undistorted, being measured by test.

But whether random, or systematic as in a cliche, or nonexistent, as in a stereotype of moral demands that everyone agrees society makes, there is plenty of evidence that such "desirability" patterns affect, at any rate, questionnaire response patterns. (Its effect on observer ratings in $L(R)$-data, however, is still insufficiently demonstrated or clarified.)

It has been pointed out earlier (p. 368) that the notion of a single social desirability factor as propounded most systematically by Edwards (1957), is a gross oversimplification, as shown in the work of Wiggins (1973), Messick and Ross (1962), the present writer (1973), and Cattell, Pierson, and Finkbeiner (1976). That an average desirability shift from the "true" anonymous mean on 16 PF factors will be significant on *most* factors in different testing situations and roles has been long known, and it has been known that it will be different for different roles, as shown in Table 8-3.

One would wish to integrate the findings regarding this profile with the above-described finding of *two* desirability factors: peer "good fellow" image and larger society "respectability" image, and with Krug's finding on a role factor in the perceptions of raters. Except for some discrepancy in factor *E*, dominance, the distortion pattern in Table 8-3 can be reconstituted on all traits as a sum of the two desirability shift patterns found by Cattell, Pierson, and Finkbeiner (1974). Furthermore, as might be hypothesized the shift found in a job-seeing situation seems to be largely the respectability-reliability distortion pattern while that when requested to depict one's personally ideal social personality comes close to the "good fellow" factor pattern.

In calling for the addition of stereotypes, either of actual or of desirable patterns in the main trait view equation (8-8) we recognize that they will not be isolated contributors but will be motivated to appear as lower-order fragments of both ordinary sentiments and roles. These essentially narrow cognitive-dynamic factors we will represent as m's, that is, subfactors within the larger M's, and tentatively we have supposed their strengths to be defined as in the last two terms in equation (8-8). That is to say, their appearance influencing behavior relates to both activation of the general sentiment or role factor to which they belong and a specific environmental situation hk, which evokes the particular cognitive perception.

In summary, an equation could be written with a trait perception (or merely trait distortion part) on the left and on the right a contextual effect from the person's traits, plus a construing effect from the judge's traits and role endowments, plus a stereotype, cliche and figment effect more specific to the evaluated trait.

8-8. Test Vulnerability Theory and Its Integration with Trait View Theory

An approach to evaluating distortion through observation instruments, which has recently appeared as a supplement to trait view theory, requires brief description here. It has been called *test vulnerability theory* and applies most immediately to the questionnaire, although it is potentially applicable to other instrumentalities, such as some mode of recording of observations by individual observers of everyday life behavior. It *supplements* trait view theory in that it takes into consideration not only the forces favoring distortion but also the vulnerability of the particular scale to motivational distortion.

The conception behind vulnerability theory was originally the purely practical one of enabling the psychologist to determine the extent of motivational distortion when he could make a measurement on only one occasion and lacked the measures on other traits necessary in using equation (8-8). If we had two scales for the same trait the vulnerability of one known to have a certain ratio to that of the other, say twice, then a comparison of scores on them would permit us, without any knowledge of the distorting forces (weights on personality traits) to infer the true score. This is easy to see if we think of two clocks, one known to become tardy twice as rapidly as the other (though at what absolute rates of retardation we do not know) then when one says 12.20 and the other 12.10 we know it is 12.30 o'clock.

The definition and calculation of what we mean by vulnerability, however, leads to a systematic, supplementary relation of trait view theory and vulnerability coefficient (VC for short) concepts which establish a more comprehensive theory of test and rating distortion than we have hitherto reached. The setting out of the argument is a little simpler if we assume we are operating with questionnaires and use equation (8-11), though it can be extended equally to observer ratings, in equation (8-8). In equation (8-11) we shall run the two terms (construing and contextual) in the brackets to a single loading—which is in any case all we can readily get in practice—and thus have a simple specification equation of what we might call the total force making for distortion. Let us call this distortion force D and suppose that in equation (8-11) we now interpose an expression for the vulnerability of a scale, a, such that the distortion occurring T_{ijk} is accounted for by a product of force and vulnerability, thus

$$T_{ijka} = V_{ja} \, D_{ijk} \tag{8-13}$$

The trait here is, of course, j, and a is a particular scale for trait T_j. We may suppose that in equation (8-11) the scale vulnerability is at unity, so that there was no need to enter it in that case and there was no need for an a subscript because we had not reached use of a particular scale form. Indeed, (8-13) may be thought of as the equivalent of (8-11) in which V_{jk} and a have become explicit and the whole specification of the various weighted sources of distorting forces has been collapsed into a single D.

It is clear that D will have the subscripts i, j, and k because this need to distort has a strength for a given individual i (depending on his trait scores), for a given trait on which he feels a special need to distort, and on a given testing situation k, which also contributes to determining the need to distort. If now we construct a series of otherwise equivalent scales, a, b, c, etcetera, for the trait T_{ji} but such that by reason of greater ambiguities of items, fewer demands on the super ego for truth, or having less chance of being objectively checked, some are more susceptible (V_{ja}, V_{jb}) to conscious or unconscious distortion than others, then we may express the analyses of effects either as in (8-14) or in (8-15).

$$T_{ijka} = b_{aj}T_{ji} + V_{ja}\,D_{ijk} \tag{8-14a}$$

$$T_{ijkb} = b_{bj}T_{ji} + V_{jb}\,D_{ijk} \tag{8-14b}$$

$$T_{ijkc} = b_{cj}T_{ji} + V_{jc}\,D_{ijk} \tag{8-14c}$$

etcetera.

where T_{ij} is i's true score on T_j; V_{ja}, V_{jb}, and V_{jc} are the differing vulnerabilities and D_{ijk} is the desire of i to distort on j in situation k.

This supposes full validity of the scale, that is, T_{jk} is entirely T_j except for the applied distortion, $V_{ja}D_{ijk}$, and since we are going to deal with these equations in a factor analytic, standard score framework we know that b_{aj} will equal $\sqrt{1 - V^2_{ja}}$.

However, the scale is unlikely to be fully valid and will usually contain (a) one or two low-loaded contaiminating common factors T_x and T_y (b) a factor specific to the scale, which we can call T_{ja}, thus

$$T_{ijka} = b_{aj}T_{ji} + b_{ax}T_{xi} + b_{ay}T_{yi} + V_{ja}D_{ijk} + b_{aja}T_{jai} \tag{8-15}$$

and, paralleling (8-14), three equations for b, c, etcetera, scales.

Incidentally it would not do to consider T_{xi} and T_{yi} as already taken care of within D_{ijk} because there they have weights peculiar to their distorting power, whereas here they are as in an ordinary specification equation.

Now all values in these equations can be determined by factor analysis of scores of a good sample of people on a sufficiency of different scales (a, b, c, etcetera) for T_j, all tested in the same situation k. This is true provided D does not split into the couple dozen factors that it packages. Since it is supposed, in testing situation k, to repeat for each scale score exactly the same combination of T's, such a split would be hard to achieve even if desired. In a particular case our interest would be especially to get the true score, T_{ij}, but in research toward helping applied psychology our interest would be in determining the vulnerability indices, V_{ja}, V_{jb}, etcetera, for the different scales, in order to perform the scoring in equation (8-16) below. However, this research determining of vulnerabilities could in turn lead to item analyzing to discover the best form for high vulnerability items, thus enabling the test constructor to put together with greater control scales of desirably high or low vulnerabilities.

The question has been raised in research groups whether the vulnerability of a scale should not be considered also to alter with the test situation, that is, to be V_{jak} rather than V_{ja}. But this, while possible, seems most unlikely, since the distorting force in the situation, D_{ijk}, takes care of situational change and effects. By analogy with, say, Young's modulus in physics, we do not need to qualify the elastic resistance of the material with what is already taken care of in the applied force. Regarding factoring possibilities let us note that it would be possible to gather scores for variables not only over different scales for the same trait in the same situation, but also over different traits and different situations. One would then get two or more D factors and two or more T_j factors, but also an awkward cooperativeness of T and D factors, since a D_j would always apply to a particular T_j. Tactically it might be well, if one cannot manufacture enough different scales of different vulnerability to take more different testing situations, k's, rather than more traits. Something could be done for experimental stability of values by designs averaging over scales or situations, always remembering that V_{ja} is a property of a particular scale, while D_{ijk} is a property of a person in distorting the trait j itself when placed in a specific situation k.

Let us now turn to the practical gain of test vulnerability theory in allowing a true score to be inferred simply from administering in the same distorting situation two different scales for trait j, of known vulnerabilities, while knowing nothing of the actual magnitude or nature of the distorting forces. If we can accept equation (8-14) a little algebra will lead us to:

$$T_{ji} = \frac{T_{ijka} \cdot V_{jb} - T_{ijkb} \cdot V_{ja}}{V_{jb} \cdot b_{aj} - V_{ja} \cdot b_{by}} \tag{8-16}$$

and since $b_{aj} = \sqrt{1 - V^2_{ja}}$ and $b_{bj} = \sqrt{1 - V^2_{jb}}$ all we need to solve for the true score, T_{ji}, is the scores on the two scales in the given situation, T_{ijka} and T_{ijka}, and knowledge of the vulnerability-coefficients for the two scales (obtainable from earlier factoring studies).

Preliminary research on the model by the present writer against real data reveals, however, as might be expected, that few scales indeed are valid enough to fit equation (8-14), and the scree test argued, as other data has, for the existence of both a specific, T_{ja}, and a couple of extraneous broad factors, like T_x and T_y (though of low loading), making (8-15) the truer general statement. Even with this, if we may argue that the contamination of scales T_{ja} and T_{jb} with the three factors T_x, T_y, and T_j (a or b) is the same, that is, that loadings are the same in the two scales, as might well be expected to happen despite differences of vulnerability, we can reach a solution minimally different from (8-16) namely

$$T_{ij} = \frac{T_{ijka} \cdot V_{jb} - T_{ijkb} \cdot V_{jb} - (V_{bi} - V_{aj}) \cdot X_i}{V_{jb} \cdot b_{aj} - V_{ja} \cdot b_{bj}}$$

$$(8\text{-}17)$$

where X_i is the totality $(b_x T_{xi} + b_y T_{yi} + b_{ja} T_{jai})$ assumed the same for both scales. This could only be entered as an approximation from previous factorings for b's and present brief scales for i's score on the factors. Only research can tell us how much this approximation affects the T_{ij} estimate and whether one can drop it and revert to (8-16). Meanwhile, so long as one deals with scales of high validity the convenience of inferring distortion-free scores from two (or for greater accuracy three) scales appears to be psychometrically practicable.

Finally, with regard to a theoretical model of distortion in psychological measurements we reach a virtually complete treatment by combining trait view theory and test vulnerability concepts, through expanding D in (8-14) into (8-11), producing a model of what may be called *trait perception distortion analysis*. This term rather than scale distortion analysis is appropriate because the concepts apply to ratings as well as questionnaire scales, in that different methods and scales offered for observer ratings could similarly differ in vulnerability.

8-9. Summary

1. Comprehensively viewed the errors in psychological observations, and in inferences to populations, concern any statistic such as a single score, a mean, a variance, a correlation, etcetera. Our central concern here, however, is how it affects the number and nature of factor patterns affecting our concepts of source traits and source states. Mere score corrections can follow only when structural problems are solved. Here, spurious effects can first be divided into ephemeral patterns occurring only in some one matrix and *perturbation factors*, which have more systematic causes.

2. An analysis is presented comprehensively categorizing all uniquely rotated factors into broad error and broad real factors. The constantly recurring broad (common) factors arising from real, non-artificial influences are then divided into (a) substantive personality and (b) perturbation factors. Perturbation factors divide again into *data treatment artifacts, instrument factors, observer-view factors,* and *subject-sampling factors.*

3. Instrument factors are a constant threat to sound conclusions in structural research, having frequently led to false concepts about the nature of personality and dynamic-structure factors. They arise almost entirely from three sources: (a) test-form conditions; (b) limited areas of observation and special conditions of situational expression of behavior (inadequate sampling of situations and people); and (c) test-administration conditions. The multitrait-multimethod (or multi-instrument) approach is a common-sense avenue to correction, but for insightful, theoretically precise concepts and corrections, and the obtaining of meaningful scores, instrument-factor theory supersedes it, as more attentive to the specific character of instrument distortions.

4. All error of measurement and some sampling error can be comprehensively conceived as associated with observers and their instruments. Studying this source of variance requires systematic consideration, hitherto not organized, of the role of the fifth (observer) coordinate in the data box. The variance and covariance associated with the fifth coordinate (observer-instrument) is open to four logical possibilities of analyzing observer-associated score matrices. Each of these has a transpose, making eight correlational possibilities. What the general psychological nature of these sources of observer error would be can be anticipated, but until research begins, no hypotheses can be proposed here as to the specific natures of the observer sources of distortion.

5. The fact that relatively poor correlations are not infrequently obtained between scores for what is believed to be the same factor measured in two different media or instruments is not necessarily a denial of the *principle of indifference of indicator*, that is, that the same traits can be found regardless of the media of observation. The identity of the source trait across media as patterns and their equality as scores are two different matters, since non-common variance from the different instruments or media reduces correlation even when the patterns are the same.

6. An instrument-free pure personality factor score is not possible, but the *instrument-transcending factor pattern* for a source trait can be obtained by factoring well loaded variables in the trait that spread

across several instrumentalities. A correct delineation of the instrument factors involved then permits a substantial *attenuation* of instrument variance in the trait score by insightful balancing of the various instrument factors. Current research shows that *instrument-transcending* personality traits exist (though sometimes at different strata relative to variables) and that the best life criterion relations are found when the trait scores span widely in the media and instrument domain.

7. The treatment of distortion of measurements from test situation has appeared under scattered, local and unconnected concepts. *Trait view theory* and the concept of *test vulnerability* present a unifying theory for what was handled under social desirability, response set, motivational distortion and lie scales, etcetera. Trait view theory also has the elegance of handling both rating and measurement by others (*L*- and *T*-data) and also self-rating (*Q*-data). Two main sources of distortion and three minor are recognized, the two first being the *construing* effect in which the observer's traits affect his rating of any trait in the subject and a *contextual* effect in which the background of other traits in the subject influence the perception of any one of his traits. The trait view equation for distortion (or the actual perception in true plus distortion) therefore has two parts, one weighting traits of the subject and one of the observer. These weights can be factor analytically determined from a matrix of scores of a set of observers on an average or single subject, and a matrix of variable scores for subjects from a single or average judge.

8. In questionnaire measurement, observer and observed become one, and although distinct construing and contextual contributions to distortion are still theoretically considered to exist, the two sets of loadings—on the traits of observer and the observed which are the same—have now to be extracted factor analytically, at least initially, as a single set of summed contextual and construing loadings. In both the questionnaire and the observer rating situations, trait view theory appears a practicable procedure because we get estimates over a sufficient number of traits and situations and factor them, to arrive at (a) the true, undistorted trait scores and (b) the weights on sources of distortion necessary to reach laws about the operation of observer distortion.

9. Beyond contextual and construing effects three others are recognized: stereotypes, restriction of behavior observation area, and the effect of role relations between observer and observed. Stereotypes (correct) and cliches (incorrect) are distinguished and both are recognized as lower order, more cognitive elements in the

dynamic structures we call sentiments and roles. They come into action from the combined effect of sentiment activation and an immediate stimulus to apperception masses. Stereotypes are cognitive maps which on the whole are tried against reality and are correct, permitting more rapid perception by filling in gaps in the perceptions of behavior of others.

10. Ratings and especially self ratings are affected not only by stereotypes of what is but also of what should be. There is no single social desirability factor but only factors giving patterns of social desirability in different contexts. Two are most important: the "good fellow" pattern for transactions with peers and the "respectable responsible person" for distortions in job seeking, etcetera. These can be added, along with cliches to role relation factors to the trait view specification equation. The "restriction of behavioral observation" effect shows in inefficient assortments of weights on variables in estimating a factor, and can be an important distortion.

11. Scale vulnerability theory is a necessary supplement to complete trait view theory, and promises also a valuable practical method of getting a distortion free scale score. It adds the quality of the actual scale, in terms of its vulnerability to distortion, to the trait view estimate of the forces of distortion, calculating the actual distortion as the product of these. To evaluate vulnerability coefficients one needs to factor several scales of different vulnerability, for one and the same trait and in one and the same test situation. Provided two scales are of high validity and different known vulnerability their joint administration in any situation of possible distortion should permit calculation of the undistorted true score. However, the unified product in *trait perception distortion analysis* has its greatest value as a theoretical model for handling self perception and mutual personality perception.

NOTE

[1] To continue in a little more detail, let it be noted that if one takes sufficiently large sample of judges, one essentially gets rid of the interobserver variance and obtains a score matrix showing how one judge, the average judge, reacts to all the different subjects. It yields, when factored, the *contextual* matrix, showing how far one judge typically misestimates, say, intelligence, when a person is more surgent, or higher in ego strength, and so on. The second, *construing* matrix deals with a fixed "averaged" person and when factored shows the extent to which any trait *in the judges* leads to misperception of the subject

trait under investigation in any subject. It tells us, for example, whether being high in ego strength (C) inclines one to see others as higher or lower in, say, superego strength (G). It will be noted that if these separate factorings are done they are reciprocal extractions (by collapsing to face matrices in two directions) of the same total three-dimensional data box as used in the combined factoring. Consequently, the b values of the two factorings bear a fixed relation to those of the total analysis.

An interesting psychological by-product of the construing analysis is that from analysis of the judgments of $>2p$ traits of the fixed subject we can estimate the personality factor scores of the *judges themselves* (on p factors) and can check the values by the judges' ratings on some second average subject. Little use has yet been made of this capability to estimate an individual's personality factors purely from his ratings of other people.

BIBLIOGRAPHY

Adcock, N. & Adcock, C. J. The validity of the 16 PF personality structure: a large New Zealand sample item analysis. *J. of Behavioral Science*, 1977, *2*, 227-237.

Adelson, M. A study of ergic tension patterns through the effects of water deprivation in humans. Unpublished Ph.D. thesis, University of Illinois at Urbana, 1952.

Aird, J., et al. Association between ABO groups and peptic ulceration. *British Medical Journal*, 1954, *2*, 315.

Allport, G. W., & Odbert, H. S. Trait-names: a psycholexical study. *Psychological Monograph*, 1936, *47*, 171-220.

Anderson, E. E. The interrelationship of drives in the male albino rat. III. Among measures of emotional, sexual and exploratory behavior. *Journal of Genetic Psychology*, 1938, *53*, 335-352.

Ardrey, R. A. *The territorial imperative*. New York: Dell, 1966.

Argyle, M., & Little, B. R. Do personality traits apply to social behavior? *Journal of Theory in Social Behavior*, 1972, *2*, 1-35.

Arnoult, M. D. Predictions of perceptual responses from structural characteristics of the stimulus. *Perceptual and Motor Skills*, 1960, *11*, 261-268.

Asch, S. E. *Social Psychology*. New York: Prentice Hall, 1952.

Attneave, F. Physical determinants of the judged complexity of shapes. *Journal of Experimental Psychology*, 1957, *53*, 221-227.

Baldwin, A. L., Kallhorn, J., & Breese, F. H. Patterns of parent behavior. *Psychological Mongraphs*. 1945, *58*, p. 5 of Chapter 6.

Bales, R. F. and Strodtbeck, F. L. Phases in group problem solving. *Journal of Abnormal and Social Psychology*, 1951, *46*, 425-495.

Barker, R. G. Ecological psychology: Concepts and methods for studying the environment of human learning. Stanford: Stanford University Press, 1968.

Barton, K. & Cattell, R. B. Changes in personality over a 5-year period. Relationship of change to life events. *JSAS Catalogue of Selected Documents in Psychology*, 1975.

Barton, K., & Cattell, R. B. *The Core Trait and State (CTS) Battery*. Champaign, Ill.: Institute for Personality and Ability Testing, 1979.

Barton, K., Cattell, R. B., & Conner, D. V. The identification of state factors through P-technique factor analysis. *Journal of Clinical Psychology*, 1972, *28*, 459-463.

Barton, K., Cattell, R. B., & Curran, J. Psychological states. Their definition through P-technique and differential R (dR) technique factor analysis. *Journal of Behavioral Science*, 1973, *1*, 273-277.

Barton, K., Cattell, R. B., & Vaughan, G. M. Changes in personality as a function of college attendance or work experience. *Journal of Counselling Psychology*, 1973, *20*, 162-165.

Bartsch, T., Barton, K., & Cattell, R. B. A repeated measures investigation of the relations of the School Motivation Analysis Test to academic achievement. *Psychological Reports*, 1973, *33*, 743-748.

Basowitz, H., Shelson, H. P., Korchin, J., & Grinker, R. R. *Anxiety and stress*. New York: Blakiston, 1955.

Bass, B. M. *Organizational psychology*. Boston: Allyn & Bacon, 1965.

Beck, A. *Depression: its clinical, experimental and theoretical aspects*. New York: Hoeber, Med. Div., 1967.

Becker, J. *Depression: theory and research*. Washington, D.C.: Winston, 1974.

Becker, W. C. A comparison of the factor structure of the 16 PF and the Guilford-Martin personality inventories. *Educational and Psychological Measurement*, 1961, *21*, 393-404.

Birkett, H. A. *A P-technique analysis of the dynamics of an alcoholic*. Unpublished M.A. thesis, University of Hawaii, 1976.

Birkett, H. A. & Cattell, R. B. Diagnosis of the dynamic roots of a clinical symptom by P-technique: a case of episodic alcoholism. *Multivariate Experimental Clinical Research*, 1978, *4*, 1-22.

Birkett, H. A. & Cattell, R. B. A comparison of motivation components in change scores with those in individual differences. (In preparation) 1978.

Blalock, H. M. *Causal inferences in non-experimental research*. New York: Norton, 1971.

Bleuler, M. The delimitation of influences of environment and heredity on mental disposition. *Character and Personality*, 1933, *1*, 286-300.

Block, J. Some reasons for the apparent inconsistency of personality. *Psychological Bulletin*, 1968, *70*, 210-212.

Block, J. Recognizing the coherence of personality. In press, 1978.

Bolton, L. S. & Cattell, R. B. What pathological dimension lie beyond the normal dimensions of the 16 P.F. A comparison of 16 P.F. and MMPI factor domains. *Journal of Consulting and Clinical Psychology*, 1969, *33*, 18-29.

Bolz, C. R. Typological theory and research. Chap. 11. In Dreger, R. M. (Ed.), *Multivariate personality research*. Baton Rouge: Claitor Publications, 1972.

Borgatta, E. G., & Cottrell, L. S. On the classification of groups. *Sociometry*, 1956, *18*, 665-678.

Borgatta, E. G., Cottrell, L. L., & Mann, J. H. The spectrum of individual interaction characteristics: An interdimensional analysis. *Psychological Reports*, 1958, *4*, 279-319.

Bramblett, C. A. *Patterns of primate behavior*. New York: Wiley, 1976.

Brand, D. A. Games theory, decision processes, and man-made interaction. Chap. 13, Pp. 417-437 in Cattell, R. B. (Ed.), *Handbook of Multivariate Experimental Psychology*. Chicago, Rand McNally, 1966.

Brennan, J. & Cattell, R. B. Why do state measures mutually correlate? In preparation, 1979.

Brunswick, E. *Perception and the representative design of psychological experiments*. Berkeley: University of California Press, 1956.

Burdsal, C., & Cattell, R. B. The radial parcelling double factoring design. A solution to the item-vs-parcel controversy. *Multivariate Behavioral Research*, 1975, *10*, 165-179.

Burdsal, C. A. Jr., & Schwartz, S. A. The relationship of personality traits as measured in the questionnaire medium and by self-ratings. *Journal of Psychology*, 1975, *91*, 173-182.

Burt, C. L. Correlations between persons. *British Journal of Psychology*, 1937, *28*, 56-96.

Burt, C. L. *Factors of the mind.* London: University of London Press, 1940.

Burt, C. L. The appropriate use of factor analysis and analyses of variance. In R. B. Cattell (Ed.), *Handbook of Multivariate Experimental Psychology.* Chicago, Rand McNally, 1966, Pp. 267-287.

Buss, A. R. Learning, transfer and changes in ability factors: A multivariate model. *Psychological Bulletin*, 1973, *80*, 106-112.

Buss, A. R. A general developmental model for inter-individual differences, intra-individual differences, and intra-individual changes. *Developmental Psychology*, 1974(a), *10*, 70-78.

Buss, A. R. A recursive non-recursive factor model and developmental causal networks. *Human Development*, 1974(b), *17*, 139-151.

Buss, A. An inferential strategy for determining factor invariance across different individuals and different variables. *Multivariate Behavioral Research*, 1975, *10*, 365-372.

Butcher, J. Three multivariate experiments throwing light on dynamic structure in eleven-year-old children. Adv. Public, No. 12, 1963, Lab. of Person Asses.: University of Illinois, Urbana, Ill.

Campbell, D. T., & Fiske, D. W. Convergent and discriminant validation by the multitrait-multimethod matrix. *Psychological Bulletin*, 1959, *56*, 91-105.

Cannon, W. B. *Bodily changes in pain, hunger, fear and rage.* 2nd ed. New York: Appleton, 1929.

Carter, H. D., Pyles, M. K., & Bretnall, E. P. A comparative study of factors in vocational interest scores in high school boys. *Journal of Educational Psychology*, 1935, *26*, 81.

Cartwright, D. *Introduction to personality study.* New York: Prentice Hall, 1974.

Cartwright, D. S., & Cartwright, C. F. *Psychological adjustment: Behavior in the inner world.* Chicago: Rand McNally, 1971.

Cattell, R. B. Experiments on the psychical correlate of the G.S.R. *British Journal of Psychology*, 1929, *19*, 357-386.

Cattell, R. B. Temperament tests, II. *British Journal of Psychology*, 1933, *24*, 20-49.

Cattell, R. B. Friends and enemies: a psychological study of character and temperament. *Character and Personality*, 1934, *3*, 54-63.

Cattell, R. B. The measurement of interest. *Character and Personality*, 1935, *4*, 147-169.

Cattell, R. B. An objective test of character-temperament. *Journal of General Psychology*, 1941, *25*, 59-73.

Cattell, R. B. Fluctuations of sentiments and attitudes as a measure of character integration and of temperament. *American Journal of Psychology*, 1943, *56*, 195-216.

Cattell, R. B. Parallel proportional profiles and other principles for determining the choice of factors by rotation. *Psychometrika*, 1944, *9*, 267-283.

Cattell, R. B. The description of personality. Principles and findings in a factor analysis. *American Journal of Psychology*, 1945, *58*, 69-90.

Cattell, R. B. *Description and measurement of personality.* New York: World Book, 1946.

Cattell, R. B. Confirmation and clarification of primary personality factors. *Psychometrika*, 1947, *12*, 197-220.

Cattell, R. B. The primary personality factors in women compared with those in men. *British Journal of Psychology*, 1948, *1*, 114-130.

Cattell, R. B. The discovery of ergic structure in man in terms of common attitudes. *Journal of Abnormal and Social Psychology*, 1950, *45*, 598-618. (a)

Cattell, R. B. *Personality, a systematic theoretical and factual study.* New York: McGraw-Hill, 1950. (b)

Cattell, R. B. On the disuse and misuse of P, Q, Qs and O techniques in clinical psychology. *Journal of Clinical Psychology*, 1951, *7*, 203-214. (a)

Cattell, R. B. A factorization of tests of personality source traits. *British Journal of Psychology Statistics Section*, 1951, *4*, 165-178. (b)

Cattell, R. B. *Factor analysis.* New York: Harper & Row, 1952.

Cattell, R. B. *Personality and motivation structure and measurement.* New York: World Book, 1957.

Cattell, R. B. The dynamic calculus: Concepts and crucial experiments. In Jones, M. R. (Ed.), *The Nebrasks symposium on motivation.* Pp. 84-134. Lincoln: University of Nebraska Press, 1959.

Cattell, R. B. Theory of situational, instrument, second order and refraction factors in personality structure research. *Psychological Bulletin*, 1961, *58*, 160-174.

Cattell, R. B. The relational simplex theory of equal interval and absolute scaling. *Acta Psychologika*, 1962, *20*, 139-158.

Cattell, R. B. The structuring of change by P-technique and differential R-technique. In Harris, C. W. (Ed.), *Problems in measuring change.* Pp. 167-198. Madison: University of Wisconsin Press, 1963.

Cattell, R. B. Objective personality tests: a reply to Dr. Eysenck. *Occupational Psychology*, 1964, *38*, 69-86. (a)

Cattell, R. B. The parental early repressiveness hypothesis for the authoritarian personality factor, U.1.28. *Journal of Genetic Psychology*, 1964, *106*, 332-349. (b)

Cattell, R. B. Higher order factor structures and reticular-vs-hierarchical formulae for their interpretation. In Banks, C., & Broadhurst, C. L. (Eds.), *Studies in psychology in honor of Sir Cyril Burt.* Pp. 223-266. London: University of London Press, 1965. (a)

Cattell, R. B. The configurative method for surer identification of personality dimensions. *Psychological Reports*, 1965, *16*, 269-270. (b)

Cattell, R. B. Confactor rotation: Some problems and tentative solutions. *Laboratory of Personality and Group Analysis.* University of Illinois Advanced Publication No. 20, 1966. Given at Oxford University meeting of the Society of Multivariate Experimental Psychologists, 1966. (a)

Cattell, R. B. Patterns of change: Measurement in relation to state-dimension, trait change, liability and process concepts. In Cattell, R. B. (Ed.), *Handbook of multivariate experimental psychology.* Chapter 11. Chicago: Rand McNally, 1966. (b)

Cattell, R. B. (Ed.) *Handbook of multivariate experimental psychology.* Chicago: Rand McNally, 1966. (c)

Cattell, R. B. The theory of fluid and crystallized intelligence checked at the 5-6 year old level. *British Journal of Educational Pyschology*, 1967, *37*, 209-224.

Cattell, R. B. Taxonomic principles for locating and using types (and the Taxonome program). In Kleinmuntz, B. (Ed.), *Formal representation of human judgment.* Pp. 99-148. Pittsburgh: Pittsburgh University Press, 1968. (a)

Cattell, R. B. Trait view theory of perturbation in ratings and self-ratings (L BR and Q data). Its application to obtaining pure trait scores estimates in questionnaires. *Psychological Review*, 1968, *75*, 96-113. (b)

Cattell, R. B. Comparing factor trait and state scores across ages and cultures. *Journal of Gerontology*, 1969, *24*, 348-360. (a)

Cattell, R. B. Is field independence an expression of the general personality source trait of independence, U 1.19? *Perceptual and Motor Skills*, 1969, *28*, 865-866. (b)

Cattell, R. B. The isopodic and equipotent principles for comparing factor scores across different populations. *British Journal of Mathematical and Statistical Psychology*, 1970, *23*, 23-24.

Cattell, R. B. *Abilities: Their structure, growth and action.* Boston: Houghton-Mifflin, 1971. (a)

Cattell, R. B. Estimating modulator indices and state liabilities. *Multivariate Behavioral Research*, 1971, *6*, 7-33. (b)

Cattell, R. B. The 16 P.F. and basic personality structure: A reply to Eysenck. *Journal of Behavioral Science* (Durbin, South Africa), 1972, *1*, 169-187.

Cattell, R. B. The interpretation of Pavlov's typology and the arousal concept, in replicated trait and state factors. In Gray, J. A. (Ed.), *Biological Bases of individual behavior.* Pp. 141-164. New York: Academic Press, 1972. (b)

Cattell, R. B. Real base, true zero factor analysis. *Multivariate Behavioral Research Psychology Monogram* No. 72-1, 1972. Fort Worth: Texas Christian University Press. (c)

Cattell, R. B. An analysis of state and trait change factors in pathology by dR technique on the CAQ. *Indian Journal of Clinical Psychology*, 1974, *1*, 34-40. (a)

Cattell, R. B. How good is the modern questionnaire: General Principles for evaluation. *Journal of Personality Assessment*, 1974, *38*, 115-129. (b)

Cattell, R. B. A second order analysis of state and trait change factors by dR technique on the CAQ. Laboratory of Personality and Group Analysis. University of Illinois Advanced Publication No. 21, 1974. (c)

Cattell, R. B. Third order personality structure in Q-data: Evidence from eleven experiments. *Journal of Multivariate Experiment and Clinical Psychology*, 1975, *1*, 118-149.

Cattell, R. B. Structured learning theory applied to personality change. In Cattell, R. B., & Dreger, R. M. (Eds.), *Handbook of modern personality theory.* Chapter 18. Pp. 433-472. Washington, Hemisphere, and New York: Halsted, 1977. (a)

Cattell, R. B. Personality and culture: General concepts and methodological problems. In Cattell, R. B., & Dreger, R. M. (Eds.), *Handbook of modern personality theory.* Pp. 473-476. Washington, Hemisphere, and New York: Halsted, 1977. (b)

Cattell, R. B. The grammar of science and the evolution of personality theory. Chapter 1 in Cattell, R. B. & Dreger, R. M. (Eds.) *Handbook of Modern Personality Theory.* New York, Wiley, 1977. (c)

Cattell, R. B. Lernfahigkeit, Personlichkeitstruktur und die Theorie des strukturierten Lernens. In Nissen, G. *Intelligentz, Lernen und Lernstorungen.* Berlin, Springer Verlag, 1977. (d)

Cattell, R. B. *The scientific use of factor analysis.* New York: Plenum Press, 1978.

Cattell, R. B., & Baggaley, A. R. A confirmation of ergic and engram structures in attitudes objectively measured. *Australian Journal of Psychology*, 1958, *10*, 287-318.

Cattell, R. B., & Bartlett, H. W. An R-dR technique operational distinction of the states of anxiety, stress, fear, etc. *Australian Journal of Psychology*, 1971, *23*, 105-123.

Cattell, R. B., & Barton, K. Changes in psychological state measures and time of day. *Psychological Reports*, 1974, *35*, 219-222.

Cattell, R. B., & Bjersted, A. The structure of depression by factoring Q-data in relation to general personality source traits. *Scandinavian Journal of Psychology*, 1967, *8*, 17-24.

Cattell, R. B., Blaine, D. and Kameoka, V. N-way factor analysis and the description of the personality's environment (In preparation).

Cattell, R. B., and Brennan, J. The practicality of an orthogonal confactor rotation for the approximate resolution of oblique factors. *Multivariate Experimental Clinical Research*, 1977, *3*, 95-103.

Cattell, R. B., & Butcher, J. *The prediction of achievement and creativity*. Indianapolis: Bobbs-Merrill, 1968.

Cattell, R. B., & Cattell, A. K. S. Factor rotation for proportional profiles: Analytical solution and an example. *British Journal of Statistical Psychology*, 1955, *8*, 83-92.

Cattell, R. B., & Child, D. *Motivation and dynamic structure*. New York: Wiley-Halsted, 1975.

Cattell, R. B., & Coulter, M. A. Principles of behavioral taxonomy and the mathematical basis of the taxonome computer program. *British Journal of Mathematical and Statistical Psychology*, 1966, *19*, 237-269.

Cattell, R. B., Coulter, M. A., & Tsujioka, B. The taxonometric recognition of types and functional emergents. In Cattell, R. B. (Ed.), *Handbook of multivariate experimental psychology*. Chapter 9. Chicago: Rand McNally, 1966.

Cattell, R. B., & Cross, K. Comparison of the ergic and self sentiment structures found in dynamic traits by R- and P-techniques. *Journal of Personality*, 1952, *21*, 250-271.

Cattell, R. B., DeYoung, G., & Barton, K. A check on the validity of motivation component measures of ergic tension, by manipulation of the hunger erg. In Press, 1977.

Cattell, R. B., DeYoung, G. E., & Horn, J. L. Human motives as dynamic states: A dR analysis of objective motivation measures. *Journal of Multivariate Experimental Personality and Clinical Psychology*, 1974, *1*, 58-78.

Cattell, R. B., & Dickman, K. A dynamic model of physical influences demonstrating the necessity of oblique simple structure. *Psychological Bulletin*, 1962, *59*, 389-400.

Cattell, R. B., & Dielman, T. E. The structure of motivational manifestation as measured in the laboratory rat: An examination of motivation component theory. *Social Behavior and Personality*, 1974, *2*, 10-24.

Cattell, R. B., & Digman, J. M. A theory of the structure of perturbations in observer ratings and questionnaire data. *Behavioral Science*, 1964, *9*, 341-358.

Cattell, R. B., & Dreger, R. M. *Handbook of modern personality theory*. New York: Hemisphere-Halsted, 1977.

Cattell, R. B., Dubin, S. S., & Saunders, D. R. Personality structure in psychotics by factorization of objective clinical tests. *Journal of Mental Science*, 1954, *100*, 154-176.

Cattell, R. B., & Eber, H. W. *The music preference test of personality*. Champaign, Ill.: Institute for Personality and Ability Testing, 1966.

Cattell, R. B., Eber, H. W., & Tatsuoka, M. *The 16 personality factor test handbook*. Champaign, Ill.: Institute for Personality and Ability Testing, 1970.

Cattell, R. B., & Gorsuch, R. L. The uniqueness and significance of simple structure demonstrated by contrasting organic "natural structure" and "random structure" data. *Psychometrika*, 1963, *28*, 55-67.

Cattell, R. B., & Gruen, W. The personality factor structure of 11-year-old children in terms of behavior rating data. *Journal of Clinical Psychology*, 1953, *9*, 256-266.

Cattell, R. B., & Gruen, W. The primary personality factors in 11-year-old children, by objective tests. *Journal of Personality*, 1955, *23*, 460-478.

Cattell, R. B., & Horn, J. L. An integrating study of the factor structure of adult attitude interests. *Genetic Psychological Monograph*, 1963, *67*, 89-149.

Cattell, R. B., Horn, J. L., Sweney, A. B., & Radcliffe, J. *The motivation analysis test, MAT*. Champaign, Ill.: Institute for Personality and Ability Testing, 1964.

Cattell, R. B., & Horowitz, J. Objective personality tests investigating the structure of altruism in relation to the source traits A, H and L. *Journal of Personality*, 1952, *21*, 103-117.

Cattell, R. B., & Howarth, E. Hypotheses on the principal personality dimensions in children and tests constructed for them. *Journal of Genetic Psychology*, 1962, *101*, 145-163.

Cattell, R. B., Kawash, G. F., & DeYoung, G. E. Validation of objective measures of ergic tension: Response of the sex erg to visual stimulation. *Journal of Experimental Research in Personality*, 1972, *6*, 76-83.

Cattell, R. B., & Killian, L. R. The pattern of objective test personality factor differences in schizophrenia and in the character disorders. *Journal of Clinical Psychology*, 1967, *23*, 343-348.

Cattell, R. B., & Klein, T. W. A check on hypothetical personality structures, and their theoretical interpretation at 14-16 years, in T-data. *British Journal of Psychology*, 1975, *66*, 131-151.

Cattell, R. B. & Kline, P. *The scientific study of personality and motivation*. New York, Academic Press, 1977.

Cattell, R. B., Korth, B., & Bolz, C. R. Behavioral types on pure bred dogs objectively determined by taxonome. *Behavioral Genetics*, 1973, *3*, 205-216.

Cattell, R. B., Lawlis, F., McGill, J., & McGraw. A check on the structure and meaning of primary motivation components. In press, *Multivariate Experimental Clinical Research*, 1978, *4*, 1-

Cattell, R. B., & Nesselroade, J. R. The discovery of the anxiety state pattern in Q-data and its distinction in the LM model from depression, effort stress and fatigue. *Multivariate Behavioral Research*, 1976, *11*, 27-46.

Cattell, R. B., & Peterson, D. R. Personality structures in 4-5 year olds, by factoring observed, time-sampled behavior. *Rassegni di Psieologia Generale e Clinica*, 1958, *3*, 3-21.

Cattell, R. B., & Peterson, D. R. Personality structure in 4- and 5-year olds in terms of objective tests. *Journal of Clinical Psychology*, 1959, *15*, 355-369.

Cattell, R. B., Pierson, G., & Finkbeiner, C. Proof of alignment of personality source trait factors from questionnaires and observer ratings: The theory of instrument-free patterns. *Multivariate Experimental Clinical Psychology*, 1974, *4*, 1-31.

Cattell, R. B., Radcliffe, J., & Sweney, A. B. The nature and measurement of components of motivation. *Genetic Psychological Monograph*, 1963, *68*, 49-211.

Cattell, R. B., & Rickels, K. The relationship of clinical symptoms and IPAT factored tests of anxiety, regression and asthenia: A factor analytic study. *Journal of Nervous and Mental Disease*, 1960, *146*, 147-160.

Cattell, R. B., Rickels, K., Weise, C., Gray, B., & Yee, R. The effects of psychotherapy upon measured anxiety and regression. *American Journal of Psychotherapy*, 1966, *20*, 261-269.

Cattell, R. B., & Saunders, D. R. Musical preferences and personality diagnosis. A factorization of one hundred and twenty themes. *Journal of Social Psychology*, 1954, *39*, 3-24.

Cattell, R. B. & Scheier, J. H. *The meaning and measurement of neuroticism and anxiety*. New York: Ronald Press, 1961.

Cattell, R. B., Schmidt, L. R., & Bjersted, A. Clinical diagnosis by the objective-analytic personality batteries. *Journal of Clinical Psychological Monograph Supplements* No. 34, 1972.

Cattell, R. B., Schmidt, L. R., & Pawlik, K. Cross cultural comparison (U.S.A., Japan, Austria) of the personality structures of 10 to 14 year olds in objective tests. *Social Behavior and Personality*, 1973, *1*, 182-211.

Cattell, R. B., & Schuerger, J. *The objective analytic (O-A) personality factor kit*. Champaign, Ill.: Institute for Personality and Ability Testing, 1978.

Cattell, R. B., & Schuerger, Jr. Second and third order factor structure in objective test measures of personality (In preparation).

Cattell, R. B., Shrader, R. B., & Barton, K. The definition and measurement of anxiety as a trait and state in the 12-17 year range. *British Journal of Social and Clinical Psychology*, 1974, *13*, 173-182.

Cattell, R. B., & Stice, G. F. *The dimensions of groups and their relations to the behavior of members*. Champaign, Ill.: Institute for Personality and Ability Testing, 1953. Republished Ann Arbor, Michigan, University Microfilms International, 1976.

Cattell, R. B., Stice, G. F., and Kristy, N. F. A first approximation to nature-nurture ratios for eleven personality factors in objective tests. *Journal of Abnormal and Social Psychology*, 1957, *54*, 143-159.

Cattell, R. B., & Sullivan, W. The scientific nature of factors: A demonstration by cups of coffee. *Behavioral Science*, 1962, *7*, 258-262.

Cattell, R. B., & Sweney, A. B. Components measurable in manifestations of mental conflict. *Journal of Abnormal and Social Psychology*, 1964, *68*, 479-490.

Cattell, R. B., & Tatro, D. F. The personality factors, objectively measured, which distinguish psychotics from normals. *Behavioral Research and Therapy*, 1966, *4*, 39-57.

Cattell, R. B., & Vaughan, D. E. Alignment of OAQ scales with second order HSPQ factors. Adv. Publication No. 40, Laboratory of Personality Analysis, University of Illinois (In preparation).

Cattell, R. B., & Vaughan, D. E. A large sample cross check on the factor structure of the 16 PF by item and parcel factoring. Adv. Publication No. 41, Laboratory of Personality Analysis, University of Illinois (In preparation).

Cattell, R. B., & Vogelmann, S. Second-order personality factors in combined questionnaire and rating data. *Multivariate Experimental Clinical Research*, 1976, *3*, 40-64.

Cattell, R. B., & Vogelmann, S. A comprehensive trial for the scree and KG criteria for determining the number of factors. *Multivariate Behavioral Research*, 1977, *12*, 289-325.

Cattell, R. B., & Warburton, F. W. Objective personality and motivation tests. A theoretical introduction and practical compendium. Champaign, Ill.: University of Illinois Press, 1967.

Cattell, R. B., & Watterson, D. A check on the seven missing personality factors in relation to 16 P.F. space. *Multivariate Experimental Clinical Research*. In press, 1979.

Cattell, R. B., & Wenig, P. Dynamic and cognitive factors controlling misperception. *Journal of Abnormal and Social Psychology*, 1952, *47*, 797-809.

Cattell, R. B., & Williams, H. F. P-technique: A new statistical device for analyzing functional unities in the intact organism. *British Journal of Preventive and Social Medicine*, 1953, *7*, 141-153.

Child, D. *The essentials of factor analysis*. Longon: Holt, 1970.

Clemans, W. V. An analytical and empirical examination of some properties of ipsative scores. *Psychometric Monographs* No. 14, Pp. 87. 1966.

Cohen, M. R., & Nagel, E. *An introduction to logic and scientific method*. New York: Harcourt Brace, 1934.

Comrey, A. L., & Duffy, K. E. Cattell and Eysenck factors related to Comrey personality factors. *Multivariate Behavioral Research*, 1968, *4*, 379-392.

Cornfield, J., & Tukey, J. W. Average values of mean squares in factorials. *Annotated Mathematical Statistics*, 1956, *27*, 917-949.

Cottle, W. C. A factor study of the multiphasic, Strong, Kuder and Bell inventories using a population of adult males. *Psychometrika*, 1950, *15*, 25-47.

Coulter, M., & Cattell, R. B. Principles of behavioral taxonomy and the mathematical basis of the taxonome computer program. *British Journal of Mathematical and Statistical Psychology*, 1966, *19*, 237-269.

Craik, K. H. Environmental psychology. In *Annual Review of Psychology*, 1973, 404-421.

Crissy, W. J., & Daniel, W. J. Vocational interest factors in women. *Journal of Applied Psychology*, 1939, *23*, 488-494.

Cronbach, L. J. The two disciplines of scientific psychology. *American Psychologist*, 1957, *12*, 671-684.

Cronbach, L. J., & Furby, L. How should we measure "change"—or should we? *Psychological Bulletin*, 1970, *74*, 68-80.

Cronbach, L. J., Gleser, G. C., Nanda, H., & Rajaratnam, N. *The dependability of behavior measurements: Theory of generalizability for scores and profiles*. New York: Wiley, 1972.

Cross, K. P. *Determination of the ergic structure of common attitudes by P-technique*. Unpublished M.A. thesis, University of Illinois at Urbana, 1951.

Curran, J. P. *Dimensions of state change, in Q-data, by chain P-technique on twenty women*. Unpublished M.A. thesis, University of Illinois at Urbana, 1968.

Curran, J. P., & Cattell, R. B. *Handbook for the 8 state battery*. Champaign, Ill.: Institute for Personality and Ability Testing, 1976.

Dahlstrom, W. G. The roles of social desirability and acquiescence in responses to the MMPI. Pp. 157-170 In Messick, S., & Ross, J. (Eds.), *Measurement in personality and cognition*. New York: Wiley, 1962.

Delhees, K. H. The abnormal personality; neurosis and delinquency. Chap. 27. Pp. 629-652. Cattell, R. B., & Dreger, R. M. (Eds.), *Handbook of Modern Personality Theory*. New York. Hemisphere: Halsted. 1977.

Delhees, K., & Cattell, R. B. The dimensions of pathology: Proof of their projection beyond the normal 16 P.F. source traits. *Personality*, 1971, *2*, 149-173.

Delhees, K.H., & Cattell, R. B. Seven missing normal personality factors in the questionnaire primaries. *Multivariate Behavioral Research*, 1973, *8*, 173-194.

Dermen, D., French, J. W., & Harman, H. H. Verification of self report temperament factors. Princeton, N. J. Educational Testing Service, Technical Report No. 6, 1974.

DeYoung, G. E., Yoon, G. H. Y., & Cattell, R. B. Sexual motivation: comparison of drive, reinforcement and random response models. In press, 1978.

DeYoung, G. E. Standard of decision regarding personality factors in questionnaires. *Canadian Journal of Behavioral Science*, 1972, *4*, 253-255.

DeYoung, G. E. A causal model of effects of personality and marital role factors upon diary reported sexual behavior. *Convention Handbook, 91st annual convention of the APA*. Montreal, Canada, 1973, *8*, 357-358.

DeYoung, G. E., Cattell, R. B., Gaborit, M., & Barton, K. A causal model of effects of personality and marital role factors upon diary-reported sexual behavior. Proceedings 81st annual convention of the APA, Montreal, Canada, 1973, *8*, 357-358.

Dickman, K. *The factorial validity of a rating instrument*. Unpublished Ph.D. thesis, University of Illinois at Urbana, 1960.

Dielman, T. E., Cattell, R. B., & Kawash, G. F. *Three studies of manipulation of the fear erg*. Laboratory of Personality and Group Analysis. University of Illinois Advanced Publication No. 14, 1971.

Dielman, T. E., & Krug, S. E. Trait description and measurement in motivation and dynamic structure. In Cattell, R. B., & Dreger, R. M. (Eds.), *Handbook of modern personality theory*. Chapter 5. New York: Hemisphere: Halsted. 1976.

Digman, J. M. Principal dimensions of child personality as inferred from teachers' judgments. *Child Development*, 1963, *34*, 43-60.

Digman, J. M. Child behavior ratings: Further evidence of a multiple factor model of child personality. *Child Development*, 1965, *25*, 787-799.

Digman, J. M. Interaction and non-linearity in multivariate experiment. In Cattell, R. B. (Ed.), *Handbook of multivariate experimental psychology*. Pp. 459-475. Chicago: Rand McNally, 1966.

DiMascio, A., et al. An evaluation of Isoquinazepan. *Current Therapeutic Research*, 1967, *9*, 517-521.

Dreger, R. M. *Fundaments of personality*. Philadelphia: Lippincott, 1962.

Drevdahl, J. E. Factors of importance for creativity. *Journal of Clinical Psychology*, 1956, *12*, 21-26.

Edwards, A. L. *The social desirability variable in personality assessment and research*. New York: Holt, 1957.

Endler, N. S. The case for person-situation interactions. *Canadian Psychological Review*, 1975, *16*, 12-21.

Endler, N. S., & Hunt, J. McV. Sources of behavioral variance as measured by the S-R inventory of anxiousness. *Psychological Bulletin*, 1966, *65*, 336-346.

Endler, N. S., & Hunt, J. McV. Generalizability of contributions from sources of variance in the S-R inventories of anxiousness. *Journal of Personality*, 1969, *37*, 1-24.

Endler, N. S., & Magnusson, D. Towards an interactional psychology of personality. *Psychological Bulletin*, 1976, *83*, 956-974.

Endler, N. S., & Magnusson, D. *Interactional psychology and personality*. Washington, D.C.: Hemisphere Pub. Co., 1976.

Eysenck, H. J. *The scientific study of personality*. London: Routledge, 1952.

Eysenck, H. J. *The structure of human personality*. London: Methuen, 1960.

Eysenck, H. J. *Readings in introversion and extroversion*. London: Staples, 1970.

Eysenck, H. J., & Eysenck, S. B. G. *Personality structure and measurement*. San Diego: Knapp, 1969.

Eysenck, H. J., & Prell, D. B. The inheritance of neuroticism. *Journal of Mental Science*, 1951, *97*, 441-265.

Eysenck, H. J., & Rachman, S. *The causes and cures of neurosis: an introduction to modern behavior therapy based on learning theory and the principles of conditioning*. San Diego: Knapp, 1965.

Eysenck, H. J., & Rachman, S. *The effects of psychotherapy*. New York: International Science Press, 1966.

Eysenck, S. B. G. Neurosis and psychosis: An experimental analysis. *Journal of Mental Science*, 1956, *102*, 512-529.

Fahrenberg, J. Physiological concepts in personality research. Chap. 25. Pp. 585-614. In Cattell, R. B., & Dreger, R. M. (Eds.) *Handbook of Multivariate Experimental Psychology*. New York, Hemisphere: Halsted, 1977.

Farber, I. E. Anxiety as a drive state. In M. R. Jones (Ed.), *Current theory and research on motivation*. Nebraska Symposium on Motivation. Lincoln, Nebraska: University of Nebraska Press, 1954.

Feigl, H., & Scriven, M. (Eds.), *The foundations of science and the concepts of psychology and psychoanalysis*. Minneapolis: University of Minnesota Press, 1956.

Ferguson, L. W., Humphreys, L. G., & Strong, F. W. A factorial analysis of interests and values. *Journal of Educational Psychology*, 1941, *32*, 197-204.

Fischbein, M. Attitude and the prediction of behavior. In M. Fischbein (Ed.), *Readings in attitude theory and measurement*. New York: Wiley, 1967.

Fisher, R. A. *The genetical theory of natural selection*. Oxford: Clarendon, 1930.

Fiske, D. W., & Maddi, S. R. (Eds.). *Functions of varied experience*. Homewood, Ill.: Dorsey, 1961.

Frederiksen, N., Jensen, O., & Beaton, A. E. *Prediction of Organizational Behavior*. New York: Pergamon Press, 1972.

Frederiksen, N. Toward a taxonomy of situations. *American Psychologist*, 1972, *27*, 114-123.

French, J. W. *The description of aptitude and achievement tests in terms of rotated factors*. Chicago: University of Chicago Press, 1951.

French, J. W. *The description of personality measurements in terms of rotated factors*. Princeton: Educational Testing Service, 1953.

Freud, A. *The ego and the mechanisms of defense*. London: Hogarth, 1937.

Freud, S. *General introduction to psychoanalysis*. New York: Liverright, 1920.

Friedman, J., & Katz. J. *The psychology of depression*. New York: Wiley, 1975.

Glass, G., & Hakstian, A. R. Measures of association in comparative experiments: Their development and interpretation. *American Educational Research Journal.* 1969, *6*, 403-414.

Glass, G., Willson, V., & Gottman, J. *Design and analysis of time series experiments.* Boulder: University of Colorado Associated Press, 1975.

Goldberg, L. R. Some recent trends in personality assessment. *Journal of Counselling psychologists*, 1972, *36*, 547-560.

Goldberger, A. S., & Duncan, O. D. *Structural equation models in the social sciences.* New York: Seminar Press, 1972.

Golding, S. Flies in the ointment. *Psychological Bulletin*, 1975, *82*, 404-418.

Gorsuch, R. L. *Factor analysis.* Philadelphia: Saunders, 1974.

Gorsuch, R. L., & Cattell, R. B. Second stratum personality factors defined in the questionnaire realm by the 16 P.F. *Multivariate Behavioral Research*, 1967, *2*, 211-224.

Gruen, W., & Cattell, R. B. The primary personality factors in eleven year old children, by objective tests. *Journal of Personality*, 1955, *23*, 460-478.

Grinker, R. R., Nunnally, J., et al. *The phenomena of depressions.* New York: Hoeber, 1961.

Grinker, R. R., & Spiegel, J. P. *Men under stress.* Philadephia, Blakiston, 1945.

Guertin, W. H., & Bailey, J. *Introduction to modern factor analysis.* Ann Arbor: Edwards, 1970.

Guilford, J. P. *Personality.* New York: McGraw-Hill, 1959.

Guilford, J. P. Factors of personality. *Psychological Bulletin*, 1975, *82*, 802-814.

Guilford, J. P., Christensen, P. R., Bond, N. A., & Sutton, M.A. A factor analysis of human interests. *Psychological Monographs*, 1954, *68*, No. 4, 53-111.

Guilford, J. P., & Michael, W. B. Approaches to univocal factor scores. *Psychometrika*, 1948, *13*, 1-22.

Gundlach, R. H., & Gerum, E. Vocational interests and types of abilities. *Journal of Educational Psychology*, 1931, *22*, 505.

Hake, H. W. The study of perception in the light of multivariate methods. In Cattell, R. B. (Ed.), *Handbook of multivariate experimental psychology*, 502-534. Chicago: Rand McNally, 1966.

Hakstian, A. R., & Cattell, R. B. The checking of primary ability structure on a broader basis of performance. *British Journal of Educational Psychology*, 1974, *44*, 140-154.

Hakstian, A. R., & Cattell, R. B. *The comprehensive ability battery.* Champaign, Ill.: Institute for Personality and Ability Testing, 1977.

Hakstian, R., Rogers, C. W., & Cattell, R. B. An empirical evaluation of the scree test for number of factors on a variety of plasmodes. (In preparation)

Hammond, S. B. Personality studied by the method of rating in the life situation. In Cattell, R. B., & Dreger, R. M. (Eds.), *Handbook of modern personality theory*, 43-69. Washington: Hemisphere, New York, Halsted, 1977.

Harman, H. H. *Modern factor analysis.* Chicago: University of Chicago Press, 1976.

Harris, C. W. (Ed.). *Problems in measuring change.* Madison: University of Wisconsin Press, 1963.

Haverland, E. M. The application of an analytical solution for proportional profiles rotation to a box problem and to the drive structure in rats. Unpublished Ph.D. thesis 1954, University of Illinois.

Hebb, D. O. *The organization of behavior.* New York: Wiley, 1949.

Helson, H. Adaptation level theory. In Koch, S. (Ed.), *Psychology: A study of a science.* Pp. 561-619. New York: McGraw-Hill, 1959.

Helson, H., & Bevan, W. (Eds.). *Contemporary approaches to psychology.* Princeton: Van Nostrand, 1967.

Hemphill, J. K., & Weste, C. M. The measurement of group dimensions. *Journal of Psychology*, 1950, *29*, 325-342.

Horn, J. L. Motivation and dynamic calculus concepts from multivariate experiment. In Cattell, R. B. (Ed.), *Handbook of multivariate experimental psychology.* Pp. 611-641. Chicago: Rand McNally, 1966.

Horn, J. L. State, trait and change dimensions of intelligence. *British Journal of Educational Psychology*, 1972, *42*, 159-185.

Horn, J. L. The structure of intellect: Primary abilities. In Dreger, R. M. (Ed.), *Multivariate personality research.* Pp. 451-455. Baton Rouge: Claitor, 1972.

Horn, J. L., & Cattell, R. B. Age differences in primary mental abilities. *Journal of Gerontology*, 1966, *21*, 210-220.

Horn, J. L., & Cattell, R. B. A culture fair intelligence test (Form B) composed of new types of subtest. Champaign, Ill.: Institute for Personality and Ability Testing (In preparation).

Horst, P. *Factor analysis of data matrices.* New York: Holt, 1965.

Horst, P. An overview of the essentials of multivariate analysis methods. In Cattell, R. B. (Ed.), *Handbook of multivariate experimental psychology.* Pp. 129-152. Chicago: Rand McNally, 1966.

Hudson, W., & Cattell, R. B. A 10 factor objective analytic personality source trait battery for children of 8-14 years. (In preparation)

Hull, C. L. *A behavior system.* New Haven: Yale University Press, 1952.

Hundleby, J., Pawlik, K. & Cattell, R. B. *Personality factors in objective test devices.* San Diego: Knapp, 1965.

Hunt, J. McV., Ewing, T. N., Laforge, R., & Gilbert, W. M. An integrated approach to research on therapeutic counselling, with samples of results. *Journal of Counseling Psychology*, 1959, *6*, 46-54.

Huntington, E. *The character of races.* New York: Scribner, 1927.

Huntington, E. *Mainsprings of civilization.* 3rd ed. New York: Wiley, 1964.

Hurley, J. R., & Cattell, R. B. The Procrustes program: producing direct rotation to test a hypothesized factor structure. *Behavioral Science*, 1962, *7*, 258-262.

Insel, P. M., & Moos, R. H. Psychological environments: expanding the scope of human ecology. *American Psychologist*, 1974, *29*, 279-188.

IPAT, *The IPAT culture-fair intelligence scales, 1, 2, and 3.* Champaign, Ill.: Institute for Personality and Ability Testing, 1949, 1955, 1975.

Ishikawa, A. Trait description and measurement through discovered structure in objective tests (T-data). In Cattell, R. B., & Dreger, R. M. (Eds.), *Handbook of modern personality theory.* Chapter 4. New York: Hemisphere, Halsted, 1976.

James, W. *Principles of psychology.* New York: Henry Holt, 1890.

Janet, P. *The major symptoms of hysteria; fifteen lectures given in the medical school of Harvard University.* New York: Hofner, 1965.

Johnson, D. M., Johnson, R. C., & Mark, A. L. A mathematical analysis of verbal fluency. *Journal of Genetic Psychology*, 1951, *44*, 121-128.

Jöreskog, K. G. Some contributions to maximum likelihood factor analysis. *Psychometrika*, 1967, *32*, 443-482.

Kaiser, F. Factor analysis of the image correlation matrix. (In press)

Kaiser, H. F., & Caffrey, J. Alpha factor analysis. *Psychometrika*, 1965, *30*, 1.

Kaiser, H., Hunka, S., & Bianchini, J. Relating factors between studies based upon different individuals. *Multivariate Behavioral Research*, 1971, *6*, 409.

Kameoka, V. A check on the independence and second order structure of Cattell's eight depression factors. (In preparation)

Kameoka, V., & Sine, L. An extension of Bargmann's tables and a computer program for testing the significance of simple structure in factor analysis. (In preparation)

Karson, S., & O'Dell, M. *The clinical use of the 16 P.F.* Champaign, Ill.: Institute for Personality and Ability Testing, 1976.

Kawash, G. W., Dielman, T. E., & Cattell, R. B. Changes in objective measures of fear motivation as a function of laboratory-controlled manipulation. *Psychological Reports*, 1972, *30*, 59-63.

Kelley, H. H., & Thibaut, J. W. Group problem solving. In Lindzey, G., & Aronson, E. (Eds.), *Handbook of social psychology*. Vol. 4. Reading, Mass.: Addison Wesley, 1969.

Kline, P., & Grindley, J. A 28 day case study with the MAT. *Journal of Multivariate Experimental Personality and Clinical Psychology*, 1974, *1*, 13-22.

Knapp, R. R. Objective personality tests and sociometric correlates of frequency of sick bay visits. *Journal of Applied Psychology*, 1961, *45*, 104-110.

Knapp, R. R. The validity of the Objective-Analytic Personality Test Battery in Navy settings. *Educational and Psychological Measurement*, 1962, *22*, 379-387.

Knapp, R. R. Delinquency and objective personality test factors. *Journal of Applied Psychology*, 1965, *49*, 8-11.

Knapp, R. R., & Most, J. A. Personality correlates of Marine Corps helicopter pilot performance. United States Navy Medical Field Research Laboratory, *Research Reports* No. 18, 01.09.1.3. Pp. 10-28. 1960.

Koch, H. L. A. factor analysis of some measures of the behavior of pre-school children. *Journal of Genetic Psychology*, 1942, *27*, 257-287.

Kretschmer, E. *Körperbau und Charakter.* Berlin: Springer, 1921.

Krug, S. An examination of experimentally induced changes in ergic tension levels. Unpublished M.A. thesis, University of Illinois at Urbana, 1969.

Krug, S. *Personality assessment in psychological medicine.* Champaign, Ill.: Institute of Personality and Ability Testing, 1977.

Krug, S. E., & Cattell, A. K. S. Second order structure in dynamic traits. (In press, 1978)

Krug, S. E., & Cattell, R. B. A test of the trait view theory of distortion in measurement of personality by questionnaire. *Educational and Psychological Measurement*, 1971, *31*, 721-734.

Krug, S. E., & Laughlin, J. E. Second order factors among normal and pathological primary personality traits. *Journal of Consulting and Clinical Psychology*, 1977, *45*, 575-582.

Lacey, J. I., & Lacey, B. C. Verification and extension of automatic response-stereotypy. *American Journal of Psychology*, 1958, *71*, 50-73.

Lawley, D. N. The application of the maximum likelihood method to factor analysis. *British Journal of Psychology*, 1943, *33*, 172-175.

Lawlis, G. F. *Motivational aspects of the chronically unemployed.* Unpublished Ph.D. thesis, Texas Technological College, 1968.

Lawlis, G. F. Motivational factors reflecting employment stability. *Journal of Social Psychology*, 1971, *84*, 215-225.

Lawlis, G. F., & Chatfield, D. *Multivariate approaches for the behavioral sciences.* Lubbock, Texas: Texas Technological Press, 1974.

Levine, R., Chein, I., & Murphy, G. The relation of the intensity of a need to the amount of perceptual distortion: A preliminary report. *Journal of Psychology*, 1942, *13*, 283-293.

Lindzey, G. *Assessment of human motives*. New York: Rinehart, 1958.

Lindzey, G., & Hall, C. S. *Theories of personality*. New York: Wiley, 1975.

Lord, F. M. Elementary models for measuring change. In Harris, C. W. (Ed.), *Problems in measuring change*. Pp. 21-38. Madison: University of Wisconsin Press, 1963.

Lord, F. M. A strong true score theory, with applications. *Psychometrika*, 1965, *30*, 239-270.

Lorenz, C. *On aggression*. New York: Harcourt, 1966.

Lorenz, C., & Leyhausen, G. *Motivation in animals and men*. New York: Van Nostrand, 1970.

Lurie, W. A. A study of Spranger's value types by the method of factor analysis. *Journal of Social Psychology*, 1937, *8*, 17-37.

Madsen, K. B. The formal properties of Cattellian personality theory. In Cattell, R. B., & Dreger, R. M. (Eds.), *Handbook of modern personality theory*. Chapter 31. Washington: Hemisphere, New York, Hemisphere & Halsted, 1977.

Magnusson, D. The person and the situation in an interactional model of behavior. *Scandinavian Journal of Psychology*, 1976, *17*, 253-271.

Magnusson, D., & Ekehammar, B. Anxiety profiles based on both situation and response factors. *Multivariate Behavioral Research*, 1975, *10*, 27-44.

Maslow, A. H. Appetites and hungers in animal motivation. *Journal of Comparative Psychology*, 1935, *20*, 75-83.

Maslow, A. H., & Flanyb, M. S. The role of dominance in the social and sexual behavior of infra-human primates. *Journal of Genetic Psychology*, 1936. *48*, 310-338.

Maugham, W. S. *A writer's notebook*. Garden City, New York: Doubleday, 1949.

Mausner, B. The specification of the stimulus in a social interaction. In Sells, S. B. (Ed.), *Stimulus Determinants of Behavior*. New York: Ronald Press, 1963.

May, D. R. *Psychiatric syndrome classifications checked by taxonome*. Unpublished Ph.D. thesis, University of Illinois at Urbana, 1971.

May, D. R. An application of the taxonome method to a plasmode. *Multivariate Behavioral Research*, 1973, *8*, 503-510.

McClelland, D. C., Atkinson, I. W., Clark, R. A., & Lowell, E. L. *The achievement motive*. New York: Appleton-Century-Crofts, 1953.

McDonald, R. P. A general approach to non-linear factor analysis. *Psychometrika*, 1962, *27*, 397-415.

McDougall, W. *The energies of men*. London: Methuen, 1932.

McQuitty, L. L. Rank order typal analysis. *Educational and Psychological Measurement*, 1963, *23*, 55-61.

Mead, M. Anthropological data on the problem of instinct. *Psychosomatic Medicine*, 1942, *4*, 396-397.

Meredith, G. M. Observations on the origins and current status of the ego assertive personality factor U.I. 16. *Journal of Genetic Psychology*, 1967, *110*, 269-286.

Messick, S. Multivariate models of cognition and personality: the need for both process and structure in psychological theory and measurement. In Royce,

J. R. (Ed.), *Multivariate Analysis and Psychological Theory*. Pp. 265-303. London: Academic Press, 1973.

Messick, S. J., & Ross, J. (Eds.) *Measurement in personality and cognition*. New York: Wiley, 1962.

Miller, K. M. *Manual for the Rothwell-Miller Interest Blank*. Windsor, Eng.: National Foundation for Educational Research, 1968.

Mischel, W. *Personality and assessment*. New York: Wiley, 1968.

Mischel, W. Continuity and change in personality. *American Psychology*, 1969, *24*, 1012-1018.

Moos, R. H. Sources of variance in responses to questionnaires and in behavior. *Journal of Abnormal Psychology*, 1969, *74*, 405-412.

Morgan, C. L. *An introduction to comparative psychology*. London: Scott, 1894.

Morton, N. E. Analysis of family resemblance. I: Introduction. *American Journal of Human Genetics*, 1974, *26*, 318-330.

Mowrer, O. H. Animal studies in the genesis of personality. *Transactions of the New York Academy of Science*, 1938, *56*, 273-288.

Mulaik, S. A. Are personality factors raters' conceptual factors? *Journal of Consulting Psychology*, 1964, *28*, 506-511.

Mulaik, S. A. *The foundations of factor analysis*. New York: McGraw-Hill, 1972.

Murray, H. A., et al. *Explorations in personality*. New York: Oxford University Press, 1938.

Nelson, E. A., Grinder, R. F., & Mutterer, J. L. Sources of variance in behavioral measures of honesty in temptation situations: methodological analysis. *Developmental Psychology*, 1969, *1*, 265-279.

Nesselroade, J. R. *The seven state objective test battery*. Champaign, Ill.: Institute for Personality and Ability Testing, 1960.

Nesselroade, J. R. *A comparison of cross product and differential R-factoring regarding cross study stability of change patterns*. Unpublished Ph.D. thesis, University of Illinois, 1967.

Nesselroade, J. R., & Bartsch, T. W. Multivariate perspectives on the validity of the trait-state distinction. In Cattell, R. B., & Dreger, R. M. (Eds.), *Handbook of modern personality theory*. Chapter 8. New York: Hemisphere, 1977.

Nesselroade, J. R., & Cable, D. Sometimes it's OK to factor difference scores— the separation of trait and state anxiety. *Multivariate Behavioral Research*, 1973, *8*, 1-18.

Nesselroade, J. R., & Reese, J. (Eds.). *Life span developmental psychology*. New York: Academic Press, 1973.

Nichols, K. E. Collation of second and third order studies of personality structure in the high school period. *Laboratory of Personality Research*. University of Illinois Publication No. 55, 1973.

Norman, W. T. Toward an adequate taxonomy of personality attributes: Replicated factor structure in peer nomination personality ratings. *Journal of Abnormal and Social Psychology*, 1963, *66*, 574-483.

Nunnally, J. C. *Psychometric theory*. New York: McGraw Hill, 1967.

Passini, F. T., & Norman, W. T. A universal conception of personality structure. *Journal of Personality and Social Psychology*, 1966, *4*, 44-49.

Pawlik, K., & Cattell, R. B. Third order factors in objective personality tests. *British Journal of Psychology*, 1964, *55*, 1-18.

Pervin, L. A. A free-response description approach to the analysis of person-situation interaction. Princeton: *ETS Bulletin* RB-75-22, 1975. (a)

Pervin, L. A. Definitions, measurements and classifications of stimuli situations and environments. Princeton: *ETS Bulletin* RB-75-23, 1975. (b)

Pervin, L. A. *Personality: Theory, assessment and research.* New York: Wiley, 1975. (c)

Pierson, G. R., Barton, V., & Hey, G. SMAT motivation factors as predictions of academic achievement of delinquent boys. *Journal of Psychology*, 1964, *57*, 243-249.

Porter, R., & Cattell, R. B. *Handbook for the child personality questionnaire.* Champaign, Ill.: Institute for Personality and Ability Testing, 1974.

Price, P., Cattell, R. B., & Patrick, S. Diagnostic separation of depressives by significant differences on four IPAT O-A Kit factor battery measures. *Multivariate Experimental Clinical Research.* In press, 1979.

Proshansky, H. M., Ittelson, W. H., & Rivlin, L. G. (Eds.) *Environmental psychology: man and his physical setting.* New York: Holt, Rinehart & Winston, 1970.

Rao, C. R. Estimation and tests of significance in factor analysis. *Psychometrika*, 1955, *20*, 92-110.

Rao, C. R., Morton, N. E., & Yee, S. Resolution of cultural and biological inheritance by path analysis. *American Journal of Human Genetics*, 1976, *28*, 228-242.

Raush, H. L., Dittman, A. T., & Taylor, T. J. Person, setting, and change in social interaction. *Human Relations*, 1959, *12*, 361-378.

Raush, H. L., Tarkman, I., & Llewellyn, L. G. Person, setting and change in social interaction II. A normal control study. *Human Relations*, 1960, *13*, 305-332.

Ribot, T. *La psychologie des sentiments.* Paris: Alcan, 1896.

Rickels, K., et al. Drug response and important external events in the patient's life. *Diseases of the Nervous System*, 1965, *26*, 782-786.

Rickels, K., & Cattell, R. B. The relationship of clinical symptoms and the IPAT factored tests of anxiety, regression and asthenia: A factor analytic study. *Journal of Nervous and Mental Disease*, 1968, *146*, 147-160.

Rickels, K., Cattell, R. B., Wiese, C., Gray, B., & Yee, R. Controlled psychopharmacological research in private psychiatric medicine. *Psychopharmacologia*, 1966, *9*, 288-306.

Roback, A. A. Psychology of character. New York: Harcourt Brace, 1927.

Roby, T. B. On the measurement and description of groups. *Behavioral Science*, 1957, *2*, 119-127.

Roff, M. A factorial study of the Fels parent behavior scales. *Child Development*, 1949, *20*, 29-45.

Rogers, C. R. *A therapist's view of personal goals.* Wallingford, Pa.: Pendle Hill, 1960.

Rokeach, M. *The open and closed mind.* New York: Basic Books, 1960.

Rorer, L. G. The great response style myth. *Psychological Bulletin*, 1965, *63*, 129-150.

Ross, J. The relation between test and person factors. *Psychological Review*, 1963, *70*, 432-443.

Royce, J. R. (Ed.) *Multivariate analysis and psychological theory.* London: Academic Press, 1973.

Royce, J. R. The relationship between factors and psychological processes. In Scandura, J., and Brainerd, C. J. *Structural Process Theories of Complex Human Behavior*, Leiden, Holland: Sijthoff International Publishing Company, 1975.

Royce, J. R., & Buss, A. R. The role of general systems and information theory in multi-factor individuality theory. *Canadian Psychological Review*, 1976, *17*, 1-21.

Rummel, R. J. Dimensions of conflict behavior within and between nations. *General Systems Yearbook of Society for General Systems Study*, 1963, *8*, 1-50.

Rummel, R. J. Domestic attributes and foreign conflict. In Singer, J. D. (Ed.), *Quantitative international politics*. Pp. 43-85. New York: Free Press, 1968.

Rummel, R. J. *The dimensions of nations*. Beverly Hills, Calif.: Sage Publications, 1972.

Rummel, R. J. *National attitudes and behavior linkage dimensions*. Beverly Hills, Calif., Sage Publications, 1978.

Sargent, F. (Ed.) *Human ecology*. New York: American Elsevier Publishing Company, 1974.

Saunders, D. R. Moderator variables in prediction. *Educational and Psychological Measurement*, 1956, *16*, 209-222.

Sawyer, J. Dimensions of nations: Size, wealth and politics. *American Journal of Sociology*, 1967, *73*, 145-172.

Schaie, K. W. On the equivalence of questionnaire and rating data. *Psychological Reports*, 1962, *10*, 521-522.

Schaie, K. W., & Goulet, L. R. Trait theory and verbal learning processes. In Cattell, R. B., & Dreger, R. M. (Eds.), *Handbook of modern personality theory*. Chapter 24, pp. 567-584. New York: Hemisphere: Halsted. 1977.

Scheier, I. H. Confirmation of objective test factors and their relation to other variables. *Journal of Mental Science*, 1958, *104*, 608-624.

Scheier, I. H. *The eight parallel form anxiety battery*. Champaign, Ill.: Institute for Personality and Ability Testing, 1959.

Schmidt, L. R. *Objektive Persönlichkeitsmessung in diagnostischer und klinischer Psychologie*. Weinheim: Belz, 1975.

Schmidt, L. R., Hacker, H., & Cattell, R. B. *Objective Test-batteries: OA-TB75*. Weinheim: Beltz, 1975.

Schneewind, K. R. Personality and perception. In Cattell, R. B., & Dreger, R. M. (Eds.), *Handbook of modern personality theory*. Chapter 23, pp. 551-566. New York: Hemisphere, 1977.

Sells, S. B. (Ed.). *Stimulus determinants of behavior*. New York: Ronald, 1963.

Sells, S. B., Demaree, R. B., & Will, D. P. Dimensions of personality; 1. Conjoint factor structure of Cattell and Guilford trait markers. *Multivariate Behavioral Research*, 1970, *4*, 391-422.

Sherif, C. W., Sherif, M., & Nabergill, R. E. *Attitude and attitude change: The social judgment-involvement approach*. Philadelphia: Saunders, 1965.

Skinner, B. F. *The behavior of organisms*. New York: Appleton, 1938.

Sokal, R. R., & Sneath, P. H. A. *Principles of numerical taxonomy*. San Francisco: Freeman, 1964.

Spearman, C. E. *The nature of intelligence and the principles of cognition*. London: Macmillan, 1923.

Spence, K. W. Cognitive-vs-stimulus response theories of learning. *Psychological Review*, 1950, *57*, 159-172.

Spielberger, C. B. *Anxiety and behavior*. New York: Academic Press. 1966.

Spielberger, C. B. *Anxiety: Current trends in theory and research*. New York: Academic Press, 1973.

Stephenson, W. *Q-technique and its methodology*. Chicago: Chicago University Press, 1953.

Stern, G. G. *People in context: the measurement of environmental interaction in school and society.* New York, Wiley, 1970.

Stogdill, R. M. Leadership, membership and organization. *Psychological Bulletin,* 1950, *47,* 1-14.

Stogdill, R. M. Leadership and morale in organized groups. In Hullett, J., & Stagner, R. (Eds.), *Problems in Social Psychology.* Pp. 140-152. Urbana: University of Illinois Press, 1952.

Stogdill, R. M., & Koehler, K. *Measures of leadership structure and organization change.* Columbus: Ohio State University Research Foundation, 1952.

Strong, E. K. *Vocational interests of men and women.* Stanford: Stanford University Press, 1949.

Studman, L. G. Studies in experimental psychiatry. W and f factors in relation to traits of personality. *Journal of Mental Science,* 1935, *81,* 107-137.

Sweney, A. B. Objective measurement of strength of cynamic structure factors. In Cattell, R. B., & Warburton, F. (Eds.), *Objective personality and motivation tests: A theoretical introduction and a practical compendium.* Pp. 127-185. Champaign, Ill.: University of Illinois Press, 1967.

Sweney, A. B. *Descriptive manual for individual assessment by the motivation analysis test.* Champaign, Ill.: Institute for Personality and Ability Testing, 1969.

Sweney, A. B., & Cattell, R. B. Dynamic factors in 12-year-old children as revealed in measures of integrated motivation. *Journal of Clinical Psychology,* 1961, *17,* 360-369.

Sweney, A. B., & Cattell, R. B. Relations between integrated and unintegrated motivational components examined by objective tests. *Journal of Social Psychology,* 1962, *57,* 217-226.

Tatro, D. F. *The interpretation of objectively measured personality factors in terms of clinical data and concepts.* Unpublished Ph.D. thesis, University of Illinois at Urbana, 1967.

Tatro, D. F. The utility of source traits measured by the O-A (Objective-Analytic) Battery in mental hospital diagnosis. *Multivariate Behavioral Research,* 1968, Special 3, 133-150.

Tatsuoka, M. M. *Discriminant analysis: The study of group differences.* Monograph No. 6. Champaign, Ill.: Institute for Personality and Ability Testing, 1970.

Tatsuoka, M. M., & Cattell, R. B. Linear equations for estimating a person's occupational adjustment, based on information on occupational profiles. *British Journal of Educational Psychology,* 1970, *40,* 324-334.

Thompson, R. F. The search for the engram. *American Psychologist,* 1976, *31,* 209-227.

Thorndike, E. L. The interests of adults: 2. The inter-relations of adult interest. *Journal of Educational Psychology,* 1935, *26,* 497-507. (a)

Thorndike, E. L. *The psychology of wants, interests and attitudes.* New York: Appleton-Century-Crofts, 1935. (b)

Thurstone, L. L. *Multiple factor analysis.* Chicago: Chicago University Press, 1947.

Tinbergen, N. *The study of instinct.* Oxford, Clarendon Press, 1951.

Tolman, E. C. Cognitive maps in rats and men. *Psychological Review,* 1948, *55,* 189-208.

Torr, D. V. A factor analysis of 49 variables. Annual *Research Bulletin,* 1953, Human Resources Research Center, ARDC Lackland Air Force Base, Texas, 53-67.

Tsushima, Y. Failure stress in examinations related to anxiety factor scores. Unpublished M.A. thesis, University of Illinois at Urbana, 1957.

Tupes, E. C., & Cristal, R. C. Recurrent personality factors based on trait ratings. United States Air Force, ASD Technical Report No. 61-97; Lackland, Air Force Base, Texas, Personnel Research Center, 1961.

Uberla, K. Faktorenanalyse. Gottingen, Hogrepe, 1965.

Uhr, L., & Miller, J. G. Drugs and behavior. New York: Wiley, 1960.

Undheim, J. D. Ability structure in 10-11 year old children and the theory of fluid and crystallized intelligence. Journal of Educational Psychology, 1976, 68, 411-423.

Vandenberg, S. G. The primary mental abilities of Chinese students: A comparative study of the stability of a factor structure. Annals of the New York Academy of Science, 1959, 79, 257-304.

Vaughan, D. S. The relative methodological soundness of several major personality factor analyses. Journal of Behavioral Science, 1973, 1, 305-313.

Van Egeren, L. F. Experimental determination by P-technique of functional unities of depression and other psychological states. Unpublished M.A. thesis, University of Illinois, 1963.

Van Egeren, L. F. Multivariate statistical analysis. Psychophysiology, 1973, 10, 517-532.

Van Egeren, L. F. Multivariate research on the psychoses. In Cattell, R. B., & Dreger, R. M. (Eds.), Handbook of modern personality theory. Pp. 653-674. New York: Hemisphere, Halsted, 1977.

Wardell, D. M. A multivariate study of extraversion. Unpublished Ph.D. Thesis, University of Alberta, Edmonton, 1976.

Wardell, D., & Yeudall, T. A multidimensional approach to forensic disorders. 1. The factor analysis. Edmonton, Alberta: Department of Neuro-Psychology, Alberta Hospital, 1976.

Weckowicz, T. E., Cropley, A., & Muir, W. An attempt to replicate the results of a factor analytic study in depressed patients. Journal of Clinical Psychology, 1971, 27, 30-31.

Wedding, D. Personal communication from University of Hawaii Psychology Department on use of the Curran 8 state Battery, 1978.

Wenger, M. G. Inter-relations among some physiological variables. Psychological Bulletin, 1940, 37, 466-476.

Wenig, P. The relative roles of naive, autistic, cognitive and press compatibility misperception and ego defense operations in tests of misperception. Unpublished M.A. thesis, University of Illinois at Urbana, 1952.

Wessman, A. E., & Ricks, D. F. Mood and personality. New York: Holt, Rinehart & Winston, 1966.

Wiggins, J. S. Personality and prediction: Principles of personality assessment. London: Addison Wesley, 1973.

Wilde, G. J. Trait description and measurement by personality questionnaire. In Cattell, R. B., & Dreger, R. M. (Eds.), Handbook of modern personality theory. Pp. 69-103. New York: Hemisphere, 1977.

Williams, H. F., & Cattell, R. B. P-technique: Functional unities found in the intact organism. British Journal of Preventive and Social Medicine, 1953, 7, 141-153.

Witkin, H. A., et al. Psychological differentiation: Studies of development. New York: Wiley, 1962.

Young, P. T. Motivation and emotion. New York: Wiley, 1961.

Zeeman, E. C. Catastrophe theory. Scientific American, 1976, 221, 65-83.